Love and the Art of War

War

by Dinah Lee Küng

Eyes and Ears Editions
eyesandears.editions@gmail.com

1. Küng, Dinah Lee 2. Sun Tzu 3. The Art of War 4. fiction 5.
humor 6. family 7. romance 8. The Thirty-six Stratagems
I Title

By Dinah Lee Küng

A Visit From Voltaire
Under Their Skin
The Wardens of Punyu (Vol. I, The Handover Mysteries)
The End of May Road (Vol. II, The Handover Mysteries)
The Shadows of Shigatse (Vol. III, The Handover Mysteries)

To my husband Peter

Here in the mountain village
Evening falls peacefully.
Half tipsy, I lounge in the
Doorway. The moon shines in the
Twilight sky. The breeze is so
Gentle, the water is hardly ruffled.
I have escaped from
Lies and trouble. I no longer
Have any importance. I
Do not miss my horses and
Chariots. Here at home, I
Have plenty of pigs and chickens.

Lu Yo

TABLE OF CONTENTS

PART I

'Act quickly when perceiving the advantage. Halt when there is no advantage. It is too early to act an instant earlier and too late to act an instant later.'

Summary of Military Canons, Wu Jing Zong Yao

Chapter One, Trick the Emperor Into Crossing the Sea

Surrounded by YouTube, I-Pad, Android, and Skype people, Jane Gilchrist prided herself on remaining a book person. Not that anyone noticed Jane these days. They were too busy Tweeting.

She lived with Joe in a secluded square in NW1 along with her mother, the American-born actress Lorraine King, and their teen-age daughter, Samantha. Unlike Chalkwood Square itself, advancing from litter-strewn bohemia to celebrity-sodden hideaway, the Gilchrists were no longer a young couple in television with more good things before them. They'd peaked.

Joe's career at the BBC was still afloat, in a drowning-not-waving sort of way. Years ago, Jane had binned her telly job for managing the quiet stacks of their local library. She had always lived for books—real books. Lately, she'd lived more and more *inside* books, her mind cluttered with characters waving at her from printed pages. No one conversing with Jane suspected that she was thinking, *So very Widmerpool, that pushy boy,* or *She's headed for the gutter, like Zola's Nana.*

Was Jane's drift into a fictional universe getting worse with the years? Or was the world just abandoning its love of literature to stubborn holdouts like Jane?

Teenagers from the estates across the Camden Road Rail slouched into the Chalkwood Library every Monday, Friday, and Saturday afternoon. Although deafened by earbuds to Jane's cheery welcome, at least they still used the library's services—if not the printed volumes. Skulking past Jane's desk, they slithered in their fleecy hoodies straight for the Internet Alcove, where they clicked away like zombies until Jane or her colleague Chris signalled closing time.

Books had saved Jane from the miseries of her own teenage years. She'd read her way from homely backstage child into plain and womanly helpmeet to her actress mother. In her late forties,

Lorraine had left Broadway for a life in England with Jane's father, the beloved thespian Jack King. Thanks to Jack's mentoring, Lorraine had even enjoyed a second career on the West End.

Jane mourned her father's painful death from cancer privately and deeply but Lorraine had moved on, imposing on Jane a sequence of legal stepfathers and less official 'uncles.' A life spent watching her mother from the wings forecast a future of only supporting roles for the daughter.

Then crusading documentary producer Joe Gilchrist whisked shy Jane into his arms and supplanted Lorraine as the glamour end of the pairing but unlike her mother, the Canadian was everything Jane needed. Joe was kind and funny—and on top of loving Jane—someone she could believe in. Joe faced down deceit and pursued justice. He dropped filming a sequence midway to wade into waist-deep floodwaters and save a child's life. He donated the earnings from his exposé on adulterated milk powder to an entire Chinese village. People applauded Lorraine, but they loved Joe, so it seemed natural that Lorraine dropped from lead to featured player.

Still, there was a catch. Jane's own casting didn't improve—she remained a planet, not a star, and went from helpmeet to helpmate, cheering on two high flyers instead of one.

The library was the safest place for Jane. She hovered around the computers, ready to recommend a book, even a software manual, to ignite a visitor's page-turning habit. Despondent, she spent more time changing ink cartridges and loading printer paper these days than lending books. All the more precious to Jane then, when a tiny borrower, having tumbled to the promise of exiting the library with an armful of free picture books, queued between the DVD-toting teens and clucking pensioners.

At such moments, Jane whispered to Chris, 'One more little soul saved from the pixels.'

So, when her crisis with Joe hit Jane that blustery September, she first scoured the self-help brochures at her branch and researched the how-to manuals. The experts knew best and their words would save her again, but it wasn't enough.

Finally, forty-three, frizzy-haired, and desperate, she queued along with the other 'late registrations' for an evening class in 'Mending Marriage, Sane Separation, and Decent Divorce,' (anything to delay asking Joe about that text on his BlackBerry that had provoked such a knowing performance from Sammie.)

I'm a coward. I've panicked at the first hint of trouble. After all these years, you'd think I could simply ask him 'So, who's the girlfriend sending you tacky messages?' Instead, I've run off like some silly Jane Eyre fleeing the bad news up in the attic.

This wouldn't have happened if Sammie had stuck her nose in a book instead of her father's mobile. Jane wouldn't have overheard her daughter: 'What is this? "I'm simmering. You keep me on the boil?" You getting off with someone, Dad?'

If only Jane hadn't looked up from that delicious new biography of Eleanor of Aquitaine to catch Joe's nervous glance. If only she hadn't been gob-smacked with the unexpected but sure intimation that darling Joe, her best friend for life, Sammie's father, was having an affair.

Pre-registered students had grabbed the best slots. The latecomers jostled Jane aside, who was too busy fighting back tears to defend her place in the queue. But she couldn't go home. She needed advice from the pros. Didn't Joan Didion promise, 'Information is control'?

If only Sammie hadn't played tag with Joe around their living room, waving that silly text message, Jane wouldn't have panicked like this. She wouldn't have invaded Joe's closet to discover a new jacket, pair of trousers, and a French sports jersey with the tag still dangling, all stashed out of sight. Shamefaced, she checked Joe's credit card receipts. He'd paid for three separate lunches at Ma Maison—all in the same August week Jane was escorting the authors of 'The Big Gay Read' around Manchester libraries.

She tried calling Joe's office at unexpected times only to end up chatting with poor Rachel Murty, Personal Assistant to cooking star Bella Crawford who was busy on the set of *The Travelling Kitchen*.

'They're shooting right now, Jane,' Rachel explained; in other words, exactly what Joe was supposed to be doing.

Jane felt idiotic standing in this queue and was turning away when the registrar grabbed her form with a perky, 'No reason to shake, love—nothing frightening. Most don't even set homework. Oh, hang on a mo', might be full up, but then, would be, wouldn't it? Let me see, 96B Working with Clients at Suicide Risk, 96C Women Loving Women, 96D Psychobabble, Where It Starts and Stops . . . Here you go, 96F, Mending Marriage, Sane, rhubarb, rhubarb. What not to talk about in front of the kids, how to get a good lawyer . . . Well, one place left. Meant to be. Most Friday classes are all full.'

This stranger's sympathy humiliated Jane. She said, 'It's actually the Mending Marriage part that I—'.

'Course it is, love. We could all use a little mending.'

Someone pushed past her with a question for the clerk. This reprieve lasted just long enough for Jane to succumb to tears. She'd be better off sipping a hot milky drink of denial back home.

Too late. The printer slugged out her registration card while the clerk commented, 'Poor Psychobabble, they'll need a sixth person or they'll have to close. Need to blow? Wait, don't I know you? From the library?'

'Yes, possibly.'

''Course. You are so wonderful! My Greggie wouldn't have made it through his A-levels without you! He pointed you out, said that's the one who keeps me at it and keeps the other blokes quiet.'

'Greg. Yes, of course. Doing all right?'

'Lovely, just lovely, dear. Here's your card. Next, please? Polymers? Sorry, all full.'

Jane brandished the computer card ahead of her like a wand illuminating the unfamiliar corridor. She took a breath and opened the classroom door.

Six faces glanced up at her stubby figure. From behind a desk a skeletal teacher with iron-grey hair slicked against a high forehead broke off mid-sentence.

'Slightly late, but ladies' privilege.' He gave her a tolerant smile. 'Welcome. I'm Richard Baldwin.'

'Jane Gilchrist. Sorry, last-minute registration.'

She laid her cluttered satchel on the floor. A young Chinese man sporting pink and white stripes through his hair eyeballed her. He struck Jane as a Ma Jian *Noodlemaker* type. She gave him the same frown she shot kids sticking gum under a reading table.

Professor Baldwin tilted slightly to one side, like a battered ship with its sails folded and its wooden masts splintered after a fatal storm has cleared. Ladies privilege indeed! Jane's indignation subsided when she realized she was the only female in the class. Mending Marriage was taught by a man. Worse, was she supposed to confide her personal failures in front of Zebra Boy?

'As I was saying, we start with the most basic principle from which all the others more or less follow.' Baldwin wrote in bold letters on the board, 'Win as much as possible without fighting.' He slid Jane an encouraging smile. So far, so good, she thought. The last thing Jane wanted was to fight Joe.

Then Baldwin veered off on a very odd vein: 'For your purposes, this might mean capturing as much of the market as possible without destroying it. Expending capital only on sure investments, protecting assets, and including your staff's energies as well as material holdings.'

A Canary Wharf type jotted notes in a neat outline. Jane could well imagine divorcing him.

'Keep those general principles in mind as we move to the specifics of the Thirty-six Stratagems, listed on this handout. I've also set you a short reading list—nothing you can't find at Waterstones or Amazon, starting of course with the master, Sun Tzu.'

A mobile near Jane's feet burst into 'The William Tell Overture'.

The pink-striped Chinese stuttered, 'W-W-Winston, Winston Chu. Sorry.' He fumbled around the bottom of his briefcase until he located the criminal instrument. Rossini chirped on, defying the young man's fumbling thumbs. The pinched note-taker bristled disapproval while a burly, dark-haired man reached across to help. 'Hey, pal, let me arrest the Lone Ranger for you there.' Jane detected an American accent. New Jersey? Brooklyn?

Baldwin nodded. 'Blessed silence. Thank you. You are?'

'Dan. Dan O'Neill.'

'Mr O'Neill, would you distribute these lists, please?'

Hands came forward. Not one of Jane's five fellow students wore a wedding band. In fact, there was a distinctly un-connubial air about this little gathering. Winston looked like a boy on his first date. Dan O'Neill was quite attractive in a muscle-bound way and might have stepped up to the altar at some point. Still, he struck Jane as breathing awfully easily for a man fending off maintenance payments. And the well-dressed suit in the centre was too self-absorbed to notice his marriage needed a mate, much less any mending.

Of course, Jane hadn't expected the cosy camaraderie of her senior citizens' reading club at the library but still, something felt off. Mending Marriage was not for her.

Raising a timid hand, she caught Baldwin's eye, but he said, 'I'll take questions just before our break, if you don't mind. Tonight, we'll take the first two of the six so-called Winning Strategies and continue with two a week until we've covered all thirty-six.' Then to her astonishment, Baldwin sang out, '*Man Tian Guo Hai.*'

Jane had had enough. 'There's been a mistake—'

Baldwin smiled, 'Feeling panic, Mrs Gilchrist? I don't expect anyone to speak Chinese, unless Mr Chu would enlighten us?'

Winston stuttered, 'I-I-I took Cantonese as a kid, but never learned classical—'

The sturdy Dan rescued Winston again, 'Trick the Emperor Into Crossing the Sea.'

'Excellent!' Baldwin shot a curious glance at O'Neill before embarking on a fairy tale about a Chinese emperor who balked at crossing the Yellow Sea to attack Korea.

He concluded, 'His frustrated generals told their cowardly emperor that a merchant was giving him a banquet and lured the recalcitrant ruler into a merchant's "house". They drank and toasted, until the emperor heard the wind pounding on all sides. The candelabra swung back and forth.'

Baldwin swayed back and forth in front of his desk. 'Finally, the dizzy Emperor opened the curtains and he saw nothing but the thrashing sea.' His skinny hands spread out on both sides. 'The house was a camouflaged ship carrying them to the Korean front.'

The turmoil of the ancient storm settled around them. Winston Chu's mouth hung open.

'Conceal your real objective, disguise your course, camouflage your purpose,' Baldwin intoned. 'Sneaking about in the darkness or lurking behind screens only attracts suspicion. To lower an enemy's guard, act in the open, hiding your true intentions behind everyday activities.' The professor took in the half-circle of tired expressions. Dan O'Neill's five o'clock shadow looked closer towards midnight. 'Any business examples come to mind?'

The stiff businessman raised his hand.

'Yes, you're Mr Deloitte, I believe?'

'Maintaining "business as usual" with a target company, but using a third party to buy share parcels? The third party might be an outside bank, perhaps Swiss, certainly never your house bank— to avoid driving up prices—until you've got control?'

'A very good start, Mr Deloitte.' Baldwin straightened the packet of registration cards on the desktop. 'Coffee for ten minutes outside, toilets at the end on the right. We'll resume with Stratagem Two at ten past.' Amid the scraping of chairs, Baldwin turned his bony frame in Jane's direction. 'Now, Mrs Gilchrist, what's troubling you?'

'I signed up for Mending Marriage, Sane Separation, and Decent Divorce. I don't think your emperor has much to offer me.'

Baldwin fished Jane's registration card out of the stack. 'Ah. My class is China's Military Genius for Maximizing Management. Mouthful, isn't it? I suggested The Warlord Way to Waging Profit.' He wiggled his wiry eyebrows in jest, 'But there we are.' He glanced into her rueful eyes, 'And here you are.'

'Quite. I was very clear at registration.'

'Yes, the room number's mine, but my code is 96E, not F.'

Jane gathered up her satchel. 'I'll go back and sort it out—'

'I'm sorry about this, but, well, perhaps you might take my class?'

'Why?'

'Well, why did you sign up for this?' He snapped her card with disdain.

'Really, I can't bother you with—let's just say I'm a part-time librarian whose mate is straying. Or in danger of straying.'

'And you think a class of discarded wives can teach you how to mend your marriage?' Baldwin leaned back against the edge of his desk. If Jane expected a hand extended in gracious farewell, she was disappointed: 'You'll find no solutions next door—unless you're looking for bridge partners!' He braced his narrow shoulders. 'My class could save you. I think. Plus,' he tossed a glance at the six empty chairs, 'the teacher-student ratio is a lot better here.'

'But isn't this a management class?'

'Well, that's only how I'm forced to package it and as you see, still not much turnout. Not quite the old days at Hong Kong University. The point is, in my class you won't learn anything particularly decent. You'll learn how to win.'

'I don't want to fight.'

'That's not what I said. Oh, I see. You think training up for the competition would be, what? Vulgar? Well, competition is a natural response to danger.' His expression softened. 'You are in danger?'

'Well, I'm quite upset. I'm sure the other class will give me advice I can use, some degree of . . . control.'

Now the tears broke through in full force. Embarrassed, Jane blinked up at the holes in the cork ceiling and then searched Baldwin's polished black shoes through a wet daze. 'I've never done anything like this without Joe knowing. When I switched from the television research department to get my librarian degree, whenever I tried something new, it was Joe who egged me on. He rallied my courage. Oh, sorry—'

'A good blub might be a healthy start,' he smiled, 'Although, Mrs Gilchrist, as my students go, you're pretty wet.'

Baldwin fetched a roll of paper towelling. 'We don't cry in my class. Emotion clouds reason. It gives your enemy a damaging weapon against you.'

'Joe? The enemy? Oh, if you only knew him! He's worked all his life for the underdog—'

'How noble. I'm not saying he's wicked. It might be like in doctors' families—children all runny noses, spouse shattered with exhaustion? And yet somehow Dr Do-Good never notices? People can love us, but still be so galvanized by their higher calling, well, maybe they forget not to hurt us. I mean, a hero can be so busy saving the entire world, he doesn't realize he's just wounded the person standing right next to him.' He paused. 'So we won't let him. You'll win without Joe even realizing what you're doing for his own good.'

'You mean, not even explain about this class? Trick Emperor Joe into crossing the sea?'

'For starters.'

'I suppose . . . I could say it's a management class.'

'Yes, a class in Managing Joe. You might have a knack for this. Just add the skill of Sun Tzu. You've heard of him?'

'Um . . .'

Baldwin sighed. 'Sun Tzu was a Chinese general who lived during the Warring States Period around 400 BC. This little book, *The Art of War*, is the sum of a lifetime's experience winning fame and power for his warlord. Applying his principles two centuries later, the Emperor Qin Shihuang united China for the first time. Mao Zedong used Sun Tzu to defeat Chiang Kai Shek in 1949, as well as the Thirty-six Stratagems based on Sun Tzu's principles over the centuries to the benefit of everyone from Sony Corp to General Schwarzkopf.'

'Well, Joe's hardly Saddam Hussein,' Jane sputtered.

'So, China's greatest warlords have nothing to teach you?'

'Well, I'm trying to keep a family united, not all of China.'

Professor Baldwin took a deep breath. 'But all of Cathay isn't as important to you as that family.' He cocked his head. 'Here come the others. Just remember Sun Tzu's warning: Battles are dangerous affairs. He who struggles with naked blades is not a good general.'

He fixed Jane with steady, grey eyes: 'You know, each autumn, I take on a batch of men whose aim is to nab the corner office from the wally in the next cubicle. What a fresh challenge—to transform this dormouse of a librarian into a fearless warrior woman! To gird your loins, forgive the expression, with powerful weapons and to array you in the silken protection of the Thirty-six Stratagems. Under my tutelage, the advantage will be yours without Jim ever guessing. He mustn't know you even suspect him of cheating—'

'Joe.'

'You're a librarian? Trust the Written Word.' Baldwin had located Jane's soft spot.

A natty fellow leapt back into the classroom and struck a kung fu pose. Keith Phipps, a reinsurance salesman, introduced his friend, the ginger-haired Kevin Filgrove, a sales manager at Marks and Sparks. The over-tailored Nigel Deloitte worked at a bank so private that when he mumbled its name like a secret incantation, no one dared ask him to repeat it.

'Coffee, Mrs Gilchrist? Watery and tasteless!' Keith handed Jane a polystyrene cup and swizzle stick.

'Well, we've all made friends,' Baldwin observed. 'Now, Number Two. Encircle the Wei Kingdom to Rescue the Zhao.'

'Take that, Swiss Re!' Keith gave his chair a karate chop.

Dan O'Neill wiggled his eyebrows, and with a gallant bow, offered Jane one of the wooden chairs.

Chapter Two, Encircle Wei, Rescue Zhao

Joe didn't ask why Jane snuck under the duvet well after ten. His Friday had been fraught enough; *The Travelling Kitchen*'s razor-toothed celebrity, a Zubatec fish known as the 'King of the Adriatic,' had missed his ice-cushioned flight from Dubrovnik. PA Rachel Murty had rushed to the fish wholesalers to buy a last-minute understudy. Unfortunately, the best she could find was a tuna with glaucoma. They'd managed to shoot around his whitened stare, but it pushed their taping well into overtime.

Now Joe was recovering with a long Saturday lie-in, while Jane welcomed the dawn from his wooden swivel chair next to the tall windows overlooking Chalkwood Square.

This was the throne of Joe's understandable discontent from which he drafted his memos begging transfer to a news programme. His pile of script proposals lay on the desk next to her, their pages stained with coffee rings. Yellowing business cards fringed his blotter and curling Post-its festooned his dog-eared pitches: *Al Qaeda's Women, Sudan's Secret Swiss Fortunes, Sons of the KGB...* each a failed effort to ditch cuisine for Current Affairs. Meanwhile Bella—*The Travelling Kitchen's* queen bee—racked up successes with her effortless stir-fries, apron freebies, and spice-house endorsements.

The three of them had travelled far since Joe won his big award from the British Academy of Film and Television Arts as *Panorama's* coming man. The BAFTA made him, momentarily, London's favourite Canadian. His congenial persistence and broad shoulders carved a spot in the media circus. Jane had been his adoring researcher earning her librarian credentials part-time. And Bella? She'd been a mere secretary with unkempt dark curls who was always wearing shoes that outran her budget.

Joe and Jane had paired off. Bella had moved up to personal assistant, then program announcer. Trapped in perpetual singlehood, Bella had been Jane's choice for Sammie's godmother, but in fact, Bella was never exactly forlorn. With a curious deftness at spotting the main chance, she'd grabbed a stint as front girl for an early evening chat program and finally, stardom as a domestic goddess. Manolos replaced Russell Bromleys.

And how those shoes had marched Bella's ambitious feet so many social levels above Joe and Jane! She'd worked hard for her celebrity glow. Unfortunately for Joe's career, at this stage she represented more a black hole. Bella brooked no defections beyond her gravitational pull. The program's budget included allowances for cashmere twin sets, book tours, podiatrist, and masseuse. Even her guest chefs, foreign kitchen studs *The Financial Times* had tagged Bella's 'unique selling proposition,' travelled whole continents just to fricassee at her side. Even if her exotic food adventures never left the BBC's set or her privately installed Battersea studio kitchen, Bella kept a watchful eye on her franchise, her producer included.

If Joe intended to survive Bella now, he must stay supine until his escape hatch from her mother ship was primed.

Jane sipped her milky coffee and checked the postmark on a card from cameraman Fergus in Kabul, just the sort of location shoot to rankle Joe mired in the salt mines of *The Travelling Kitchen* while Fergus slung satellite dish kits on and off Heathrow luggage belts.

How still the square was this morning! The Georgian window frame leaked a cool draught. Jane curled her toes into Sammie's woollen coat, and pulled out Baldwin's handout. After all, it wasn't as if reviewing the Second Stratagem committed her to continue with his class. In 374 BC, the state of Wei laid siege to the weaker state of Zhao. Zhao appealed to the Zhi kingdom, which enjoyed the counsel of Sun Bing. Sun Bing, not Sun Tzu? *She must keep those straight. Except, who cared?* Jane would switch class next Friday.

Jane stared north towards Primrose Hill. The weekend was starting: a dark-haired young man in a long white tunic and trousers unlocked the shuttered religious bookstore at the upper corner of the square. A fish lorry sped up to Odette's, a lunchtime trysting spot for media couples. Saturday shoppers hurried between the bollards marking the square's dead end from the High Street beyond as they headed to catch the Northern Line.

Each year the commuters dressed better but acted less neighbourly. In the old days Jane and Joe could only afford No. 19's attic flat, but at night they gazed across the grey rooftops towards London Zoo in Regent's Park. Lorraine had the attic now, and insisted the stairs were nothing to a gal who had once partnered Astaire in a black-and-white television special. 'Fred said I was better than Cyd Charisse,' a mantra that Sammie always mouthed behind her grandmother's back.

Everything seemed so normal on this chilly morning, everyone on the right pillow, the breakfast tray almost ready for Lorraine and the library's Saturday routine waiting. Suddenly her suspicions of Joe seemed unthinkable. Perhaps he'd have a perfect explanation for it all. A man who kept a secret in order not to upset you only ended up upsetting you by acting secretive. True, they hadn't had sex for quite some time, a month or two, perhaps even three?—but only because *The Travelling Kitchen* was filmed three nights a week before a live audience smirking at Bella's *double entendres* with her chefs. Joe didn't get home until Jane was fast asleep, book in hand and tucked in by her fictional friends.

Jane battled her creeping discomfort with the courage of a mouse donning cat's armour. She busied herself by dusting off his BAFTA award with a corner of her bathrobe.

'What are you doing with that, honey?'

She hadn't heard him pad in. A Casanova flush with illicit lust didn't jive with this sight of good old Joe in checked flannel. You could take the hero out of Winnipeg, but his hunting-lodge p.j.'s came with him.

'Just dusting it. There's coffee.'

'Yes, I need a jolt.' he said, rubbing his bristles. 'I want to finish something before lunch.'

'*James Callaghan's Political Grandsons?*'

'No. *Mothers of Death, Seeds of Jihad*—Don't give me that stern librarian look.'

'Sounds more Roger Corman than Jeremy Paxman.'

He replaced the BAFTA mask on the shelves above his desk. 'I put a World Service researcher from the Urdu section on it. Poor child, she thinks television is "more the thing" than Bush House.' He booted up his laptop.

'I'm sure you told her television is the graveyard of promise, the shoals on which great talent flounders and the abyss where good ideas become clichés.'

'I told her it could be a worthwhile career if she works hard and wants it enough. And I still believe that, Jane.' There was always another memo flying off to a documentary chieftain or Current Affairs warlord, another interview to hang tight for, another excuse, like the latest cut in political programming for more humiliating reality shows. Joe's reality was humiliating enough without *Big Brother*.

'How was your night class?' He scanned his e-mail.

Jane started with, 'You wouldn't believe it, but—' when Baldwin's voice popped into her head: Stratagem One. *Disguise the course. Don't tell Joe.*

'Wouldn't believe what, sweetie?'

She hesitated. Could she lie to Joe? 'It was surprising, actually.'

'Library management, surprising?' He fished around his briefcase.

'Yes.' She buttered toast for Lorraine's tray. 'Um, new inventory . . . reader databases . . . reservation systems for borrowers, oh, and an online network for housebound borrowers, summer schemes for early readers, that sort of thing.'

She held her breath, waiting for his swift detection, but he only nodded, 'Always good to have new skills.' He checked the news pages online. 'You never know when things might change.'

Jane shifted Lorraine's tray to her hip. 'What might change, Joe?'

He hitched up his pyjama bottoms. 'You might want a promotion, or more responsibility, or even a transfer—'

'Not while Sammie's such a handful.' This sounded like a conversation Jane didn't want—a conversation about her becoming more independent, about *change*. She left with Lorraine's tray.

Lorraine wasn't an invalid. At seventy-nine, she could shop on the High Street, cook, and bathe herself, but years of dressing room suppers and breakfasts to be delivered no earlier than noon had locked Jane into caregiver habits. She set the tray outside the front door on the attic landing, knocked, and left the ancient hoofer-turned-Shakespearean-hack to her snooze under the eaves. While Joe grabbed the bathroom before Sammie, Jane returned to her class notes with a guilty level of renewed interest.

After their coffee break last night, Professor Baldwin had resettled his bony hips against the edge of his desk.

'Strategy Two uses an ally, perhaps a second company, to distract your competitor. Virgin Atlantic succeeded in taking on British Airways where bigger airlines had failed because Virgin used the brand recognition of their records and Cola products to launch a multi-pronged assault from entertainment and food markets—where British Airways had no ready defence.'

Jane hadn't noticed any battle between British Airways and Virgin. Nor did she recognize the Starbucks case trotted out by Nigel Deloitte. The banker was certainly keen, but Jane found Baldwin's ravaged good looks and penetrating instruction more riveting. And through her puffy-eyed discomposure during the second part of Friday night's class, she'd at least retained: The enemy can't be superior in all things. When he's too strong to be confronted head-on, attack something he holds dear. Find the gap in his armour . . .'

'The Achilles Heel approach?' Nigel had interjected.

'Precisely, Mr Deloitte.'

Joe interrupted her reading with a shout, 'Jane? This bathroom latch is looking pretty wonky—'

'They stopped making them in 1910. Sir Bernard says our doors are worth a fortune.' Sir Bernard, knighted for designing a museum and a railway station, lived next door.

Joe emerged in damp terry cloth, drying his hair. He lowered his voice, 'You know, Jane, I've been thinking, wouldn't it be better for Sammie to try boarding? Her GCSE's were a disaster.'

Jane faced Joe. He cast a dark silhouette against the autumn daylight now shining through the tall windows.

'Send her away? Sammie needs us more than ever, Joe. She's so thin and stressed.'

He rubbed his stubble. 'There'd be fewer distractions. Just a thought. Working today?'

'As always.'

'Well, that's my point. Sammie might do better with more supervision.'

Only later, after a morning spent on a 'stock workshop' with Chris, did Jane recall Joe's words with alarm. Weirdly, the previous evening Baldwin had urged: 'Attack the relatives or dear ones of the enemy to weaken him psychologically.'

Joe couldn't be serious about Sammie boarding. Their back-talking, spiky-haired girl-woman had always been Joe's darling and her grandmother's outright pet, and these days, Jane felt she was almost the last person Sammie turned to for advice or affection. Of course, girls that age tended to reject their mothers and favour their dads. Was Joe planning to remove Sammie to isolate Jane? Was he preparing to dismantle their household by incremental stealth?

Baldwin had said every Chinese stratagem had a defensive option. What was it? Should Jane hold tighter to Sammie, to put Joe under siege?

Suddenly she felt like looking at those strategies again, but Baldwin's handout was back home.

'Chris, which branch has the best Asian collection?'

'*Londinistan? Sari Shop? Brick Lane? In the Kitchen? Mango Season? Inheritance of Loss?*'

'I meant Chinese—'

'Oh, right, right. *Stick Out Your Tongue? Colours of the Mountain? Balzac and the Chinese Seamstress? Sky Burial? Red Dust? Bound Feet and Western Dress? Concise Chinese-English Dictionary for Lovers*—?'

Jane shook her colleague by the shoulders until the straight sheets of his blond hair flipped out of his eyes. 'Chris, snap out of it! I was only wondering, if we don't have *The Book of 36 Stratagems*, could we get it?'

Chris narrowed his pale eyes at Jane through the centre-parted droop of a blond Afghan hound. 'How about a promotion called New Hong Kong Voices? With Jackie Chan posters? You know, like they told us at that librarians' seminar. Think "branding," like with breakfast cereals, so the borrowers come back for more.'

'Right.' Jane threw up her hands, 'Branding it is. How shall we brand Charles Dickens? I mean, he didn't win the Man Booker or the Orange or the Whitbread.'

'Best Violence,' Chris said. 'Penguin's Best 100 ranked *Tale of Two Cities* as Best Violence.'

'Talking about Best Violence, here come the Rhyme-Timers,' Jane quipped. These rambunctious vandal-borrowers were as well organized as five-year-olds could manage until a shoving match broke out over *Agent Z* and *Penguin from Mars*. Jane faced a freckled urchin who thrust up *Tales of the White Snake Woman*. A sinuous serpent woman dressed in fuchsia silk brandished a curving sword.

'She looks fierce,' Jane said.

'Because she en't really a woman. Got a spell on her.' The urchin's eyes widened to round grapes.

'You've already read it?'

'Course. And when her prince husband finds out she's a great, fat snake, the stupid git drops dead. She fixed him with her magic potion, see, coz she's so stupid she loves him.'

Who was Joe's serpent woman and how soon could Jane prove to Joe that his mystery seductress was just a great, fat worm?

Heading home after work, Jane ran through the possible serpents poisoning her Eden with their interest in Joe's rough-hewn charms. There was a blonde trainee who'd chatted him up for a job at a rather wet barbecue in Islington. Or was it the elementary school teacher Janice, married to an adulterous *Money Programme* presenter who thought being on telly made his mole-strewn face irresistible off-camera? Irene, yes that was her name.

Hadn't Irene recently consulted Joe over an arugula salad dressed with tears about her chances of wreaking revenge via a job on *The Travelling Kitchen*? How far had the distressed Irene taken her appeal for Joe's support?

And then there was Rachel, Bella's PA: crisp ginger hair, vintage frocks that had been discarded for good reason, and winter or summer, bare white-asparagus legs. 'Rachel Murty, not too purty,' was Joe's dismissive joke about Rachel. But was he covering up something?

If it hadn't been for the sexy little BlackBerry texts, Jane would have said that Joe's problem wasn't illicit love. Winning that BAFTA award for his *Afghanistan Vet Suicides* was the turning point. She should never have allowed a tipsy Joe to cradle the award home, kissing the sightless Greek mask as if it were an infant leaving the maternity ward. Those lifeless malicious lips had passed him the contagion of professional vanity.

On the surface, Joe was still the same—hardworking, committed, relishing his 'full British' of fried tomatoes, floury beans, and puffy sausages with his camera crew in the canteen, each morning. But strangely, after the BAFTA glory, nobody's ideas were quite as good as Joe's and no reporter quite up to repeating his masterpiece. No editor—Steenbeck virtuoso or digital whiz—was quite sharp enough for Joe Gilchrist. His anxious supervision in the cutting rooms gave those dry-eyed pros a headache. Joe's innocent star began to sink as low as his responsibilities piled up: Sammie's crippling school fees, plus a hefty mortgage over two floors of Number 19 picked up by Lorraine who now roosted under their eaves.

Not quite sure why his high standards put people off, Joe learned to take what he could get. Finally, all he got was an offer from loyal Bella to produce her show.

Brooding over all this, Jane locked up the library and headed back across the square.

Lorraine's separate front door stood ajar. Her mother's canary-bird hair and red lips popped over the banister. 'Saw you coming.' It was more a summons to the attic than an invitation.

'Sammie doing her homework?'

'Grandma's on the job.'

'Thanks.' Jane spotted some black-rimmed invitations standing sentinel on Lorraine's kitchen shelves. 'Don't tell me—'

'Yet more final curtain calls. Outliving the rest of the cast can be so lonely. One of them is a memorial for Esther Redfern.'

'Oh, dear Esther.' Jane fondly remembered Esther cheating at backgammon in a New York dressing room. 'I'll send flowers. The 800-Flowers Special?'

'No, the Ophelia number for Esther. The usual card, you know, Rosemary for Remembrance, yadda yadda. Thanks so much, darling.'

Always devoted to Joe's career, Lorraine was right now viewing a *Travelling Kitchen* episode. She'd turned off the sound, leaving a mute Bella dropping something white and creamy on to the end of her pointed tongue. Lorraine wagged a finger at the screen. 'Tell Bella that finger-licking business is getting tired.'

Jane watched as Bella batted her eyelashes at a slim black African wearing a majestic toque. The chef threw back his head in a laugh so wide his pink palate caught the glare of the lights hanging overhead, the 'babies.' It looked too much like a training film for dentists, the director cut to the jib camera hovering over the worktable—what cooking shows called 'Doing a beauty.'

'The usual smutty jokes?'

'Very gassy humour today. *The Wonderful World of Beans.*' Lorraine hooted, 'In my day, beans for dinner meant a show was about to fold. This is about as subtle as *The Three Stooges.* Watch— see that? I've counted five close-ups of her lip gloss smacking away and the camera panned right across her cleavage and nearly fell in, twice.'

Lorraine herself was cooking, cigarette holder in left hand, wooden spoon in right. 'Grandma's cooking' at Number 19 meant: dried onion soup stirred into sour cream for dipping Ritz Crackers, Blender Hollandaise poured on flank steak, a 'side' of tomatoes on iceberg and Rocky Road ice cream. Lorraine never apologized for her cuisine—she couldn't trundle much home in her trolley and anyway, there were too many matinees to catch, too many lunches with old darlings needing 'fresh air,' and her nightly DVD.

Her conversation was as straightforward as her menu. 'Your mother has got no side to her,' was Gerd's generous exit line to Jane as he abandoned them for life with a boy in Vienna. 'No discretion, no reticence, no taste, no subtlety, but certainly no side.'

Gerd followed Jane's father Jack in the romantic line-up, and preceded a road show Falstaff and a few others. Now the curtain had fallen on Lorraine's frenetic stage, leaving only the critic's gimlet eye.

'Jane, you know that religious bookstore at the corner? It is very odd.'

'You mean Muslim.'

'No, in addition to that. Odd. The window display gathers dust. Men come and go at all hours, but no one ever buys a book.'

'Perhaps they have to observe special prayer time or something,' Jane muttered.

Lorraine peered through the leaves of her avocado plants across the square. 'They make me nervous.' Lorraine went back to whirring up guacamole.

Jane shifted magazines and letters on to the sideboard and opened a bag of corn chips. She laid out her mother's plastic 'A Season of Gershwin' place mats. The Al Hirschfeld caricatures of Broadway personalities were half-scrubbed off.

'Darling, a serious talk.' Lorraine stopped.

Jane cued her, 'Line?'

'Well. Apparently, Sammie isn't studying hard enough.'

'Everything's . . . fine.'

Lorraine lit a fresh cigarette and snapped her monogrammed lighter shut. Fur boas, evening clutch bags, swizzle sticks, and cigarette lighters—Lorraine had always hogged the glamorous props and the good stage business. Jane worked a paper napkin into pathetic little squares.

'Joe thinks the child needs more reassurance and stability. He hinted something to me about boarding school.'

'*Et tu, Brute?*'

'He looked in yesterday morning, after you'd gone to work. He wafted school fees suggestively through the air, waiting for a certain Fairy Grandmother to catch on.'

'You'll hold off on that.' Jane added, 'I know you're always happy to help.'

'Why hold off? If it's just to get her through these A thingies? You were a mess when you studied for the SAT's, and for what? Why we didn't bring you back to boarding school here in England, I don't know. You never wanted to stay in the States but why wouldn't you say so flat out? Instead, you just killed yourself studying for those damned things. You were all covered in zits and—'

'That was thirty years ago.'

Lorraine stubbed out her cigarette. 'Jane, I've never dodged reality, especially if I couldn't put a show over. I've weathered the turkeys along with the sell-outs. Now you're different from your daughter. You prefer your books. I respect that—'

'No, you don't. "I chose books, you chose looks",' Jane paraphrased Roald Dahl with a rueful smile.

'As if I had a choice! While you were reading *Theatre Shoes*, I was doing three shows a weekend. While you were reading *Othello*, I felt like strangling Jack's sitcom bitch. While you ploughed through the *Anna Karenina*—'

'*Emma Bovary*—'

'I was steaming up my dressing room with Gerd—'

'And your point is?'

'My point is, however I lived my life, I always picked up the tab. I never hid behind the covers of a book. Or threw myself under a moving train. Or got me to a nunnery. Or was found strangled, for that matter.'

'And you think I—?'

'I never folded my act. I curse the day I bought you that stupid Nancy Drew. Now what's going on downstairs? You're hiding away in the library.' Lorraine reached out and clasped her daughter's fingers in support.

'I don't know,' Jane burbled. 'Something's wrong with Joe. Not just the job. Sammie saw some sexy message on his mobile. She asked if Joe was having an affair. He threw a wobbly, but he didn't actually deny it.'

'Big deal.' Her mother shrugged.

'He's bought a bunch of new clothes.'

'New clothes?' Now her mother frowned. A new wardrobe signalled a new show. 'I thought he was just worried about her grades.'

'Well, aren't we all? But he sounded strange about Sammie, as if she were in his way.'

And that wasn't like Joe, who adored his child-woman. What was that second stratagem she'd been reading this morning? Rescue Zhao by encircling Wei. Sammie was the weak chink in Joe's armour. If Zhao was her life with Joe, then Wei, the weak city, was Sammie. Jane should play for time and encircle Sammie to pin down Joe.

Jane ripped the paper napkin into little pieces. 'Sammie can't board. As long as she stays here, Joe won't leave.'

'That bad, huh?' Lorraine tasted her guacamole and squeezed in more lime juice. Lorraine liked her acids straight. 'That's it, then, no boarding school fees.'

'Remind him that her college fees have just trebled, thanks to Lord Browne. If Joe persists, um, you tell him you want to keep a closer eye on her yourself. Maybe we all need to stop treating her like, like—'

'Second Banana. Or in this case, Fourth.'

'Anyway, no boarding, please, Mum.'

'Oh, we're talking Mum now.'

'Even if Joe offered you an interview with Piers Morgan.'

'I'll just tell him to have his people call my people,' Lorraine brushed away Joe's fantasy bribe. 'I'm perfectly happy to spend more time with Sammie,' Lorraine hesitated, her pride only faltering at the frumpy grandma casting, 'Unless my agent calls, you understand.' She winked.

Chapter Three, Kill with a Borrowed Knife

Thanks to a bomb scare delaying the Northern Line, Jane was late for Baldwin's second class by a full twenty minutes. The other five students were listening to him explain Stratagem Three, the "alibi" or "substitute" stratagem.

'Kill with a Borrowed Knife doesn't mean using real knives—you laugh, Mr Filgrove, but I teach these tactics in a prison where it's a genuine proviso. The Knife refers to an outside agent to eliminate your opponent, or to win your objective.'

'Like when Zelda got her best friend to bring me to the pub one Friday night. Zelda fancied me, but used her friend to lure me into her clutches,' Kevin beamed.

'Good, Kevin! You attack borrowing the strength or allure of another, because you lack strength or you want to save your own ammunition for later.'

The men had left a seat in the middle ready for Jane. The relief on Winston Chu's face at her arrival was obvious; how could she extricate herself now, thus squeezed between Keith and Kevin on one side and Winston, Dan and Nigel on the other? Not since playing 'pretend' princess in Lorraine's cast-off costumes had she felt so enthroned, no longer a middle-aged mother with temples of grey frizz that Sammie kept insisting she should rinse out. Now she felt like royalty buttressed by aides and bodyguards on both flanks. Fumbling with her notebook, she shrugged off the silly image; it must be those Lang fairy tales she'd re-shelved this afternoon.

'Another example, Mr O'Neill?'

'Sure. Reminds me of something Stalin did to eliminate the Polish underground defending Warsaw. He used the German army as his knife.'

Young Winston Chu crossed his eyes at Jane, mouthing 'Stalin?'

'Indeed, he did. Please explain to Mr Chu.'

Dan turned to Winston. 'In July 1944, Stalin's first tank unit reached Warsaw. The Polish underground thought okay, great, help's on the way, now's the time to kick out the Germans. They rose up, but the Soviets ground to a halt on the city outskirts. That left the Germans free to throw all their fire against the Polish Resistance. Roosevelt and Churchill begged Stalin to save Warsaw, but the Russian forces just sat on their butts. They let the Germans mop up anybody who might give the Allies trouble later on.'

'Are you some kind of historian?' Winston ventured.

Nigel Deloitte commented. 'Hardly a business example.'

'This is a management class, but each of you might have different things to manage. We'll get to the business models in good time,' Baldwin said.

'How could Number Three be used in a business context?' Nigel persisted. His manicured fingers hung poised over a leather notebook embossed with his bank logo.

'Certainly.' Baldwin leaned against his desk. 'Once upon a time, there was a company called Coca-Cola . . .'

Happily back on track, Nigel, Reinsurance-Keith and Marks-and-Sparks-Kev copied out Baldwin's account: Coca-Cola broke the Nutra-Sweet aspartame monopoly by building up a rival, the Home Sweetener Company, and threatening to switch their business away from Nutra-Sweet once Monsanto's patent expired.

'Then before the Home Sweetener chaps could begin selling their aspartame, both Coke and Pepsi leveraged better contracts with Monsanto.'

'What happened to Home Sweetener?' Keith asked.

'They were just a pawn, you see, a borrowed knife.'

The others laughed. Jane imagined the poor betrayed Home Sweetener manager fallen on the steppes of Asia. Long spears rose from his fallen corpse, ragged banners with the Monsanto logo snapped in the breeze, and a Mongolian cavalry sang the Coca-Cola theme song. "I'd like to teach the world to sing in perfect harmony," over his sightless eyes . . .

'Jane, another example?'

Jane started, her reverie torn away from the steppes. Who could be her knife against Joe's unknown girlfriend? How could she use Joe's infatuation against him or find an agent to ferret out Joe's secret? Anyway, who else would care? People committed adultery every day.

Keith made a stab: 'Lobbying insurance regulators to change government rules to fit your new policies?'

The corridor bell jangled. Baldwin said with a smile, 'Now after the break, we're doing Stratagem Four, Preserve your Strength, and Take Your Ease while Waiting. So go off, now, and take your ease for fifteen minutes.'

Nigel bustled away to answer calls on his iPhone. Winston loped along with Dan towards the glass-fronted case of cling-wrapped sandwiches and stale pastries.

What did her rival even look like? Iago was right. Jealousy was the green-eyed monster. It gnawed at Jane, but its feline eyes stayed myopic as long as her rival stayed in shadow. If anything turned in on itself, it was Jealousy, poisoning its victim with self-loathing. She shouldn't have cut off her long hair. She shouldn't have gained weight.

Memories of her looks during her courtship with Joe on a *Panorama* recce flooded. She'd been slim then, with glossy curls and ethnic jewellery. As his researcher Jane was happy to help lug files and equipment for Joe Gilchrist, so determined to bring in his exposé on arms sales to El Salvador under budget. What glee they had shared at cadging a few reels of spare film off *World About Us* so Fergus could sneak cutaway shots of liberation nuns on the run! They'd been inseparable, night and day, Joe brushing the stray wisps off Jane's forehead while Fergus shot stills of her in the last light of day—that moment cameramen tagged the 'magic hour,' which took the world from the saffron sun to salmon dusk. It gave a poetic definition to the homeliest profile.

That photo now gathered dust on Joe's desk at the Beeb.

Baldwin had told the class that the ancient Chinese had a term for the alliances formed in youth, when young scholars wore simple robes of cotton cloth. Jane and Joe had forged a cloth-gown friendship, along with Bella, Fergus and a few others, but their cloth-gown bond lay in tatters these days. Not that her wardrobe had moved from cotton to silk. Come to think of it, maybe her clothes were a turnoff?

Making her way to the coffee bar, Jane imagined herself with a more youthful spring in her step, an imaginary waist-length braid brushing a damask silk jacket, like a character from a kung fu novel. How did those Hong Kong filmmakers get their heroines springing into the air twenty feet high, twirling a glinting rapier over their heads without cutting off their own braid swinging high, up, up, into the—?

Someone tapped her shoulder. Startled, she scattered her notes all over the linoleum.

'Oh! I'm—sorry, just wanted to say hello.' The Chinese boy scuttled around, collecting pages off the floor. Because his father had enrolled him in the class, Professor Baldwin had nicknamed Winston, 'Chu the Younger.'

'—Rather irritating, that, as there isn't any other Chu in the class.'

'It's only a joke, showing respect for your elder.'

'Look, I've lost my bibliography already. Could I copy yours, rather than risk another wisecrack from Balding the Sage?' Winston fumbled for a pen at the bottom of a computer case full of tangled cables.

'Shall I get us something to drink? Tea? Black or green?'

'People always assume I want tea. What I would really like is,' he grinned, 'a Red Bull.'

By the time Jane returned with their drinks, Winston had copied out the titles of five books.

'So you're Chinese and don't drink tea?'

'Tea is the least of it. I'm a genetic aberration. Drives my father round the twist. I'm allergic to peanut sauce,' Winston ticked off on his fingers, 'Fish sauce, shrimp paste. Just looking at a crab gives me hives. You try getting your kid through a Cantonese wedding saying, "Sorry, none for our little Winston," for thirteen straight courses. After a while, my parents just left me at home.

My poor mother told everybody I was studying physics. Another fantasy. She died hoping I would become some big shot in technology.'

'Anybody can be allergic.'

'To an entire culture? And it's not just food. I am the least numerate Asian on the planet. Forget the abacus, I can't even manage a calculator. And you can forget martial arts. At five, I broke my wrist in beginner's karate.'

'Wow, you must have been enthusiastic!' It was the first time Jane had laughed outright in weeks.

'No, I caught it in the locker door. You've seen how adept I am with my mobile? I froze it trying to program the calendar alerts.' Winston slipped Jane a business card, reading, '*Chu Printers, President, Chu "Lucky" Lok-lo.*'

'That's Dad's card. He says it's never too late to learn Chinese wisdom, even from a *guay-lo* like Baldwin. That's Cantonese for white devil. Dad's idea is that by learning a few management skills, I catch up with the shining sales figures of my Cousin Nelson. He opened a sub-department in our shop, the "Lychee Computer Corner." I can't tell whether Dad likes it or hates it. Probably both.'

'Has Nelson mastered the Thirty-six Stratagems?'

'Doesn't have to. He read applied maths at Leicester. If you mention something like, say, Audio Hijack Pro, he gets hot. He breathes Voip, Skype, or web cam installations like oxygen. The only music to his ears is an iTunes update. Nelson is everything I'm not. He'll inherit Dad's business instead of me and I'll be out on my arse.' Winston shrugged, 'The worst part is, Nelson's nice. It's hard to hate him.'

'Maybe you need a knife strategy to use on Nelson.' She didn't think Winston wouldn't take it to heart.

'Exactly!' Winston exclaimed. 'If you think of anything really tricky, let me know? And I'll help you. Why are you here? You're not a businesswoman.'

'Oh, you know, getting ahead in the library world.'

'Oh.' Winston paused. 'Are libraries so competitive? Our Belsize branch is a little redbrick retreat.'

Jane brushed back her frizz with bravado and rolled her eyes. 'Oh, you can't imagine, Winston. Lots of bells and whistles to hook the younger readers. We're talking e-books, now. And there are the book clubs we manage and, believe me, they can bring out the enemy in some readers.'

Dan O'Neill was approaching their table. On seeing Winston bend his head towards Jane in conspiratorial confidence, the American turned away. Jane felt disappointment.

'Who could be an enemy in a book club?' Winston asked.

Jane blurted out, 'Carla Smythe' with an indiscreet vehemence that sent Winston leaning back in his chair. Know-it-all Carla Smythe, armed with her formidable pile of reviews, was indeed ruining Jane's group for senior borrowers, The Bookworms. Ninety-year-old Mrs Ruth Wilting was Carla's favourite target. Mrs Wilting dared not dispute Carla's pronouncements, much less admit she'd enjoyed a good read. For diversion, Carla might turn on the asthmatic, giddy Alma, or Alma's best friend, the robust but half-deaf Catherine. Catherine didn't catch many of Carla's putdowns.

Rupert Sitwell was their second-oldest member after Ruth, and the only male. He'd got a First from Peterhouse College, Cambridge University. Carla treaded carefully with Rupert, but as he confessed to Jane, even he felt a bit thick when dissecting inter-textuality with Carla.

Listening to Jane's description of the Bookworms, the sympathetic Winston nodded.

'So, Winston, I'm starting to think of Mrs Carla Smythe as a force of totalitarian diktat, sort of Karla, rather than Carla. And I'm no George Smiley.'

Winston pulled on his pink forelock. 'Couldn't any of the other Bookworms be your knife against Carla?'

'Hmm. Rupert does have Carla's breadth of literary reference but Rupert is too well-bred, like the warden in *The Barchester Chronicles*, sort of fading in the fray.'

'Well, charge his batteries and boot him up,' Winston urged. 'Sharpen him for the cut-and-thrust.'

'He's so gallant. Perhaps he would answer the appeal of a librarian in distress.' Jane mused. 'And what might be your knife against Nelson?' Suppose he got a better offer? From a rival company? Any around?'

'Maybe Sultana Software, a Malaysian outfit that sells P.C.'s off the back of a lorry down Havistock Hill. Dad would hit the roof if he thought Nelson was talking to them.'

'Why, Winston. You wouldn't.' Jane insinuated.

'Well, not until I took this class,' admitted Winston. 'If you use the knife strategy this week, then I will, too. You're coming back, aren't you? You're a very easy person to talk to, Jane. You give me courage.'

They shook hands on their pact. Jane resolved she would indeed use the knife strategy. And not just on Carla Smythe.

Chapter Four, Preserve Your Strength, Await the Enemy's Exhaustion

Baldwin concluded the second class by assigning Stratagem Four, 'Set the pace, keep the other side tense and preoccupied,' as homework for the following Friday. This idea was simple—just put your feet up and wear your enemy out with waiting.

There didn't seem much pace Jane could set for Joe. He worked late, and anyway, he'd made himself tense and preoccupied for months without Jane's help. Whenever he did finally thud up the stairs and come through the front door, he dumped his things near the umbrella stand and, without a word, slumped into his chair to stare out the windows. If Joe really did have some woman 'on the boil,' it was a miracle she hadn't spilled over in a froth of frustration at his depression and inertia by now. He cosseted only one item: the BlackBerry aligned next to his placemat over supper, transferred to his nightstand at bedtime, and returned in the morning to watch guard over his coffee. It was a silent succubus draining all his energy without delivering a single 'yes' in return.

He waited from morning to midnight for a producer to call with a commission. Especially welcome would be an assignment from BBC queen bee Camille Harper. His former colleague had promised 'when she had a mo,' to review a pitch—an exposé of corporate charity projects going diabolically wrong—that Joe and Fergus had patched together over free weekends and late nights.

How apt the title for that one, Jane thought, *Projects from Hell*. They faced another silent evening. Sammie was in bed, sulking over limits to her Facebook time.

'Oh, Joe, put away your Crackberry, please, just for five minutes. Then maybe work yourself up to ten. Add an extra minute every day, like those twelve-step recovery programmes for drinkers.'

Joe ate his lasagne without savouring the béchamel sauce he used to praise. When had his prairie-wide laugh shrunk to a sliver of Arctic deep-freeze? Where had it gone, that big spirit that once tackled huge issues with confidence and courage?

She cajoled, 'How about we go for a walk up Primrose Hill? I've read somewhere that a watched mobile never vibrates. You baby-sit that thing like a night nurse in a preemie ward.'

He actually slept with the wretched device, setting its alarm on vibrate so he could rise at dawn to work on *Drunken Grannies, A Shocking Look at Alcohol Abuse Among Respectable Pensioners.*

If only she could get a few seconds alone with it, Jane remained convinced she would find more hidden among Joe's messages than sherry-bingeing grandmas.

Idly, she reached for the BlackBerry. Joe's hand shot out and clutched it to his chest. If Jane hadn't been so shocked to see the anger knitting his dark brows, she would have felt sorrier for him. She couldn't resist, 'Sorry, Gollum. Keep your Precious. Anyway, Camille's probably shopped your idea to the same geniuses who produced *Freaky Eaters* or *Skateboarding Ducks.*'

'You're right, there,' Joe brooded. 'Maybe she already called Fergus and he didn't tell me. Would he go behind my back with some other producer?'

'Not Fergus. You two go all the way back to Enoch Powell's deathbed interview.'

'If Fergus double-crosses me, he'll float down his own river of blood.'

Joe ate less and less, subsisting on reserves of bitterness that fuelled his spiritless shuttle between the square and *The Travelling Kitchen.* What with Joe so snappish, it wasn't easy for Jane to apply Baldwin's lesson to curb her comments while making no foolish moves. One night he'd almost kicked their cat, Bulgakov, out of his path—and he loved Bulgakov, feeding him choice bits of dinner under the table despite Jane's protests.

Waiting for Joe to arrive at exhausted vulnerability might prove impossible—the jumpier Joe got, the greater Jane's tension.

It wasn't exactly homework you could hand in to a classroom of Nigels and Winstons. Jane decided to concentrate on Sun Tzu's principle of preserving her strength until she knew her enemy's identity. As she walked out of the classroom the previous Friday, the lanky Sinologist had taken her upper arm very lightly. He intoned, 'Remember, Jane, when water flows, it avoids the high ground and seeks the easiest, lowest path. Make your enemy tire herself out while conserving your own energy. My assignment to you this week is to flow like water. Lie low. Do not confront or interrogate Joe. Promise me?'

Instead, she tired herself out at work trying to sort out the new database while all the while fighting off horrific visions of Joe and his unknown beauty twisting their naked bodies into Kama Sutra pretzels. Her nightmares turned lurid and literary. Joe metamorphosed into D.H. Lawrence's randy gamekeeper Oliver Mellors with an elusive paramour in Lady Chatterley tweeds. Passionate scenes from Flaubert, Ibsen, and Chekhov wracked her in turn. Jane hadn't yet found hotel receipts in Joe's drawers or smelled a strange perfume in the Volvo, but while Joe survived on Swedish crackers and gall, her fears fed gluttonously in the absence of hard evidence.

Fighting without fighting proved very difficult. Whoever her rival was, Sun Tzu commanded Jane sit this woman out. Would all of Baldwin's lessons require such self-discipline?

'Choose the time and place for your battle, so you know when and where the battle will happen, while your enemy does not,' Baldwin had said. 'Stratagem Four is the only one of the thirty-six stratagems that we can trace back to Sun Tzu himself—the others were all developed over the two millennia since his death.'

Out of the corner of her eyes, like a Len Deighton spy, Jane scrutinized Joe as he emptied his pockets at night, changed into his pyjamas, and said little more than, 'Thank God the *ristafel* episode is in the can. The Indonesian chef was so short he had to stand on a crate behind the prep island.'

Over the weekend she faltered more than once by mentioning one woman's name or another's—say, a comely researcher Joe had openly admired, now long departed to the brainier stretches of Horizon. Or that Japanese chef, Madame Norita, he drove all the way back to Heathrow through a chilly pounding rain? Joe showed not a flicker of guilt nor paid any attention. He nodded at Jane's comments, (mined as they were by the names of sexy acquaintances,) his eyes scanning his computer or BlackBerry for the summons that never came.

Jane sought distraction in her library chores; during a 'Love Libraries' event, it transpired that few borrowers loved the dingy walls of the Chalkwood branch so it now reeked of fresh paint. To avoid triggering Alma's allergies, Jane relocated Monday night's Bookworm meeting to Rupert's Hampstead home.

After all, why shouldn't Jane test Baldwin's strategies on the unsuspecting old dears? It might build her confidence, like all that duelling practice Alexandre Dumas gave his Musketeers. Moreover, she and Winston had a pact. Suddenly she got a wicked idea for using Strategies Three and Four. Before she locked up the library, she made a strategic telephone call . . .

Walking after work through the frozen dusk to the Northern Line, Jane halted beneath a ladder propped against the corner house that straddled the square and Chalkwood Road. A man in spattered dungarees stood perched on the uppermost rung. He was painting a mural on the long dark window by the light of an electric bulb swinging from a thin cord in the breeze.

'Wouldn't it be easier to work by daylight?' she called up.

'I work during day,' he mumbled with an unidentifiable accent.

The man had a wispy blond beard, paint-flecked hands, and ripped trainers. On the window, Jane made out an enormous painted wing with feathers in luminescent salmons, peaches, and pinks. 'What's your painting going to be?'

'A message for them.' He gestured over his shoulder at the Arabic bookstore facing them.

'What's that music playing? It's quite beautiful but eerie.' She pointed to the boom box perched on the windowsill.

'Penderecki's *Requiem*.'

He worked in silence. Jane moved on, only to experience a stranger encounter at the tube station. Dan O'Neill stood in the ticket queue. His tie was loosened, and although he carried no briefcase, he exuded the relaxed satisfaction of a man finishing a good day's work. He gave Jane a warm smile. She anticipated some kind of comment about living or working around Primrose Hill, but instead he said, *sotto voce*, 'Safest time to ride the subway. Evening prayer time, *Salatul Isha*.' He headed off toward the southbound platform.

'Curiouser and curiouser,' she thought, and descended down the rabbit hole to the northbound platform.

Rupert lived in a narrow book-lined house overlooking the heath. John le Carré once lived nearby. Jane liked to pigeonhole London's nooks and crannies with the delicious knowledge that had she dared, she could knock on a particular author's front door and one of their characters would answer. You could even play the game on nearby Chalcot Square. Knock on Number 3 and Sylvia Plath's ghost peered through the front window. Stroll a few metres southward toward Frederick Forsyth's old digs and bump into the Jackal cleaning his gun in his dressing gown. London was full of authors, the dead ones commemorated by blue plaques for mere civilian readers, but still breathing for a librarian. The whole world around Jane shimmered with invisible dimensions, angles, and parallel realities created by writers.

Rupert's polished front door stood ajar for his fellow Worms. Jane had never been here before. The entry hall was papered in maroon and gold stripes and hung with nineteenth century engravings. From his worn Melton overcoat hanging near the hat rack to the gleaming hall table and the China-trade porcelain lamp stand, everything was as refined as their host. He'd laid a tray of hot cheese puffs and anchovy *hors d'oeuvres* alongside a drinks trolley laden with carafes of juice and chilled wine.

Ruth Wilting struggled up the steps behind Jane, her walker bumping through the doorway and her two solid shoes stepping up behind. 'Jane, dear, could I have a word with you?'

'Let me help you, Mrs Wilting. You must be winded. We won't make a habit of this, I promise. The paint fumes will be gone by next week.'

Jane helped the older woman out of her thin mackintosh and lowered her into a brocaded chair. They swapped her rubber-soled walking shoes for cracked patent pumps. Perspiration reduced Mrs Wilting's face powder to a sheen. Hampstead was a marathon trek for the old dear. It was a familiar story among Jane's older borrowers: the Chalkwood Library was constructed in 1961 on a purpose-built ground floor of a small building set in a side-turning off Regents Park Road. Mrs Wilting lived in a sheltered housing block for retirees not many steps away. Many older people with mobility problems shared the sad reality: the daily walk to Jane's bookshelves was the only outing they could manage independently.

'Oh, this makes a nice change. What nice cheesy bits, as Hilda Rumpole would say. No, I wanted to apologize because I must explain to you, Jane dear, why this might be my last meeting.'

'Oh, please don't! I saw this coming, but I want to reassure you, you're an important part of our discussions. Without you, Catherine and Alma might get discouraged.'

'Oh, I don't know about that.' Ruth fished her copy of *The Great Fire* out of a canvas tote bag. "I suspect Catherine just comes for Rupert's cakes. She never gets even halfway through the books and just reads the last few chapters on Sunday night. And I think Alma would come if we read the gardening column from *The Telegraph*. She has a little crush on Rupert, you know. Well, she's young.'

Just then, Alma, seventy-five years young, could be overheard twittering over Rupert's ornithological watercolours in the library beyond.

'You mustn't let on. Alma would be mortified to think we'd noticed."

'We must make it more worthwhile for you, more than cakes and Rupert's charms. Why did you join?'

'Oh, the library's home service was perfectly nice, but Mrs Goodchild—my home help, you know—she saw I liked to read and write. She said I should get out once a week, have a bit of a stroll, see other people, get my hair seen to—'

'Yes, I like the way they've done it.'

'I want to look nice for the club. Yes, well,' Ruth gathered her forces, 'As I said, I don't like to name any particular person but—'

'Well, let me spit it out for you. You aren't looking forward to Carla's lectures. I've spoken to her but as the librarian, I really can't exercise censorship. Still, she is such a killjoy—'

'That's it, Jane! All my life I've loved to read, ever since I borrowed *The Little Princess*. Now each book is spoilt by anticipating how that woman will ruin it. Why does she poison every meeting, Jane? It's as if every volume she picks up is a weed that needs uprooting, until there isn't any lifeblood left in it and there's no opinion still standing but her own. If she doesn't enjoy what she reads, why doesn't the silly cow take up knitting?'

They took a few *hors d'oeuvres* off the tray. Ruth added, 'You know, I would have liked discussing that Safran Foer boy—'

Carla's voice boomed up from the steps. 'Oh, you couldn't possibly mean that, Ruth. A clever-clever sixth-former playing with his word processor fonts.'

'It's original, do admit.'

'Do admit. Hah! Don't use that Mitford slang with me. I don't admit any such thing. So many of these younger writers think that cutting and pasting e-mail on to the page is literature. Well, is everyone in there? Let's get on with Shirley Hazzard.'

At first, it seemed, everyone had enjoyed *The Great Fire*.

Catherine said, 'I admire the eloquence of that quiet death of the worn-out POW! And the Japanese soldier's suicide, the two deaths juxtaposed—oh, clumsy me, sorry.' She plucked a crumb of salmon-and-cress sandwich off Rupert's Persian carpet. 'These are yummy, Rupert. Did your lady make the mayonnaise by hand or blender?'

Alma tried to raise the bar above nibbles. 'Her language was lyrical. I've tried writing poetry but it's so hard not to over-egg it—'

Ruth nodded. 'I've written a bit myself and—'

Catherine wasn't interested in Ruth's senile scribbles. 'Rupert, did you find Hazzard's prose too feminine to represent Aldred's point of view?'

Alma asked, 'Yes, what do you think, Rupert? As a man.' Her bird-eyes darted to their host sitting on his padded footstool. He'd left the battered leather sofa to the broad-hipped ladies. Jane caught the vestigial flirt in Alma's ageing features folding in and out of themselves, like a cushion of soft, powdered flesh. *Mrs Wilting was right—the septuagenarian Alma was in love.*

Rupert said he thought Aldred's rescue of Helen was in keeping with the times. Robbed of his youth by war, Aldred was attracted to Helen's innocence. 'Otherwise, it might have felt wrong, their age difference—'

Carla snorted. 'Well, thank you, Rupert! At last! Aren't the rest of you tippy-toeing around the obvious?'

Carla leaned forwards, freezing Catherine mid-air in a grab for the last sandwich. Catherine's husband had left her for a much younger woman. 'Didn't you find it shocking, Catherine? A thirty-two-year-old preying on a seventeen-year-old?'

Alma gave her friend a supportive pat but Catherine only shrugged, 'As Rupert says, a lot of men lost their youth during the war, and wanted to catch up. And didn't Shirley Hazzard do war work at sixteen? I bet she knew someone just like Aldred.'

'Well, it bothered quite a few reviewers. This was no *Transit of Venus*. It was a big disappointment to many.' She shook her sheaf of clippings.

'They always are, aren't they?' Ruth Wilting murmured.

'What do you mean by that?'

Rupert argued, 'You're too harsh, Carla—'

'—John Banville! Won the Booker in 2005!' Carla hooted down her bosom at him. 'Banville says, "Hazzard's elliptical style will try the patience".'

'Well, Banville's wrong.'

Carla stared down at Rupert. 'Phwf! Strip this story down and it's just a Harlequin romance!'

'Closer to Rilke than Barbara Cartland.'

'Well, that's just your opinion, Rupert.'

'Actually, it's not. It's from *The New York Review of Books.*' Rupert batted his sparse lashes. '*The Guardian* said, "A very fine novel." *The Observer* called it gravely beautiful and utterly attentive.'

Ruth Wilting was grinning.

Jane jumped up, 'Right, we agree it's just one stroke short of a masterpiece. Bravo, Ms Hazzard. Next week, *The Tiger's Wife.*'

Carla sputtered and banged shut her copy of *The Great Fire*, but the others bustled past, cleaning up the battlefield of napkins and crusts. All but Jane trundled out the front door, a woollen octopus of extending umbrellas, capes, hats and scarves, their greying heads comparing bus timetables.

Jane exclaimed, 'Brilliant, Rupert! You pulled the sting right out of Carla's "stilted." I thought Ruth would crow with happiness.'

'You used me Jane, and I enjoyed every minute.'

'Too bad we can't do her in every month, but she'd twig soon enough.'

'I don't think she suspected our little plot tonight. Was I all right? Not too brutal?'

'Carla deserves it. She called my senior manager this week to say my reading choices weren't good enough.'

'Stabbed in the back?'

'Indeed. So, I thanked Carla by phone after I faxed you those reviews. I asked her to give a close reading of *Ulysses*, *A Suitable Boy*, and Byatt's *Frederica* trilogy—to see if we might benefit from her judgments.'

Rupert passed a hand across the parchment skin of his brow. 'Jane, that must be at least two thousand pages. You'll wear the woman out.'

'It's a tactic, so that I can relax for at least a week,' Jane said. An exhausting read it would be, if she could count on Carla's literary hubris to force her through all the volumes in time.

As he said goodnight to a triumphant Jane, Rupert's wireless spectacles on his small, white face gleamed as sharp as a knife catching the overhead lamp. She had used the knife strategy twice over—if you counted Rupert's expert at *The Times* as one knife, and Rupert himself as another. Wearing Carla out was Stratagem Four.

Flush with martial confidence in Sun Tzu and his disciples, Jane strode back to the Hampstead tube station. The rumble of the train pulling into the Northern Line platform sounded like a drumming roar in her ears, a call to the battlefield. For one whole week, she'd taken her ease and preserved her strength.

The night air coming off Primrose Hill promised a wet winter. She crossed paths with a breathless pair of lovers descending from the view at the top of the Hill of the lights spreading from St Pauls' all the way to Canary Wharf. Joe and she used to do that.

She braced her shoulders as she marched down Primrose Road towards the bollards at the top of the square, that perfect enclave, empty and peaceful. The spattered painter in the shaggy cardigan had retired and his ladder rested on the grass below the window.

He had started a painted angel. After finishing the two wings, he'd filled in a Renaissance face framed by yellow ringlets. The bottom half of the figure was missing, but there were two muscular shoulders and sleeves of sapphire blue and shimmering emerald green spanning the twin panes. Jane recognized the features of a fierce Michael guarding the square. His hair might be curled, but his eyes weren't gentle and the mouth was clenched tight.

Jane hurried to the warmth of Number 19. Lorraine's blue television glow spread on to the roofs outside the dormer window.

Her mother's watchful silhouette retreated from the window as Jane crossed the square. Lorraine worried, Jane knew, not only about her daughter's safety in the metropolis, but also about Sammie, about their loving quartet. Jane wanted to reassure her mother that if Baldwin were right, the roiling waters would settle at some tidemark of emotional ease. Her sharp suspicions of Joe's meandering had given way to days of unfocussed doubt.

The evening's success in diminishing Carla's force gave Jane a surge of capability. She didn't have to defend all of heaven like that angel, just this little corner of a square in NW1, but she too was preparing for battle over her small patch of peace. She had been girding her loins for the moment of exhaustion, looking for the opening for attack.

She knew what she had to do. Wait for the moment. Bide her time. And when Joe was totally exhausted, her forces would seize a hostage.

She was going to kidnap his bloody BlackBerry.

Chapter Five, Exploit the Fire to Commit Robbery

'Number Five! The vulture strategy! Sun Tzu teaches us that when your enemies are confused or weakened, we must swoop down at the first opportunity and seize them.'

Baldwin rubbed his long palms together as though preparing to strip the bones of the six work-weary adults slumped in front of him. Jane admired the enthusiasm of his style, but with that long nose, high forehead, and bony shoulders, he looked a bit too vulture-like right now.

He'd hinted at a stint of teaching at Hong Kong University but those times had 'changed for good.' He'd returned to London after the 1997 handover of Hong Kong to Beijing's control. Before that? That was one story they couldn't coax out of him. In England, he'd found a home of sorts and a teaching position. So why did the forceful, hawkish Baldwin strike Jane as so vulnerable? Perhaps it was because he so obviously needed students—not as groupies for his ego—but as fellow enthusiasts. Timeless in those droopy tweeds, almost weightless, he gave off the whiff of an absent pilgrim 'returning' to find an England more foreign than the ex-colony he'd left.

Jane pondered as to which author would have created Baldwin; he was too brisk for a brooding Brontë, but not quite aristocratic enough for one of Trollope's Pallisers. Leonard Woolf? Cervantes? There was an Asian reticence to his pedantry and formality. As he struggled to engage their tired imaginations, Baldwin appeared in Jane's imagination in long black silk robes, fraying around the edges, topped by a scholar's cap shiny with wear. Anyway, when not animated in lecture, his expression seemed scarred by some honourable defeat in some intellectual marathon with the powers that be.

He wore no wedding ring. Yet Jane had detected no leanings towards the boys. Quite the contrary, after only two classes, he'd singled Jane out as the object of a dusty gallantry. You could imagine Baldwin like an English version of Van Gulik's detective Judge Dee, hiding in his study from his four gracious but managerial mandarin wives. He lived for the old tales.

'. . . Suddenly, the states of Qin, Wei, Zhao and Chu were all embroiled in a war over the Han—'

'Sorry, but are we expected to remember all these Chinese names for the final?' Nigel asked.

'It would be nice, Mr Deloitte, but for my purposes, it's the tactics that count. Here's a story from that Chinese classic, *The Three Kingdoms* . . .'

'My father used to tell me all these Monkey King stories, but I preferred *Curious George*,' Winston muttered to Jane.

'That's why your father sent you to this class,' Jane whispered.

'. . . SO, Mr Chu, in order to foil the monks' plan to burn the Monkey King and steal his magic robe at night, the monkey stays awake and gets a fireproof blanket—'

'Harry Potter's Invisibility Cloak!' chimed Kevin.

'Similar, yes. He calls up a strong wind to fan the flames that devour the entire monastery and the evil, greedy monks. But the Mountain Demon sees the chaos, and steals the magic robe when the Monkey King isn't looking.'

Kevin was confused, 'I don't get this. The Mountain Demon won? The Monkey King lost his friend's fancy dressing gown? Isn't the monkey supposed to be the hero? I can't lose our Christmas bathrobe order.'

'Yes, could we get to the business models, please?' urged Nigel. He had closed his bank-issued notepad minutes before.

'The moral of Strategy Five is: When the enemy country is beset by internal conflicts, when disease and famine ravage the population, when corruption and crime are rampant, then it will be unable to deal with an outside threat. This is the time to attack. So, Kev, imagine you're walking the shop floor. Two tipsy shoppers start arguing over a dress. Suddenly, they realize their handbags are gone. Got it? You, Keith, give us another.'

'Two hot salesmen in a branch office keep slagging each other to the boss. The quiet guy waits until they're really over the top, makes his move, and gets the big transfer upstairs to headquarters. Easy.'

'Now last week's homework, Three or Four. Nigel?' Baldwin's bird-of-prey eyes zeroed in on the banker.

Nigel Deloitte had his example of Borrowing a Knife at the ready, a description of many months' snarky conniving. Long-frustrated at the refusal of a small but feisty analysis house to come in under his bank's umbrella, Nigel had arranged a bogus offer from a sister bank at an irresistible price. The little company's board voted to sell and take their profits, at which point Nigel's secret allies yanked the rug out, leaving no other suitor but a leering Nigel, his low-ball offer the only thing left on the table.

'We not only used a knife, but we twisted it, because we strung out the talks until the founder's marriage was on the rocks,' Nigel said.

'Oh, nice touch, Deloitte,' said Dan O'Neill. He shook his head and glanced at Jane.

Jane confessed how she'd armed Rupert with a sheaf of reviews to sap Carla's domination of the Bookworms. This drew a satisfied verdict from Baldwin, 'Very original.'

Winston's stab at Number Three had gone wrong. When Chu the Elder heard Sultana Software was wooing Nelson, he challenged Nelson, who of course denied any dealings with the Malaysians. Old Mr Chu had lost so much face, he'd given Nelson a raise and more floor space for his Lychee promotions.

'It helps if your knife is more solid than a concocted story,' Baldwin said. 'And Nelson used tonight's Number Five on you Winston, whether he knew it or not! The country beset by internal conflicts was your own father-son relationship. Nelson saw your father was embarrassed and knew it was the ideal moment to make his move.'

Baldwin continued, 'Don't get discouraged, Winston. Try to see all your situations from an Eastern point of view—in constant change, without stasis, *wu chang*. No defeat is permanent—'

'So no victory is permanent,' Dan said.

'Unfortunately, also true,' Baldwin nodded. 'Your plan should not look so much like a linear chain of cause and effect,' he drew a straight line across the board, 'as a cycle in endless flux, where you try to obtain as many advantages as possible.' He drew a rolling spiral from left to right.

'Oh, Lord. We might be in this classroom forever,' Kevin quipped, weaving his torso back and forth, 'in a state of endless flux.'

'Well, you certainly will, Kevin, if you don't contribute more. You'll tell us your homework after the break.'

Jane noticed that Dan's repeated comments prevented Baldwin from asking the American to serve up his own homework. She found Dan an odd combination of congeniality and opacity. She was more used to Americans like Lorraine's visiting stage buddies—personalities as legible as the poster billings they craved.

Dan asked her to share the break with him. From the canteen's corner, Jane and he watched Keith and Winston swallowed up by the Sane Marriage matrons and Polymer engineers. Dan was a Gulf War I vet who now worked for the New York City Police Department. He was in London for professional consultations, 'to keep an eye on opportunities for the NYPD over here.'

Dan was a welcome change from the hapless Winston. He wasn't tall or photogenic like Joe, but rougher around the edges with an easy confidence that Jane found sexy despite herself. Dan said nothing more about his liaison work, but asked Jane a slew of questions. Perhaps police interrogation technique had contaminated his talent for small talk, but he was a good listener to Jane's work problems:

'. . . Becoming more of a social centre than a library, if it keeps going like this. At least, that's the fear of some library campaigners. They're planning to cut our book budget again.'

'Who's they? Aren't the librarians in charge?'

'For policy, *they* are the Museums, Libraries and Archives Authority. And the local council's in charge of money. Of course, there'll always be some readers. And the independent bookstores are putting up a good fight . . .' Dan's eyes wandered across the crowd.

'Do you live around that tube station?' he said, suddenly turning back to her.

'Not far. Chalkwood Square. Yourself?'

'I told you, a service apartment near Oxford Circus. How long have you lived up there?'

'Forever. When Joe and I first arrived, the square was derelict. The railings were still gone, torn up for scrap during the war. Garden a ruin. Now look at it! Chockablock with the chattering classes.'

'Chattering classes? Funny phrase. Like my sixth-grade class with Miss Gravelstein. Anyway, it's a very, very nice neighbourhood. I jogged the other evening on Primrose Hill. That's one expensive butcher.'

'Did you see the price of Hampstead Heath Honey in the Melrose and Morgan window? It's all right for Jude Law. We shop at Tesco.'

'Interesting bookstore.'

'Bookstore? Primrose Hill Books?'

'No, I mean the other one.'

'Oh, that one! They don't sell many English-language books. Chris—he's my colleague in charge of our community outreach— he asked them once if they wanted to do a cross-cultural event with our branch.'

'No takers?'

'They were polite but no. On the other hand, the Primrose Hill Books people are really lovely. They lined up Alan Bennett for us.'

'Did they.'

'The playwright? He lives in St. Marks Crescent, so it was just a stroll for him. Look, don't be offended, but you don't remind me of a typical American cop. You make me think of a watcher,' Jane blurted out. 'You know . . . listeners and forgers, something, something, how does it go? Couriers and watchers and seducers, and something, something balloonists, and, oh yes, lip readers.

That doesn't mean anything to you? It's le Carré. Sorry, I always stick people into books. Or pull them out. Occupational reflex.'

'Put me in Ed McBain.' Dan tossed their empty cups into the bin.

><><

When Jane opened the front door that night, she found Joe stretched across the sofa, his mobile stuck to one ear.

'No, I don't think we could rear our own calf on location, no matter what they do on *River Cottage*.' It was only Bella. Joe looked pained. 'The show has to stick with foreign food. No foreign, no show. You're not Delia Smith.' He chuckled, 'Luckily. Oh, hi, sweetie. Nice class? Uh, uh. Look, Bella, I have to hang up now. I know, I know . . . No, it's not a problem, go on . . . I know, I know, I know.'

'You know a helluva lot,' Jane giggled from the kitchen.

Joe nodded, 'I know . . . Bella, do you think this could keep 'til tomorrow?'

But he kept listening to the whinging running into his ear, creasing his brow, and emerging out the other ear.

Poor Bella. It was hard to grudge her Joe's time. How many romances had she gone through now, and yet there she was, still alone at nights. It was typical Bella to expect the Gilchrist *ménage* to be there for her, night and day. Yet surely, she had enough moments during the day to cry on her producer's shoulder. It was hard to draw a line when they were all such old friends. Bella was like one of the family, descending on Sammie with godmother gifts that were always OTT, carried off to school next day for showing off to friends and rivals.

This particular conversation must have been going on for hours because Joe's baritone had worn down to a lovable growl, drowned by Lorraine's hairdryer whining down through the ceiling boards. This ballooning gold lame headdress was a contraption that Lorraine pulled on over a Medusa's head of curlers and earphones plugged into Stephen Sondheim or Leonard Bernstein.

As she emptied the dishwasher, Jane admired Joe's patience. Well, better Joe spent his evening listening to Bella's complaints about the guest chefs, the menus, the publicity department, than pining after Rachel Murty, the goggle-eyed redhead who trailed around with a clipboard of continuity notes. Rachel had resurfaced as Other Woman Suspect.

Hercule Poirot's phantom features hovered over the can of scouring powder on the sink counter. '*Oui*, my little grey cells tell me, Jane: the youthful fumbling Rachel, this one has the means, she has the opportunity, and most of all, my friends, she has the motive. This ageing Joe, he can help the helpless Rachel, is it not so?'

Joe was forcing things to a close, 'Look, I really have to say goodnight,' when they heard a scream from the attic floor.

'Jane! JOE! HELP!'

Joe ran up the twisting stairs, three steps at a time. Through a blur of smoke, Jane saw Joe jump full on top of a choking, coughing Lorraine, now screaming under his thick torso muffling the burning bonnet. Jane ran to the bedroom and grabbed a blanket. Joe wrapped it around Lorraine and pounded at the orange flickerings in Lorraine's chiffon night. Ashy flakes floated and drifted into the shag carpet.

Lorraine rolled back and forth, open-mouthed with fright. Jane emptied Lorraine's rubbish bin on the floor, and filled it with water. Joe dowsed Lorraine and lifted her clear of the smouldering headgear. The three stared at the blackened gunk pooling into the rug.

'Oh, oh, my God,' Lorraine sobbed, her hands flailing at the back of her head. 'The heat—'

'Bend over, let's check the damage.' Jane pushed aside the bristly curlers. Underneath the singed hair, a scorched patch of skin was turning purplish at one end of her nape and translucent white at the other side.

'I'll go get ice and disinfectant,' Jane said. 'Luckily the curlers absorbed most of the heat but you'll have to trim that bit off.'

'Oh, dammit,' her mother exploded. 'Christ, what if I get a part?'

It was so typical of Lorraine to worry about an audition call-up.

'Why didn't I buy those fire extinguishers?' Joe said, scraping at the sticky, black plastic.

Jane ran downstairs to her ice trays. 'What if I get a part?' she muttered to Bulgakov who'd already claimed the sofa warmth left by Joe. She was banging ice chips into a salad bowl, wondering at the aged person's ability to live in the past, when she caught sight of something blinking under the coffee table.

Joe's BlackBerry lay like prey, its code opened and its secret innards exposed. Jane heard them upstairs—Joe's measured reproof, then the old-lady refusal to take the blame for clinging to a twenty-year old hairdryer with frayed wires.

'I'm not a complete idiot, Joe. It could happen to anyone. Oh, God, look at my hair!'

Jane was alone downstairs. Joe's BlackBerry lay there, beckoning to her, winking, coy and impish from behind a table leg.

The temptation was too great. Laying the ice to one side, Jane approached the instrument with stealth. She punched 'messages,' 'inbox.' Like the Mountain Demon's swift move on the magic robe, her theft wouldn't take more than an instant. The Monkey King need never know.

And there they were, (oh, foolish Joe!) all his received messages stacked up, one after another. Most of them were 'call me's,' but others were 'miss you's,' 'can't wait's,' 'don't hold out,' 'act on our feelings,' and the very worst, 'For her own sake, tell her things have changed!!!!!' Really, five exclamation points. How old was this girl? She probably dotted her i's with little hearts.

With seconds remaining to her before Joe became suspicious, Jane ran her eyes down his caller list. She checked Rachel but there was no match. Anyway, Joe's seductress must be a worthier foe than the gauche Rachel.

She heard Lorraine upstairs fluttering back and forth between her bathroom and tiny sitting room. 'Where's that ice?' Joe yelled down the stairwell.

Jane's thumbs punched and hovered, checking numbers against names, running through Beeb regulars, Fergus, Olivia, Phil, his brother Sterling in Winnipeg, their Polish ex-housekeeper—she still there?—Bulgakov's vet, Sammie's orthodontist, the Volvo garage and even that old standby, department head Camille Harper—though why should somebody so obviously giving Joe the professional finger say in her next breath, 'I dream of your body?'

She heard Joe stomping down the stairs, seconds from finding her with the Blackberry in her guilty hands! But before she could toss it back under the coffee table, his footsteps continued right past their open doorway, carrying Lorraine's charred negligee down to the rubbish bin.

Desperate, she punched the BlackBerry one last time, asking for 'details.'

It spread into a mocking grin, its window a luminous green eye expecting her horrified reaction. The person sending Joe all those panting love pleas read out in five horrible little letters: BELLA.

Chapter Six, Noise in the East, Attack to the West

Why would Bella steal Joe, old Joe, past-his-prime-Joe, waist-deep-in-mid-life-petulance Joe? Why would any celebrity, even one dumped by a Parisian fusion chef via the pages of Vanity Fair, look at Joe?

Perhaps someone stole Bella's mobile and sent those messages?

Night after night, rigid beside Joe on their well-worn mattress, Jane stared sleepless at the wall. She trod to the library in a daze. She set Lorraine's dinner tray in a trance. Through a fog of numbness, she coached Sammie for her A-levels. She wanted to cry, but she'd done that. Sheer incredulity bricked up any tears.

From the earliest days at the Beeb, Bella had distanced herself from the chorus line of assistants and researchers hoping to get on the box. Her amorous ambitions aimed well beyond the middle-class hunting grounds of Shepherd's Bush to the lusher expanses of dinner parties in Mayfair and weekends in the country.

Bella had never bothered with Joe. Joe wasn't wealthy, famous, chic, or edgy enough. Jane recalled Joe's own derisive, 'Bella greets every producer with open legs.' Had he been hiding pique?

Eaten up with professional anxiety, Joe now looked a seedy, under-shaved has-been, a wraith of wasted self-sabotage. What could he possibly offer Bella at this late date but acrimony, maintenance headaches, and package hols?

It couldn't be sex. Bella boasted she could get enough of that whenever she wanted. Jane gnawed her way out of her shock to get at the truth of why Bella's flame was licking at Joe's toes.

><

'There can never be too much deception in war.' Baldwin pulled a ping-pong bat from his battered case. 'China's national table tennis team uses Stratagem Six in major tournaments. Watch carefully.'

He tossed the white ball to within an inch of the ceiling, then slammed it through the air over their heads against the back wall. It rebounded, smacking the back of Nigel's ear.

Winston sniggered, 'Good shot.'

'Sorry, Deloitte.' Baldwin now stood next to Keith, three yards from where he'd tossed the ball. 'Did any of you notice me dart over to the window?'

Returning to the board, he traced four ideographs in swooping lines with a squeaky felt pen. *Sheng dong, ji xi*. Give it a go, Mr O'Neill?'

'Noise . . . East, well, I guess that would be something like, make a noise in the East and launch an attack in the West.'

'Very good,' Baldwin said. 'Now all of you were too busy watching the ball and smirking at Nigel's misfortune to see me shift position. Stratagem Six looks a bit like Stratagem One. In both tactics, you mask your preparation for the real attack, but Six is less passive. You attack where there is no defence, stage an alert in the east, but strike in the west. Pretend to be weak or soft, withdraw without warning, be incomprehensible, and force the enemy to make wrong preparations.'

'Like shoplifters!' said Kevin. 'One kid pretends she's going to throw up if she isn't shown the loo, while her friend pockets a necklace.'

Nigel spoke up: 'Last month our so-called partner set a lot of conditions that turned out to be a complete distraction, nothing to him at all. Meanwhile, he screwed us on a currency technicality that cost us fifteen per cent.'

Baldwin smiled at Jane. 'Make sure your enemy finds himself or herself attacked where she didn't expect it. The element of surprise gives overwhelming advantage.'

Later, lying in bed listening to Joe's snores and snorts, Jane wondered how she could surprise Bella. Bella had surprised her. How could Jane distract Joe any more than he already was? Bella was working on him in the office by day and via BlackBerry by night.

In the pre-dawn hours, Jane's shock fed most avidly on her ballooning fears. In her imagination, Bella's celebrity lips, glossed up for the camera, turned vampire-like. Her coiffure spread wilder and her nails turned a deeper scarlet, always stirring, picking, and shelling Joe like a fresh prawn.

Jane would drag herself exhausted from their bed at dawn. Coffee mug in hand, she stared out at the chilly, grey square, its familiar railings more a prison enclosure than a sanctuary. It was small comfort that one of the glimpsed text messages implied Joe had yet to succumb! Bella knew Jane's weak points, especially her inability to change Joe's fortunes. At least Bella was only the face of *The Travelling Kitchen*. Had she been the assignments editor on *Newsnight*, Joe might have stripped off his compunctions along with his trousers and socks at her bedside months ago—just for a chance to produce, what was it now? Oh yes, *Underground Iran*.

Baldwin had lectured, 'Sun Tzu takes this tactic further; Not only make one false move to lull the enemy. Repeat the false move as genuine.'

Yes, to feint, not faint. *Keep on pretending you know nothing. Keep on pretending, pretend, pretend.*

Jane would focus on setting the date for Lorraine's eightieth birthday party and agreeing on a guest list. Lorraine believed her fan club numbered more than one hundred and fifty 'luvvies.' She handed Jane a list that Leporello would have tripped over. It would be impossible to produce half that many actual bodies for her mother's shindig. Many resided in a home for ageing theatre people, but the manager haggled over the staff needed to haul them to NW1. The more dogged of the remaining candidates were taking supper theatre to outposts like Singapore and Johannesburg, or 'resting' between jobs in private digs Jane couldn't locate. Some were too plain gaga to recall Lorraine King or their halcyon days playing the Porter to Jack King's MacDuff.

Worst of all, Lorraine had listed Sir Brian MacKelling at the very top. He was neither gaga nor gone. Sir Brian not only going strong. Sir Brian was 'huge,' filmed and fêted from New Zealand to LA. MacKelling! Why not bring back Olivier and Gielgud from their graves? What the hell! Hamlet's murdered father, let's not forget him!

Sammie mimicked her grandmother as she helped Jane clean Lorraine's flat. 'Just call his agent, darling, or run down to Lime House. Tell him he looks buff, and he'll be your slave. Eeeyew. Look at this ashtray. Disgusting old bat.'

'Sammie! She's your grandmother.'

'I love her absolutely, but look at this!' Sammie kneeled on the carpet. 'Is this a dead spider? Oh, yuk! It's one of her false eyelashes, all gummy. Did you see the cigarette scorches on her bedside table? That hairdryer explosion was just a foretaste of the Last Inferno. I hope I'm not still living here when she burns down the whole house. She's a menace.'

'I'll remind her. But not the same day I tell her that Sir Brian can't come.'

'Grandma says it was Grandpa Jack's supporting role in that production of, oh, whatever it was, that made Sir Brian's career.'

'Nobody made Sir Brian but himself, by hard slog.' Jane turned off the Hoover just in time to hear Lorraine's steps coming up. A lifetime of dance warm-ups and a sturdy banister was keeping her mother upright and steady.

The old gal entered, rosy-bright with cold, the veins of her pert nose slightly the worse for a life of Green Room cocktails.

'Mother, did you walk to the butcher and back without a coat?'

'Well, I didn't expect to be so long. I couldn't find it. Joe left it at the cleaners.'

'It's right here, Grandma. Why don't you wear your glasses? A trip to the High Street isn't an audition.'

'LIFE is one long audition, child. Be prepared to go on at all times. I only got chilled because I was held up. There's some iman giving a performance outside—'

'Mother, you mean imam. Iman is Mrs David Bowie.' 'Well, look out the window and you'll see who I mean.'

The three of them crushed together on the window seat and looked across the roof. Blocking the cul-de-sac at the top of the square were half a dozen neat rows of rear ends turned up to the darkening sky.

'Pretty tight choreography for amateurs,' Lorraine said. 'I've seen more ragged chorus lines in the West End.'

'Why are they in our square?' Sammie demanded. 'Shouldn't they pray at the mosque over on Park Road?'

'They're on tour,' Lorraine said. 'A matinee arranged by that religious bookstore.'

'Listen to them chant,' Sammie said.

'I couldn't cut my way past their holy heinies, they were crooning so loud. I just stood there behind the leader, clearing my throat, you know, really projecting that kind of meaningful cough you aim at the back stalls. The preacher gave a cue and they all dropped to their knees and one of them did a pratfall right across my trolley. My eggs are probably scrambled already.'

'Just so long as they don't do more than pray,' Jane said.

'Or make me wear a headscarf.' Sammie tossed Lorraine's coat over her head, arms outstretched, chanting, 'I'm pure. I'm a virgin! I can't breathe!'

A key turned in the lock downstairs. Jane steeled herself. Did she have the courage to execute her feint tonight?

After Joe, Jane and Sammie had eaten their defrosted stew together, Sammie retreated to do her 'graphs and functions.' Jane put on a pistachio kimono she'd picked up from a Camden stall. The swaying sleeves lent a willowy feeling. Curling seductively into the sofa cushions, she gazed at Joe hunched over his papers.

Time for Stratagem Six.

'Joe, let's talk for a minute.'

'What about?' He shuffled his pitches into two piles: rejected and to-be-rejected. He didn't notice Jane's slinky robe.

'About Rachel. I know, Joe, about you and Rachel.' She forced conviction and hurt into her tone.

He didn't even swivel to face her. 'Rachel Murty?'

'You two are having a fling, aren't you?' She tried to sound hurt, playful, and superior all at once.

Now, Joe looked straight over at Jane. 'Rachel? What's there to know? She's Bella's assistant and so . . .'

At the word Bella, Joe's eyes dropped down to his story pitches.

'You know, I haven't entirely lost touch with the old crowd. You should be more careful. Things don't stay secret for long. There's always some frustrated biddy at the Beeb who thinks she's doing you a favour pulling the proverbial wool away from your eyes. I'd have thought you'd been around long enough to know better.'

'Me getting a leg over Rachel? For God's sake, as if I had the time.'

'How reassuring to know fidelity hangs on scheduling. At least you could leave me the dignity of not letting me be the last in all of London to know.'

'Don't be ridiculous. Rachel's a nincompoop, a twit. Bella only keeps her on staff so she can bully her.'

Jane waited for him to say more, but real reassurance lay lifeless on the floor between them, refusing to do its traditional turn in the cabaret of mated life. Lorraine King's daughter was quick to spot a missed cue.

'Joe?'

'Gimme a break, Jane. Don't I have enough problems on my plate?'

'At Ma Maison? You wouldn't spend money like that on Fergus. Sort of fits in with the new shirt you're saving for something special and the late hours . . .'

Joe finally rose and took her in his arms. 'I've been distracted. I've got to get things back on track.' He kissed her.

The pistachio silk began to fall away. She kissed Joe back with all her passion and then—the BlackBerry chirped from the kitchen table. To Jane's dismay, Joe gave her forehead a kiss and took the call.

'Oh, that's great! Yes, that works fine. Ciao.'

'*Drunken Grannies* lurched on to Camille's shooting schedule at last?' Red-faced, Jane refastened her kimono belt.

'No, that was Bella. God, I'm bushed.' He headed off to bed—without Jane.

How that terse exchange with Bella had brightened his mood! Still, he exuded a new wariness. Jane had made her Noise in the East, so to speak, without him knowing where or how she'd opened her Western front. Now he'd be careful around the studio, especially around poor Rachel who innocently adored him, but the most Jane could hope for was that he'd warn Bella to back off, that Jane suspected something—in this case, the wrong thing.

She retreated to her side of the bed, crumpling her flimsy kimono with Joe's dismissive peck burning her worried brow.

In her dreams, the green silk crêpe stiffened, its hem lengthened to the ground like a tent, and the sleeves spread into embroidered wings. She took flight, like something between a kung fu movie star and that painter's blond avenging angel.

She soared back and forth past the house facades of French blue, dove grey and pale yellow. She jumped lightly from post to post along the railing. A 'dream' Bella wearing her trademark apron watched from the far side of the square. Jane sailed around the trees, which had mysteriously changed from sturdy plane trees into supple bamboo. With Strategy Six, she'd slowed things down, perhaps even gained the upper hand—with a little humiliation but without a battle, just as Baldwin had promised.

Chapter Seven, Create Something Out of Nothing

On the night devoted to Stratagems Seven and Eight, furious gusts blew Baldwin's shivering students straggling into the classroom. Nigel secured his charcoal cashmere overcoat at a safe distance from Kevin's clownish ways with coffee cups. Winston scurried in, soaked to the skin in a flimsy athletic jacket, and blew on his hands to warm them. Dan strode in late, with no apology for either his tardiness nor for the neon-green anorak that made him look like a giant lime on steroids.

Compared to his soggy, raw-faced students, Baldwin looked sprightlier than ever. Thanks to the old-fashioned heaters, his lank hair floated in a static aura around his temples. A crimson tie hung down his white shirt like a bright exclamation mark. He stroked it now and then to check it was still centred on his chest. Perhaps the silky adornment was new.

He opened class with the cryptic: 'Things in the world arise from existence. Existence arises from non-existence.'

'Whoah,' said Kevin, 'Spacey, what?'

'Yes, Kevin. Spacey.'

Keith burst out laughing, 'Got you there, mate!'

Baldwin resumed, 'Space. Emptiness. Nothingness. Before anything came into existence, it was non-existent. That is, it came from nothingness, the basic premise of Laozi, sixth century BC.'

'Daoism,' Winston nodded. 'Dad's a Daoist. I think. Sort of a capitalist Daoist. Well, maybe just a capitalist with a naff Daoist shrine in his shop.'

'Even in the West, we think of Laozi's work as more than interior decorating, Winston. He's profoundly philosophical. However, in China, Laozi's *Tao-te-ching* is read as a military tract. And as you will see, Nigel, it offers ample uses for business.'

At which point, Nigel Deloitte finally uncapped his tortoise-shell Dupont.

'Strategies One through Six were the Winning strategies. The next six are the Enemy Dealing Strategies. Number Seven is about lying. What some of you,' he fixed on Dan, 'might term disinformation. Sun Tzu uses Number Seven when destroying the enemy's reputation. I'll let you ponder that while I hear last week's homework. Any Noises in the East?'

'Supposing you were watching a, uh, competitor?' Dan began. Everyone leaned forward. At long last Dan was offering something besides a stale historical anecdote.

'You don't want this competitor to know you're watching his business, or in contact with one of his employees?' The American chose his words with care. 'So, you make it really obvious you're following the activities of another one of his employees.'

Nigel picked up Dan's thread. 'You might arrange to be seen lunching with one of his staff? Or send him indiscreet communications through the office systems?'

'You got it, Deloitte. Incriminate the wrong guy.'

'A perfect example of Noise in the East, Attack in the West,' Baldwin nodded.

'Exactly what kind of business are we talking about, Dan?' With his perky pink spikes, Winston looked like a parrot poking his little beak out the bars of his cage.

'Religious publishing,' said Dan, not missing a beat. 'It's more competitive than you might think, Chu. Important to know what's being pushed into the market.'

'I never took him for a spiritual guy,' Winston whispered to Jane. 'I mean, a Gulf vet and all—'

'And your homework, Mr Chu?'

Winston's glance dropped to his purple Converses. 'Well, Professor Baldwin, it went all wrong.'

'As usual,' Nigel sniffed.

'I tried to distract a customer with such a dazzling array of print options, they wouldn't see how I doubled their page run, but when they went to sign the order, they did notice and complained to my father. So the Noise in the East became a roar in my face, if you see what I mean.'

Kevin and Keith grimaced as one.

'But,' Winston rallied, 'I've got a story that makes up for it. I don't know if it counts as homework—'

'Have a go, Winnie,' Kevin cheered. Of course, nobody had heard any homework from Kev yet.

'It's about three of my grandmothers—'

'Hold on, mate,' Keith said. 'You can't have three grandmothers, just not on. Or at least, don't try taking out insurance on the third!'

'My grandfather was a very wealthy Hong Kong manufacturer of a camphor balm to ward off colds,' Winston said, eyeballing Keith. 'My own grandmother was a concubine or Number Four, actually, the youngest and prettiest. Our whole clan lived in a big villa on Peak Road. Each woman had a floor for herself and her children. My grandfather got the ground floor.'

'Five floors?' Kevin asked.

'Six. He was the kind of man who planned ahead,' Winston said.

Kevin jibed. 'Hardly likely to get Zelda to sign on for that! I'm just going upstairs, dear, for a week or two.'

'Perfectly normal and legal in Hong Kong then,' Winston insisted. 'Well, Grandma Number One was terribly jealous of Grandma Two—not that either gave a toss about the old boy. When he took on my grandmother, he gave Grandma Two a brilliant racehorse. She was crazy for animals.'

'Kind of a golden handshake?' Nigel asked.

'What about Mrs Three?' Kevin blurted out.

Winston shook his head. 'She was never the same after a tram accident in Wan Chai. Lived on opium after that.'

'Was that legal too?' leered Kevin.

'Grandma One didn't get any presents, so she hated Grandma Two even more. She threatened to pay somebody to break the horse's leg or give him spoiled feed. The more races he won, the more Grandma Two worried. She even hired an extra boy to sleep in Waterloo's stall.'

'Waterloo being the steed in question?' Nigel rapped his pen on his desk.

'One day Grandma One invited Grandma Two to a dinner. And served her a very special dish of brains in the old Manchu Imperial style.'

'Not Waterloo?' Jane panicked.

'Worse. Grandma Two's beloved pet monkey. All covered in scallions and black bean sauce.'

Kevin exploded and Nigel looked about to gag, but Baldwin was thrilled: 'Perfect Stratagem Six, Winston! Grandma One distracted her rival with threats to Waterloo just long enough to kidnap——?'

'Wellington. An evil creature, always pulling my hair.'

Nigel broke off Winston's reminiscence. 'My homework was rather complicated, so I printed it out.' He outlined his bank's indirect attack on a private company by first staging a direct acquisition of shares, 'That was my Noise in the East.' Nigel cleared his throat. 'And the bid for shares prompted the target's board into defensive action, ruling no shareholder could have more than five per cent of the total shares outstanding. Meanwhile, I took on partners who bought up shares in three different lots, giving us indirect control of fifteen per cent.' He looked down his nose at Winston. 'My Attack in the West.'

'In just one week?' Jane asked.

'Finance moves a little faster than library management, Mrs Gilchrist.'

'You swallowed up a company that didn't want anything to do with you?' Jane asked. Nigel seemed a pinstriped roach who shouldn't be armed with an automatic pencil, much less Sun Tzu.

'Well, they don't have to deal with us. Yesterday, we sold our shares and we're walking away with double our investment.'

Jane protested. 'But you didn't produce or improve anything. You just moved shares and people around like chess pieces. Didn't you learn anything from Jacob Marley?'

'A City bloke?' Keith asked.

'There were two of them, Keith,' Winston said. 'Jacob and Robert Marley.'

Jane sighed, 'Oh, Winston, don't you read books? There were two Marleys only in the Muppet version.'

'You mean Bob Marley?' Kevin asked. He hummed a reggae beat.

Dan sighed. 'You're all jerks. Jane meant the greedy ghost in *A Christmas Carol.*'

Nigel had understood Jane only too well. He said with the gratitude of an ice cube, 'If I find myself turning into a door knocker anytime soon, Jane, I'll let you know.'

Jane appealed to Baldwin. 'Aren't we bound by some Confucian ethic or Daoist principle to use these tactics for good, not unmitigated profiteering? She shuffled through her handouts. 'As a matter of fact, I'm not sure I'm comfortable with Number Seven, this creating something out of nothing . . .' She read, 'The four stages of rumour against an enemy: blacken his name politically, attack him as financially dishonest, allege he conducts an immoral life, accuse him of excessive pride. In short, Professor Baldwin, play dirty. Lie.'

'Jane raises an important question. I'll give credit on the final exam to the ethical implications or otherwise of strategic exploitation. It's not a moral judgement on my part, but a strategic consideration; later in the course we'll discuss the risks of putting these tactics to immoral use.'

Winston groaned; none of his homework had worked so far. The idea of extra credit was beyond him. It seemed unfair, he whined to Jane and Kevin during the break, that even though he was the only Chinese in the class, he couldn't make the Sages work for him.

'Chinese? Winston, you're one-hundred-percent-NW3,' Kevin chided. 'Hey, maybe Seven could solve my belt problem.'

Jane saw nothing wrong with Kevin's belt.

'I over-ordered canvas belts for spring. So, I'll create a demand for canvas belts out of nothing. Get our stylist to put them in the ads, on all the mannequins, and get some B-list celebrity to wrap them around her tits. What'd'ya think, Chu? Hey, Chu! Wassup, bro?'

'Nelson's sales figures, that's what's up.' Winston crumpled his Styrofoam cup. 'Last week my cousin sold twenty-two office computer set-ups, at least half with peripherals the customer didn't know he didn't need. You know how many print orders I took? Three.'

'Cousin Nelson probably had these strategies drummed into him in his high chair,' Jane said. 'Now concentrate, Winston. How can you make something out of nothing?'

The three of them brainstormed over uses of Nothingness. Finally, Jane had an inspiration: 'How about I come into the shop and order save-the-date cards for my mother's eightieth birthday party next February?'

'Am I invited?'

'No, Kevin, you are not.'

'Wouldn't that be Something out of Something? I mean, you really do need cards, don't you? Why would that impress Dad?'

'Well, Winston, I do need invitations, but the save-the-date cards are a new thought. I come into your shop just before closing time. Of course, I toss a really foul look in Nelson's direction. I'm hysterical. I have to have these gold-edged, embossed cards on heavy paper as of yesterday because another shop did a cheap and nasty job on their computer. I throw an absolute fit.'

'Until Dad comes out of the back room to see what's wrong.'

'That's what's so brilliant. You tell him, "I can take care of this she-bat from hell." You work a miracle—say, produce these cards in ten minutes. I write a slobbery thank you to your father saying your shop offers the best old-fashioned service in London, that Smythson's had better lock up their client lists,' Jane beamed, 'And you get all the credit.'

'How do I produce this Buckingham Palace order in ten minutes?'

'I place the order now, silly. You run them off when nobody's looking and tuck them out of sight.'

Winston sucked in his breath. 'That's brilliant.'

It was easier than working up some outrage over the nothing of Rachel Murty and Joe in a non-affair. How could she step up her mock jealousy of Bella's personal assistant? Joe was amazed, not dismayed, that Jane suspected him of cavorting with a girl with a Ronald McDonald hairdo.

Only one thing assisted her ploy: Rachel had nursed a crush on Joe for years. Jane and Joe had more than once shook their heads over Rachel's ability to botch a simple task, her penchant for sweet cocktails at lunch, and the 'before' outfits that only a makeover artist could love. Joe took to calling her the What-Not-to-Wear-Girl, and after, Rachel lost the scrambled eggs with sea-urchin butter recipe stolen off Gordon Ramsay, she became the I-Don't-Know-How-She-Doesn't-Do-It-Girl.

Next morning, while Lorraine finished her Saturday morning buttermilk pancakes, Jane squirreled away in her mother's bathroom to meditate. She concentrated very hard on Number Seven: Something out of Nothing. Sitting cross-legged on the turquoise shag next to Lorraine's marabou bed slippers wasn't as Zen as a Shaolin temple. Still, before Lorraine had slurped up the last of the Aunt Jemima, Jane had worked herself up to quite an artificial pitch of poisonous rage. Gentle librarian indeed! She was channelling the incarnation of a jealous consort of the Ming dynasty. Surging with sufficiently vengeful vibes worthy of Winston's Grandma One, she marched downstairs.

Joe grunted such a miserable good-morning that Jane's resolve was shaken. Then she thought of cowardly Winston and supercilious Nigel at next Friday's class, and taking courage in hand, started the tongue-lashing: 'What's on for you today? More beating up a dead story idea with Fergus or just whinging into the mobile with Rachel about your hard lot?'

Joe's hollowed eyes peered at her through swollen bags of sleeplessness, 'Don't start up again.'

So she kept at Joe, nagging like a shrew after her Saturday shift at the library. Playing the wrong wicket about Rachel started to feel like fun. How was Rachel these days? Any boyfriends, she asked, besides Joe, of course? Had she taken to wearing Joe's favourite colour? Did she settle for lunch and tea breaks with him the entire week?

Love and the Art of War

Saturday night, the four of them took in a movie at the Curzon Soho and then stopped for a bite. Halfway through, Jane murmured, all saccharine understanding into Joe's scorched ear, 'If you want to step out to make a phone call, we won't mind. I can't imagine Rachel's doing anything special if you're here with us.' Sammie and Lorraine looked at her in bewilderment. Joe scowled at his fish and chips.

Jane's battle plan flagged Sunday morning because, in a way, it was working. Joe tried to soothe her with affection, but her objective was to wear him down on a false front, not to sue for peace. So, she crawled away from him and by the dawn of a winter Sunday rising over the square, murmured chants to sustain her inner Warrior Woman, *I am, who am I? I am, let's see, I am the White Snake Lady, all-powerful. No, I don't want to be a reptile. I'm the Lotus of Revenge.*

And as the Lotus of Revenge, Jane tortured Joe on Sunday over a rain-soaked tennis net in Regent's Park. It was obviously the last game of the season, and rightly so: they spent more time missing and chasing balls in a sulk than rallying. After one of Jane's backhands landed with a sucking thud in Joe's stomach, he bellowed from the backcourt, 'Give it a rest, Jane. I'm not shagging Rachel. Whoever fed you a story that I fancy that whitewashed bag of bones is giving you a load of crap. Why don't you believe me?'

It was odd to see Joe's expression shift, from battered to indignant to bewildered, as she sank her Rachel-sharpened teeth in his ankle. Sunday evening, Jane jested one minute, hissed the next. Stratagem Seven emboldened her; it wasn't Jane tormenting Joe, it was a sinewy court beauty with almond-shaped nails dipped in venom, for whom intrigues and histrionics were daily fare. It was downright cathartic for Jane to create something out nothing, especially as Joe turned cowed and defensive.

Monday morning they returned to work in a state of frozen politeness. Jane felt an unusual serenity as she unlocked the front door of the library branch.

The downside of Stratagem Seven was that Joe assumed Jane was eaten up with rumours about the gawky PA, so his phone conversations with Bella grew more blatant. He dragged in quite late both Monday and Tuesday evenings. Only on Wednesday morning did Jane dare resume the attack over Nothing Rachel. 'Well, if it's nothing more than a crush The Murty has on you, I'll still have to deal with it for my own peace of mind. I think I'll lunch out on the subject.'

'Oh, you do that, with my bloody blessing, if it gets you off my back. I haven't seen *la femme fatale* Rachel for more than five minutes all week. She's late again with the planning schedules. And in the unlikely event that she's struck down by the lightning of a genuinely decent programme idea, kindly jot it down on a napkin.'

'Oh, I'm not lunching with Rachel. I'm going to ask my old friend and ally Bella for advice. I'm not the first wife dealing with a seductive PA—'

'Bella—? Why Bella?'

'Who would know better how to deal with a clingy PA on the make? After all, she graduated from that school *magna cum laude*.' The Lotus of Revenge narrowed her gaze. 'And there's another rumour, Joe. This one you might want me to check out. Bella might quit *The Travelling Kitchen*.' If Stratagem Seven worked so well, why not double the dose?

Joe dropped a trainer on the floor.

'I read it in a woman's mag at the dentist's. Marketing men and those demographic gurus they interview are saying that no matter how exotic the show, people turn off the tube and then go cook Delia Smith. *Mee krob* out. Elderberry compote in.'

'I don't believe it. She would've told me.'

'If you've spent the last six months trying to ditch her sinking ship, why wouldn't she?'

Jane enjoyed knowing that Joe would spend all morning at the studio listening to Bella's explosive denials.

Jane had whipsawed Joe for four straight days with Somethings from Nothing. She had really put her back into Stratagem Seven.

She left Joe sitting in the kitchen quite still, staring unseeing into Bulgakov's piss-fresh gravel box.

'Why wouldn't she tell me first?' He looked pierced by an invisible spear thrown expertly from a blind angle. The Lotus of Revenge was ready for the next skirmish.

Chapter Eight, Openly Repair the Path, Secretly March to Chencang

Reality at the library didn't so much bite that week as gnaw; by Thursday Jane managed to finish the autumn stocktaking without Chris, in bed with flu. Finally, he returned to do the little ones' reading session, half of them queasy themselves with the same plague.

'One of the Rhyme-Timers just lost her yogurt.' Chris bore off the *Series of Unfortunate Events* placard for a quick rinse-off in the Gents'.

'Don't worry. That's what is meant by an unfortunate event.'

As usual, Baldwin had given his class two different strategies for that week's homework, but Jane had no time left to test Stratagem Eight, the Secret March to Chencang. She looked in the washroom mirror and saw new wrinkles on her upper lip erupting with a sore red spot. She hadn't had a pimple since John Major held office. She felt closer to Mrs Wilting than the Lotus of the Revenge.

Of course, the previous Friday, Baldwin made Strategy Eight sound as easy as, well, mooncake: 'Number Eight is the normalcy strategy. You tie up the enemy's main force with a frontal attack he expects, while you move in by a secret detour.'

'I can't attack my cousin Nelson, not head-on,' Winston protested. 'I'd rather short-circuit all his soundboards by dead of night. He thinks I'm his biggest fan. Last week I suggested we team up on tutorial classes for customers. He'd do software and I'd demonstrate printer installation, the maintenance of ink cartridges, whatever I could. He apologized. Turns out he'd already got a class going already, every Friday night. My father even leaves the keys with him so he can lock up.'

'Oh, dear,' Keith grimaced with pity. 'Nelson's got a set of keys.'

Winston's pink spikes were wilting. 'Even Mum never got her own keys.'

Baldwin's beetle eyebrows shot up. 'So, Mr Chu, repair any bridges you burned in retreat while planning your backdoor attack. Remember, the direct and obvious attack for which the enemy prepares his defence.' Baldwin's marker swooped across the board, 'And the second, indirect and sinister attack,' his pen skittered delicately from a second direction, 'Which causes the enemy to divide his forces and energies, so, *voilà*! Confusion and disaster.'

Nigel wrote in caps, 'Confusion. Disaster,' and drew a rectangle around them.

Dan raised a beefy hand. 'How about Operation Fortitude, the diversionary preparations for the Normandy landing which made the Pas de Calais the obvious site for the Germans to prepare for defence?'

'Excellent, Dan, a very famous example, but of Stratagem Six rather than Eight because the Germans put their Panzers there, but no one landed. No frontal attack tied them up.'

'How's this, then? You have a situation you might think is criminal.' Dan paused. 'You round up a few of the gang for questioning. That's a genuine frontal attack.'

Baldwin nodded.

'And while the leaders are doing their damnedest to find out if their members are spilling the beans under questioning, you step up the activity of the informer you planted inside their operation.'

'Much more subtle and absolutely correct. You've made two attacks, one overt and one secret.' Baldwin moved on to Kevin. 'Does Marks and Spencer's have any enemies?'

Nigel interrupted, drumming his fingers. 'Wait a minute. I don't see much difference between Noise in the East and this Repairing The Bridge business.'

'Very perceptive. They're both examples of *shang bing wu bing*, or indirect attack, more typical of Eastern than Western warfare. I expect you like board games, Nigel? Chess as we play it today demands direct attack, rather like establishing a line of fire and then pulling the trigger, while the Chinese game of Go depends on indirect attack. The player surrounds the opponents' pieces to win.'

'I still don't see much difference between Six and Eight,' Nigel pouted.

'Ah, well, in Six we threatened a false attack to make the enemy look the wrong way. In Eight, the emphasis lies on two genuine attack points, the second using very unorthodox means or downright impossible routes while the competition is actually defending the orthodox path.'

It was now time for Stratagem Eight over lunch with Bella who'd booked a table at a Malaysian eatery. Joe didn't know their ladies' lunch was a long-standing appointment but even so, Jane was making good on her threat to test the waters. If Bella felt a scrap of guilt over trying to poach Joe or if Joe had warned her to cool off, Bella was too clever not to be on her guard against an orthodox attack. *Either she'll expect me to play dumb, which is the easiest defence, or she'll be ready to hide her play for Joe, if she thinks I have the guts to probe her. I must think of something totally different. I'll do a frontal attack but not the one she fears. Meanwhile I'll build my road to Chencang . . . Wherever that is.*

However, Jane found it hard to sharpen her mental weaponry when riding to lunch in a cab through a London that seemed one vast panoramic postcard documenting years shared with her erstwhile friend. It was in the zoo café that Jane had confided that she was pregnant with Sammie. Bella had begged to be godmother. There was Mayfair where the two women had passed a tipsy afternoon at Harry's Bar and swaggered over to Thomas Goode's to register chinaware for Bella's coming five-star wedding—Farm Street Jesuits and Orangerie in Holland Park, Bermuda honeymoon and all—just days before she caught her betrothed in bed with his Lexus mechanic. Of course, Ms Crawford apologized to her guests for the cancelled nuptials but kept the Spode.

Jane overheard the headwaiter's general alert, 'The Ego Has Landed,' and looked up to see you-know-who checking in her coat. Bella waved hello to Jane across the dining room and brushed her long, dark curls off her shoulders with just a dollop of insouciance, drawing the attention of everyone in the room.

Watching her weave her hips in jeans of cherry velvet between the closed-packed tables of the Hill Station Café, Jane longed for the old days, when Bella was amusing or at worst, an irritation and merely an exercise in forbearance. Was it possible to fear and revile someone without losing some stubborn affection for them? Jane couldn't bear the idea of Joe sleeping with Bella, but it was almost too late to change her basic opinion about Bella—that she was a silly who couldn't help herself.

Heads turned, eyelids dropped, and glances moved sidelong with murmurs acknowledging that the celebrity was garbed in the latest. In her rattan chair, Jane squirmed, wearing the earliest. Jane was a dab hand at deciphering the waffle of a book publicist's blurb, but wondered if her fashion dyslexia at the footnote of a new shoe heel prompted Bella's secret scorn. Their fellow diners must think them an incongruous pair—*Daily Mail* diva and dowdy librarian.

'Bella.'

'Jane, darling.'

Bella had contracted the 'darling' from a Sotheby's tapestry expert circa 1998 and never found a cure. The two women air-kissed and then paused. Bella scanned Jane's face for a second and sighed. Jane searched for traces of guilt or guile. She detected only faint lines fanning out from the ends of two large black-lashed eyes under a bat-like brow. It had been almost nine months since they'd seen each other to discuss Sammie's birthday present, so what was so ageing that Botox couldn't freeze it into submission?

Of course, Bella came armed, as was obvious once the waiter had taken their orders. Her defence was a flow of Godmother Natter, making Sammie the focus. Jane played along, chatting about Sammie's horrendous exams in such trigonometric detail, irregular French hilarity, and Ciceronian period length that Bella began to glance left and right, desperate for the distraction of more than chicken *rendang*. But she didn't dare shift into any subject that might steer them closer to Joe. Unfortunately, that also ruled out the one essential topic that riveted her attention—herself.

Having gauged with what Herculean endurance Bella was determined to prolong the Sammie marathon, Jane launched her frontal attack before dessert. Joe would have warned Bella that Jane was planning to accuse Rachel of on-set shenanigans. What she was about to say wasn't in anyone's war games.

'Bella, I want to talk to you about Joe.'

All sympathy, Bella nodded. 'Tired-looking. I know, I know.'

'I'm worried about him.'

'A bit off, but probably just worry over the programme.' Bella said. 'He's told you, I suppose, that our ratings are slumping like a collapsed soufflé?' She paused, 'Why, darling? What else could be the trouble?'

'He's restless. You know the show isn't really him.'

Bella reared back with mock astonishment. 'Why, Janie, you're usually such a loyal girl! I wasn't expecting you to confess his Dark Secret to me.' Another giggle. 'You think I don't know about his secret pitches to *Panorama*? They won't have him. He's Yesterday's Man. But I'm not going to hurt him. I appreciate his talent.'

'You've talked to the other department heads about Joe?'

'All the time, darling.'

The bitch. All these months, Bella had been queering Joe's hard-wrought pitches with a few well-aimed words of faint praise. Jane readied her thrust for a direct attack with greater conviction. 'When I said restless, maybe I should have said discontented.'

'Same difference.' The television star picked with her camera-ready manicure at the chenille fringing around the rattan chair's chintz pillow. 'Discontented how, exactly?'

'Oh, not what you think—'

'Jane, you're not worried about my poor little Rachel—?' Bella shoved her grilled mangoes with caramel sauce aside, ready to parry Jane's frontal attack on the normal route.

'Oh, I know about her little pash, Bella. That's not it. Joe's handsome, and kind to people, and what's more, he's still determined to make television count for something. Being a crusader only adds to his sex appeal. Lots of women fancy Joe.'

'Do they?' Bella's nose shot lower down to the trail, zigzagging like a hound, hunting, and sniffing the conversational minefield.

'He's been watching other chefs, not other women.'

'Well, the show always needs fresh meat, ha, ha. We've had to call in that nouveau sushi git four times now, "by popular demand." He's done the same meal each time and still, nobody understands a word he says.'

'I think,' Jane paused, twisting her dessert blade in the air to admire its glints bouncing off the restaurant lighting, 'Joe is looking at another lady cook.'

'As my guest?' Bella pursed her plump lips, 'Oh, that would alter the dynamic too much.'

'That's not ex-act-ly what I mean.'

'Well, that's just cobblers! Joe wouldn't do that to me. He couldn't. Apart from the fact that we're a team, I mean old mates and all, he can't! I AM *The Travelling Kitchen*. When Chadwick took over the department, I got him to hire Joe—not the other way around. I don't mind reminding you, it was a favour to you both to rescue Joe from Obituaries. I raised him from the dead!'

'Well, no one can stay grateful for ever . . . unless there's something else he should be grateful for?'

Jane deflected the sparks of alarm flashing across the table with: 'It's not about cooking skills, Bella. Joe says it's about incandescence.'

'I'm not incandescent? I see. What about Transcendent? Fluorescent?'

Jane warned, 'It's about country food now, quick cooking, you know, plain old English food.

'You mean what people out *there* really eat?' Bella waved a perfect manicure towards Kensington High Street. 'Space Raider crisps, banana Nesquik—'

'Jamie hoeing his allotment. *The Ministry. 30-Minute Meals.*'

'So, Joe doesn't like my Norwegian Christmas idea? Not even with more close-ups of my tongue in slo-mo saying I looooooovve the taste of aquavit in Christmas pud? I just crave huskily evocative aniseed threaded through the oranges in my stocky? Oh, and some soft-focus of me nipping down to the kitchen for a late nosh, my boobs peeking out of a satin negligee?'

'I admit your male viewers don't complain.'

'No, Jane, I'm not going any farther down that road. Anyway, I'm not stranded on some foreign food island. Remind Joe that I was on the cover of *Olive* last month. Bloody hell, I'm designing my own kitchen scales for the BellaBrand.'

'No. Really?'

'Oyster with optional turquoise. Fifties retro with the "BCs" in black. My initials, no one else's. Unless Joe can find another star with the initials BC.'

'I doubt that.'

'You tell him I need streaming Internet video, like Xanthe on the *Telegraph* site. He won't listen to me.' Bella tucked her blouse tighter across her ample bosom. 'And they'd better not mention reality television to me one more time. Gordon can humiliate failing restaurants, but look what's happened to him.'

Jane repositioned. 'I know, I know.' There was a pause so deep and pregnant between the two old friends, it begged for a sonogram. Was Bella trying to reconcile this unsettling warning with her secret pursuit of Joe?

'It doesn't make sense,' Bella rounded on a hovering waiter, 'Take this away!'

'The chef sends his compliments—'

'It's totally fierce, cutting-edge,' Bella favoured the sweating boy with a set of gnashers gleaming so white, he floated away in a trance after which her beam shut down faster than a power grid failure. She was seriously unsettled. She had come to betray Jane over her entrée and even before Jane's lemon grass sorbet with almond jelly had wilted under its mint, Jane had disclosed that Joe might betray her.

Jane added absentmindedly, 'It might be a passing idea.' She slashed up her jelly like so many Tang dynasty foes. 'I'll talk him out of it. Knowing your career depends on it.'

'How?'

'Oh, I'll think of something, darling,' Jane said with a vague and very unconvincing shrug. She wasn't about to retire her weapons that easily. She hadn't forgotten Stratagem Eight. Bella would waste her afternoon phoning around while Jane prepared her Secret Way to Chencang.

A worried Bella broke her heel on the doorjamb as they made their exit to the kerb, hailing separate taxis. Jane realized that her old friend was the only person she'd never assigned an author because Bella was such a changeling, her narcissism propelling her from gauche and servile nobody to nose-in-the-air chef. Perhaps Charles Darwin was the appropriate choice, including an evolutionary chart showing Bella rising from a badly dressed knuckle-dragging assistant to fully upright Celebritipithicus Pain-in-the-Neckus.

Joe was warier now, too. He finally made good on his long-delayed promise to take Jane back to a B&B that had played a large part in their courtship. Jane would have preferred Devon, with all its Agatha Christie connotations of scones buttered with literary murders, but their personal history dictated otherwise: one of Joe's political shoots of yore had coincided with their first 'dirty' weekend. Hence, it would be again East Sussex, which to Jane conjured up nothing sexier than Rudyard Kipling and Winnie-the-Pooh.

Jane mused, 'I wonder if our room has changed much?'

'Let's just hope they changed the sheets.'

'Even the lampshades were damp! Remember how that MP didn't bother to show up for your interview?'

'So, I turned the camera on his wife and she Told All. Every bribe, every mistress. *The Times* fell on it like ravenous dogs.' Joe bucked up at the memory of an ancient triumph.

'The whole time, Fergus's telephoto focussed on that log pile she was chopping into firewood. Her axe, so dainty, as if every stick was her husband's scrawny neck. Brilliant. Wait. I think we should have turned back at that green pub sign.'

'I know the way, Jane. So . . .you had that lunch with Bella.'

The sun dipped behind a rain cloud.

'She told me she never heard such gossip-mongering. I'm silly to be jealous over a broomstick like Rachel.'

The old Volvo navigated through drizzle along an unfamiliar lane riddled with muddy potholes.

'How much did this startling revelation cost me? Bella hasn't paid for a lunch in years. God, Jane, it would have been much cheaper to believe me. Rachel is a gormless nonentity. It should be here, somewhere . . .'

Forty minutes later three stalwart hikers, gave directions to the Soggy Dog as, 'Back a ways, turn at the green pub sign.'

At least each revolution of the engine carried Joe farther from Bella. Jane prayed it wasn't too late to forge her secret path back to Joe's heart.

That evening, even before dinner, as the wintry winds blustered outside, they made love. Married love-making, where the timing was well-synchronised, there were no embarrassing bloopers, and nothing that made the cylinder roar loud enough to disturb anybody in the next room. Yet it bestowed a welcome relief. Lying afterward in the claw-foot tub, Jane actually believed their life could fall back into place. Everything seemed to be slipping along the path to Restorationville when Joe paused in admiration of his apple *confit* in pistachio *filo*.

'Bella should do this guy's stuff on the show. I expect East Sussex doesn't qualify as travelling too far but the chef is French. Maybe I should give her a tinkle.'

Pulling away from the kerb of Chalkwood Square, Jane had resolved that his first reach for his Blackberry would be her clarion call to arms. Battle banners snapping in the wind now shot up along her emotional horizon. She must launch the rest of Number Eight and March to Chencang.

'I've got an idea, Joe.' She laid both her palms on the polished table. 'It's been what, four years now? None of your pitches has found a home, because each one is totally news-pegged with a short shelf life. And they don't fit it in with the cooking thing you're doing—'

'Temporarily. Always temporarily.'

'Four years is not temporary. You're dealing with a whole new team of producers who don't remember the old Joe Gilchrist. They hear Gilchrist and think "Gilchrist, food, boring." So, I suggest you take the aikido approach—'

'The what?' Joe wrinkled his nose.

'From a new book we got at the library. Aikido, the Asian defence strategy.'

'Oh, yeah, sure,' Joe frowned, 'Like judo, right?'

'Harnessing the energy of your opponent in the direction you want, by seizing the momentum. You seize the shaft of your enemy's weapon and flip the spearhead around on him.'

Joe trailed down Jane's path, his large brown eyes warming to her in the candlelight.

'I'm amazed neither of us thought of it before. If you're stuck with this cookery label, spin it into something meaningful! Work up an idea about food price inflation or famine or aid problems. The destruction of crops from global warming and climate change? Rice shortages? Ethanol eating up corn production? New arguments about genetically modified foods? Parlay your cooking contacts into the kind of thing you really want to do. Do you still have the card of that woman who works for the Food and Agriculture Organization in Rome? Get on to her.'

'Frame the food story my way? So, some department head can assign it to his flavour-of-the month producer.'

'No, Joe, here's the hook. You pitch it as a Special, go around the heads of regular programming. Only you can bring in the chefs to make it a sort of humanitarian celebrity road show. Time it for a one-off, a G20, any kind of summit.'

'You mean, don't run it by Camille?'

'Bella's queered your pitches with Camille and everybody else on that floor, Joe. She damns you with foodie praise.' Jane's path to Chencang narrowed. 'Bella doesn't want to lose you.'

'What do you mean by that?'

'You turned *The Travelling Kitchen* around. She'll derail anything that distracts you. Make sure she doesn't get wind of this.'

She had launched her frontal attack over that silly Rachel Something Out of Nothing and lured Joe down her Secret Path to Chencang.

How easy it was, being strategic—or deceitful? So far, all her lies had been little ones, and it was so simple because, after a lifetime of being straight and nice, no one expected Jane to be devious.

Driving home Sunday afternoon through rain glistening on the windshield, Jane and Joe chatted about which chefs might do an exposé on the collapse of the food chain. Exhausting that topic, they chatted about Lorraine's futile hopes of landing Sir Brian as guest at her February birthday bash. Joe promised to spend time going over Sammie's maths. He agreed now, shunting Sammie off to boarding school was premature. He couldn't recall where the idea had started.

Jane had now guessed the answer to that, but Bella's plan to remove Sammie was thwarted.

The sun broke through as they turned into the square. Jane felt as warmed as the foliage rustling orange and yellow opposite their front step. She might even apologize to Carla for imposing that reading marathon. She'd go to the Chu family print shop to order save-the-date-cards. She looked forward to Stratagems Nine and Ten. The Warring States Period couldn't have been so very bad if everyone managed as adroitly as this. She hopped out of the Volvo and hurried upstairs to put on the kettle.

Unfortunately, she missed Joe's secret scrutiny of missed calls on his phone.

Chapter Nine, Watching Tigers Fight from the Mountain Top

'They're at it again!' Lorraine shuddered. 'Do they have a permit to block off the end of our street like that?' She tottered on the window seat and leaned dangerously over the dormer windowsill.

Jane turned down the heat under Lorraine's casserole of ground beef, cumin, sour cream, black olives and tortillas, the South of the Border recipe the teenaged Lorraine cadged from the ancient screenwriter Anita Loos.

Together, they peered over the clogged gutter and across the square. October's melting frost turned the leaves to rotting muck. Beyond the northern railing, three rows of praying male bodies doubled over in prayer, filling the end of the street right up to the bollards on the kerb and bowing somewhere in the direction of Mecca, via the dubious sanctity of Camden Town. In the sunny centre of the grassy park, two yummy mummies on wooden benches advertised their indifference.

'The Chorus Line from Kabul again. Why do it here?' Lorraine whined.

'Sir Bernard says the bookstore owner moonlights as a preacher,' Jane explained. The architect next door had called the police. A wary officer on duty said the situation was 'In hand, Sir.' Not only long-term residents had weighed in. The OBE rock star remodelling the lavender house facing south had 'expressed concern' to a local councillor only to get limp assurances that 'things would probably taper off.' The result of such phone calls was in evidence. Three Bobbies stood expressionless at attention in front of the bowing white figures.

'I don't envy those policemen,' Jane said. 'They must feel ridiculous, presiding over prayers they can't even understand.'

'As foreigners, they should show more respect to local ambiance.'

'Foreigners like yourself, Mommie Dearest?'

'But I assimilated! I worked for years to fit in! And I did them one better! Remember my *As You Like It*? Didn't *The Times* call my Rosalind a breath of fresh air? I certainly don't recall the words "immigrant travesty" on my West End billing.'

'Don't pretend you did it all alone. I was there. I heard Jack coaching your diction late into the night. Lorraine, why don't you ever give my father some credit?' These angry words slipped from Jane's lips without warning.

Lorraine turned slowly, doing her stage pivot with the lifted eyebrow. Jane had seen even polished actors falter in the middle of a climactic speech when Lorraine aimed this slow-motion laser on them.

'Give Jack King credit?'

'He paved your way. He corrected your accent. He purged the tap-dancer from your entrances. He sold you on the boards decades before Jerry Hall or Kathleen Turner tried it. You rarely share the credit with anybody but never with my father.'

'Well, I gave Jack something to work with, didn't I? I embraced the local culture. I'm practically the senior poster girl for American theatre imports. This is my neighbourhood now. Those guys down there treat me like I'm some kind of trespassing infidel.'

Lorraine clambered off the window seat and fetched a cigarette from her kitchen table. Jane's spirited summoning of Jack's ghost had raised her old hackles, like Hamlet's father strolling in through the door. Jack had turned his Broadway hoofer into a Shakespearean hack—a novel swerve in her career path (or a novelty act, depending on the critic). Jack's months of training had carried Lorraine through that difficult middle stage of an ageing thespian's life. Only offstage, Jack soon found other 'protégées.' In retaliation, Lorraine had tested her husband's patience by helping Caliban 'with his lines' once too often.

The chanting out on the street subsided. Lorraine puffed hard on her cigarette and muttered, 'Maybe that angel has something to do with it.'

'What angel? Your last angel bailed you out of the *Homage to Fred and Ginger* disaster.' Jane checked their meal. 'Oh, you mean the angel painted on the window.'

'Of course, that's what I mean. Oh, hell, my bladder's giving out again.'

From behind the bathroom door came much rustling and grunting. Returning to the kitchen, Lorraine threw Jane a game smile. 'You know they can make you a new bladder? I saw it on ITV. They take your cells and grow them on an armature in the lab. I'll give mine a name, Bill the Bladder, and I'll visit him in his little crib 'til he's ready,' Lorraine warbled, 'Because he's just my Bill.'

The trip to the loo had worn her out. Daughter helped mother remove various pieces of outerwear. Jane served up the casserole and set up Lorraine for an evening with *Irma la Douce*.

They heard shouts outside. Lorraine mounted her sentry post again, bare heels digging deep into the faded cushions, her head sticking out of the roof. 'Whoops, the cops are breaking it up! Look, they're taking down IDs. Leave the casserole on warm, Janie. I'm not missing this!'

It wasn't much of a scuffle, the worshippers being too full of grace or just anxious to get their own dinner.

Back downstairs, Jane watched Sammie sulk her way through a chop and microwaved potato.

'Why can't I spend the weekend with them?'

'Because I'm tired of hearing from your teachers about your unfulfilled potential. Because I've never met these people. I've never even heard of them.'

'You don't know any of my friends anymore. You're always at the library or looking after Grandma. You never go shopping with me or let me fix your hair.'

'What's wrong with my hair? Don't answer that. What happened to your old girlfriends? You just mope around and you don't eat enough. Are you depressed, honey? Where's May-lin? I bet she's studying.'

'She's so wet.'

'Amy?'

'As if. She had an alcoholic coma. Her parents are making her pay off the ambulance fee.'

'Could you at least take out those earphones while we eat? I can hear that buzzy sound from here. You'll go deaf.'

'Anyway, I'll take a gap-year teaching in Malawi. Natalie's Googling all the best options.'

'Your mother is a librarian but you're too lazy to research your own gap-year? Why Malawi? You'll be sorry when you come home with malaria, yellow and shaking with fever.'

'—Or some other place, then. I've got time. Speaking of time, where's Dad?'

Jane shrugged. 'Friday-night wrap-up drinks.'

'Yeah.' Sammie slowly sliced her potato skin into miniscule threads, a bit of stage business worthy of her grandmother.

'You're going to your evening class, Mum?'

'That's right. Will you do the washing-up, for once? I've got to run an errand before class.'

This earned an indifferent shrug. Still, the girl had queried Jane's plans. She was keeping tabs on her parents with her little searchlight heart, tapping along the walls of pregnant silences for cracks, taking soundings. The kitchen lamp's light reflected off Sammie's shiny chestnut hair. Wonderful how young girls' hair shone. Jane gazed with love unobserved, not just at her daughter's soft mane, but the pimple medicine smeared near the hairline, the eyeliner gone wonky, and a smudge of ordinary pencil lead on the earlobe. Sammie was a svelte sophisticate in comparison with the teen Jane who once waited for Lorraine backstage, but she was much thinner than Jane had been at that age. How had the child lost so much weight without anyone noticing? But then, perhaps Lorraine had worried as she watched her ugly duckling Jane surface, not as a swan, but just a smarter, quieter duck?

Her *A-Z* in hand, Jane headed off to find Chu Printers. By the time she'd rounded the square, she'd resigned herself to teenage girls yet again. It was a Sisyphean task, because every time Jane rolled the boulder of hope for Sammie's future to the heights of a place at a decent university, the child kicked it over the precipice. Then Jane would soften. It was bound to be a bad season, with Sammie's academic insecurity made worse by girlfriend sagas of shifting loyalties and betrayed alliances worthy of Henry II's court.

She cinched her mac tighter against the wet wind whistling off Primrose Hill. Reaching the far corner of the square, she stopped to look up at the Window Angel, his colours aflame from the lamplight within.

His wingspan caught a pinkish gleam and his cornflower hair was now flecked with gold. Despite these baroque flourishes, he looked Miltonian—a hardened survivor of celestial showdowns. Gaunt lines segmented his cheeks—a few brushstrokes had added a decade. Worse, the angel's Roman nose and soft lips were now disfigured. Painted blood trickled from his calloused feet.

A mutilated angel—what did it mean? Ageing the angel over the passing days recalled *The Picture of Dorian Gray*; instead of corruption and evil surfacing from a seductive facade, the beautiful angel had morphed from youth to war vet.

A door latch clicked. A young man emerged from the bookstore across the street. He looked like all its customers— dark-eyed and swarthy despite a close shave and wearing a white tunic covered with a cheap windbreaker over a pair of jeans.

'Nice evening for a stroll.' he said. Jane felt pinned down.

'I was just admiring the angel.'

'St Michael? His body is covered with fine hairs, each one of them like a tongue, imploring the Mercy of Allah on behalf of sinners.'

He smiled and headed southward. That was that, disconcerting Jane, as if it were he, not Jane, who belonged there at night, watching the square, identifying who was passing, and offering cultural explanations to the passing English tourist. Who was the interloper?

Jane had passed Chu Printers without seeing it, dozens of times. London was full of immigrant shops you only noticed when you needed them. The air inside the jangling door reeked of machine oil, seafood takeaway and stale jasmine. A red and gold

Love and the Art of War

Chinese shrine hung on the wall next to the counter facing the entrance alongside a free calendar from the Hong Kong and Shanghai Banking Corp. Inside the shrine's shabby niche, tangerine rinds bristled with nubs of blackened incense sticks interred in a sand-filled bowl labelled Moggy.

Winston waited behind the counter, right on cue. Enemy Nelson was bent over his table in the 'Lychee Corner.' The evil genius was conducting an autopsy on the bowels of a laptop. Nelson didn't look anything like a millennial threat to the future of the Chu dynasty.

'May I help YOU?' Winston plunged across the counter at her.

Jane suppressed her laughter. Nelson's eyes stayed fixed on his electronic innards.

'I need this card printed out right away,' she ordered. 'Heavy paper with embossed lettering.'

Winston flipped his pink spikes towards the darker recesses of the shop. 'No problem,' he shouted too loud, '*Mei you wen ti.*' They both could have used some of Lorraine's acting tips. The audience for their little theatre piece, Chu Patriarch, was a scrawny man just visible between hulking printing presses and copiers as big as refrigerators, way at the back of the shop. His right hand snapped the beads of a rackety abacus up and down, column by column, while he smoked. He took no notice of Winston's new customer.

Jane played to the gallery. 'I know it's Friday, but could you have them ready for pickup early Monday morning?'

'MonDAY? Waaaah, short notice! We're so busy!' Was Winston so eager, he'd blow it by pulling the pre-printed invitations out from under the counter, right then and there?

'Oh, no! It has to be Monday, or I won't place the order. No other shop can do it. It's a very, VERY, important event, involving a lot of busy people who need tons of advance notice.'

'Okay, lady, let's see what I can do.' Winston spread out a battered ring binder of samples from which to select the spongy paper, fancy typeface, and various borders. Jane fought the urge to laugh. She'd decided all of this a week ago. Winston calculated

92

the price of paper, coloured ink, gold edging, and Sunday overtime.

'BIG Job, but I can do it, special for you!'

'Oh, you are a prince! I'll recommend you to all my friends from Hampstead to Sloane Square.'

As Jane fished out the cash deposit, Cousin Nelson detached himself from his surgery. Inching the weedy Winston off centre stage, he leaned towards Jane. Nelson was taller and far better looking than poor Winston, who was all spotty stubble and flakes of hair gel. They were related through their mothers; Nelson's sire was quite different from the wiry abacus-clacker. Poor Mr Chu conjured up one of those downtrodden peasants in The Good Earth, while Nelson's smooth brow and shoulder-length mane of glossy black hair inspired the erotic *Dream of the Red Chamber*. There was no denying that when the ancient dikes of the Yellow River flooded the paddies and Chu Senior was swept clinging to his hoe into the muddy torrent past a powerless Winston, Nelson would breaststroke against the raging currents to retrieve his uncle on his powerful shoulders.

'Have you considered an electronic invitation?' Nelson murmured. 'So much faster and you get instant R.S.V.P.'s. Better for planning.'

'Oh, no, no, it's going to be quite a formal occasion. One shop has already let me down with their digital silliness.' Jane said. 'That's why it's so last-minute.'

'Our shop can do personalized video messages,' Nelson persisted with a sibilant accent so different from Winston's native English. 'Let me demonstrate. Your guest downloads his e-mail containing the hyperlink,' Nelson reached for a handy computer keyboard, 'He clicks here to register any dietary concerns. He downloads a map to your venue and,' Nelson smiled dazzling white teeth, 'He can even play an MP3 or QuickTime video of you saying how much you look forward to seeing them.'

Nelson's fingers were strong and graceful. 'We can do the video shoot in half an hour, right in your own home. Or, I could do it right now, with this camcorder.'

Oh, God, Lorraine would just adore slapping on the Max Factor for Nelson's camera. Poor Winston was jogging up and down on his toes behind Nelson's shoulder, wagging his head, 'No, no, no!' Had he forgotten this was a charade? Didn't he have those cards under the counter?

Nelson's sample video was a lot more fun than any stodgy cards; Nelson in a rented tuxedo purred from a little video frame, 'So plan a very private function. Your own.'

Something out of Nothing was going terribly wrong. Winston was waving his head and hands at Jane like a frenzied marionette. There was a phlegmy smoker's cough from the shadows as Chu Senior left his swivel chair and came up behind his gesticulating son. The old man swore under his breath, '*Diao ne*,' and returned to his abacus, shaking his head at Nelson's panicked tarantella.

Jane held her ground. 'If I wanted a video of my mother, I assure you my family could do that perfectly well. What I'm looking for is a good old-fashioned printing service.' She also knew that most of Lorraine's guests might think 'download' referred to a private function best conducted on the toilet.

Nelson's sales spiel was making Winston and Jane late for Baldwin's class. Finally, she peeled herself away and Winston joined her around the corner of the shop in a state. 'You see? He's all-powerful. That stupid demo mesmerized you!'

Jane raced him to the tube. 'Oh, ye of little faith. I'll be back Monday morning to pick up the cards. You impress your father with your cool handling of my emergency. Somehow, I don't think he noticed anything but your St Vitus Dance.'

'None of these strategies works for me! And I'm Chinese!' Winston despaired.

'But you're not, really, are you, Winston?'

Winston thrust his face inches from Jane's nose and pointed at it. She refused to give in. 'Looking Chinese doesn't mean you have the mind of Sun Tzu. What's that chirping?'

'The latest iPhone. Dad asked me to test it.'

'Oh, hand it over. I'll turn it off.'

At the tardy appearance of the two conspirators, Nigel raised one overworked eyebrow. Baldwin was mid-lecture. 'Tactic Nine. Watch Tigers Fight from the Mountain Top. Delay entering the field of battle until all the other players have worn themselves out with squabbling. Then attack and just pick up the pieces.'

Kevin crowed, 'This one's easy! Like watching H&M wage a pre-Christmas price war with Zara and diminish their margins during the best sales season of the year. Then we mop up with after-Christmas blow-outs.'

Winston leaped up, anxious to forget his bickering with Jane.

'Yes, Winston?'

'Epson wanted to jump into the laser printer business but when they offered a laser printer at five per cent below market price, they triggered a price war with other companies. That move brought the whole laser printer range into competition with their core business—dot matrix printers. As a result, dot matrix was forced out of business.'

'Dot matrix printers,' sighed Nigel. 'Quaint, weren't they?'

Baldwin folded his hands, 'Excellent, Winston. Sometimes it's best to do nothing. Inaction can be an aggressive weapon. For example, Intel held back on PDA and mobile phone business to protect its trusted relationship as supplier with other large electronic companies.'

When Baldwin saw how happy this business citation made Nigel, he added, 'But I prefer the Cao Brothers story.' His eyes glazed over as he murmured, 'Year 200, AD.'

'C. E.?'

'If you insist, Nigel. 200 Christ's Era.'

'With all respect, not Christ. CE stands for Common Era.'

'*Do unto others* hardly being a banker's motto,' Winston muttered.

'King Yuan Shuang dies, leaving behind three sons. He bequeaths his throne to the middle son. Angered, the eldest tries to reclaim his birth right, but when their enemy Cao Cao stages a frontal assault on them, the three squabbling brothers unite in defence. So, class, what should Cao Cao do?'

'Pull back. His attack united the brothers.'

'Exactly, Dan! And when Cao Cao withdraws, the Yuan brothers go back to quarrelling. Cao Cao whittles away four of their provinces over the next three years. Finally, he picks off the eldest son.'

'Yes, we do that when the share prices are driven down far enough,' Nigel commented.

'The two remaining Yuan brothers flee to the distant tribe of the Gongsung Kang. Cao Cao asks the Gongsung Kang for the Yuan brothers' heads. Shortly afterwards, two boxes were delivered to his gate.'

Jane tried to imagine Bella's head in a box.

'You see, Cao Cao knew any attack would have forced the Gongsun Kang into a alliance with the Yuan brothers. Instead, he just waited for Gongsung Kang to do them in.'

Winston squeaked: 'This is our homework?'

'Yes,' Baldwin chirped. 'Coffee now?'

Sammie's silence at Jane's blithe reference to *The Travelling Kitchen*'s weekly wrap party had stuck in her mind. Jane decided, half-listening to the second strategy of the evening—something about knives and honey—to meet Joe at the studio. She texted him to that effect and was rather startled to get his welcoming, 'i'll tell reception xx j.'

The weekly wrap party was in full swing, the 'swing' being more of a slow-motion heave, thanks to litres of Antilles punch from the show. Rachel was thrusting her shallow bosom at the guest chef and rattling at him like a machine gun. Still dressed in her studio uniform of Burlington cashmere and signature apron, Bella had weighed anchor at the far end of the Green Room, hair-sprayed curls bent in conference with the chef's PR woman.

Looking bored, Joe leaned on the bar near the door and watched as Jane was introduced to the chef. She waved to Bella who returned a neutral salute.

'Bit frosty, that,' Jane observed to Joe over the lip of her wine glass.

'She cheesed off at some rumour you heard that I'm going to replace her with someone else. Where do you hear such things? I can't be bothered—I've got a title for your idea: *Famine to Feast.* What'd'ya think?'

Jane watched Bella carefully. 'What happened to *Feed the World?*'

'Too tired. Besides, I couldn't get Geldof's people to return my calls.' Bella's prow turned slowly in their direction. The whole room felt the shifting tide as Bella ploughed through the chef's adoring claque to reach Joe and Jane.

'Leaving soon?' This directed entirely at Joe.

'I'm shattered. Mr Steel Band over to you.'

'There's something we have to discuss, Joe. Call you later.'

'How about *Chefs Without Borders?*' Joe suggested during the drive home. When Jane didn't respond, he tried, *Recipe for Hope?* The blue glow from Lorraine's window reminded Jane to run upstairs to cover her mother's snoring form with a blanket and turn off the floating DVD 'bonus features.' Even as she descended back towards their front door standing ajar, she wondered if Bella could bear to wait even half an hour.

But no, Joe's BlackBerry rang. 'Tell her I'm in the bath.' He grumped holding the phone towards Jane. She didn't take it. He threw it on the rug at their front door and pulled at his hair, 'Didn't you hear me? I don't want to talk to her! Pick it up, God dammit! I don't care what you tell her!'

She was tempted to do just that—push Bella aside. Then she saw the way Joe pulled his temples up at both sides, his green-brown eyes reddened by booze and stress. It was nothing more than a histrionic director's pose, which showed off his still-luxurious hair, and for a decisive second, he resembled a snarling tiger full of ego and impatience. This wasn't her Joe; it was something Bella would do.

Suddenly Jane knew she must resist the temptation to play along.

It was time for Number Nine: Let the tigers fight.

She stepped daintily over the BlackBerry.

The telephone row lasted fifty-five minutes by Jane's bedside clock. Joe shouted that first: he could be away and if possible, would be away on an independent project for six weeks without jeopardizing Bella's "career comfort level," whatever that was, and second: that anyone, even Sammie could produce her rubbish, and (after a worrying silence,) no, that didn't change anything, he'd make sure the frontal shots weren't fattening, keep the camera moving, (after another long tirade from Bella's end) and third, (his voice rising) his new project actually wasn't any of her business, she didn't run his whole life any more than he ran hers, and as far as she was concerned, it could be a show about gourmet dog food . . .

Jane fell into an uneasy slumber, as Joe's snarling, muttering, and cajoling in the living room continued. Yes, inaction could be aggressive indeed, if it left Joe's raw frustration wrestling with one of the best battlers in the business. Would letting the tigers fight at last burn out this magnetic dance of loathing and desire that was waltzing into focus more clearly every day? Joe's passion as well as persistence, even muffled by the bedroom door, warned Jane there was no easy victory in sight. By the time his heavy form settled into its customary trough in the mattress, Jane had already suffered one nightmare—of Bella's disembodied head staring up out of a breadbox tethered to a horse's saddle ridden by the majestic Nelson Chu.

'Would you like this on Blue-Ray?' Nelson smiled, lifting Bella's head up by her long hair.

Jane stood facing him, surrounded by a great emptiness across a windy field and answered, 'No, thanks, Nelson, just embossed.'

Chapter Ten, With Honeyed Mouth, Carry Sword in Belt

Jane began her workday Monday exploring rumours that her colleagues in the Camden office would have refused to deny; Chalkwood's three-days-a-week might be cut back even further.

Jane endured a morning of polite evasion on the phone. Dispirited, she begged off Chris's invitation to test a Japanese vegan menu. Neither her morale nor her sinuses felt up to wasabi.

Chris's menu preferences matched his book recommendations—more exploratory than soul satisfying but very hot with adolescent poets who sought his obscure recommendations. The head-tripping novelists among Chris's 'Best Of' favourites had won over the slightly older Gen-X'ers. Jane even trusted Chris with the Rhyme-Timers on condition he didn't give *Winnie-the-Pooh* another postmodernist spin—one mother had complained when Chris told the pre-schoolers that Eeyore needed 'mood-enhancing medication,' and Tigger was 'probably ADD.'

Chris was even less successful with the elderly, or as he called them, The Brillos. The previous spring, he'd moderated a short-story workshop for the elderly until his dispassionate deconstruction of Colonel Armstrong's memoirs was more than that upright soldier could stomach. With regret, Jane dissolved their Pensioner's Prose Workshop. The oldsters' short stories lay forgotten in a storeroom drawer.

Chris took the Bookworms once while Jane was down with a cold. He sent Mrs Wilting off with the doorstopper, *Gravity's Rainbow* as well as William Gibson's *Zero History*. Predictably, Thomas Pynchon and Mrs Wilting came to no good end, as was clear when poor Ruth slid her *Gravity* back to Jane across the counter.

'It was like climbing Everest without any oxygen.'

'Did you reach the peak, Mrs Wilting?'

'Yes, Jane. Gibson was fun, but is Pynchon worth the cerebral frostbite? Do us a favour, dear, and keep him out of Carla's reach.'

Today Jane had a personal reason for declining Chris's Japanese fest. She was meeting Dan O'Neill for lunch in Chinatown. It wasn't a romantic appointment—he called it a study session—so she didn't mind his suggestion they meet in a restaurant that had never seen better days. A ray of feeble sun shot dust motes dancing through the steam from the kitchen. The clatter of cheap porcelain behind the swinging doors made the atmosphere safely unseductive.

Shaving cologne wafted off Dan, although already at midday, the smoothness of his morning deforestation was wearing off. It was a nice enough aroma, even if it hinted of overeager American hygiene. He read off his Baldwin's handout, 'Use flattery, plan evil, speak with forked tongue.'

'Funny, your suggesting this place.' Jane remembered it as a serviceable but never fashionable eatery.

'Listed in a guidebook. "Pretend you're going along with your enemy's programme. Charm and ingratiate yourself. When you have gained his trust, you move against him in secret".' Dan sipped his beer and topped up Jane's white wine. 'Why funny? Chinese food in Chinatown. Hey, don't snap that glass in two.'

Jane stopped twisting the fragile stem. 'I haven't been down here for years.' She kept to herself the memory of a raucous dinner in this very dining room years ago. They'd eaten with some of Joe's crew until ready to burst with fortune cookies and brew. Unable to interest a passing cab, they'd stood laughing out on the kerb in pouring rain, enjoying post-production euphoria. Their group strolled together until they reached the ornamental gate at the entrance to Gerrard Street where Joe slumped to the base of a lamppost while Jane went back to the Lee Ho Fuk to telephone for a hire car.

It had seemed carefree at the time. Jane now remembered it as boring and uncomfortable. The evening had gone on far too long for a new mother. Her nursing pads had soaked up the rain, puffing into two soggy lumps in her bra. Why had Joe drunk so much that night? What sorrow was he pickling, even then?

It was nice to be out with a man, she thought a little shyly to herself. She imagined kissing Dan, which in itself was a novel fancy after so long with Joe. But wait—they were just two continuing education students reviewing their materials. Jane decided nonetheless to make some effort at acknowledging her companion's gesture. 'You're doing your homework right now, aren't you? You're going along with the programme, being charming and ingratiating, and winning my trust? You're on to Number Ten already, Mr O'Neill.'

'Well, better I do the charm bit than the pig variation, right?'

The first version of Stratagem Ten advised smiling like honey to hide a knife, while the second recommended acting as stupid as a pig—compliant, dull, and hardworking—until the moment to strike.

'I'm going to choose the second variation,' Jane joked, 'I'm going to make a pig of myself. Those dumplings look delicious.' A trolley of taro rolls and shrimp buns rolled up. Dan selected a series of little dishes. He was, suddenly, too expert for Jane's comfort.

'Dan, why are you taking our class?'

He split open his pair of wooden chopsticks and stabbed a *haw gow*. 'Just like you—learning something new.'

'You know these tactics backwards.' What author created the Dan's of this world? She'd tested Joseph Wambaugh, but Dan kept popping back out. 'Dan, you recite Sun Tzu by heart and you aren't trying to maximize any quarterly profits.'

'And you aren't trying to thwart the forces of literary snobbery in a book club.'

'No.'

'So, what's your secret? Starting a business?'

'Certainly not. It's all I can do to work the library's inventory software. I couldn't even run a used-book stall, and books are something I do know.'

'I'm sure you'd do it very well.'

There was so much noise, their awkward silence melted into a cheerful soy-saucy bustle, with clanging woks replacing bronze gongs.

'So, Dan, how do you know all those modern applications of the stratagems?'

'Army War College. Between Kuwait, early retirement, joining the force. For a while I thought teaching might be the answer. You're right—the business angle doesn't grab me. I'm not sure it's going to help Keith much, either. Kevin's pretty funny. That Nigel is scary.'

'If anyone uses Baldwin's lessons for the Dark Side, it'll be Nigel.' Jane imitated Nigel's frantic note taking—writing with one hand, twisting his eyebrow into a knot with the other.

'Oh, everybody'll get something out of the class. Once you know the stratagems, you're hooked. You see opportunities everywhere. You catch yourself doing something stupid and say, wait, I don't have to fall for that anymore—'

'Yes, yes! But everything around me is turning into a wacky kung-fu movie. The rumble of the tube before it gets to the platform makes me think of war drums. A silk shirt in the John Lewis window makes me want to wear embroidered robes. My kitchen chopper looks like a movie prop. And last week, I actually had to stop myself from buying a rice cooker. That isn't the real me. I'm a pyjamas and spaghetti girl.'

'Tell me your secret and I'll tell you mine. More rice?'

So Jane told Dan about The Gilchrist Warring States Period. She tried to stay calm and at least she didn't burst into tears. The nicest surprise, after disclosing that Bella's cross-hairs were aimed at Joe, was Dan's confused: 'She's big on local TV?'

'Everyone in this room would know her name,' Jane said. She gazed at the lonely clerks, chattering Chinese shop girls, and quartets of noodle-gobbling mainland currency traders—and she apologized, 'Well, maybe not this room. But I assure you, the average English housewife considers her a star.'

'Well, if it makes you feel better, I never heard of her and you're lookin' at one hot grill-meister here. Come on, give me that little smile, the one you toss me in class when Nigel's being a real asshole.'

'I was afraid I'd start crying, but you make me feel better. You really never heard of her?'

How wonderfully big was the world beyond NW1 and Shepherd's Bush, the Bookworms, Lorraine's luvvies and Bella's stew pot—there was a whole planet beyond Jane's domestic woes! Were the Dan's of this world just visiting from parallel universes, like Philip Pullman characters cutting with their Subtle Knives from one dimension to another? Was London unique in its self-devouring *amour propre*? Was this the only city where Bella could freeze Joe's loving soul with a shard of a vanity mirror trapped in his eye—like the chip of icy glass that alienated the boy Kay from his love Gerda in Hans Christian Andersen's *Snow Queen*?

Dan's dimension seemed like a simpler, cachet-free sanctuary. Could she ever live in such a place? Or, might it turn out the same, just trapped in parallel grids of celebrity references, job pettinesses, shrinking budgets, tumbling house prices, and diminishing vision?

'To tell you the truth, it's a surprise to me she's chasing him, after all these years of being platonic friends. He's wonderful, but he's not amazing. I don't know what she sees in him.'

'Whatever you saw in him.'

Jane recalled the first bolts of shock at Joe's attentiveness and his logrolling, tree-felling, hockey-playing body stretched out in bed alongside her plump nakedness.

'Bella wants money, A-lists, country weekends, recreational drugs, free designer rags. I wouldn't put *Dancing with the Stars* past her. Anyway, that's not Joe.'

'I'll bet it's the Triangle Effect.' He explained. 'You two are buddies, right?'

'Were.'

'So this Bella sees Joe through your eyes. Your love enhances his value. Like the way Kevin gets women to buy weird fashions. You wouldn't be caught dead in a dress, then you see it worn by your best friend and suddenly you gotta have it. Anyway, he's still coming home every night? Maybe it's just your imagination or her wishful thinking.'

That gave Jane more to chew on with her sugared seaweed. Meanwhile, Dan dove into the food. He seemed a hungry sort of person. Was he Tom Jones lusty or Mr Pickwick gluttonous?

'And your secret, Dan?'

'Oh, it's not so secret, just a secondment to cooperate with my local counterparts. Lots of New York cops work liaison in foreign offices.'

'Fraud? Internet porn?' She fished.

'An American boy has got in over his head over here with some Muslim preachers. Everybody knows these terrorist websites are global and viral. We're worried—not just about what he's doing here, but what he's feeding back to buddies in the States.'

Jane was duly impressed. Wambaugh wasn't his author after all, nor was Ian Fleming—Dan didn't have the tuxedo body or dry martini lips. Really, what kind of a librarian was she turning into, if she couldn't muster the name of one cheerful thriller writer with a good appetite?

'Who's your favourite author?' she blurted out.

'You mean, for research?'

'No. Poolside reading.'

'Don't have a pool. Okay, I'll play. Nelson DeMille. Elmore Leonard. Don DeLillo. Richard Ford. And it might surprise you, Chinese poetry.'

'So why are you taking this class?'

'Because I'm lonely, okay? Over here for six months, working all day with no one to talk to at night. My son Skypes and my ex-wife sends me one little postcard about her nifty scuba-diving in Crete, but I was just looking for something familiar. Sun Tzu's an escape.'

'Not a refresher for your job?'

Dan emptied his rice bowl with quick shovels of his chopsticks. 'Maybe.'

'Can you talk about it?'

'Nope.'

Jane nodded.

'But I can give you a theoretical. There are about thirty plots being cooked up in the UK and agents monitoring more than 1600 potential terrorists. The local help is stretched way beyond belief.'

'But they hired lots of new security agents—'

'And they can always use more, especially when it involves an American. For example, imagine an American boy in the back rooms of an informal prayer meeting in Trenton seduced by CNN glory, hot-and-cold running virgins, the usual bait for one of the Lost Boys. Suddenly Jersey Boy gets a trip to London, all expenses paid. You'd want to keep an eye on him, wouldn't you? Watch where he turns up.'

'Theoretically?'

'Just hypothetical. Stratagem One. Persuade the emperor to cross the sea without knowing it? You cultivate one of the Muslim good guys, a moderate imam working up in Luton. He's already refused to host two inflammatory preachers to these green shores. You get your Good Imam to recommend to the owner of the London outfit that he hire his "nephew" as a low-paid salesclerk.'

'That nephew being your New Jersey boy?'

'No, no, no. That nephew being a second-generation local. His parents were booted out of Uganda. Let's call him Gilbert Sullivan.'

Jane smiled at the reference. 'For He Is An Englishman. Any London outfit I might recognize?'

'Let's say, for argument, a religious bookstore.'

'I begin to see.'

'Stratagem Two, Besiege Wei to Rescue Zhao? Harass the Park Road mosque, keep'em distracted, just to eclipse little problems cropping up over at the bookstore—missing files, mislaid pamphlets. Then, Number Six comes in handy: Clamour in the East, Attack in the West. That might mean a little visit to install surveillance equipment during a prayer meeting out in the street. Break it up, gently, issue a warning, tie them up taking down ID numbers . . .'

'I saw that meeting! It is our bookstore! My mother got pushed around during that,' Jane exclaimed.

'Must be a coincidence. I'm just talking what if's. Three, Kill with a Borrowed Knife? Our Gilbert plays the impassioned new acolyte. He gets the bookstore owner all worked up over different interpretations of the Koran with the neighbouring mosque—pushes the bookstore owner into accusing the mosque leader of apostasy. We make sure the mosque hears about that.' Dan snapped a rice cracker in two.

'Why am I not surprised? I felt fear, but I assumed it was fear fed by prejudice—'

'Just your imagination. I'm making this all up.'

'Four, I forget, what was Four? Exhaust the Enemy?'

'Oh, that's easy. Dog the rival imams with security tails that break all the rules of competence. That's what the Pakistani security services do to make'em nervous. Give the mosque guy trouble with his outdoor prayer permits. Harass our own Gilbert on visa details. Tell each one it's the other's guy's fault for screwing up the community profile but then, we jump to Number Nine, watching tigers fight it out.'

'Goodness.'

'Just a theory.'

'I understand. How about Number Five, Loot the Burning House?'

'Computer hacking. I couldn't go into that, even if I understood it, but it's about data theft. I'm sure Winston's cousin would get it.' Dan smiled at his private vision of a destructive computer worm. 'Here come the sizzling prawns, I thought they'd forgotten those. Hmm, smell those babies. Thanks.'

'Don't stop, please.'

'Okay, let's see, more Clamour in the East . . . distractions to deflect any suspicion that we're watching Jersey Boy by hassling our poor Gilbert out in the street, making a huge scene in plain view, sticking him in the cooler overnight. Result? Gilbert gets heat for what he might have squealed and God knows that's enough. Meanwhile, we're slowly approaching our genuine little convert with velvet gloves.'

'I love the way you link these all together. Something Out of Nothing, Number Seven? Winston and I tried to impress his father with a last-minute printing order, but it was all Winston could do to play the game.'

'Something Out of Nothing,' Dan examined the halo of unfashionable frizz surrounding Jane's tired blue eyes widened in awe. 'Maybe I'll start a rumour you're dating Winston.'

When Jane laughed, he added, 'I warned you, I get bored in a rented room, watching reality shows that have nothing to do with reality.'

'And what about the Honeyed Knife?'

'Oh, that one.' He arched his back and adjusted his belt, a very primate move. 'Well, lunch, courtesy of the New York taxpayer? Charming patter? I've done my best. What do you think I have in mind, Mrs Gilchrist?'

That took Jane's breath away. She hadn't set her heart on flirtation, but she had wondered whether lone wolf Dan's motives were romantic. Then he continued: 'I'd like you to keep your eye on that bookstore.'

Ouch. So that was the reason he was cutting with his honeyed knife through her lunch hour. Jane felt awash in sadness. Women like her glamorous mother got long romantic runs, but Jane's season had been a short one, it seemed, starring only Joe.

She sighed. 'Well, if I see anything really odd, I'll tell you. Why don't we split the bill?'

'No way. It's always nice to have a couple of eyes on the spot 24/7.'

She got back to the library on time.

'Carla was just in here,' Chris whispered. 'She's rounding the last lap. Returned *A Suitable Boy* and the *Frederica* trilogy.'

Jane rubbed her palms. 'How did she look? Nicely haggard, grey of pallor, bleary-eyed, off her feed?'

Chris grinned. 'I'd say a mere shadow of her former self, but then there was a lot of her to start with.'

On the way home, Jane stopped in front of the suspicious bookstore. She heard male voices, at least three. Although they didn't sound sinister from where she stood on the darkened kerb, they certainly weren't selling books behind those shuttered windows.

Overlooking the street, the Painted Angel stood guard. His sword tip had turned into a painter's brush that was just tailing off at the end of a phrase, worked in translucent blues, reds, and yellows.

It read, *Thou Shalt Not Kill.*

Chapter Eleven, Sacrifice the Plum Tree to Save the Peach

Chris swore at their new coffee machine—a trendy but tetchy donation from Westminster culture czars who voted extra money for those libraries that pulped old books to speed their devolution towards juice bar status. As he settled down to his hard-won post-prandial cappuccino, Jane was released to set off for a place famous for a set lunch of hefty steak sandwiches—it was either that or an inedible baked potato with mince from the Cypriots down the road.

The steak was stringy. The curtains smelled of carbonized protein while the greasy menu card conjured up visions of stale Trollopian indulgence. The dank dining room fit Jane's pessimistic outlook for The Bookworms session coming at the end of the day. The reading selection wasn't the problem—they'd agreed on Orhan Pamuk's *Snow*, which Jane hoped to finish now over her meal. She savoured its setting, the snowbound Kars, a Turkish town full of wilful 'headscarf girls.' But when the Bookworms finished with Kars, they'd still have to deal with Carla and her 'new approach' for coming selections.

Jane couldn't concentrate on Pamuk. Stratagem Eleven kept niggling: Sacrifice your silver to protect your gold. There are circumstances in which you must sacrifice small things to gain the long-term goal. Or let the scapegoat suffer, so that the others do not.

Jane didn't want anyone to suffer. She wasn't willing to sacrifice silver, gold, nor so much as a blade of straw. Everything in sight was dear to her—Joe, Sammie, her job—and hadn't she fought during the last budget row to keep the evening hours open for the Bookworm meetings? The Bookworms were the canaries down the mineshaft, the last bulwark against MP's branding libraries as 'kaleidoscopes of culture.'

Chris was planning pre-emptive action—eliminating which books might have to go in advance of criticism that their stock was too fusty to be relevant. Jane had even caught Chris sacrificing their entire Noel Coward collection as he intoned, 'Coward must go so that John Osborne might live.' Stratagem Eleven under her very nose.

Jane realized that a sacrifice would be called for if she wanted to save the Bookworms during the next budget skirmish. Not that the old dears cost a lot of money—a bit of extra heating and electricity, a few beverages, and Jane's overtime didn't amount to much—but Central Libraries had already reduced Chalkwood to three days a week, and now served Jane notice that the Bookworms' membership hovered at the critical limit.

That evening, she found a shivering Rupert and muffled Carla squabbling outside the locked entrance.

'—Debate, fine. Opinion, fine. But why discourage someone's passion for reading!' Rupert argued through chattering teeth.

'I'm not interested in mere feelings. Authors must be judged in an informed context,' Carla retorted.

Jane flicked on the strip lighting. The remaining Bookworms weren't far behind, age being appreciative of punctuality versus squandered minutes.

Pamuk turned out to be a crowd-pleaser—topical of course, but universal enough to allow for Catherine—who never read a newspaper—to express her mere feelings. Carla offered much background on the Turkish genocide of Armenians but, for once, omitted citing *The Dustjacket*, an obscure blog devoted to new fiction. To Carla's delight, *The Dustjacket's* blogger often put paid to any Bookworm. *Dustjacket* expressed his opinions with an authority that Jane could never quite pin down. Moreover, *Dustjacket* was absolutely impossible for Jane to locate, although Carla had waved a long trail of hyperlinks down the narrowing footpaths of cyberspace.

Rupert suggested they next tackle *The Literary Review's* Bad Sex Prize Shortlist. Alma giggled. Catherine turned her hearing aid back up. Jane agreed a Bad Sex List was an unorthodox but original route to some very good authors. Even ancient Mrs Wilting seemed game for some light-hearted fumbling.

Carla's knuckles bleached white with tension as Rupert read from a clipping, 'One winner compared a character's breasts to a pair of Danishes, and another's to "Two Space Hoppers".'

'What are Space Hoppers?' Ruth asked.

'A big balloon toy with handles. You sit on it and bounce around on your—,' Jane paused, 'your you-know-what.'

Carla sputtered. 'I've spent hours and hours vetting the books Jane suggested we do next. I thought Doris Lessing's—'

'Oh, Carla, let's give Rupert's list a try!' Catherine burst. 'I'm getting rather tired of these worthy sessions. Alma?'

Alma fluttered her eyes with loyalty for Rupert and fear of Carla. In confusion, she turned to Jane. Four pairs of eyes came to rest on the librarian.

Alarm bells rang in Jane's minds: *if Carla bails out we're no better off than if Ruth does; we'll be too few to retain the room. I can't let Carla know she wields that kind of power.*

Jane would have to sacrifice silver to save the gold. 'I'm sorry, Rupert. I must take some responsibility as monitor, especially as I did ask Carla to spend so much time reading ahead for us all.'

Three pairs of woolly shoulders slumped. 'You're not proposing we do the entire Lessing *oeuvre*, are you, Carla?' Jane pleaded. 'We could zip through *The Golden Notebook* and jump to *The Cleft*?'

'No bad sex?' Alma whimpered.

'Well, *The Golden Notebook* is full of sex,' Jane said.

'Good sex?' Alma asked.

'Well, not always,' Jane admitted. 'Some of it is quite unsatisfactory.'

'Bad sex isn't any fun.' Alma rallied to Rupert's sally against Carla, without realizing the stakes. 'Bad sex writing does sound fun.'

'Rupert can share his list later, dear,' Catherine comforted her friend.

Rupert looked stricken. He'd assumed his support for Jane in Hampstead had earned endorsement for his bouncing Danishes. He carried his cake plate home in silence.

Lorraine was waiting up for Jane's return. Even before Jane had shut the door to the street, her mother wailed over the banister, 'Where's Sammie? Has she texted you?'

'Isn't she home? Where's Joe?'

'The child's mobile is dead. Just nothing. I expect she ran the charge down texting to her girlfriends all day. "I'm here. You're there. We're all teen-agers on Planet Stupid." Now I can't find her.'

'Mother, don't panic!'

'You see! You see! You just called me Mother! You're panicked, too. Don't blame me. When she wasn't home by nine-thirty, I gave her five extra minutes and then I started calling and calling and—'

'Did she check in after school? Where'd she say she was going?'

'Going round to study, she said. I assumed she meant with that pierced troll, Amy, but—'

'What's the number?'

'Don't bother. I've rung. She never went there. Amy's parents laughed in my ear. Amy is in bed. Should we call the police?'

'I don't know. If she walks in the door in the next half hour, we feel like a couple of loonies, but if she never walks in the door again? There was that Suffolk maniac and that fifteen-year-old stabbed with a knife ten times outside Waterloo Station.'

Joe pounded into the flat, his heavy shoes glistening with rain. 'Is she back?'

Lorraine detailed the sequence of frantic phone calls she'd made in the last twenty minutes to a list of girlfriends, 'Including that Goth-y creature she studies Latin with.'

'I'm calling the police. What was she wearing this morning?'

'What ten thousand other kids are wearing, Joe,' Jane said. 'Fleecy hoodie, striped muffler, jeans, trainers.'

Joe rang the station. The three of them waited from Lorraine's attic sitting room. If only Sammie's slender silhouette would appear between the bollards at the northern end of the square but only drizzle in the streetlights reflected off the square's iron fencing. They listened in vain for the reassuring chug of a taxi engine passing the church and coming up Chalkwood Road.

Lorraine poured herself another tonic-flavoured gin. When the phone did ring, it was the police checking to see if Sammie had turned up.

Sammie rebelled all the time, in irritating ways, but she had always been level-headed about the basics. She might worry Joe or Jane on purpose, but never her grandmother, who had defined the acceptable parameters of bad behaviour for the entire family.

Jane ran down the entire list of Sammie's friends, flipping through a dog-eared book of numbers. Goth Girl had seen her after school heading for the tube. Amy couldn't be roused. Mrs Kwok insisted that May-lin shouldn't be disturbed—she had a flute audition the next day. Sammie had been missing for almost five hours on a Monday night.

It was what happens to other parents.

Black-and-white photos of Lorraine watched over their vigil from the mantelpiece: a thirtyish Lorraine leaning on Jack's shoulder in his dressing room celebrating a small triumph in his Trevor Nunn *Macbeth*, or Lorraine in a Pucci mini with Gerd at a Bond Street art exhibition. The silver frames were tarnishing. The room smelled of Mitsouko, nicotine and things soured and old.

Around ten-thirty, Joe's mobile rang—the caller Bella. 'Keep off the line. For God's sake, we have an emergency,' Joe shouted at her and clicked off.

At the second and third persistent tries, he only glanced. 'Bella again.' Then Jane's mobile received the text: 'SAMMIE WITH ME. ON OUR WAY. BELLA.'

An exhausted Lorraine was whisked off for one final trip to the bathroom and one of her 'helpful' blue pills, and then tears and comforting washed with the histrionics of relief. Below, Jane heard the taxi, the front door bell and Joe's footsteps lurching downstairs followed by Bella's operatic explanations echoing up the stairwell. Jane tucked in Lorraine, picked up her gin glass, and went down to their flat.

Bella was sweeping around the living room in a camel-coloured cashmere coat loosely belted over a tomato satin negligee.

'She tried hair dye with one of her little friends, who then persuaded her to give it a trial run in the local before coming home. Somebody bought her some "pop," and got her completely sizzled. They came to my flat after closing time, to ask for god-motherly shelter and a pot of coffee.'

Bella's famous white bosom heaved with the exhalation of self-importance and the excitement of all that loving concern, exposure to cold wind, the *deshabillé* costume and the rescuer's soliloquy.

Clumping up the stairs, half- slumped over the banister, her mascara streaming, her green nail varnish chipped, and her lovely hair a lifeless shade of blueberry, came Sammie.

Jane threw the girl across the stuffed toys, CD's, and magazines scattered across her duvet, slammed the bedroom door and took a deep breath. Her anger at the first physical contact with Sammie was already overwhelming. How much more humiliating to suffer Bella's intimate commiseration for at least the next half hour?

Bella leaned towards Joe on the sofa. 'Really, Joe, she'd be better off boarding. Get her away from all the stress.'

'What stress, Bella?' Jane interrupted from the doorway.

'Her studies, for one.' Bella said, turning half-unbelted across the back of the sofa. Jane felt as awkward as an eavesdropper. 'She's desperate, darling. Can't cope with the maths. Flunked the modules. And watching her grandmother deteriorate is upsetting her. She needs to get away.'

'It's called adolescence, Bella. But she's going to stop seeing this friend. Bingeing is not something we do.'

Joe and Bella both stared at the dirty glass in Jane's hand, the one that had contained Lorraine's bottomless gin and tonic throughout the evening.

><>>~<><

Next morning, Sammie snored through the CD player she used as an alarm. Joe pulled the plug on the White Stripes song and pushed her out of bed and into the bathroom. Parental panic had had a good night's sleep and woken up as tough love.

'You take offence, Jane, but Bella had a point. At least, I take Sammie with me on the recce to Rome? It's her half term. She can revise her classics while I see the Food and Agriculture Organization lady, then we see the tourist traps, you know, father-daughter bonding and all that . . .' He kept his eyes fixed on the cream clouding his coffee.

Lorraine's head hurt too much for anger. 'Really, Jane, consider yourself lucky. I kept seeing our poor darling with a knife stuck between her ribs. Oh, imagine.'

'I can't believe neither of you is as furious as I am.' A mushy calm hung over the memory of last night's terror.

'I won't play the heavy. If Joe's going to be forgiving, I'll do him one better and be understanding.'

'Lorraine, please butt out?' Joe was showing less amiableness with Lorraine of late.

'Jane wasn't rebellious, but I was. Sammie just got in over her head. Speaking of head, I hope the Dracula Do washes out.'

'Lorraine, are you laughing? No wonder I can't discipline my own child. She'll always find a safe haven with one or the other of you.'

'You know, Joe, I kept waiting for Jane to bust out, smoke dope, get arrested in some street protest, iron her hair, for God's sake, but—'

'Very funny. All's well that ends well?'

'No,' Lorraine paused. 'She won't do it again.'

'I still say Bella had a point.' Joe stared out at the square.

'Will you shut up about Bella?'

'I can take Sammie with me to Rome, you know, bring the classics to life.'

Lorraine loved Joe's idea. 'Yes! Steep her in ancient culture. *Ben-Hur, The Robe, I, Claudius, Spartacus, Samson and Delilah*—'

Jane feared Sammie be left neglected in a hotel while her father discussed famine with well-fed bureaucrats, but she was outvoted. She was going to have to let Sammie, go, just like in Stratagem Eleven, sacrifice Sammie's interests in the hope Joe would come back with a food project and a new direction for his life.

As the week progressed, the recce proposal lost shape. It was less about investigating a famine-and-food special for Joe and now a group excursion to Italy for *The Travelling Kitchen*. By Friday morning the Italian departure included not only Sammie, but also Bella, a soundman and cameraman, as well as Reston the Stylist who would test the effect of the Mediterranean winter light on grapes and tomatoes glued back on the vine.

Jane packed Sammie's little carry-on, and swallowed her dismay that Bella had insinuated herself into the trip, but she still challenged Joe who rose early to review the design for online promos of *The Travelling Kitchen's* 'Tuscan Winter' special.

'It's supposed to look romantic,' a glum Joe said, staring at photos of granite-cold kitchens, abandoned terraces, and gnarled farmers in threadbare jumpers.

'Miserable. You haven't told Bella about the documentary idea?'

'No, she hasn't twigged. I've talked to a Dutch press officer at the FAO and she's lined up a full afternoon of meetings—biofuels, drought warnings, Ban Ki-Moon's call for lifting supply by fifty per cent, fuel costs, grain speculation, Chinese consumer demand—anyway, I'll be busy while the others sleep off their pasta.' He reached out to hug Jane's waist, 'Trust me, I've haven't forgotten the plan.'

The heavier Joe's luggage got, the more his depression lifted. Jane saw the old Joe, happily overwhelmed and short on time, ticking off lists and heading out of town for a quickie shoot. Taking Sammie as a talisman of good behaviour loosened his reserve about enjoying Bella's celebrity connections and must-eat menus.

Only Rachel Murty was honest or gauche enough to call Jane at the library that morning. How had Joe's request for a break from the schedule mushroomed into a storyboard featuring Bella strolling Tuscan vineyards out of season?

'You're going too?' Jane gasped. 'I thought Bella had you chained to your desk phoning restaurants to warn them she was making a spontaneous appearance.'

'Well, I'm a sort of chaperone.'

'Since when do Bella and Joe need a chaperone?' Jane bit her tongue.

'I'm chaperoning Sammie, you silly. I just wanted to know what her homework is. Actually, Jane why don't you come? It might be fun, like old times.'

Not quite, Jane thought. Not quite.

><><

Returning to Baldwin's class felt like retreating between the safe covers of a book. Nigel said she was looking rather tired, but no one pinpointed Jane's anxiety.

Winston explained his homework of Stratagem Eleven; he'd sacrificed two days off to impress Chu Senior with his newfound work ethic.

'You sacrificed your own weekend—?'

'To promote myself,' Winston preened. 'Sacrifice the plum tree to save the peach tree.'

'That makes no sense, Winston,' Professor Baldwin said. 'What are you, the plum or the peach, or both? I really think you're better off with the preventive versions, which in this case, is just to make sure nothing goes wrong.'

'As in, your father might sacrifice you as a scapegoat to save Nelson's peachy behind,' said Jane. She thought, I'm sacrificing my daughter without a fight. She's actually going off with Bella and Joe together, getting tangled up in Bella's nearly public seduction of her father. But Baldwin says you get something in return for your sacrifice . . .

Baldwin stepped back from the board, reading: 'Sun Tzu: When your competitor hands out too many punishments, he's lost control of his people. When he hands out too many rewards, he's lost his ability to motivate his followers.'

'So Joe's lost?'

'Sorry, Jane?'

Jane masked her gaffe. 'Sorry, you're saying that when the enemy has handed out too many rewards, he's actually lost the entire war?'

'Not necessarily the entire war, Jane, but it's a certain sign of weakness. And, indeed, it's just as telling if he's too harsh. It's a sign he fears losing control. Either way, your opponent has lost his balance.'

Nigel said, 'Last year we faced off with another lender who was offering interest rates so high, on a short-term . . .'

Joe was bribing Sammie with this trip to Italy and he was letting Bella rope him into a very different outing from the one Jane suggested could save him. Baldwin would say Joe was losing his balance.

'Jane? Need a drink? You look awfully sad.'

Jane found herself sitting in the canteen, listening to Dan's use of Stratagem Eleven, 'Then we'd have to sacrifice our informer. Gilbert's a pro, so he knows he might end up a scapegoat. Suspicion that he's a weak link is growing all the time—after all, that's our idea—so nobody realizes our real target is Jersey Boy, sitting there watching training videos.'

'Can't you pull out Gilbert at the last minute, if he's in danger?'

'If we can warn him in time, Jane. But these people are careful. They might ask him to make the ultimate sacrifice, blow himself up first, as a test.'

'He could say he tried and the bomb didn't go off?' Jane found Dan's applications of Professor Baldwin's strategies were getting uncomfortably dangerous.

'If they suspect him, they'll make sure things go off without a hitch.'

By now, Bella and Joe would have checked into their Italian hotel. Jane accepted Dan's offer of a taxi ride home a stroll through the winter night towards the square.

'A night like a Tang poem.' Hands buried in his anorak, Dan recited: 'Shine bright moon, your gleaming rays whiten my bed. One in despair cannot sleep, dull, dull night so long, soft breezes blow the bedroom curtain . . . that's a pretty loose translation.'

Jane didn't know where to look. How to make a graceful exit? Even a tired, middle-aged librarian didn't just turn her back on spontaneous Chinese love verses! She slowed her steps at the bollards, unwilling to pass under the bright street lights of the square with Dan—it was too much like stepping on a stage witnessed by all her neighbours.

'You're an unusual man, Dan.'

'Just a cop with a bookshelf of Penguin paperbacks.' Dan shrugged and waved her safely across the square. 'Sleep well, Jane.'

Chapter Twelve, Lead the Sheep Downstream by the Hand

Joe returned from the Italian shoot in a suspiciously ebullient mood. He even smelled different. A bottle of shaving cologne redolent of cedar resin and fresh figs now stood on the bathroom shelf. Despite the rigours of wintry weather and an ailing soundman, the Tuscan sojourn sounded like one long swan drenched in sunny tempers and vintage Montalcino. Wafting a disconcerting air of contentment on his very first Saturday back home, Joe tackled mundane chores he'd put off for years. While Jane worked overtime at the library, her kitchen cabinet hinges were tightened, the Hoover hauled off for service, and the worn washer on Lorraine's bath tap finally replaced.

Joe also pushed aside his pile of miserable pitches to tutor Sammie on the contributions of the Enlightenment Philosophers. Sammie reported later to Jane that she could 'relate to' Diderot.

Joe took them all out to dinner—not to divulge the full horror of the tour, but to celebrate the predicted success of the Tuscan episodes. These had been spun like cotton candy by the publicity people into a quickie booklet of recipes slipped into *The Telegraph's* Sunday edition, along with an offer of pasta utensils.

'The pink colander is out of stock already!' Joe shook his head in wonder. He tucked into his shepherd's pie with gusto.

Sammie ate little, said less, and seemed preoccupied with her Italian present from Bella, a pair of red Italian boots soft as glove-leather. It seemed caddish to wonder whether the Italians had subjected Joe to a Lobotomy à la Lorenzo the Magnificent. Afterward, the family took a slow walk to the top of Primrose Hill so that Lorraine could smoke her allotted one cigarette of the day.

'Joe's a new man. Did you need a new man, Jane?' Lorraine tossed a cryptic glance at her granddaughter. 'Was your father this lively in Italy?'

'He was very busy.'

'How did you like Rome? See the Coliseum? Where they kept the wild animals?'

'He said it was just an overnight trip for that meeting with the food experts. So he left me with Bella and Rachel.'

Sammie took careful strides between mother and grandmother, as if keeping them in lockstep would fend off more of Lorraine's cross-examination. 'We learned how to make real pizza in a stone oven and squeeze the black ink from a squid's sac.'

'You'll have to show me that sometime real soon, kid,' Lorraine muttered.

Bella had stopped ringing Joe at home. Was the new Joe planning secret forays to the world's hellholes of hunger? Or had he finally found a way to make *The Travelling Kitchen* interesting? Could Jane let herself hope that nothing had happened in Italy and that somehow, Joe had come to appreciate his family? Or at least come to his senses? Jane pondered Joe's upbeat mood, though Lorraine kept referring to Joe as 'Your Stepford Man.'

The muddy square lay dormant, the sky hung colourless, and even Regent's Park Road's traffic sounded somnolent. The wintry mist filling the square turned the tall windows into grey sentries filtering the silvery half-light by which Jane huddled in her bulky cardigan a few feet from the kitchen space heater as she wrote out her homework for Professor Baldwin.

After learning the six 'Winning Strategies,' the class was now finishing the six 'Enemy-dealing Strategies.' Next week they would launch into the six 'Attacking Strategies.' To Jane they were all 'Coping with Joe' Strategies.

While testing the thirty-six stratagems, (or in Winston's case, where the stratagems rebounded on his sorry head) there were always the Master Sun Tzu's basic principles to learn, simpler than the tricky tactics that evolved later. Sun Tzu didn't employ cute metaphors about monkeys, snakes, bridges, and honeyed knives. Take his Principle Six: Seize the Day, as easy to remember as *carpe diem*, Lorraine's lifelong excuse for seizing her leading men by their codpieces between Acts II and III.

Sun Tzu also fit Jane's budget. Keep things simple, effective, and inexpensive. If Sammie managed the miracle of three A's in her A-Levels, or even two A's and a B, it would still be a stretch to meet soaring university fees without taking on more library hours at another branch. Jane cringed, imagining herself clocking in at the five-day-a-week, state-of-the-art Kilburn Library Centre with its plasma movie screens.

What was the alternative? Lorraine would offer to send Sammie off to her dream campus in the US, but for the first time ever, Jane chafed at yet more charity from upstairs; had Sun Tzu planted a little seed of rebellion where only gratitude had grazed for decades? Had Joe ever resented Lorraine's support, but held his tongue?

She repeated to herself, yet again, 'Attack is the secret of defence; defence is the planning of an attack.' Sometimes these proverbs made sense. Sometimes they just made her head hurt.

Clearly Sun Tzu knew Jane's psychic limits. Do a lot of simple things very well. So, every day Jane did very simple things, but not well at all.

Stay ahead so the competition must react. Her eye followed a shivering sparrow navigate the bare treetops outside the French doors leading to their tiny kitchen balcony. Stay ahead of Bella? In the aftermath of the Tuscan shoot, the entire Bella threat had fallen away, like a bad dream dissolving at dawn, or a line of ancient warriors on the horizon retreating in the dusk. The Cooking Queen's early winter madness, perhaps a late hormonal surge unable to find a lightning rod more appropriate than good ol' Joe, had magically passed over, it seemed, or found a more suitable target?

Was the nightmare over?

Had Jane won?

Was there any point in continuing with Baldwin's class?

It seemed a shame to quit—to abandon Winston to Nigel's barbs and stick Dan with lonely walks back to his bedsit. They'd become friends and what's more, Jane felt they both needed her. Baldwin's final instruction as he wrapped up the most recent class was, 'Sun Tzu says, remain flexible. Take advantage of any opportunity that presents itself, however small. In a nutshell, that's also Stratagem Twelve, Lead the Sheep Downstream by the Hand, the ruse of serendipity.'

He continued: 'That means, Nigel, avail yourself of any profit, however slight. As the CEO of Southwest Airlines said, "Be ready for change." The objective is fundamental alertness to every possibility on the battlefield.'

Scanning her battlefield, one drooping banner on the skyline caught Commander Jane's eye. Foot soldier Sammie was not herself. She was skinnier than ever, but she wasn't sullen anymore. Neither was there any more back-talking or flippancy or, sadly, Bolshie light-heartedness. Sammie had buckled down to her homework with an industry that should have heartened her mother.

One day, Jane found the Italian red boots crushed at the bottom of the bathroom bin.

'Was it fun rooming with Bella in Italy?' she asked.

'I shared with Rachel.'

'I thought Bella was going to share with you, you know, for a little godmother quality time.'

'No. Bella did play cards with me when the light was "off" and they couldn't shoot her butchering baby lambs the Italian Way. Just as messy as the English way, if you ask me.'

'What did you play—Hearts?'

'Gin rummy. She cheats. But I still won. Anyway, her mind wasn't on the game. She called it, "Our chance to have a little talk".' Sammie avoided Jane's gaze and looked at the kitchen floorboards.

'Talk about what?'

'She hasn't fulfilled her promise.'

'To do what?'

'Not to do, to be. I don't know. Something about being a true symbol of hope, instead of a cooking icon. Or was it about being a true woman? Maybe she said a true human being. Anyway, she spent a lot of time talking to Dad about it *in their room.*'

The teenager's brave banner swayed and tossed in a sudden emotional wind, as if the French doors in the kitchen had just been blown in on them by a freezing gust walloping the air.

Jane looked at her Sammie's lowered head and realized the tremendous courage her daughter had just showed with those three indiscreet words—protective, pitying, and wise beyond even her grandmother's years. Jane's shoulders shook with the stress of months of repressing her fears.

She burst into violent tears and reached for Sammie. Sammie fell, sheepish, down into her mother's outstretched arms and huddled over her mother's head as if she could protect her from all the heartbreak raining down. She enveloped Jane's face in her fleecy midriff smelling of Top Sixty perfume.

So far from Joe, Jane hadn't felt this close to Sammie in years, not since a frightening night spent at the Royal Free's emergency room after a close shave between Sammie's bicycle and a meat delivery van.

'Don't hate him, Mum. Please don't hate him.' Sammie stroked her mother's hair through her own sobs. 'That telly scene is awfully seducing. Strangers are always slobbering to please you. Everything laid on by other people. There's no faffing about, no queues, no aggro. Celebrities don't live on our planet. After all these years, Dad couldn't help himself.'

'I see.' Jane clung to her daughter's tiny waist. At least she had her daughter back, heart and soul. Was it a consolation to cling to the sheepish girl and press on her all this adult despair? She moaned her misery into Sammie's comforting fleece and knew her tears weren't wrong when she heard Sammie's apologetic: 'I wasn't fair to you, Mum. Of course, I like it better when Grandma and Dad let me do what I want. I always feel like I'm disappointing you—'

'Oh, Sammie, no, no—'

'You want me to be smarter and read more and work harder.' Sammie choked through her own bitter tears, 'But I didn't understand until now, that's because you love me. You never tried to buy me off with a rubbishy pair of boots. I don't care if Bella is my godmother. I realize now she's a selfish bloody cow. Sooner or later, Dad's going to realize it, too. And that's my promise.'

PART II

After the rulers of the Zhou Dynasty were compelled to move east to Luoyang in 770 BC, they gradually lost control over the feudal lords. The next three hundred years, the Spring and Autumn Period, unveiled a turbulent drama of usurpation, annexation, treason, and murder, but also wisdom, courage, and loyalty.

Chapter Thirteen, Beat the Grass to Startle the Snake

Even on the rare nights Joe now made it home for dinner, conversation at 19 Chalkwood Square congealed like stale gravy. Jane had promised Baldwin that she wouldn't confront Joe, but since Sammie's confirmation that Joe and Bella shared a room in Tuscany, this silence required Olympian willpower. It was at last real war, after a Phoney War of false accommodation and denial.

More evenings than not, Joe excused himself entirely from the family table, saying he'd already grabbed some mash at the Beeb's canteen. His clothes smelled of the far more exotic scraps of *The Travelling Kitchen*. Each night, he crawled under the bedclothes with a theatrical yawn, in case Jane still lay awake.

Jane laced her frosty lack of interest in any studio anecdotes with only the most impersonal bulletins about Lorraine's health or Sammie's maths scores.

The Gilchrists' ability to trundle along this joyless plain disconcerted Jane even more than Joe's depression had oppressed her. At least sharing his career miseries had kept them intimate. They must've subsisted for years on nursing his fractured self-esteem. Somewhere along the way, Joe had taken his distance from Jane's concerns—leaving her more and more to Lorraine as confidante—and taken his parental pleasures raising Sammie on a parallel track. He hadn't registered that Jane's Bookworms were threatened by a shrinking Council budget. He hadn't once noticed that since September, she'd been following an 'information management class' that required not one single textbook.

Worse, Joe knew it, of course, and resorted to clumsy gestures. He brought Jane imported tulips—out of tune with both the season and her spirits—and then Sammie let out that they were used flowers from the 'New Ideas for Dutch Ovens' episode. Jane hid her fury behind the covers of *The Hare with the Amber Eyes*.

Most painful, Joe displayed a more generalized, (if glazed) contentment than Jane had seen in him in years. You'd think their mantelpiece had sprouted a regiment of BAFTA masks, Golden Globe statuettes, Screen Actors' Guild trophies and Critics' Circle accolades. Instead, now all it took to thrill Joe down to his new sienna cashmere socks from Italy was the news that Jacques Pepin was descending from the culinary clouds for Bella's week of 'French *Saveurs du Nord.*'

'The Italian week turned us around. Did you see our *Barb* figures? The show's picking up!'

Jane wasn't interested in Broadcasters' Audience raves for Bella. 'Any news from the food people in Rome? I thought they liked our idea.'

'Absolutely, sweetheart, they were very keen. Still in the works. Just takes time. I've got another phoner lined up for next week.'

The world seemed to demand nothing of Jane but tongue-biting endurance. The throes of jealousy, betrayal, and frustration were like a persistent thrumming underneath each day's countable hours—an engine of hurt grinding its gears at the pit of her stomach.

Some mornings after Joe left for work, Jane set herself a written list of things, starting with: get out of bed, brush teeth, wash hair, make bed—easier to follow instructions than leave herself any choice. Pretty soon she'd hire a personal trainer to keep herself breathing.

Then she cried herself back into a temporary calm, all her wailings well-muffled from Lorraine's ears by Polish carpenters hammering at 17 Chalkwood Square's basement wall. In the afternoons, Jane heated quick soups and instant noodles, set Lorraine's tray, and dished up Sammie's supper, her exposed nerves frayed by Green Day's bass line pounding from behind the girl's locked door.

It was a season of damp wool, churning dehumidifiers, and secret tears. It was the winter of everybody's discontent—except Joe—made even less glorious by the looming prospect of Sammie's exams.

If anyone noticed Jane's clenched heart, what could they do? Chris never remarked that her Monday morning reading of nursery rhymes sounded like a dirge or asked why her Tuesday "off" was spent in the darkened reading room scraping rocks of chewing gum from under battered reading tables. Lorraine watched in silence as Jane scrubbed away her Furies on Wednesday and Thursday, cleaning the attic flat while crying, then shopping for food while crying, and then just crying.

Her eyes were like purple gooseberries.

Despite the onset of the damp season, Professor Baldwin remained as fluffy and dry as an old drake, determined as ever to keep his shrinking class swimming along behind him through the Warring States Period; only Nigel, Jane, and Winston huddled in attendance. Kevin had accompanied buyers to Manhattan on business, Dan was late returning from a 'business trip' to Birmingham, while poor Keith hadn't been able to insure himself at any premium against a sore throat.

'Ah, the common cold, against which there is no effective stratagem except Mrs Ng's fish ball soup,' Winston said.

No sooner had they sat down to Stratagem Thirteen than one of the school's factotums had barged into their room with an order to decamp. Baldwin's tiny team found itself shunted from its large and chilly classroom into a tiny room used for tutorials.

They resettled their bags, coats, and briefcases in a space scarcely bigger than two broom closets. Nigel relegated one broken chair to the corridor as a retort to the management. They squeezed into the remaining chairs with their elbows touching. The linoleum stank of Dettol.

Jane was amazed at the professor's fortitude. It was as if Baldwin expected worse treatment and was almost relieved. 'Our ranks are thinned, our territory reduced, but nothing will deter us from launching our third group of six, The Attacking Strategies!' He punched the frigid air with frantic conviction.

You had to admire Baldwin, trying to animate three tired adults with ancient Chinese philosophy. He looked like Don Quixote without even a Sancho Panza.

'Jane, when you cannot detect the opponent's plans, what do you do?'

'Wait and see, like you keep telling me.'

Winston intoned, 'The Honourable Wily Hedgehog Librarian Stratagem. Do Nothing and Hope It All Just Goes Away. Ommmmmm,' He extended both arms into a Buddha gesture of blessing but there wasn't much room without hitting Nigel in the nose.

'Halfway there, dear lady, but there must be something to see. And you can't sit around forever. Your troops must eat, your communications might fall under attack, and the weather might turn against you.'

Winston nudged Jane to study Baldwin's chalky calligraphy on the old-fashioned blackboard.

'Oh, I don't know. Scare them with a snake?'

'Oh, dear lady! You launch a direct, brief attack! You "beat the grass" and force the snake out from under the rock to measure its weakness and shed light on its secrets.'

That afternoon, Jane had soothed her red eyes with lotion and dressed her hair for evening class, but underneath she felt so beat-up, the idea of beating anything else exhausted her. All she could do these days was weep deeper into her armchair or throw her miseries into installing a new browser in the fast-ageing library computer systems. Why couldn't Baldwin let her alone tonight? Instead he urged her at last to attack—to scare Bella or Joe himself?—into revealing their next step.

'But Professor Baldwin, whatever happened to common sense, Western-style, as in let sleeping dogs lie?' Jane asked.

'Don't stir up a hornet's nest?' Nigel suggested.

'Thanks, Nigel. That's what I meant.'

'You're recommending a warning shot, professor?' Winston asked.

'Exactly. Say you float a "sounding-balloon" or "test-run", to show your father what hell his life would become after Nelson's *coup d'état*? Those of you who know the history of modern China will be put in mind of the Hundred Flowers campaign? 1957?'

Three blank faces looked up at Baldwin.

'A call to Let a Hundred Flowers of opinion bloom? The Communist Party's device to bring critics in the open, only to cut them down ruthlessly?'

No one leapt out of a chair.

'O'Neill would know what you're on about,' Nigel said. His note taking had slackened during the last few classes.

'Really, class, you ought to be able to find a use for Number Thirteen—it couldn't be more flexible in practice. The Chinese classics say, "To ask a general to act is not as good as provoking a general to act. You can use it on your own side where the so-called snake is your own reluctant boss instead of a rival or opponent—'

'That would be combining it with Number Three!'

'Very good, Nigel. For example, your bank manager might hesitate to issue a guarantee for his client. He might need your prompting.'

At least Nigel jotted that down. Clearly the lack of Dan's erudite assistance left Baldwin exasperated. Provoked by the dullards he faced this evening, he shook his head.

'The point is, you *act*. You gain information using a well-tailored provocation. Or you protect yourself when someone starts pounding on your grass.'

Nigel shrugged. 'All rather obvious.' The cold November rain hammered outside.

Annoyed, Baldwin pounded on his rickety table. 'Commanders succeed because they get information early and use it quickly. Even in fifth century BC, Sun Tzu's army was what you bankers call information-centred. Banks should reduce the overload of unread reports and interoffice e-mail and concentrate on information flow in and out of headquarters.'

Nigel raised his voice over the pounding storm. 'With all due respect, I don't need a Chinese tactic to tell me information centricity is a basic tenet of organization theory, particularly anything associated with TQM. Sorry, Winston, TQM means total quality management.'

'Total Quality Moron,' Winston muttered to Jane.

'I heard that, Chu.'

The class broke for coffee as bedraggled as it had begun. The canteen smelled of fresh floor polish and old fried bacon. Jane's spirits rose at the sight of Dan in his soggy anorak hunting down their new classroom.

'What are you guys doing down here? What have I missed?' he whispered.

'Number Thirteen. Beating the grass—'

'—To force the snake to reveal himself.' Dan scrutinized her dark-circled eye, 'Everything okay?'

'Certainly.'

'Because you always come to class looking quite together. But tonight, uh—'

'I look not quite myself.'

Dan stood back a foot to gauge the damage. 'Not your rosy-cheeked self. More hit-and-run. Not quite drive-by, but definitely victim.'

'What a very blunt American compliment.'

'What a very cool English response. What's the problem?'

'A family drama. Teenager headaches.' Jane dumped a cube of sugar into her beige tea. Her clothes were feeling a bit loose these days, but anyway, it no longer mattered whether she grew as wide as a house. 'Let's not talk about it and say we did.'

'Oh, let's talk about it and say we didn't.' Dan forced her to sit with him, many tables away from Winston who was looking to place himself as strategically far from Nigel as possible. Baldwin sat surrounded by the biddies from Mending Marriage.

'—Your tales of woe can take my mind off the appalling misuses of Number Thirteen in the West Midlands. It seems the Birmingham police are quite capable of beating the grass, catching half a dozen baby snakes but letting the cobra slither clean away. Possession of videos, inflammatory DVD's—that's not enough. You stake out a house, surround it with armed men, risk the lives of dozens of officers, not to mention neighbourhood housewives, toddlers, and teens, but it's all no good without proof of incitement, even if it means incite on assignment.'

'Isn't that entrapment?'

Dan sighed with pity at Jane's innocence. 'Oh, shit, it's only a theory, remember? So, what's your kid's problem?'

'Her father's having an affair.'

'Your problem, then. Sorry, I don't mean to upset you. You cheat on him?"

'Never!'

'You still want him?'

'Of course! We're a family!'

Dan cleared his throat and stirred his coffee. 'Well, he must be some kind of jerk. Take this Kleenex. You're looking kind of raccoon-y.'

Jane wiped the mascara off her cheeks, and thought: why was she willing to fight for Joe? Her anger blotted out almost all her love. Of course, she'd never been unfaithful to Joe but there hadn't been any offers to refuse. No, the harder loyalty was always taking his side—even when he brought his Panorama problems on himself. Jane had convinced herself that Joe was heroic to keep on pitching and to keep on fighting for his stories to be heard.

Her voice cracked with tears: 'I admire him. He's always fought injustice and corruption—'

'—And evildoing on Planet Earth. You make him sound like Batman.'

'Yes, he adored working on *Panorama*—'

'Never seen it.'

'Like *60 Minutes,* with investigative exposés.'

'So only he could save the world? Me, Megatron Megadude.' Dan turned grave, 'It's very seductive until the day somebody outdoes you, goes off to save the world and comes back in a pine box covered with a flag. You never feel quite so heroic again.'

'Well, he has always been my hero. I loved him, for his causes, his crusades. Now he just can't accept a world that doesn't need his heroics. Take that away, and what's left is tarnished pride. He's lost all sense of his place in the world. I suppose Bella helps him find it. She might give him the audience he feels his projects deserve.'

'Well, if you're thinking of divorce, I've been there.' He paused. 'It isn't pretty.'

Jane shook her head. 'Well, that's not an option.'

She suddenly threw her head back, and gasped. Because, with his few questions, Dan had just done his 'homework' for Stratagem Thirteen on her, 'beating the grass' until she was on the verge of confessing the very thing that spiced her tears over Joe's 'adultery' with such a salty burn. She didn't stick by Joe just because she believed in him or loved him. She was proving something to the world, to herself, and especially to Lorraine.

'Oh, Dan, that's the wretched irony. I can't get divorced. When Joe proposed in the maternity ward, the very hour our beautiful Sammie was born, the happiest moment of my life, I turned down his proposal. I spurned him.'

'Why?'

'Oh, I don't know. I was so stupid! I'll never forget the look on his face. I didn't want to end up divorced like my mother. I didn't mean to reject him, just the idea of being married. Of course, I told myself I was hip, independent, cool—but Joe didn't see it that way. He said he'd never ask me again.'

'So. You never got married.'

'No. I was self-destructive and fearful, and now it's too late.'

Chapter Fourteen, Borrow a Corpse, Return a Soul

Since Jane's admission to Dan that she was, technically, a single woman, the air between them buzzed with heightened static. Baldwin's mood was also much improved by caffeine or perhaps the flattery of Dan barrelling back in time for the second half of his class. The two men let down their guard and all but turned the discussion of Stratagem Fourteen into a Sinologist's graduate seminar. This was a lucky break for poor old Fourteen, whose ghoulish aspects would put off any amateur's enthusiasm; no matter which version Baldwin cited from the classics, Stratagem Fourteen involved some dead loser donning the decaying flesh of someone else to nab a second chance.

' . . . So we have the deceased Xu Bitao borrowing the corpse of her dead sister in order to return to life and marry.'

'Some wedding,' Winston shuddered.

Nigel sat up. 'If she can bring her dead sister's corpse to life, why can't she just revitalize her own?'

'Let's not get literal with figurative legends, Nigel. Here's another example. A corrupt official Yue Shou dies. The Prince of Hell gets ready to spear him with a pitchfork and dip him into a vat of boiling oil when the Immortal Lü Dongbin asks that Yue be handed over as a disciple. The Prince of Hell says why not? Unfortunately, back up on earth, Mrs Yue Shou has already cremated her husband, so our dead man must borrow someone else's body. Luckily, a crippled butcher in his town has also died and his body is available. Thus, Yue Shou returns to life, but with a lame foot supported by a crutch—'

'What is the Chinese concept of the soul?' Jane interrupted. By now, Baldwin's students realized he was capable of disgorging many stories if someone didn't move the lesson along. 'I mean, if this is a Daoist story?'

'Excellent question! In these cases, the Chinese use *hun* for soul.' Tapping out the word *hun* on the board, Baldwin explained, '*Hun* is your personality. It lives on after the body's death and watches over your loved ones. The *po* is closer to the biological, electrical feeling some people feel around a deathbed.'

'That's rather useful,' Jane said, thinking Joe's *po* was intact these days, but his *hun* had left the household, while her *hun* was struggling along but her *po* had all but drained away.

'Yes, but what does all this mean?' Baldwin leaned forward on his battered desk and one of its legs broke right out from under him. He fell into Winston's arms and they tumbled to the floor. Jane and Dan untangled the two gawky scarecrows.

Nigel sneered, 'This room is a death-trap. We should get a refund on the course fees just for sitting in this dump.' He dusted off his bespoke Gieves and Hawkes trousers.

'I see I'll have to adapt my lecture style to the new environment.' Baldwin flexed his bony knee, checking for damage, and then forged on, 'Where was I? What does it mean, Fourteen? You revive something from the past by giving it a new purpose, or reinterpret it, or bring to life old ideas, customs, traditions.'

Dan said, 'I get it. You're a new leader who wants to attract followers or impress converts, so you claim the mandate of the imprisoned or exiled leader.' He winked at Jane.

'I could use this one,' Winston piped up. Jane noticed his pink-streaked hair was growing out. 'I tell my father that a family company named Chu Printers has to keep the name Chu, so his legacy is preserved for generations.'

'Good,' Baldwin prompted.

'You see, Nelson is dating that Malaysian chick Selina from Sultana Software, the one he only started dating after I mucked up Strategy Three? Now, if he marries Selina, they might rename the shop. Worse, Selina's mother might take over everything. You know how Malaysian-Chinese women can be? Wah! Watch out! My father's legacy would go from being Chu Printers to a subsidiary of Sultana Software.' Winston turned to Nigel, 'Those Malaysians undercut everybody. Suppose I employ Fourteen? I borrow the weight of ancient custom—that's the idea, isn't it, Professor?'

'What? Ten years of honourable printing in Belsize Park?' Nigel sniggered.

'Well, Nigel, it means something to my father,' Winston spat back. 'The patina of the old must be preserved. Or my father's business ends up named after a raisin wearing an orange turban.'

Baldwin said, 'But Winston, this tactic asks that the old be borrowed, forgotten, or discarded, not legitimately inherited, like your name; that you take an institution, a technology, or a method from elsewhere for your own purpose. But I quibble.'

Nigel perked up. 'Like a shelf company? Could the corpse be a shelf company?'

'Yes, Nigel! Perfect!'

'A shell game?' Winston was miffed his ruse hadn't pleased Baldwin more.

'No.' Nigel sighed. 'A shelf company is a pre-registered business entity. It has no assets or liabilities and has never done business. It's registered with the sole purpose of being sold.'

'Well, what's the bloody point of that?'

Nigel sighed. 'I thought you were a businessman, Chu.'

'Well, funny, that. We actually run a business. We don't just shuffle options and warrant things around. We add value. We provide a service. And would you stop calling me Chu? You're not head boy. You may call me Winston.'

'Fine, Winston. A shelf company is the fastest way of getting a business up and running. There are whole warehouses of such companies sitting in cemeteries of usable corporate corpses. You buy one, appoint new directors, open a bank account, and start trading.'

'Trading. Trading.' Winston took no notice of Jane's calming hand on his arm. 'You mean pushing assets around in circles so you can take a juicy cut? At least in my business we deal in real print, real paper. We're not financial parasites.'

The lesson was stumbling towards its end. Jane regretted her admission to Dan even before Baldwin previewed the next week's assignment. Sweating in that silly anorak, (so unnecessary in the unseasonable November warmth that unleashed torrents of rain day after day,) Dan spent the final hour gazing at her oddly. She did look a sight.

During her rackety tube ride home, the mortification still stung. Given the normal energy level on the Northern Line after ten p.m., no one would notice a mousey woman with unkempt hair, fringed ethnic scarf, and frazzled expression. Inside, Jane was afire with shame. Would Dan think her confession was a pointed hint that she was more available than he'd assumed?

She'd never felt less available in her entire life. She was becoming less substantial with each passing day. Soon she'd look in the mirror to find she'd turned semi-material, like some pale Henry James ghost in black Victorian mourning dress found weeping on the Bridge Approach, like in *The Turn of the Screw*.

During Sammie's infancy, Lorraine had begged Jane to marry Joe. She had cajoled Joe behind Jane's back as it dawned that she, Jane's much-married mother, had debased the institution in Jane's eyes and she was right. The very word marriage summoned up in Jane a vivid brew of potent romances, sterile separations, and Act III curtains slamming down hard on her youthful sensitivities.

Back in the early days, Jane had stoutly defended her unmarried state to Lorraine as independent and liberated. The tussle had died down. Over the years of play dates, work shifts, and retirement from television research, Jane's decision rusted into vestigial irrelevance. Most people assumed Jane and Joe were married, anyway, Lorraine finally rationalized. In the end, Jane stopped insisting on her maiden name.

As threatened, Joe never proposed again. So now she couldn't whimper like some suburban discard, 'How can you do this to me? After all, I'm your wife!'

Walking home through a moonless night, Jane imagined what any wedding would have looked like at the height of her passion for Joe, and what any ceremony might look like now—a cringe-making middle-aged 'celebration,' all gathered together before God to toast loyalty, not love, and everyone getting sloshed and fighting the urge to remark how the 'bride' has weathered well.

Wouldn't any ceremony now resemble Baldwin's reheated corpse, rouged up and warmed-over in a bid for resuscitated romance? Talk about reviving a dead body to reclaim a soul! Taking vows now would be all about claiming legitimacy. That's not how she wanted to keep Joe. Even if by some miracle, he did dump Bella and ask just one more time . . .

She didn't like Stratagem Fourteen. She'd skip any homework involving snakes or corpses and move straight on to Fifteen and Sixteen.

The rain was letting up and a warmish night falling against the soft thrum of the city from the south. Crossing the Bridge Approach, Jane heard a set of footsteps some twenty feet behind her. She didn't panic, just kept up a steady stride across the metal bridge, then hastened a little. The Council Estates weren't far away and only one station north of Camden Town, all the gentrification in the world couldn't bar the nightshades of addiction from having a grab at her wallet.

The steps didn't hurry. She turned left on to Berkley Road, and was just passing Eglon Mews, when she chanced a backward look and gave a sigh of relief.

It was only the painter trudging in her wake, with his beard pressed into his chest under an overloaded backpack jutting up behind his shoulder blades.

She would have continued straight into the square, but with her momentary stop at his darkened window, he caught up with her and asked, 'Seen this?'

The Painted Angel's glass feet were smashed in.

The artist dropped his pack on the wet sidewalk. 'I got to the hardware store before it closed.' Plywood was roped to the bottom of the pack and the sharp angles of tools poked from inside of the canvas. He shrugged. 'It's happened before, back home.'

His cadence—Continental, thick, northern?

'I painted an angel on my studio window in Rotterdam with "Thou Shalt Not Kill' after the murder of Theo van Gogh. Some guys walking past my window, they see the painting and they get

141

mad. They even come to the door, *ja*, and tell me wash off your painting. Wash off your racist words.'

'The Sixth Commandment being a racial affront?'

The Dutchman smiled. 'The Rotterdam police call me. They don't want trouble, community sensitivities, *ja, ja, ja*. So finally, even the mayor orders me; Joop, wash off your angel. I say, no way! He sends firemen with big hoses. The pigs start to wash off my fucking angel. And the crowds are yelling, the Muslims yelling, and the old women, everybody yelling for my angel. Which was much better than this guy . . . Better aqua.'

'You're making this up?'

'No, I'm telling you. Everybody comes, even the TV guys. A reporter says, I come to talk about your angel, but when he sees the hose, he tries to protect my painting, you know, because he's so famous, nobody going to spray him. And he gets fucking arrested! Then they put this video of him and me and the angel on YouTube, and man . . .' Joop sighed.

'What happened then?'

'Oh, the mayor apologized to the reporter who made the mayor apologize to me, but he made me apologize to the Muslims, except some Muslims on my side made the police apologize to the community. Everybody won.'

'Except the angel.' Jane looked up at St Michael's scarred face. Was this a new angel, or the Rotterdam one reborn, borrowing the washed-off form of the other version to offer his message of peace new life?

Like Baldwin's lesson, borrowing a corpse.

The Dutchman pulled on his soft blond whiskers. 'The police tell me I'm in the shit with the mosque guys, real shit. They say, one morning, you watch out. You're going to be on your bicycle and somebody will stab a message into your chest just like with Theo. So, I come to visit here with my uncle.'

'I like the electric blue door. Wasn't it brown before?'

'You should have seen my aunt's face when that rock hit her flat-screen TV! I tell her, man, the fucking news is not on that box, the fucking news is coming through your window.'

Jane said, 'You make me laugh. Make your angel laugh. He looks so vindictive that way. Laughter conquers all.'

'*Ja*,' the painter nodded. '*Goed, goed* idea. He will be a laughing angel.'

Jane carried Joop's wash of laughter into the square and up the stairs. She checked on Lorraine, who'd fallen asleep while watching Sammie do her homework.

She returned downstairs and started her bath in preparation for a long, good read. While the bubbles mounted, she went to hang up her jacket. It was only then she saw a letter on her pillow and realized that while grandmother and granddaughter had whiled away their evening in peace and ignorance in the attic above, Joe had stealthily moved out.

Chapter Fifteen, Lure the Tiger Down Off the Mountain

The rest of Jane's Friday consisted of shock and slow-moving numbness at the sight of a long wooden rod holding only jangling clothes hangers.

She took a very hot bath—the kind favoured by *Tale of Genji* heroines—scalding steam and purging loofah—then crawled into bed.

She would survive the empty darkness with the help of books. Folding her broken spirit between the pages of a book hadn't failed her yet. Not when Lorraine forgot to pick her up from Grand Central Station at the close of summer camp nor when a rejected Joe had raced off in anger from the maternity ward to shoot some reaction footage on a police-beating-suspect verdict in LA.

She'd been abandoned before.

Like a watchtower of paper and cardboard comfort, new library books sat stacked on her bedside table. A story set in the Canadian wilderness just reminded her of Joe. No more Joe.

Bulgakov pumped the soft furrows of the duvet with his claws.

Jane stroked his coat. 'What's wrong with you, furball? Why haven't you walked out too?'

She spread the other books across her lap: Ian Rankin, a new Will Self, and a hefty royal biography. Nothing suited. Her Great Wall of Solace threatened to give way.

She hunted down a much-thumbed *The Severed Head* that she knew made light of adultery. The two draped bedroom windows curtained her off from the cold world outside like two reliable guards. Instead of seeming emptier without the smells and sounds of Joe's settling his labours to rest, the space contracted. She hadn't really *seen* their bedroom—the chipped bookcase, exercise dumbbells, twisted shoe tree and the armchair with its loose stuffing—for years.

The bedside phone rang at eleven. It was Joe. His voice was muffled by remorse or drink as he announced he was spending that night away. Not in Bella's plumed and downy boudoir, it turned out, but in Fergus's spare room. If the guest bed matched the Fergoid wardrobe, Joe was facing a lumpy slumber.

'I think you know what I'm trying to say.'

'No, Joe, I don't.'

'You read my letter?'

'No.'

She'd dropped it unread into the bin, along with enough slimy day-old quiche to make it impossible to retrieve and told him so.

'I need to think things through, Jane. Get some perspective. I've been really confused lately.'

'I'm not confused. Telephone Sammie tomorrow.' Her dry, cool voice surprised her. Would she hold up for another sentence?

'Look, I'm sorry. Maybe I've changed too much without realizing it. I don't want to hurt you for anything in the world. We have to talk, I guess.'

She had held it all in, but any more conversation would be pushing her luck. 'Not now. I'm tired. Give Fergus my best. Goodnight.'

Total relief swamped her. A huge calm pervaded the room. A concrete slab of waiting had fallen off her back. She stretched out both arms and legs to touch both sides of the bed. Her feet caught a pair of Joe's boxer shorts wadded up at the bottom of the sheet. She fished them out and slung them on top of the quiche.

The next morning Sammie came to breakfast with swollen eyes and pushed her cornflakes around in circles. Jane was already on her second pot of coffee, figuring out how to tell Lorraine that Joe had done a bunk at last.

'Dad called me this morning. He's with Uncle Fergus. I told him not to stay there too long or he'll bring home fleas. Isn't he coming home, Mum?'

'It's just for a while.' She reached for Sammie's waist to hug her. 'He loves you more than anything in the world.'

'Yeah. So he said.' Sammie slipped from her grasp. She shared her grandmother's aversion to trite dialogue.

'He wouldn't lie to you.'

'Can you be a part-time liar, Mum? Someone's either a liar or he's honest. Dad wants to take me to *Avatar* this afternoon. I don't want to go. I've got to swot up my maths.'

'I suppose that counts as a white lie.' Jane stroked Sammie's hair. 'I have an idea. Would you like to meet my friend Winston from my evening class, instead?'

Although it was a quirky idea, it grew with the hours until that afternoon Sammie and Jane forced their way against a headwind sweeping down Primrose Hill to meet Winston for Chinese food.

'Who is this guy? You've got a friend under forty?' Sammie squealed over the Northern Line's rumble up to Belsize Park.

'You can have friends all ages. Hasn't your grandmother got friends of all ages?'

'Sure, from seventy to one hundred.'

Winston beamed with delight as they walked up to the Chu counter. A noodle feast was their reward for braving a freezing Saturday of harried weekend shoppers. Nelson was at the airport picking up a shipment of new keyboards from Taiwan, so Winston's little sister Monica would hold the fort.

They walked to the Moonbeam Restaurant nestled in a small mews half a block away from the Saturday market crowds. With its garish vermilion sign and jade green railing, the Moonbeam was a homey place to lift the bruised heart; it seemed one of those Chinese restaurants that never changes and you never remark on—until the day you need it—and then it rises out of the mists, a Brigadoon of sweet-and-sour pork. Its sweltering dining room bustled with waiters shouting orders pushing through takeaway customers loitering near the cash register, as bursts of smoke flew up from steaming woks glimpsed behind the swinging kitchen door.

'What a din,' Winston cringed. He picked up a stained menu card propped against the soy sauce cruet. 'I'm actually not very good at this.'

Sammie recoiled from a plate of glistening sea creatures landing on an adjacent table. 'Nothing with scales or tentacles, if you don't mind.'

'Don't worry, Sammie.' Winston patted her wrist. 'I don't eat squiggly things either. Anyway, you look like somebody who only eats once a month.'

'Hello, Winston.' A waitress dragged up to their table and yanked at two greasy plaits caught in her apron. Underneath a spattered bib, she wore a blue satin cheongsam that squeezed even her slender waist into two sausages of shiny fat.

' 'Lo, Cecilia. How's your mother?'

'Made me wear this stupid Suzie Wong outfit again. How's your Dad?'

Their simultaneous sighs of, 'Nothing new' told a story in itself. The weight of Chinese parental expectation clouded their brows. Cecilia ladled out steaming bowls of rice and set an oval plate of pork strips on crispy noodles on the table. Winston told Sammie and Jane that he'd met Cecilia at the age of six in Saturday morning Cantonese class. 'I would never have passed without her cheat sheets.'

Mr and Mrs Ng Chow-fat, insisted Cecilia study accounting full-time and wait on tables weekends in the Moonbeam. Winston confided that his friend's private dream was to work in 'new media.' How to achieve anything between hours of reckoning pre-tax profit margins for assorted relatives all over London and biking cartons of fried rice around the neighbourhood was the wan-looking girl's desperate dilemma.

Sammie looked with suspicion at the food. Her picky eating was getting worse. She asked, 'What's your dream, Winston? Why are you taking a library management class? Mom says you want to run your Dad's business. When I grow up, I want to write Lonely Planet guidebooks and never come home.'

Jane scowled at her daughter and shook her head, warning Winston.

'Well, actually I'm not into library technology. Not even printing. We've got a lot of cool stuff in the shop, but it doesn't do anything for me.' His expression drifted. 'It sounds corny, but I had something more traditional in mind.'

Jane imagined a Ching dynasty Winston in long grey scholar's gown with white cuffs and a pristine white collar. He was lifting scrolls of black calligraphy off a silk-screen press, when he wasn't tending bamboo plants in his orangery. Somewhere a *pi-pa* was playing . . .

Winston shattered her lovely vision with, 'My toddler years were spent in Hong Kong during the last big construction boom. You might say my earliest lullaby was the rhythm of pile drivers.' His eyes glazed over. 'My dream is to sell real estate, like my ancestors before me and their ancestors before them.'

'Winston, you're so clumsy with numbers!' Jane couldn't help herself.

Winston lost a square of pineapple off the end of his chopsticks. 'True, I'm more a people person. I'd need a partner to watch the percentages.'

They devoured a delicious lunch without a single tentacle or scale. Winston and Sammie found common cause in various food phobias and academic struggles.

'You know I tried Tactic Fourteen, Jane.'

'What's Tactic Fourteen, Winston?'

'A Chinese proverb, Sammie. You borrow tradition to give soul to your cause. 'Course, Dad agreed right away that the Chu name must carry on down through the generations. Thanked me for warning him of threat posed by the lovely Sultana mob. Nelson caught on and right away suggested the three of us work together on something fresh, something really *now* to enhance our position. Here's the result.'

A doleful Winston dangled a green plastic sweet pepper in front of Sammie's nose. 'This is a key chain prototype UPS'd from my uncle Horatio's toy factory in Foshan.'

Tiny white print circled the vegetable's waistline: 'Chu Pixels and Printers.' Sammie turned it round and round, reading, '— Packs a Peck of Peppy Products—Computers, Printers, and Service 24/7 . . .'

"Notice, pixels come first? Bad omen. Nelson had to explain to Dad what the twenty-four and seven stand for . . .' Winston pocketed the plastic vegetable.

'I'm not quite sure what to say about the key chain but this food is delicious, Winston.'

'Oh, Jane, that's just Menu One. I can't read the others. Probably dogs-up-a-tree, frogs in lotus leaves, dragon doo-doo on seaweed . . .' He played the clown to Sammie's grinning audience. He whispered to Jane, 'Fourteen flopped. I'm moving on to Stratagem Fifteen. Lure the Tiger Down Off the Mountain. Harass the hell out of Nelson this week.'

'Well, at least Sammie and I lured you out for a meal. Thanks for not telling her too much about the class. Her father thinks I'm studying library management.'

Mother and daughter strolled home with fresh breezes at their backs.

'He's Hugh Grant trapped inside this beanpole Chinese body, Mum. So sweet, all stammering.'

'Aren't you glad I don't make you slave in a print shop or kitchen all day?'

'I shall spend all tomorrow studying,' Sammie promised. 'But tonight, Grandma's taking me to *Wicked*. She and one of the dressers go waaaaay back.'

Sammie paused outside her bedroom door. 'Is Dad coming home tomorrow?'

'I think he's working on something with Fergus.'

'As long as it's with Fergus, I don't mind.' The unspoken 'Bella' hung in the air.

Monday morning Jane got to work on time, drank her coffee as if nothing had happened, and prepared for the meeting to review the Public Lending Right figures totting up the most borrowed authors. Figures were important these days in the battle to keep a branch open. Chris didn't remark on her buttoned-up demeanour but she caught her own severe reflection in a darkened computer screen. At least 'abandoned goods' wasn't blinking from her brow in neon lights.

Chris ticked off the most thumbed: 'Patterson, Cox, Steel. The usual. So, so depressing.'

'They keep us open three days a week. If our viability was based on Joshua Ferris, we'd be on the street.'

'If I position *Jamie's Dinners* next to John Thaw and Catherine Cookson, do you think anybody would get the joke?' Chris shrugged. 'I'm damned if I'm sacrificing Philip Roth for Jamie's risotto.' Chris held up a sports bio, *Black, White and Gold*. 'At least this is a good read.'

'Put it next to *My Walk to Freedom*.'

'Good idea. There, Mr Mandela, a new friend.' Chris rearranged his 'Triumph over Adversities' display to better impress the directors of The Reading Agency's Fulfilling Their Potential Initiative.

On the other side of the room, he'd set up some reading for preteens: *Love Lessons, Gossip Girls,* and *The Girls' Collection*. 'Convincing? You know, if I were a girl—'

'You're not—'

'—a girl in this neighbourhood, I'd want to escape into *Persuasion*. No more television rip-offs.' He caught Jane's glance. 'Not that there's anything wrong with watching telly.'

'Don't worry, Chris. Go ahead and insult television all you want. Joe moved out.' She shuffled the borrowing data.

'Oh, Jane. Do you want to call in sick or . . .' Chris reached for the bin, 'Or be sick . . . or something?'

'No. I'll start to feel pain in the phantom limb any minute now, but so far, I'm numb.'

'Your hair looks nice pulled back like that.'

'Thanks. One good hair day is a fair trade-off for a decades-long relationship—'

"I didn't mean—'

'I had the bathroom all to myself for a change.'

'Yeah, I like being single myself. You need something, you know, to tide you over?'

'Let's leave the drugs to our borrowers,' Jane said. 'I'm fine. Really. What time are these people coming?'

'Any minute, I expect.'

'Well, then, pull all our Dan Browns and diet books out of the back cupboard and scatter them around. Go on! I'm fine.' Her mobile rang and The Initiative Delegation walked in just in time to scowl with disapproval at Jane's ear pressed to her mobile, 'Yes, darling. That's why he's going to keep staying with Uncle Fergus.'

Chris distracted the officials with his 'Thrills and Chills' table.

'Sammie, I have to go, darling. Please, please, don't let it affect your studies. I love you, too. Oh, don't cry. Yes, I still love Daddy, too. I just don't like him one little bit.'

⫷⫸

'You mean you don't want to talk about it, or you just told Joe you didn't?' Lorraine was confused.

'There's no point in talking while he's totally embarrassed. After all, a few weeks ago, he loathed Bella. What does she see in him? I can't believe it's sex—no—don't look at me like that. If it was just a shag behind the pots and pans, I'd have lost him years ago to some ditsy PA. Dozens tried over the years.'

Lorraine listened from the window seat. 'For once in my life, I don't have any advice for you. I never got them back, not once they strayed. It was all cool disdain and alimony where Jack was concerned. As for alimony, fat chance as you're not—'

'Don't start now—'

Jane told Lorraine how she could only view Joe's entrapment like the Snow Queen's enchantment of Gerda's boyfriend Kay, and how, only after long years of searching for the Snow Queen's ice palace, Gerda's tears burned the troll-mirror's glass out of Kay's eye and heart, like an ice chip melting away under the heat of her love . . . She still loved Joe, just as Gerda had never stopped loving the boy Kay, because she knew that the boy Joe was trapped inside this middle-aged man's frustrations and fears.

'Hans Christian Anderson? The Snow Queen's ice chips? You're hopeless. The only ice chips that featured in my failed

152

romances were in the champagne bucket Jack kept chilled in his dressing room for ingénues.'

They worked for a while on the February birthday guest list, mulling over various disabilities as against conversational gifts, until Lorraine felt uncomfortable. She struggled off to change for bed. The usual pain pills weren't relieving aches in her bladder, but that didn't stop her humming in the bathroom. Lorraine had a favourite book character—Don Marquis's indomitable alley cat, Mehitabel who sang, (as recorded by a cockroach Archie jumping from typewriter key to typewriter key,) 'my youth i shall never forget, but theres nothing i really regret, *wotthehell wotthehell, theres a dance in the old dame yet, toujours gai toujours gai.*'

Yes, Lorraine had given Jane nights of adolescent tears, but *wotthehell wotthehell*, she'd also taught her daughter songs that kept the most dismal of shows on the road.

✺✺

'I don't quite follow this lure-the-tiger-out business, Professor.' Keith read from his handout, 'Stranded on the sandy beach, the dragon is teased by shrimps. Descending to the plain, the tiger is bullied by dogs. Well, what's the difference between this Stratagem Fifteen and good ol' Four—that one about tiring out the enemy while you conserve your resources?'

'A bed rest has done you good, Keith.' Baldwin stroked his forehead as he perched on a high stool in the corner. They were stuck in their tiny room and this week, all were present. Baldwin's solution was to sit above their heads, his pointed knees inches from Dan's chin. So far, it made him look—depending on the angle of Jane's chair and her mood—either like the class dunce relegated to a corner or St Peter handing down verdicts from the Pearly Gates. She finally settled on *The Land of Oz's* very intelligent Jack Pumpkin—all bones and big brain.

'Are you all keeping track of these nuances as well as Nigel and Keith? Remember, Four was one of the so-called Winning Strategies, best used from a comparatively strong position. You

153

set the pace, keep the other side tense, and attack might not be even necessary, if things go your way.'

Things weren't going Jane's way. Her half-hearted strategies had brought only temporary victories and psychological holding patterns that evaporated within days. The benefit of the class was not so much success in fortifying her family compound as providing distraction while the whole edifice collapsed around her.

Baldwin gained steam, 'Now, this Number Fifteen, Keith, is the third of the six Attacking Strategies, which are more aggressive. You don't just make your opponent anxious, you lure him, or her,' he smiled at Jane, 'Away from his source of strength. You isolate him from his support base, so that you can attack and harass him on unfamiliar ground.'

'You mean by forcing another store to try a line or collection that directly competes with where we're strongest?' Kevin asked. 'Retro-print spring wear?'

Baldwin confirmed, 'Exactly, Kevin. Retro-print spring wear, if you're particularly successful with such garments. You pull the ladies away from your enemy's fashion commitments—'

'To sportswear—' Kevin said.

'While you make your dresses the must-have garments of the season.'

'Those guys don't have the right designers,' Kevin grinned. 'They can't turn their orders around that fast. Even with the latest JIT inventory systems. But it would mean a huge outlay for us in promotion, ads, and in-house copywriting.'

'So lure them into your market. Pull out the retro stops. Luring the tiger off his terrain will mean being very alert—'

'Tightening my cycle of orders and customer-response—'

Flexibility, speed, decisiveness. All the traits Jane lacked. But one thing was clear to her even before the session broke for coffee. Instead of waiting for Joe to show his pathetic adulterer's hand, she would lure the tiger out of the cave. Not the tigress. She'd been thinking of Bella as the enemy, a size 38D fiend at the end of her spear, but that was all wrong, she realized now.

Wasn't it Joe who was thwarting her happiness? Wasn't his weakness their common enemy? She must lure Joe off Fergus' guest bed long enough to nip at his heels. Cowardly retreat might salve her pride, but she would have to just swallow her reticence and pull Joe back on her ground.

With shaking hands, she dialled his number. 'Joe, I think I'd like to talk after all,' she said. She could hear Natalie Cole crooning softly in the background amid the hubbub of a bar or restaurant. Somehow, she didn't associate Fergus with cocktails.

'Oh, Jane, I'm so glad to hear you sound okay. Yes, we have to clear the air. Considering everything I've put you through, I mean, actually, we have a lot to talk about. I haven't been quite honest with you, I'm afraid.'

'Oh, Joe, darling, I think I'm way ahead of you on that score. Let's meet at home tomorrow. Sammie's taking Lorraine to the hairdresser.'

'How about somewhere more, uh, neutral?'

'Sorry, Joe. I've only got the half hour at lunch. It's our busiest day at the library. I'll be home at noon.'

'All right, Jane. I can make it. Anything you say.'

'Yes, I have a full afternoon cleaning out all the self-help brochures. No doubt, I'll find all the marriage counselling tips quite handy now.'

'Gosh, Jane. You sound so in control. I don't want to upset you more. Maybe it's too soon?'

'Too soon? No, Joe, you won't upset me. You probably need the rest of your things, and it seems a good day. Saturdays I always clean out Bulgakov's gravel box. We can clean out your gravel, too.'

Her hand shook but her voice had held its bravado. It was less a charade than it would have been a few months before. Stratagems were all well and good on paper, but once you'd lured the tiger off his mountain and on to your territory, what could you say to make him stay? Finally, Jane's pride was raising its abused little head. She wasn't prepared to beg. It was time to attack.

Besides, she had plans, too. Heading out of class, Dan had asked her to lunch again. And this time, she was happy to think, it sounded like a proper date.

Chapter Sixteen, To Catch Something, First Let It Go

Of all the stratagems so far, Baldwin's Number Sixteen resonated most deeply with Jane. Sixteen was the only stratagem she actually feared, the one that ordained, 'To catch something, first let it go.'

Sixteen was one of Baldwin's favourites because, 'It embodies the very essence of Chinese philosophy, the constant principles of flux and flexibility between the yin and yang that make for such subtlety in Daoist thought.'

Exactly how could Jane be sure that something released from her anxious clutches could be reclaimed? She had to gamble, a prospect so unpalatable, she'd fought it off by concentrating all Saturday morning on those dog-eared leaflets, then excavating layers of index cards curling off their push pins.

She discovered Chris, nose stuck in *Black Swan Green*, hiding from such library drudgery. He was muttering to himself, 'Wow! This is so me!'

'I'm leaving for a quick bite.'

Chris looked annoyed at having to man the desk, so she added, 'Meeting Joe for a chat,' at which he nodded, 'Oh, sorry, Jane, take all afternoon if you have to.'

On the short walk home, she reviewed Stratagem Sixteen: Always leave a way of escape for the enemy. It mirrored Sun Tzu's Principle Seven; if you burned your bridges and your troops had no escape, they'd fight with superhuman strength. Although, why push your troops to fight to the death if they had no escape?

'The point being,' Baldwin had underscored, 'Cornered prey will mount a final desperate attack. When there is no way out, they stand firm. That's what you want in your own troops, but it's not what you want to confront in the enemy.'

From across the square, Joe stood visible through the tall windows, head over his mail. The sight of his broad shoulders under the battered brown suede jacket stopped Jane cold. That head of tousled brown hair only slightly thinning near the widow's peak above the familiar brow was no longer hers.

She hesitated before crossing the grass. It was all so familiar, the traffic noises fading as she rounded the bollards and the flanks of elegant houses with colourful doors like tin soldiers guarding the peace.

Yet Joe was willing to let it all go. You must let the enemy believe he still had his freedom. His will to fight will be dampened by his desire to escape. When in the end the freedom is proven a falsehood, the enemy's morale will be defeated and he will surrender without a fight. It seemed a long shot. Oh, what did the Chinese sages know about Joe, anyway?

Baldwin had said, 'Use the principle of *qi yi, qi fang,* to deceive someone by means of his own attitude or cast of mind. Leave your opponent free to remain in reality a prisoner of his own illusion.'

To recapture Joe, Jane should hide her distress, urge him off, delighted and guilt-free, a prisoner of his own illusion that he'd fallen in love with Bella? That everything he ridiculed had reversed into his ideal? She'd have to swallow her love and worry for him, and just—just—let him go?

Dan said Sixteen always worked—but that was back in New York: 'Yeah, this tactic is tried and true,' he'd told the class after last night's coffee break. 'Somebody causes this God-awful traffic accident. If you throw the book at him, he freaks out, calls his lawyer, plays for time, clogs up the legal system. So, you give him a coffee, have the nurse fuss him over while they tow away what used to be his Lexus, wait him out 'til it sinks in that he's the asshole that just killed a couple of people.'

Baldwin nodded, 'You give his guilty feelings free rein—'

'Yeah, hear the dude out, let him think he's getting off easy.'

Nigel spoke up. 'I can offer a business example.'

'That was a business example,' Dan shot back. 'We just happen to be in very different businesses.'

'Sorry, O'Neill.'

Getting Nigel to apologize was something of a first. It was getting worse than the Bookworms, Jane thought.

'We're trying to poach a manager from Citibank who has a handle on developing markets. I interviewed him, but didn't press him for an answer, just let him walk away He'll reconsider. He wouldn't have agreed to see us if his present position was good and, if I'm lucky, it'll get even worse.'

Arms crossed, Baldwin warned, 'Just keep in mind, Nigel, your Citibank quarry may be playing the same game with you. Having turned you down, he expects you to raise the stakes, a prisoner of your illusion that he's worth it.'

'Yes, yes, of course.' Nigel looked disconcerted.

'So! More historical references!' Baldwin passed out photocopies. 'Always leave an escape for the encircled enemy. That's from *A Hundred Marvellous Battle Plans*. Do not press an enemy at bay, from the *Battle of Extremity*, press forward when the enemy gets relaxed and pull back when it approaches to attack. By and by, the enemy will take its own life, etc. etc.'

Which is not what we want, Jane reminded herself as she released the latch on Number 19's front door. Joe waited upstairs, looking like a man under siege—badly shaven, with exhaustion lines cutting down each cheek. His jaw, so often clenched with frustration, hung almost slack.

'Hello, Joe.' She'd brought some groceries from the High Street and started shelving them, not wasting Lorraine's lessons in the usefulness of props during a difficult scene. 'How's Fergus?'

'Fergus is fine. I went upstairs to say hello to Lorraine but she wasn't home.'

Still the decent Canadian son-out-of-law? Why couldn't he be a complete bastard?

'Probably still at the hair salon or the dressmaker. Sometimes I think the only thing that keeps her going is opening, as she calls it, in her birthday party.'

'How's Sammie? Could I have her with me next weekend?'

He'll use Sammie, too.

'That depends. What's the head lice situation at Fergus's?'

Joe took a long time to reply, at last, 'Well, I'm not exactly at Fergus's.'

So, there it was. He wouldn't have admitted it yet if she hadn't attacked.

'I see.'

Jane examined the ingredient list on a bag of corn chips. 'I don't know how she did it, Joe. Please explain.'

Joe attempted some sort of comforting embrace but Jane squatted down to shift all the spaghetti boxes into the deepest corner of the pantry, leaving him swatting at empty air.

'Honestly, Jane, until Italy, I always thought of her as just a friend. Then, well, things changed.' Joe wore that helpless little boy expression, the one he used when Jane suggested he fold the laundry.

What changed is that you took off your clothes and bonked each other silly.

'She used to drive us crazy. She was our family joke! I see the joke is on me.'

Joe turned sullen. 'I'm surprised you noticed. You were always stuck in some book. Or upstairs dressing and undressing the Star. And by the way, Jane, you lied to me about that evening class. I just saw the receipt.'

'I lied?' Jane hung on to her spice jars for dear life. If she couldn't corner him, neither would she play defence. She laughed so she wouldn't spit in his face, and offered him some corn chips.

'Yes, you! You're not going to any management class. You're been getting counselling on how to "decently divorce" me since September.' He sounded miffed.

'I can't exactly divorce you, can I? Though no one cares more for you than me. Between devouring bestsellers, of course. No one has watched your disappointments with more pain, when I wasn't researching more ideas for you to flog, that is. So, now, the problem is that I read too much? Or is it my pathetic three-days-a-week job? My librarian's devotion to a few dwindling borrowers, that's the betrayal that herded you into Bella's bedroom?'

'Well, we've been stuck in a rut. You never seem to notice. I've been really depressed,' he argued, 'And lonely. Of course, I expect you find that unbelievable.'

'Not unbelievable. Preposterous!' Jane yelled. Good thing Lorraine was out. By now Joe had backed into the corner of the kitchen. She felt like crowning him with the reading lamp and sticking choice parts of him into the food processor.

'Bella really understands me! You find that preposterous?'

'So it was my neglect that forced you to screw our daughter's godmother under the child's nose?'

'Did Sammie say that? Bella and I were very discreet.'

This wasn't good. The cornered tiger was starting to snarl back. Bella must have prepared him for Jane as Medea and Medusa in one—all fury-headed, snakes unfurling, flying at Joe with a Banshee scream and claws bared, the ultimate Snake Women scorned.

'We never intended to hurt anybody, Jane, least of all Sammie. Bella loves her. She's absolutely terrified that this will turn Sammie against her."

'Bella cares only about Bella. That's why she's so ridiculously, predictably, ludicrous. Hilarious. Why am I not laughing?'

Joe had slipped out of the kitchen area into the living room, his back meeting one of the tall windows. If he pressed any harder, the ageing wooden sash might give way, ejecting him, arms and legs akimbo, on to the crumbling Georgian stucco work overhanging the ground floor entrance. Jane retreated to fold the shopping bags with the precision of an origami champion.

Joe peered forward at Jane with almost morbid curiosity and asked, 'What are you going to do?'

Jane reached for a mental image of Baldwin, her sage-like Yoda in worn tweed.

'Do?' She checked her watch. 'Fix myself a bite, get back to work. You know, that absorbing life I lead, dispatching overdue notices, has made me peckish.

Joe's shoulders dropped two inches. 'So, why am I here? Well, I guess I'll get some of my things.' He opened the closet near the front door.

'Actually, Joe, I'd like you to leave, but one thing first.'

Baldwin's advice held her in check like a tourniquet stanching the bleeding of her heart: Deferment must be used with caution. Make sure that one's troops can afford the delay, even when you have the upper hand. Make sure nothing can happen to change the enemy's position for the better.

'Actually, it's why I wanted to see you.'

'Sure, sure. Anything.' He paused near the front door.

'I'm asking you to be the soul of discretion, at least 'til Sammie's exams are over. Nothing official or unofficial, no *Daily Mail* exclusives, no leaks, no pap photos, no nothing. Bella is a celebrity, a particularly juicy prey. One whiff and they'll start tracking and tapping your Blackberry as fast as you can say Rupert Murdoch. Sammie can't afford to be distracted right now by a photo of her father snogging his star in public. Her whole future's at stake.'

'Oh, absolutely. Well, Jane, I . . .' He actually looked ready to kiss *her*.

'And don't forget your best friend.' She crossed the living room and grabbed his BAFTA award. She dumped the taunting mask into his arms like a sack of rotten potatoes. He looked startled and about to say something.

She slammed the front door in his face.

The sound of clapping came from the bedroom.

Oh my God, they weren't alone.

'Jane, that was the most extraordinary performance I've ever witnessed, on or off the stage.' Lorraine struggled to her feet from the depths of the bedroom, reading chair. 'All these years, I flattered myself as the family actress. But dammit, I haven't seen such guts since I saw your father do Polonius on the very same afternoon that he got his cancer diagnosis. I wonder, whose genes did you get, after all?'

'I thought you were out! Were you hiding in there the whole time?'

The old woman waggled her head, basting her lie with overacting. 'I would never eavesdrop *on purpose*. I came back after lunch and wanted to have a look at your new library books, especially that Antonia Fraser one about living with Pinter. Joe just let himself in. I couldn't trust myself not to take a kitchen knife to him. You know, the old Judi Dench double-dagger thing.' Lorraine crossed her arms at the elbows, holding up Lady Macbeth's rapiers.

'Wish you had.'

'And miss your performance? It's so very hard to play against character, don't I know it? Yet you carried the scene. You convinced me. You have all my respect, Jane.' She wobbled slightly and took her daughter into her frail embrace.

And now, how Jane sobbed.

'It was *Yu Qing, Gu Zong*, To catch something, first let it go.'

'What's that from, sweetheart? *Sayonara? Memoirs of a Geisha?*'

'No, it's from my evening class with Professor Baldwin. It's not about library management. It's about Chinese war strategies. I've been studying Sun Tzu to keep going. But what if Sun Tzu doesn't work?'

Lorraine's face turned into a white, Empress-like mask of determination. 'Well, nothing I ever tried kept things together. I could tell you sure shook Joe up. Fix me a gin and tonic, darling, and show me these strategies. Teach this old dog some new trick.

Chapter Seventeen, Toss out a Brick to Attract a Jade

'I'm afraid our branch has received some very bad news.'

'Why, Jane, dear, what is it? You look so sad. There are circles under your eyes, dear,' Ruth Wilting's palsied fingers took Jane's hand across the reading table, and wobbled it back and forth, as if she could shake Jane's bad news away.

'Well, for some time, since Florence left us last year—'

'Old people don't need pretty euphemisms, Jane. Florence croaked.'

'Thank you, Carla,' said Jane. 'Since Florence died, our numbers have held at just the minimum to keep the library open for these meetings. Of course, the Bookworms could continue to meet at Rupert's, but that's too far for some of you, and leaving the library setting makes it less likely we'll ever attract new members.'

'And they won't pay for your time at Rupert's.' Carla cradled her briefcase of books and reviews to her capacious bosom.

'Carla, I don't think Jane was ever motivated by overtime,' Rupert said, as if the word *overtime* fell in with things like ration coupons or bedbugs—not relevant.

Carla hove up like a steamer's bow. 'Well, somebody has to spit it out. Perhaps we've exhausted the potential of this particular group. I don't really mind. I know perfectly well how to read on my own.' Her lips tightened into a slash of determination.

The Bookworms needed Carla to stay, while Carla was waiting for an excuse to move on—exactly what Jane feared.

'Actually, I have a more positive suggestion.'

'Yes, Jane?' Alma whispered. Without the Bookworms, Alma wouldn't see Rupert anymore. Rupert and she were of the same generation, but came from different worlds, two whole miles, and several distinct social classes apart. Rupert's lovely Hampstead villa might as well have been in Moldova as three tube stops from Alma's modest council flat.

Alma poked her beaky face towards her friend, 'Catherine, you don't want us to break up, do you?'

'Don't be silly.' Without the Bookworms, Catherine had no further need to stitch up a fresh shirt in Liberty cotton on her vintage Singer.

Jane watched as Catherine and Alma align their two polished leather handbags on the table in a leathery bulwark against Carla's briefcase formation. What would Sun Tzu do, leading troops so divided? She would have rallied Rupert for advance support, but he was still sulking over not getting his Bad Sex List.

Well, my idea was to have a project that would help us play for time and recruit new members.'

'What kind of project?' Ruth asked.

'Well, I don't know. The Museums, Libraries, and Archives Authority is going to review the minimum service standards set five years ago. There's a possibility the council will cut our book-buying budget even more, as well as our allowance for overhead costs like this meeting. We have only a few weeks to defend ourselves. There's a senior civil servant in charge of this review. A Mr Fellowes, a former chief librarian, actually.'

Rupert read the Authority's memo over Jane's elbow, and slapped his forehead in disgust. 'Listen to the way this Fellowes covers himself, "Public libraries play a vital role in achieving their communities' social, economic, and environmental aspirations— they are much more than just places to borrow books".'

Rupert looked up at the others: 'Surely it's not one or the other?'

'Well, you'd think not,' Jane replied. 'But the trend is focussed on the young reader glued to the screen, not the page. We're lending more and more e-books, which is a good thing, I think. But if a library is going to survive these cuts, the pressure is to build up the museum idea and rename the library something like "Discovery Centre," or play up the café image. Tower Hamlets doesn't even call their branch a library anymore.'

'What do they call it, dear?' Catherine pressed a hand on her hearing aid.

'The Idea Store.'

Carla burst out. 'The word *library* terrifies Tower Hamlets?'

Catherine hooted back, 'I'm not sure I'd spend the afternoon in an Idea Store. It sounds like I have to buy a tea towel or a VDD, I mean, DVD.'

Alma said, 'Not a library at all. The first time my mother took me to the library near my grandfather's. I was, oh, just six. Let's see, that would have been in—oh, well. A low window was open. I could see the trees outside, shining a lustrous green. The floorboards were polished and reflecting the sunlight. It was so quiet. Then I saw a golden oriole sitting on the sill—'

'Oh, how lovely!' Rupert clapped his hands together.

'Yes, it was a he, daffodil yellow with that little black marking from his eye to his beak, and two black wings and a black-tipped tail, his head watching the grown-ups reading at the tables. I remember thinking we must be quiet and not disturb the grown-ups. I'm not saying orioles are essential to a library, but in my opinion, no branch should be all hustle-bustle—'

'Like waiting at the chemists,' Ruth muttered.

Alma sighed, 'A library should be like a magical door through which you could meet live birds—or dragons and witches.'

'The word "library" should sound like "treasure chest," or "safe house," especially for young people,' Catherine said.

Jane seized the baton. 'Well, you Bookworms must prove you can stick up for old-fashioned books and remain socially relevant at the same time. I don't fancy being the hostess of an Internet cafe. So, we need a book-related project that fits the Authority's social targets and at the same time waves the flag for seniors and the printed page.'

'We'll do our best, dear,' Mrs Wilting promised in a very unconvincing quaver.

They'd reached Seventeen, Toss out a Brick to Attract a Jade, which Baldwin said had the broadest use of all. Jane copied this into her notes without feeling any inspiration.

The professor sported a silk tie of hot pink, in defiance of the winter so grey and wet. Keith announced he would be missing the class on Stratagems Nineteen and Twenty. His company had ordered their middle management attend a seminar on the reinsurance response to the economic recession—at a five-star hotel in the Canary Islands.

'How is your homework? Any of you working ahead?'

Jane explained the Bookworms' dilemma. It was far easier than confessing to the class that Joe had moved out.

'Well, prepare a trap, Jane, and then lure your enemy by using bait. Yes, Kevin?'

'Wouldn't Seventeen cover any kind of advertising? Or am I just a strategy yobbo?'

'Not at all. Your uses of the tactics don't have to be obscure or convoluted. Seventeen is all about advertising, especially if you promise more than you intend to deliver. Take the tale of Quenching Thirst with a Promise of Plums.'

Baldwin had given up on the canteen's coffee-coloured swill. He poured himself a cup of green tea from a dark red clay pot freshened with steaming water from a thermos.

'Do you recall Lord Cao Cao?'

'The head-in-the-gift-box chap?'

'Very good, Kevin. Lord Cao Cao led his troops into parched terrain. When they complained of thirst, he sent round a rumour that up ahead lay a large grove of plum trees. The soldiers' mouths watered at the very suggestion. This illusion sustained the army until they reached actual water.'

Jane left the class that night as she had for weeks, still puzzling as to what attraction Joe held for Bella. Baldwin's summary of Seventeen was, 'In war, the bait is the illusion of an opportunity for gain. In life, the bait is the illusion of wealth, power, or sex.'

Joe wasn't wealthy. He wasn't powerful. His sex appeal was so visibly on the wane that Jane was sure Bella could have done better at any London media party.

⤜⤛

'Political dreams, Jane, have swollen Bella's head,' Rachel Murty spat out an olive pit. 'Like some kind of Ambition Encephalitis.' They sat squeezed on two narrow benches lining a long table in a Greek restaurant. They had to shout across the table at each other through animated conversations on both sides.

'I don't have to tell you, Jane, that woman has an astonishing sense of entitlement. She always gets what she wants, so usually she can afford to be very sweet about it.' Rachel pursed her lips. 'Though not always.'

'But why Joe? Surely, she's not short of offers?' Jane watched Rachel order her second ouzo with iced water. It was just half past noon.

Rachel pulled back her puffy bronze hair, rubbed her temples, and exploded with relief. 'Oh, I'm so happy to get this off my chest. I've felt simply awful for weeks and weeks watching her work her wiles on Joe and everybody just knowing how evil she's been to you? Not to mention using Sammie.'

Rachel let her new high-rise wedge platforms clack off her feet on to the wooden floor underneath their table. She groaned with relief. 'These things are giving me blisters. I thought the problem would be falling off and breaking my ankle, but they're just too tight.' She stabbed a *dolmadaki* with a toothpick and shrugged, 'The thing is, I think Joe's essential for the new Bella.'

'The new Bella?' Jane shouted over the noisy crowd.

'No better than the old. She's so very tired of being just a kitchen celebrity. Cooking is so shallow, given the world situation. She needs to expand. She wants to reposition herself in the market. The cover of *Good Food* isn't enough. Bringing the world into her kitchen only demonstrates her unrealized potential, I overheard her say on the phone to somebody. I think it was her

169

new image consultant or maybe it was her mother, although I've long doubted that she was "born of womankind," to quote the Bard.'

'How does Joe fit in?'

'Well, he's not just a pretty face, as you well know. He's political. He cares about the world. That's sexy. Lots of other girls have tried with Joe—and failing with him, moved on to other prey. You can't imagine the things I've overheard while using the loo. You remember that *Panorama* editor who was supposed to be at his desk in London, but kept turning up on shoots so he could shag the talent? Really irritating to the rest of the crew. The Department punished him all right—gave him *Blue Peter*, but Jane, he certainly wasn't the first or last producer to tumble. They all do, sooner or later. Perks of the job. By the low standards of our profession, Joe is . . .' Rachel searched for the best word, 'bit of a saint. Watching Bella work on him has been very upsetting for me, like watching a Great White swimming around a dolphin.'

'*You're* upset, Rachel? I wake up in the middle of the night, remember he's not there, remember where he is, and start crying.'

'Yes, you look all puffy. Pat some Preparation H on your lower eyelids. Reduces the swelling. Tip from Jenny in Make-up. The *moussaka* sounds nice. At least you're still standing.'

'Thanks to an evening class in, well, coping mechanisms.'

'That's good. Aromatherapy? Meditation?'

'Chinese proverbs, mostly.'

'Have you talked to Joe?'

'He's blaming the entire world, my mother's demands, even my job, but never himself.'

'He blames you?'

'Oh, he tried.' Jane's tone was drier than her white wine, 'Apparently I read too much.'

'You *read* too much? Well, you certainly can't say that about Bella. Forget the *moussaka*. That lemony fish looks good. I'll have some of that, may I?' Rachel handed the menu to the waiter and looked at Jane as straight as she could with her crossed eyes squinting through violet contacts from under miniature awnings of caked mascara that only rendered her complexion a bluer white.

'Reading too much? That's probably Bella's line. *The Daily Mail* is about it for her. I'm surprised she got Joe to swallow it, but then she didn't really put her back into it, so to speak, until she got Joe down to Italy and had *la dolce vita* up and running.'

'So, tell me how she's repositioning herself politically.'

Rachel nodded. 'She's got me flying in all directions on this new image-building project. You won't believe it.'

'Try me.' Bella's previous passions were Power Yoga, Pilates, Covent Garden fund-raising, and collecting modern Vietnamese paintings. Jane poured more *ouzo* into Rachel's glass.

'I really shouldn't. Thanks.' Rachel's pale cheeks flushed. 'She wants to be a goodwill ambassador.'

'A spokeswoman?'

'With a global profile. A cause. Her very own disease. Or knowing her, an entire plague.' Rachel leaned across the table. 'The truth is, she's scared. Broadcasting House is talking of moving the whole BBC Lifestyle channel—cookery shows and the like—lock, stock, and wok—up to Media City in Salford. Manchester!'

'And Joe knows?'

Rachel shrugged. 'There is no way Bella would move north. She's had me calling round the charities for weeks. Wants me to knock on doors in Geneva and offer her as a front woman for one of the humanitarian agencies, but you'd be surprised. Do-gooding is a seller's market. Or do I mean buyers? Anyway, I've tried New York, Geneva, even that UN office in Vienna. Did you know they've even got waiting lists? Mostly second-eleven types, if you ask me. I can't even get her an interview.'

'Nobody wants her?'

'Oh, don't think I didn't try' Rachel ticked off on her fingers: 'UNHCR, UNICEF, UNRWA, UN, WHO, all the cancers I could think of, swine flu, SARS, AIDS, handicapped, arthritis, thyroid, eczema, ingrown toenails. They're all taken. I got exactly one call back—The Sussex Spleen Society. The skankier the star, the keener to whitewash her reputation, so how can Bella, who has never so much as donated a rusty tin opener to her local Women's Institute, compete with Angelina Jolie? Not that Bella sees it that way.'

Rachel assumed Bella's duck-lipped *moue* and shoved her scraggly bosom on to the table in imitation of her boss's pigeon frontage. Imitating Bella's fluting tones, she protested, 'After all, I've got sooo much to offer. It's selfish of me to keep me to myself.'

Through her painful laughter, Jane suffered a horrible realization. If she didn't have a 'brick to toss' as a lure to win back Joe, she now had an inkling of the lures Bella was dangling. Rachel's account of Bella searching for her cause célèbre sounded too familiar, too perilously similar to Joe's cravings to return to hard news, to produce meaningful stories and to be pertinent again.

So it wasn't sex or celebrity passes or designer food or functional illiteracy that had lured Joe from Jane's side. No, it wasn't even some instinctive application of Stratagem Seventeen—tossing some cheap brick in Joe's path. Bella was using the most fatal seduction of all for a frustrated idealist like Joe—the proposal that together they harness her notoriety to make the world a better place. And to a good man beaten down by years of professional rejections, the possibility of Bella as part of the sales package might seem made of pure jade.

Jane despaired.

Chapter Eighteen, To Catch the Bandits, Catch their Leader

Joe came back to pack two groaning suitcases, his warped squash racket, and at Lorraine's last-minute insistence, all ten years of his beloved National Geographic archived in IKEA shelves on her attic landing. Clear skies eased his clumsy exit for two days, and then released their chilly grip with yet another downpour. The square's more wistful veterans talked of snow falling on Primrose Hill, back when.

Sammie said the clammy weather gave her an upset tummy. Looking a little green, she took to her bed for a day. Midweek dawned with the sun slanting golden shafts through smothering grey clouds, but she hid a sullen face deep in her hoodie like a wraith; the girl-woman rose, donned long mittens and low-seated jeans, and headed off for school. Jane knew things were wrong with Sammie but she simply felt too miserable right now to give the child more attention.

Lorraine was going down to Ealing to look in on her old friend St John Stevens. She took ages to get ready but such sorties to see old luvvies always did Lorraine good. She might soon have to resort to diapers for the elderly, but at least she could see where she was going. St John wasn't as lucky. He'd long ago traded in Malvolio's gold-topped walking stick and crossed yellow garters for a white cane and support socks for diabetics.

Always the grande dame before her backstage reunions, Lorraine left the house in full kit—a broad-brimmed hat and dramatic shawl, clip earrings like Colorado boulders and her battered Kelly bag. In case there was an audition call for glamorous old coots between now and dinner, she was ready to 'read.' Watching her descend the stairs, Jane spotted the *Auntie Mame* wacky exit. Her mother had a whole gallery of polished entrances and exits in her bag of tricks.

In any event, the thespian's salute to her waiting cabbie had a cock-eyed, chin-up charm. Jane needn't worry. Lorraine was capable of succumbing to many humiliations, but expiring in Ealing was not going to be one of them.

Jane faced the bathroom mirror. A web of wrinkles radiated out from the ends of her eyes, criss-crossing the freckled skin on her temples. Her neglected eyebrows crawled towards each other like lonely caterpillars, while her lashes had disappeared.

Today was the lunch with Dan. Although he wasn't handsome like Joe or even Jane's 'type,' the novelty of lunch with any man besides Chris was undeniable. She didn't look anything like a woman warrior of beauty braced for fresh combat. 'Careworn' would be kind. Her clothes didn't fit any longer. Her face needed blusher or lipstick, but when she tried to rouge up, she resembled a weathered Tibetan lady on the cover of Joe's *National Geographics*.

So it was with some self-consciousness that after a quarter of an hour's dishevelling march down to Camden Lock, she saw Dan had taken great trouble over his appearance. He'd swapped the lime anorak and boyish trainers for a grey sports jacket over a polo shirt. His overshined dress shoes reminded Jane of a sergeant on parade.

They started to walk together. If their attire didn't match, at least their legs were similarly proportioned. Taking a walk with Joe meant Jane skipping and hopping to keep up with his impatient strides.

They turned into the market. Some of the stalls were open, but the novelty T-shirts looked forlorn in the winter cold. Windy gusts rattled the jewellery and beaded handbags on display.

'Haven't been here in years and years, not since the fire. Joe and I used to come down here Sunday mornings to pick around the stalls, grab something to eat. Sometimes we'd come with another couple and have a lovely, long lunch, just the four of us.' *More often than not, Bella and Her Morning After . . . How Jane and Joe used to review that disaster zone, safe in their cosy conspiracy of happiness.* 'After my daughter was born, it got a bit difficult pushing the stroller through the crowds, stopping for feeds, or changing nappies. We finally had to give it up because Joe was in the cutting room most weekends.'

It was all the same junk for sale: embroidered pillows, Moroccan ceramics, antique tin toys, cufflinks shaped like tea pots in Roger Stone's jewellery window and souvenir T-shirts. Jane recalled a small moonstone ring Joe had bought for her from an antiques vendor—where had that bauble gone? She remembered Joe, standing right over there, thumbing through used LP's— Dylan, Sam Cooke, Joni Mitchell—asking her to hang on while he looked for an elusive Byrds album. Now here was Dan, hunting for a souvenir for his grown daughter in Hawaii. How little she knew about his personal life.

Jane recalled, for an excruciating instant, what it was like to be in untroubled love with Joe. You never saw, at the heights of such happiness, that it had to end. *You didn't stop everything and say, I'm resting right here with this happiness. I refuse to move on.* No, you just went home, made lunch and made love.

The chagrin vanished. She glanced at Dan—so painfully out of place, so Lands End American—paying for a pair of Camilla and Charles coffee mugs.

'You're joking. They're not even William and Kate.'

'My son-in-law is an insufferable architect with impeccable taste. Doesn't Prince Charles specialize in architectural criticism?'

'That's pretty cruel.'

'I wish I could see his face when he unwraps these.'

'Well, I don't see a single thing I can't live without.'

'Except lunch. Lunch never goes out of fashion.'

The weather was just clement enough for them to brave an empty terrace overlooking the stagnant waters of the canal. They ordered very simple food, guided by the smell of gravy and piecrust. Two boats floated at anchor on a sleepy ripple lapping the wall of the café.

'Distract me, Dan. Distract me from my self-loathing,' Jane stretched her arms up to the pale light.

'Why? Self-loathing's so much fun. Wallow away. I've never stopped feeling sorry for myself—and Sharon left me fifteen years ago.' Dan shrugged. 'When I got back from Kuwait, it dawned on her that separation had been better than marriage. I'd served twenty-five years so I could take early retirement and suddenly, I was out of the service and the marriage. Maybe she didn't like me out of uniform. I never was much of a clotheshorse.'

He took a long pull on his beer and smiled. 'Was that distracting?'

'Yes.' Dan's dependable voice filled dead air like a pleasant radio DJ.

'So I finally joined the NYPD. All that War College training, language school, service in Thailand, Hong Kong, the Middle East—I had to trade it in for something. The only other option was some bullshit arms-trade consultancy or service with a security firm in Iraq.'

'It brought you to London. Paid travel. An important assignment.'

He mugged, 'Yet I Am Not Happy. I've developed moping to a fine art. You ever read *Catcher in the Rye*?' He caught Jane's surprise. 'Sorry. I forgot you're a librarian. Well, I'm turning into some middle-aged Holden Caulfield, just talking to himself, completely pissed off at everything and everyone.'

He ran out of chat. He wasn't the sort of man who talked about himself for any length of time. 'So, how's Baldwin's class working out for you?'

'Totally useless, actually, but fun. Baldwin was right about the other class. What a depressing lot! But the stratagems could never change Joe's feelings.'

'Hooked, is he?'

'By that she-devil. To think she was my best friend.'

'You must have other girlfriends. You're too nice.'

'I did, but now I realize too late Bella scared them off. She's possessive about everything.'

'So defeatist? Ah, c'mon. Give Joe time. Years of misunderstanding can take a lot of time to repair.'

'Talking from experience?'

'Nope. But you say she's the evil one. You haven't given up on him?'

'She's a monster of vanity.'

'Well, I'm sure you're right, she's a monster and all that, but you've heard the old saying—it always takes two to *monst*?'

Their chicken pies steamed into the cold air. Dan pierced his crust with a fork. "Oh, that's hot. Careful. Don't forget Number Eighteen. To Catch the Thieves, Catch the Leader. So, our question is, who's the real problem here, your Joe or his Martha Stewart?'

Jane sniffed the delicious pie and looked at her broccoli dusted with butter and breadcrumbs. For the first time in weeks, she felt peckish. Was it the wine? The sun on her cheeks?

'Forget Joe. I'd rather talk about my reading club, where there's never been any doubt that the enemy is a know-it-all member named Carla. Loose her on the city and the entire library system would shut down in a mass attack of over-informed depression.'

Joe glanced at her over his plate, 'Don't change the subject.'

Jane shrugged. 'Well, Joe's left me for Bella. That's that. I'm not quite sure who's the leader and who's the follower. Maybe Number Eighteen doesn't apply much to my personal situation.'

'Sure did to mine. They all do, as you'll learn if you stick with Baldwin's class.'

Jane thought back to their last class. Number Eighteen had certainly grabbed Nigel's attention. His Dupont scribbled along as Baldwin elaborated: 'Target your action to the bulls-eye. Aim for the fat horse, not the slim rider. Defeat the enemy by capturing the chief. If the enemy keeps his men by money or threats, then if the commander falls, the rest of the army will disperse or come over to your side. However, if they're bound to the leader by loyalty, then beware; they'll fight on after his death out of vengeance.'

Kevin's objective for Stratagem Eighteen was to hijack an entire herd of dynamic H&M salesgirls.

'My mole is a window dresser who eats lunch with them. He hasn't reported back on which girl is the leader to pull the others down the road to my stable.'

'And your brick to lure these jades? Try to use the other strategies you've learned,' Baldwin prompted.

Kevin thought for a moment. 'Well, I could cobble together a management training seminar as a sort of brick to attract my girls, that's Seventeen. I won't attack too soon—I'll Await the Exhaustion of My Enemy with Ease, that's Six—'

'No, it's Four,' Nigel said.

'Oh, right, Four. Then, when I meet the H&M buyer for drinks, I'll Hide My Smile Behind a Dagger, Number Three. I'll confide that I'm downsizing floor staff, which is my Noise in the West, before Attacking in the East. That's Six.'

'Goal Kev!' Keith collapsed on his desk. 'You used five tactics in one go!'

Baldwin cheered, 'Head of the class for Kevin! You've read ahead to Stratagem Thirty-five, Chain Your Enemy's Ships Together?'

'No, professor, I swear! I'm just a natural!'

'But first, identify that key salesgirl and let's hope for the sake of your scheme, that's she's not too fat! And then gallop off with the whole team. Now, to our lovely Jane?'

'Well, I'm certainly not up to doing five in one go! Let's see. Number Eighteen reminds me of book reviewers these days. If a publisher gets *The Guardian* to favour an author, everybody else falls in behind like lemmings. If I were a publisher, I'd say the bandit chief works at *The Guardian*.'

'Good example! Winston, my good man. Name your enemy commander.'

'I sat up last night wondering who is my problem. You all know my situation. I thought my enemy was Nelson. After all, hasn't he muscled his way into Dad's good graces? He's the all-but-anointed heir.'

'Start your own business, Winston. Our bank might help you out.' Nigel was trying to be nice. Jane wished he wouldn't.

'Nelson can't help being a great programmer or a flashy salesman. He was just born better. I'm like my father—hopeless with electronics. Then it hit me: maybe the problem is my father. He's the commander. If I'm supposed to show him filial piety and all that rhubarb, doesn't he owe his own son more support?'

While finishing their chicken pies, Dan recalled Winston's outburst as well. Jane reminded Dan that Winston had left that night's class looking very alone and dejected. The Chinese boy was taking the stratagems almost as seriously as Nigel—the only thing the two of them had in common. They were both strangely eager to make something—anything—work.

Dan finished his pie with gusto. Obviously, bedsit dinners were unsatisfactory as a lifestyle. He suddenly asked Jane, 'Did you notice something that happened during the last class?'

The waiter handed them a dessert menu.

'We'd got halfway through the stratagems when Winston asked himself whether Nelson was really his enemy.'

'Yes, I remember.'

'Then Nigel had second thoughts about some rival banker he was targeting.'

'Yes, and then, Kevin wasn't sure which salesgirl was the so-called commander he needed to purloin—'

'Or whether his sales were dropping more because of a weak link on his own staff?'

'I see what you're getting at; *everyone* was re-examining their assumptions about who was their true enemy. Me too! I admit it. I found myself wondering why was I blaming Bella for everything? She's just being herself. Why am I obsessing over what she sees in him or what she wants? The turncoat is Joe.'

'Exactly. And that was when the real importance of Stratagem Eighteen hit me.'

Dan had sat out Baldwin's lively back-and-forth except for coming up with his usual historical analogy; 'The Soviets seizing Kabul with airborne troops in 1979? That sure grabbed the enemy by the throat and cleared the way for ground-based troops to come in.'

'Not that it won them the war,' Nigel corrected Dan.

Tired of wrangles, Baldwin had asserted his authority: 'Dan is correct to show how the so-called leader can be a command centre rather than a commander.'

Jane knew better than the others that Dan's war tales were beside the point, so she asked him now as they headed off to walk back to the square, 'What hit you?'

"Remember, I came over here to liaise with Scotland Yard about this New Jersey kid studying with the local imam? But that's not where it started—not as far as the locals were concerned. Surveillance of your bookstore and the two rival imams started by tracing one of the bombs that didn't go off back in 2006. For a while the Yard guys thought if they could grab the explosives expert, that would defuse the situation.' He scowled, 'Sorry for the pun.'

The deafening traffic loosened Dan's fears of being overheard. 'Of course, in time, they could just find another techie with a vengeance for second-hand slaughter. And it wasn't a problem to bring in more disciples, either. This country has as many teenagers suffering from low self-esteem and no future as the US.'

'Why don't you just arrest the imam? Isn't he your so-called fat horse?'

'There's not enough evidence. Remember, in America we were attacked from outside—so we think in terms of retaliation. We treat terrorism suspects as enemy combatants, lock'em up, ignore the rights of the individual and forget *habeas corpus*. You can thank our previous Attorney General for locking up human rights in secret prisons, black holes, and throwing away the key.'

'And here, in London?'

'You Brits know that doesn't work. It didn't work in Northern Ireland, did it? You treat terrorism as crime, which stands to reason if your attacks come from the inside. It's more like having cancer—you don't attack yourself, you look for a cure. So, the Yard keeps suspects under surveillance as long as possible before arrest, to get the intelligence, get the evidence, get something that'll hold up in a court case to support criminal prosecution.'

'And you don't have that?'

'That's my point. Why isn't there ever enough evidence? What if we hauled in this bookstore owner, only to find out we played our hand too soon, wasted all our time on some number two or three? We've got Gilbert Sullivan in place, like I told you, just raring to strap on the ol' bomber belt and run with it over to the nearest police station, but it takes more than hearsay to press charges.'

'Well, what do you need?'

'We need a top man's fingerprints on it, literally, or our Gilbert looks like just another wild kid who took things too far. And sitting there in class, listening to that fathead Nigel talk about shifting his attention to the head of the warrants department made me think, Whoa, Dan, boy, maybe we're circling around the wrong commander because *there is no commander.* That's why Gilbert can't bring us hard evidence to build a case. He just gets teases, suggestions, hints that something's going on. A lot of hot air.'

After twenty minutes' brisk walk, they reached the square. Would Dan expect to come in? With Sammie getting home soon and Fairy Queen Lorraine returning in her diesel pumpkin for an aspirin and a nap, could Jane entertain Dan? Was she ready for that? She needn't have worried.

'Sorry, I can't come in. Got a meeting.'

'It's been a lovely lunch. I'm so comfortable with you.'

'Hey, what can I say? You're feeling down. Misery loves company. Just think of the yin and yang symbols Baldwin drew on the board that first lesson.'

'Why?' \

'Remember the circle had a dark half and a light half, but the light half had a dark dot in the middle—'

'There was a spot of light in the middle of the darkness.'

'You got it. Sun Tzu writes, "Know your enemy as well as you know yourself," but Jane baby, your problem is, who's your real enemy?'

He pecked her on the cheek. He smelled of some old-fashioned shaving cream. Jane watched him until he passed the bollards and turned into the High Street and out of sight in the direction of the tube.

He never even glanced at the bookstore.

Jane was sorry he hadn't come in for—who was she kidding—tea? He was no Mr Darcy, but more like Colonel Fitzwilliam in *Pride and* Prejudice, not the hero, but someone she could have offered Sammie's fat-free biscuits and more conversation.

But his words lingered. She realized that, even after all their years together, Joe was the enemy, not Bella. She didn't want to accept it, but it was the only way to move forward. If Joe had been so ripe for the picking, did it matter whose lap he fell into?

This truth was as hard to swallow as one of those fat-free snacks, but from her windswept peak of Himalayan pain, she surveyed a new landscape.

Wandering through the shadowed valley below, she imagined Joe's tiny figure, looking not so much villainous as lost.

Chapter Nineteen, Steal the Firewood from Under the Pot

Baldwin hooted at his class with affectionate derision: 'Exams! Yes, Keith, of course there will be final exams! How else can your Zurich masters be convinced their precious francs haven't been squandered on you?'

Over the previous weeks, the school's maintenance staff had cleared out the rubbish cluttering Baldwin's bolthole. There was now just enough room for his long legs to dance a jig of amusement at Keith's impending ordeal.

'They're interested in premiums—not grades, Professor!'

'No doubt. But I expect you all will do well, whether or not your CEO's or the London library poobahs take my course seriously.'

'It's been years since I sat an exam,' Jane sighed.

'What should we expect?' Dan asked. 'Eight-legged essays? Will you lock us up for weeks, like candidates taking the Manchu civil service exam?'

'I don't mind being locked up with Jane.' Keith fluttered his eyelashes at her.

'Wouldn't we look a bit May-September?' Jane bantered.

'No, more early-June hooking up with mid-July—'

'Oh please!' Kevin broke up, 'We'd all run out of oxygen!'

Baldwin cut off the flirting. 'The exam will be timed—but not confined, Dan. First, there will be a true-false section testing your understanding of all thirty-six stratagems and what constitutes a true interpretation from a misconstruance. Part Two will ask for a one-page war plan, employing your choice of twelve tactics. Past homework exercises are acceptable unless, Winston, they failed every time. I'll give extra credit for noting risks and preventive measures, but I will deduct points if there isn't a good spread across the various stratagem groups.'

He mimicked Jane's doleful expression, 'No sticking to just Defeat Strategies, dear lady.'

The professor was enjoying himself. 'And finally, there will be a multiple-choice section on historical uses—please don't groan, Winston. God knows a little Chinese history wouldn't do you any harm. The good news is that we'll have a practice exam in February. That's it! You've noted down the anecdotes I've shared with you?'

Kevin protested, 'But I can't keep them all straight—the Jing, the Zhong, Zhang—

Keith held his ears and rolled his eyes, 'The bells, the bells, driving me mad—'

Baldwin handed out timelines for historical revision. His cheeks glowed red, giving the impression that he was getting outdoors more. Wisps of his soft brown hair danced across his high forehead as he bounced from student to student. 'Not to worry. On the right you have cross-references between the Principles of Sun Tzu and the stratagems . . .'

Keith read out, 'The Warring States Period . . .'

'This evening we move on to the Chaos Strategies. And we don't want to lose our way! Keep better track of the applications, Keith. We're exactly halfway—'

'Only halfway?'

'Yes, and I'm happy to say you all show more variety in your homework than previous groups.' He actually winked at Jane. 'Read out Number Nineteen, please, Jane?'

'Avoid any contest of strength head-on. Instead undermine your enemy's position. Remove the firewood under his cooking pot. Detach the handle of his axe.'

Nigel's Dupont was in trouble. The banker was licking the nib and scratching his pages in inkless frustration.

'Tongue's turning blue,' Winston said, giggling at Nigel.

Jane continued in her librarian tones: 'An army without food will perish. When faced with an enemy too powerful to engage directly, first weaken him by undermining his foundation and attacking his source of power—'

'Thank you, Jane. What does that make you think of, Class? Fire underneath the Cooking Pot?'

'Caffeine,' Winston answered. 'Nelson lives on caffeine. He just got a second-hand espresso machine from a Chinese restaurant in Turin. Now he's worse than a drug pusher—every customer gets a free coffee.'

Dan shrugged, 'So? Unplug his new toy.'

'No.' Nigel interrupted, sticking his invalided nib in Dan's face. 'Secretly replace his espresso with decaf, sprinkled with laxative.'

'Nigel!' Jane exploded.

'Hang on. It would take your cousin a day or two to see why he wasn't on form. His customers won't be coming back. That's combining Stratagem Nineteen with Twenty-five, Steal the Beams and Change the Pillars.'

Baldwin laughed and said, 'How refreshing to see you working as a team. Now, a business example for you, Nigel.'

His case study was about a small Minnesota soap company launching the first liquid soap for home use. Worrying that one of the 'big boys' like P&G or Colgate would move right in, Minnetonka Inc first sewed up the manufacture of the pump containers in long-term contracts.

'Minnetonka survived long enough to establish themselves as leaders of the so-called soft soap market.'

Baldwin then explained more sophisticated ways of seeing Number Nineteen: tackling a problem from the bottom up; the root-removal stratagem, cutting the ground out from under someone's feet, or sapping their morale by holding them up to ridicule, 'the enfeeblement stratagem.'

'Or defusing a conflict which is contrary to your interests in the "conflict-limitation stratagem." And all the time,' Baldwin urged his little audience, 'Protect your own material and spiritual strength—your fire—against possible enemy use of Nineteen.'

'Like installing better antivirus programs in our network. I've been telling them to do it for months—' Nigel mumbled to himself, scribbling with Jane's spare ballpoint.

'Maybe you need an outside consultant,' Winston insinuated. 'Like Nelson. Take him out of my hair for a few weeks and I won't make any more rude comments. That'd be a great use of Nineteen.'

Jane's mobile rang. Taking the call in the corridor, she heard Lorraine's panicked voice: 'Jane, darling, come home now. It's Sammie. Take a taxi.' The voice that could carry three measures of song to the second balcony cracked with urgency.

'What's happened? Drinking again? An accident?'

'She's not hurt, well, not exactly. Just come now, darling. I cannot handle this.'

White-faced, Jane bundled up her book bag. Alarmed, the rest of her classmates promised to e-mail notes on Number Twenty, Trouble the Waters to Catch the Fish.

It was a bad dream repeating itself. Lorraine again waited up on the landing outside Jane's front door. Her bare feet exposed bunions from years of dancing shoes and high stilettos. Sammie was home and her low sobs could be heard through the warped wooden joins where the stairwell ceiling met the wall of the back bedroom.

'She was throwing up again this morning. Well, I assumed, darling, that it was flu or food poisoning. But when I asked her what she'd eaten, she said to mind my own business.' Lorraine's graceful white hands fluttered like Blanche DeBois but her voice had the steel of Amanda Wingfield.

Jane dumped her bag on the landing and found Sammie lying face down on her bed.

'Go AWAY,' Sammie moaned into the pillow.

Jane leaned down to embrace her, but Sammie shoved her back. Jane tried again and got as far as hugging Sammie's bony shoulders only to be pushed away even harder.

'What's wrong?'

'I don't want to talk about it. Leave me alone . . . please.'

'Did something happen at school? What's going on?'

'Go away. I'm all right.'

'Grandma says you're sick.'

Sammie didn't answer, but pulled the fleecy sleeves of her jacket tighter over her clenched fists and shoved her arms deep into the duvet under her tiny waist, folding herself up as tightly as she could, into a hard rod of grief.

'Is it about your father and me?'

'GO AWAY.'

Lorraine was in the kitchen, her hands shaking. 'Sammie said her flu was much better, so I said to come up and keep me company. I made her some mint tea and waited, but after more than half an hour, I came downstairs to take her temperature. I found her sitting there in the corner, all dressed, doing her homework at Joe's desk as if nothing in the world was wrong. It was creepy, Jane. Remember that play, *The Bad Seed*? Patty McCormick opened in it when I was first doing that awful—oh, never mind, you get the idea. It was that creepy.'

'Mother, Sammie's not creepy. I don't understand.'

'She never had the flu, Jane. She's got that bohemia thing teenagers get.'

'Bulimia? SAMMIE?'

'Why don't you see how skinny she is? Underneath all those sweatshirts and baggy jeans?'

'She stayed home sick on Wednesday. Maybe it's a relapse.'

The mewling of Sammie's hysterics reached the kitchen table.

'Jane, she was vomiting on Wednesday and then yesterday danced out of here like June Allyson. That is not flu.'

'I was just happy she was well again.' Remorse flooded Jane. She knew she'd been too swamped for weeks with her own loneliness, and anger to focus on her daughter. Sammie's loyalties divided between father and mother had forced Jane to take her distance. It was Lorraine who'd told her Monday night that Sammie had come down with flu while Jane was managing the Bookworm meeting.

Lorraine shook, more with indignation than remorse. 'How dare she try *acting* in front of me!'

'Maybe it was just a twenty-four bug.'

'Bug my foot. You don't vomit Monday, Wednesday, Friday and skip Tuesdays and Thursdays.'

'I suppose not.'

'And there's something worse. She blamed Bulgakov for those scratches on her arm. To think I was going to have him declawed! Haven't you noticed those stupid fingerless wrist-warmers she dons night and day? She's hiding razor cuts.'

'WHAT?'

'She's been slicing into herself with a razor. Yes. It's some kind of fad. Luckily, she used a safety razor and the cuts have almost healed and you never noticed.'

Jane ran back and threw open Sammie's door. Her daughter was now propped up in bed and blowing her nose, but still wearing fingerless mittens.

'What have you been doing to your arms? Have you gone crazy?'

Jane watched with maternal horror as red-faced Sammie thrust her hands deep into the kangaroo pocket of her hoodie to keep Jane from pulling off the grimy coverings.

'Show me your arms, Sammie.'

'I won't do it again. I'm sorry.'

'How could you hurt yourself? Scar yourself intentionally?'

'I only did it once. Well, twice.'

'WHY, Sammie?'

'I don't know! I want to talk to Dad,' Sammie moaned and threw herself back into the pillows, wailing harder now and mashing her face into a pile of crumpled tissues. Jane lifted one mitten and saw the little web of cuts, shallow but not the work of a playful cat.

This horror was too alien to their small family. One almost glanced at the door to see what evil influence had infiltrated their peace. Tears streamed down Jane's face for all four of them. Sammie's little bingeing escapade had worried them for a night, but was eclipsed by Joe's defection. Now it was obvious that the nightmarish pleas of Sammie's soul had taken a more subterranean dive. With her own body fluids, the child was summoning her father home.

Jane returned to the kitchen to find Lorraine shaking her head. 'When I think of what Joe spent on car seats, bike helmets, swim

188

vests, trainer wheels, knee pads, wrist braces—every time that kid rode her trike, she looked like Robert Taylor in *Ivanhoe*, all armoured up to joust with George Sanders. Then, one day she sticks a finger down her throat and grabs a razor.'

'She wants Joe. You'll have to call him. Go ahead.'

Lorraine did as she was ordered.

'Sammie wants to see you tonight, definitely. But alone, Joe,' she glanced over for Jane's reluctant approval. If ever Joe and she had to mesh as parents, without recrimination or bitter grudges, it was now, although she felt an almost uncontrollable certainty that Joe's affair was to blame.

Soon enough Jane heard the slam of the very car door that had once signalled happiness at Joe's return from a long shoot. Lorraine's murmurs sounded up the stairwell and then Joe's baritone response and Lorraine's hushed explanation. How much Joe's timbre pained Jane.

Damn Bella! Damn celebrity, ambition, travel and perks, accolades, and awards, and all the enticements that Joe's sagging esteem had fallen prey to.

She grabbed a tissue to blow her nose but before she could hide the shredded mess or smooth her mashed hair, she started at Joe's silhouette framed in the door.

Joe was fat.

Given her distress, it was not the first thing she expected to notice. But there he was—chubby, flabby, pudgy, inflated—you name it, it was all sitting on Joe's belt, as if every pound lost by his daughter had zeroed in on the father's waist. He'd popped a button off his old cotton chinos and then disguised the eruption by tightening his buckle over the empty buttonhole. Even his chiselled nose had gained flesh. Here he was to thrash out the issue of Sammie's eating disorder, but as far as Joe was concerned, a little anorexia might not be a bad idea. He'd never suffered a weight problem on the prosaic menus of 19 Chalkwood Square, but then again, Jane must get used to a new Joe—bloated on *Travelling Kitchen* leftovers.

'I can't believe she's doing this. Didn't you talk to her about this stuff?' He pulled wildly at the back of his hair, the way he always did when trying to sort out a knotty shooting schedule or a screw-up at the airport with a stranded crew.

'Not surprising, really,' Jane replied more coolly than she felt. 'It's all about food, you see, rejecting the world of food. We know what that's about.' To refuse food—its taste, variety, sustenance, even glamour—was to reject the fabulous world of eating à la Bella.

'You're saying this is my fault?' Joe roared at Jane and turning his back on her, he practically threw himself into Sammie's room after a perfunctory knock on the door. His appearance triggered fresh wails from Sammie followed by Joe losing his temper with that roiling mix of love, distress, and horror that Jane shared.

What was said was so ugly that Jane covered her ears. After a quarter of an hour, Joe came back to the sofa where Jane sat, her insides like molten metal with the knowledge Joe wouldn't take responsibility for Sammie's collapse.

'She promises she's stopped, but I don't think she can handle this alone. I'd rather she stayed here where Lorraine can keep an eye on her.'

Jane had missed a beat somewhere. 'Where else would she be?'

'Well, isn't that why I'm here? She just said she wants to live with me. I mean, I thought you knew that. Jeez, I don't know what to do. There's a spare room at Bella's, but it'd be really strange. Weekends, okay, but all the time? Would I have to drive her to school every morning?'

'Live, with you and Bella?' Jane felt kicked back into the cushions and compressed from three dimensions into two with all her breath ripped out of her. Why would Sammie, whose discoveries about Bella's relationship with her father had so recently given her loyalties a jolt, now ask to live with them?

Jane had mugged up in the library all week about the effects of separation and divorce on children. How often had she pointed out the family guidance and adolescent counselling books to bleary-eyed dads, dog-haired mums or anxious grandfathers spending an afternoon on their own, 'hoping to make a little contribution' to peace at home? Jane had handed out all the info on hand—on ADD, weight control, skin problems, paraplegic 'Teens On Wheels', the alcoholic spouse, the late learner . . .

Well, now, it seemed it was the helpful librarian who was the late learner.

'I'm not sure how Bella will feel about it . . .' Joe said in a strained voice.

'Oh, she adores her Sammie,' Jane said in a voice frosted with ice.

'Of course, Bella loves Sammie, but—'

'Well, Sammie comes first.'

'Yes, of course.'

'If Sammie eats Bella's cooking better, well, that's the solution, obviously. At least for a few weeks.'

'I don't understand this at all. I didn't plan this,' Joe said, riled. 'You're blaming it all on me? I mean, what's happened since I left? She was pissed off at me.'

'She is *very* pissed off at you Joe. She truly loathes Bella. Just the other day, she called her a cow. But she wants to live with you. You're her father and she's worried about you.'

'But I'm not sure—I mean, how?'

There was a paperweight on the table at the end of the sofa, within Jane's grasp. She wanted to hit him with it, bash him back into her old Joe, wake up the comatose person she still loved inside, the barely visible, loveable, bewildered man she'd been happy with for so long. In a moment of madness boiling up inside of her, she reached out, intending with all the force of one of Baldwin's famous warriors, to smack it into Joe's pudgy mug.

Only the thought of the gentle Baldwin stayed her hand, reminding her that she could only win *without fighting*, no matter how strong the urge to splatter her outrage all over Joe's feeble hesitations. She'd just come from a class where the lesson was to steal the fuel from under Joe's cauldron, but the fiery depths were boiling inside her own soul. How could she stanch that inferno while imagining Sammie with a razor in her hand?

But she wanted to win. Baldwin had made her promise to try.

'Perhaps it's not entirely all your fault,' she said, hardly believing it could be said or believed. She turned on the light switch and returned her hands to her lap.

And at that, Joe's wild confusion burnt out. He did something Jane had never seen before. He broke down, crumpled with shame, and wept, head in his hands. The Joe she loved, her Joe, was still inside there, somewhere.

Jane rose from the sofa and went into Sammie's room. Listening to her father's racking sobs, the child looked wide-eyed at her mother. Jane stroked Sammie's forehead, creased and red, and fetching a cool flannel, patted the swollen eyes with love.

Why not let Sammie go, at least for a few weeks? Watching her mother mope day after day wasn't doing her any good. Jane couldn't cut Sammie in half or make her feel Joe was any less her father now that he'd moved out of the square. If Sammie wanted to abandon the Good Ship Mum, Jane hadn't the heart or the energy to object. She told Sammie in so many words.

What more, the strategy of Number Nineteen suddenly came into play. The thought of Sammie's unromantic presence tamping down all the flames back at Bella's love nest held a definite, if underhanded appeal. Jane smiled to herself and returned to the living room.

'So, she's moving in with you. She promises to stop all this eating and cutting nonsense and I believe her.'

'You think so?'

'Yes, I do. I'll send her over tomorrow with all her stuff. And you'll have to work out a way to get her to school on time.'

Joe said a sheepish goodnight to them both. He tossed a wistful glance back at the kitchen table, that humble Sunday morning altar of waffles and cream cheese on bagels lost to him forever.

'Jane, I'm glad we can still agree on—well—we're still her parents.'

'Forever, Joe. That won't change.'

Jane said it with such tenderness, Joe leaned towards her, and after hesitating with a glance up at Lorraine's door, planted an awkward kiss on Jane's cheek and then left.

Joe had come pounding over to the square to take up a defensive position, knowing Sammie had summoned him for some kind of accounting, but with one feeble puff of emotional exhaustion, Jane had taken their pot off the boil. The bluff that had disarmed him during their last round was spent. This time, with one kind phrase that contradicted her sense of justice but worked like a uniting balm, something deep had passed between them.

Her friends would be home from evening class by now. Perhaps Winston was worried Sammie had been in an accident? Maybe Dan was thinking of his own wife or grown son, off in the States, too far even to get a call should something go wrong. She'd left them all thinking the worst had happened, when it was only garden-variety misery. Misery for Sammie but oddly tinged with tenderness for Joe amid that lingering sensation of a precious quiet as they managed their daughter's woes.

Something had been defused by her struggle. Something had happened to draw Joe to her side, if only for a precious hour. By stifling her righteous jealousy and anger, and with fortitude struggling all over her plain face, the fuel for Joe's defensiveness had died out. He had stopped backing off. He had, even briefly, held her hand with a naturalness he hadn't shown in months.

Like a weary survivor, Jane sank into a scalding bath. She had preserved her strength and awakened the enemy's exhaustion. Joe would insist that Bella, as well as he, would watch closely over Sammie. Their honeymoon was already over.

Tonight, Jane had finally seen that Baldwin's stratagems were more than just a diversion or distraction. Bravely applied, they worked.

And there were seventeen more in the ammunition pile.

Chapter Twenty, Muddy the Waters to Catch the Fish

After a few days of moving rock posters, *Twilight* volumes, and her hoodie collection into Bella's pristine guest room just done over by Kelly Hoppen, Sammie returned to the square for the rest of her schoolbooks. Now exposed as a serial upchucker to the double-barrelled scrutiny of both mother and grandmother, the girl worked at bits of porridge on the end of her spoon with self-conscious regularity, but most of the time, waved it in the air while she chatted.

'. . . And these guys just kept, you know, smirking like this,' Sammie imitated a drooling teenage boy, 'And I was going, what's wrong? What's wrong? Until Lucy told me they did the same thing to her. Nothing was wrong! It was a stupid trick. I kept checking to see if my jeans were unzipped or I had pimple medicine showing on my forehead. They just kept pointing at me, sniggering.'

'Well, that's boys. They got ya,' Lorraine checked the maple syrup level.

'Well, I'll get them back.'

'Don't bother. Listen to this old trouper. You know what bugs men most? Ignoring them.'

Sammie nodded. Sailing on this relaxed matriarchal gust, the child swung her jib a little closer to shore. 'You know, Mum, those two fooled us, too. Not just you. Grandma and me, too.'

'Who are you talking about now, pumpkin?' Lorraine gobbled up her spaghetti with the greed of the old for both food and gossip.

Jane stayed where she was, clearing the sink of dishes and scrubbing the countertop. She had to stop staring with eyes brimming with anxiety while her daughter was 'eating.' Sammie had tolerated only one spoonful of tomato sauce on her pasta. After asking for porridge instead, she was barely touching that, but Jane also knew the child had gobbled up half a jar of Nutella as soon as she'd dumped her sack of dirty laundry inside the front door. Apparently, Bella's Polish 'girl' refused to take on more dirty knickers. Jane wanted to ask how Bella was adapting to Sammie's arrival, but decided she would judge by the results. Already she noticed a strange payoff to Sammie's part-time defection: as if from behind the anonymity of a confessional screen, Sammie was blossoming with unexpected disclosures.

Lorraine pointed an arthritic forefinger at Sammie's forced intake. 'Promise me that stays down in your tummy 'til Exeunt, Act III.'

Jane rubbed her daughter's shoulders a little too anxiously. 'Dr Landis says you'll be sorry if you do any more throwing up. Your teeth will rot. You'll get ulcers and kidney—'

'I'm talking about Dad and Bella, of course. It started a long time ago—'

'Well, I don't think it started until Italy. At least Rachel told me—'

'Oh, Mum. They fooled Rachel, too. In Italy, they reshuffled their bags as soon as the crew unpacked the van. Suddenly, there we were, Rachel and me, roommates. I mean, it all was done in an awful rush, even if Dad was randy—'

'Sammie!'

'Horny men!' Lorraine snuffled from the depths of her pasta.

'Mother, that is Not Helpful.'

Sammie sculpted some porridge round the spoon with her tongue. 'All right, not randy, not horny, lusting for the Unthinking Man's Crumpet of the Kitchen—even if he was whatever you want to call it, he acted in Italy more like somebody who knew he already had it in the bag. And she is a bag. There.' Sammie shoved her bowl towards Lorraine. 'I've finished.'

'Well, we won't force you.'

Jane took her daughter's left forearm in her hands and stroked the crisp, spidery scabs. There were no new cuts. Sammie had slathered the lingering traces with cheap makeup, a childish camouflage effort that actually cheered Jane. Was Sammie's spirit as resilient as her epidermis?

'Exactly why do you think—?'

'They've been at it for months and months.' She yanked down her shirtsleeve. 'Even when Dad was still living here and making all those faces during dinner, 'member? Because he had to take her phone calls in the other room? When he complained she was in love with her own reflection? That she'd caught the Egola Virus? That was all a cover-up, Mum. 'Course, the Egola part is, like, so true.'

'I wondered . . .' Lorraine mused, smacking lips coated with syrup.

Jane kept her expression neutral. 'And since when did two and two make eight?' She lined up dirty utensils in the dishwasher. A fork, a knife . . .

''Member that night I went to her house because I was too out of my skull to come home? Well, Bella kept saying, "Let's ring your father, let's ring your father." And even totally blotto, I was wondering, well, Dad always calls you an over-hyped bag of Botox. And he'll throw a wobbly when he sees me. Why don't you call Mum? She's your best friend, or at least Grandma?'

'At the absolute least,' Lorraine snickered.

'But no. Bella kept insisting: "Let's call your father. Like they had some special understanding and while she went into her bedroom to get her coat, I went to the bathroom, and there was a bottle of aftershave on her dressing table, the same brand as Dad's . . .'

'A bottle of aftershave doesn't prove—'

' . . . Then we got to this charming hotel in Italy, she says, oh it's so charming, darling Joe, yeah, right, sure, with the antipasto in the buffet rotting in the sun half the day. Mum, my bed had a trough running down the middle that made me feel like a human hammock. Rachel couldn't stop crying, she was really, really shattered by packing up the whole kitchen set-up for taking on location—'

'About Bella and your father?'

'Oh, yeah, well, as far as they were concerned, this dump with the dripping taps was the Muppets' Happiness Hotel. I caught them sucking face in the corridor just after Bella threw a wobbly at Phil—'

'The cameraman with the limp?' Lorraine was ever particular about the *dramatis personae* of any anecdote . . .

'He's the one. Phil said Bella's *vitello tonnato* gave the crew heaves and zap! Dad was right there to comfort her.'

'Then he never wanted to get off that show?' Jane said. 'All those pitches I helped him with, they were all just to cover up his affair? I don't understand. When Bella and I had lunch, I had the feeling that she wasn't that sure of him.'

Sammie bit her lip, 'No, no! You were right, Mum. She is totally insecure, about everything, especially about her job. Bella wants Dad to get back into Current Affairs even more than you do. Because she wants to ditch *The Travelling Kitchen*. She's going to reinvent herself.'

'You mean this crazy idea of being a celebrity do-gooder? I thought that was just a fantasy non-starter.'

'No, Rachel was right. She's been nourishing a Lady Di fantasy for years. She sees herself in a safari jacket cuddling little Africans or sitting on the board of The Prince's Trust or getting a gong for saving the world from—'

'Indigestion!' Lorraine thrust a fist into the sky. 'Solve the Middle East with a polenta recipe!'

'It's not funny, Grandma! Don't you two see? It isn't just that Bella wants Dad. I mean, she wants every man she meets—to want her. She just doesn't love Dad the way we do, you know, for the wrong reasons, like, he lobs all his tennis balls until you're laughing yourself sick—'

'And wraps my Christmas presents with duct tape—' Lorraine nodded.

'—And rereads the footnotes to *The Annotated Sherlock Holmes* every single summer vacation,' Jane added with fond regret.

'Bella knows Dad has talent,' Sammie explained. 'She reckons with her face and figure and his documentary connections, Dad could—wait, wait, let me remember, oh yeah—"share her high-altitude view to frame her new concept".'

'Oh, stop!' Jane burst out laughing despite herself. Bella had not only stolen her man, she'd battened down her man's escape hatch. Jane's wonderful scheme that Joe rustle up his chef contacts to produce an exposé about famine, diet, and the food industry, his escape route out of the pressure cooker of *The Travelling Kitchen*, his abandonment of Bella to her crazy reductions, concoctions and conniptions—it was all now hijacked by Bella's Bono fantasies?

Lorraine patted Jane's hand. 'Joe can be such a sweet mug. He reminds me of Lloyd in *All About Eve*. Like a fly in her sticky web. I can just see Bella now, rehearsing her Nobel Peace Prize speech in front of her mirror . . .'

'Sammie, why are you rubbing all this in? You know how much it hurts.'

'Because you're so passive, Mum! All my life, you've had your head in a book or a library meeting or now, that stupid evening class, for months, for years even! I'm just trying to wake you up! Doesn't anything make you mad enough to do something? Don't you still love Dad?'

'That's not fair, Sammie! I'm not passive, but I'm not going to get anywhere by throwing hysterics day and night like Mrs Rochester in her attic!'

Lorraine considered, 'Personally, I always thought Mrs Rochester was the meatier part . . . underwritten perhaps, but full of good stage business, setting the whole house on fire—'

'Lorraine, please! Sammie, I have to use my brains, as well as all my courage and all my heart. I'm hurt and angry with your father right now. I still love him.'

'So why didn't you get married when you had the chance!' Sammie shot to her feet, her skinny, scratched-up arms pounding the air.

'Sammie!' Lorraine reprimanded.

'Well, they should have got married. You also said so to me. I should have proper parents. What difference would it have made to you? You still have to share me. You still have to raise me. Do you think I really want to spend all my Saturdays in Knightsbridge with Bella, just to see how many times she stops to autograph somebody's Green Planet shopping bag, "Oh, you're really too kind, I really must move on, you know. I too have my little errands to run, just like you, you poor nonentity, but you're turribly, turribly, turribly sweet to watch my show." And you wonder why I want to spew?'

Lorraine clapped her hands together. 'Oh, she has my talent for mimicry. You do see it, don't you Jane? They say genes jump a generation.'

'You're not making any sense. So why did you move to her flat, if Bella's so sickening? Just to play Peeping Tom?'

'Oh, Mum, the romance is way over already. Bella called Rachel from the bathroom last night. I can hear everything from the guest room. Bella said Rachel would end up as a PA on *Hell's Kitchen* if she didn't step up the search for her charity to push her image upmarket. On and on about The Vision. She accused Dad of being loyal to everybody but her, his lack of vision, not to mention Rachel's inability to embrace the vision. Bella was shouting about the synergy of their three visions.'

'Lordy. Sounds like a weekend at Fatima.' Lorraine shrugged and said, 'I know, I know. Not Helpful.'

'Bella says we're stakeholders in The Vision, and problems are only challenges. It's not so hilarious when you have to listen to this stuff over breakfast, Grandma. Dad needs me there. And you know what?'

'What.'

'Hang in there, Mum. They row every single day. She's trying to change Dad's accent when he says "about" and "boat." She criticizes his clothes. One of these days, she'll go too far.'

'Over his accent or his lack of vision?'

Sammie shook her head. 'She's wearing Dad out, grinding him down, and if she doesn't get her new show mounted with award-winning Gilchrist production values *and* if she doesn't get a new vehicle "pre-prepared" to go forward for the autumn season, well, she might spit him right back in your direction.'

'All chewed up,' Jane said. 'How appetizing, but unlikely, Sammie.'

'Jane, you should never have bought her *The Parent Trap*.'

Sammie hugged her mother's waist and shook her. 'Mum, do something! Move in on her. Dad's so tired out. He's hurt from all those rejections. He's confused. So confuse him more. You always wrongfoot Dad in tennis and then when it's deuce, you let him win with his silly lobbing. Just do that in real life. Get yourself a new look or even a new guy. Then when everyone thinks you're happy and safe and full of forgiveness, move in on her when nobody's watching.'

'She's the devil's spawn,' Lorraine rejoiced. 'Aren't you proud of her, Jane?'

'Thanks, Grandma. Count on me, Mum, and never forget, I'm your man on the inside.'

Were Sammie and Baldwin in telepathic communication? Or was Stratagem Twenty, the second of six Chaos tactics, just good old common sense: before engaging your enemy's forces, create confusion to weaken his perception and judgement. Do something unusual, strange, and unexpected. This will arouse the enemy's suspicion and disrupt his thinking. A distracted enemy is more vulnerable.

For once, Baldwin wouldn't be cluttering their chaotic notebooks with too many Chinese warlord stories.

' . . . So that's Number 20 in a nutshell. Muddy the Waters to Confuse and Catch the Fish. Sun Tzu advises the same tactics with, as usual, a bit less poetry: Confuse the enemy, conceal your strength, jumble your orders, convert your banners, ease off the enemy's vigilance by hiding what it fears or offering what it likes. Provide distorted information . . .'

It was worth a try, a desperate try, Jane thought, now committed, despite her reclusive leanings, to muddy the waters into emotional sludge.

During the next coffee break in Baldwin's class, she blurted at Dan, 'Would you come over tonight? I mean, would you like to come over, for a late snack, or just a night-cap?'

Dan stood, stunned, in the middle of the corridor. 'Um, I was planning on catching a late game on satellite. Uh, gee—'

'Oh, I understand, I really do. Joe always likes his hockey games "Live from Winnipeg." Maybe some other time. No problem. Really.'

Dan waited for a more definitive cue, perhaps a mating call like a coquettish giggle.

He fumbled, 'Um, yeah, sure, why not? Maybe a quick one? A snack, uh, that would be fine. But you don't have to cook, just a snack. Sure, cool.'

Jane called Sammie's mobile. 'Darling, there's been a change of plan. I know you were going to keep Grandma company, but I want you to stay there with Dad tonight—'

'Mum, I can't. Bella's having a dinner party tonight. The guest of honour is that F-word chef, so she told Dad it's bound to be absolutely-X-rated-fabulous. She doesn't want a kid hanging around once the drinking gets going.'

'Well, you tell Bella, that I'm also having a friend over.'

'So what? You're having a friend over. Winston? To do homework? I can still watch telly with Grandma. Otherwise, Bella'll make me hide in the kitchen to put little slices of things on other little slices of things.'

'Your grandmother is visiting her friend Charlotte. And it's NOT Winston. It's someone else from my class, an American, on secondment for some antiterrorism work.'

There was an appreciative silence, then, 'Wow, Mum. Cool. Can I drop that on Bella?'

'Please do just that.'

'Only she'd try to hire him as a bodyguard for her charity trips. Is he hunky? What if Dad finds out?'

'Sammie, your mother is a single woman past her prime facing Friday night in a lonely flat. I can invite someone for a drink, I suppose?' Jane sounded braver than she felt.

Dan paid the taxi fare for them to get back to the flat in record time, but it was an awkward ride. Whereas he'd turned up for lunch nicely dressed and primed with anecdotal patter to soothe the aggrieved classmate, he'd already invested tonight's energy in a six-pack in the fridge and game statistics. He was finding it hard to switch channels at the last minute.

'How do you do?' Lorraine said, sweeping down from her own front door as Jane led Dan up the stairs. Jane recognized her mother's Gloria Swanson swoop from *Sunset Boulevard*. Lorraine paused long enough to tell Dan that her dear friend Charlotte in Islington was one of life's permanent understudies—spending years waiting for a chance to do Helena Charles in a revival *Look Back in Anger*.

'Poor Charlotte never got called, and she has been looking back in anger ever since 1986.' Lorraine's hoary old Charlotte chestnut was wasted on Dan. He shifted his workaday leather case from one hip to the other, nodded, and promised to read Osborne 'real soon.'

Dan got his cold beer anyway and drank on the edge of the sofa where a week ago, Joe had sobbed over Sammie's razor madness.

As she whipped up omelettes, Jane heard herself chattering too much—about Baldwin, Winston's failure to exploit anything or anybody with things Chinese, the Bookworms' fractiousness, and even her BBC career cut short by Sammie's birth.

'There we are,' she said, placing two hot plates of scrambled eggs on the kitchen table with the very best wine from Joe's collection. 'So, how's your operation going? I mean, whatever you can tell.'

He stared at the label. 'My, my, your usual plonk? Thanks. Well, something has to break. To tell you the truth, things are still quiet on the inside. Maybe something's tipped them off. It's making everybody nervous. Like those westerns where they say, "Quiet out there. Yeah. Too quiet".'

'Well, you can't just do nothing, can you? MI5 can't afford another spate of headlines screaming, where did they go wrong?'

'Bingo. But what can we do? Scotland Yard can watch these guys down the road,' he gestured behind him at the square, 'download bomb recipes. Our guy inside, Gilbert, sits there with them, eating chips and zapping through DVD's promising virgins, grapes—choose your translation—in exchange for suicide. He meets guys who met guys who knew guys convicted of plots, or they've travelled to Pakistan but—'

'Arrest them!'

'There's no actual plot. Say, do you have some Tabasco? That'd be great, thanks. No evidence, no target, no crime, no conviction. Scotland Yard couldn't give these guys a parking ticket. You could hold them for 42 days—or 42 years—there's nothing.'

'But there's a law against incitement, isn't there?'

'Yup, but hooting with laughter at a beheading on DVD isn't a crime, Jane.'

Dan ate his meal with obvious appreciation. How long had it been since a woman had cooked for him? They drained Joe's vintage bottle as Dan ticked off all the trials and precedents that might affect their surveillance of the bookstore. Soon, Jane had lost track in a bewildering summary of local boys with ties to Morocco, the United Arab Emirates, Pakistan, Jamaica, and Brooklyn.

She made coffee in a subdued mood. Dan's allusions to plots thwarted or even only suspected were chilling. It was a still night outside under the street lamps of Chalkwood Square, but after listening to Dan's stories, Jane's corner of London felt like the still eye at the centre of a hurricane of nerves.

'People have no idea, do they, Dan? It's hard to imagine every morning that someone wants to hurt you. And that hundreds and hundreds of people are always on duty to protect you.'

'That's why I love Baldwin's class.' Dan's undistinguished features broke into a smile. 'Once a week I'm reminded that things are always in flux and always in play. 'Kind of cheers me up. Things must be getting better if they're getting worse.'

He cleared his plate to the sink and walked with his wine glass over to gaze out the tall windows.

'Pretty pricey corner of London, huh?' Jane detected a note of the have-not. 'But then, what isn't to a divorced guy with a one-bedroom condo in Fort Lee?'

She nodded, 'When Joe and I moved in, we were gentrifying pioneers. The houses were built in the 1850's but over the years this part of London got run-down. Everybody muddled along. There was a batty opera singer who held court on the kerb and was looked after by all the neighbours. There were committees and street fairs. Then we started to get film stars, rock stars, even an Attorney General who got arrested for kerb crawling. He committed suicide, poor man. A psychiatrist lives over there. A singer from Led Zeppelin in the grey one. And the daughter of a Tory peer in the basement of the blue one. A Russian billionaire lives opposite—'

'The pink one with the red door?'

'No pun intended, unfortunately. Or maybe he bought it for the red door. Anyway, Lorraine says three thugs check the street before he dives into the back of his car.'

'I bet your mother doesn't miss a leaf dropping.'

'She fights with the cat over who gets the sunny spot on the window seat.'

'Wish she could tell us who pays the bookstore's rent.'

There was a long silence. Sir Bernard emerged from the house next door, keys in hand, and drove off, a blonde granddaughter taking the back seat.

'He was knighted for redesigning a railway station,' Jane said. 'Or a Sainsbury's. I forget which.'

'Oh. I guess that's a big deal.' Dan emptied his glass. The conversation drained away too. 'Well, it's probably time for me to go.'

She studied his sturdy features—the six o'clock shadow, the thick neck, and the collar he'd ironed in his bedsit to save on *per diem*. The evening was young and he didn't move. Jane shared his confusion as the muddy waters swirled around them.

'Um, I'd sure like to kiss you before I go,' he said finally. Yet he didn't budge a centimetre in her direction. 'The fact is, I'm a little out of practice. Anyway, I had the impression that you're still, you know—oh, what the hell!'

He took her into his arms with awkward enthusiasm and kissed her hard. Jane felt awash in the sensations that came from not-Joe kissing, not-Joe smell, not-Joe chest, and not-Joe ferocity of longing. Dan wanted her very much. She kissed him back, her breasts mashed against his barrel chest and her legs pulled tight against his thighs.

She was just relaxing into this brash exploration of things not-Joe, when she heard a key turn in her front door. Dan didn't hear it, so Jane's struggle to break his embrace succeeded too late by a few crucial seconds.

Joe stood bug-eyed in the doorway. 'I thought you were at an evening class.'

'Aren't you hosting a dinner party?'

'Yeah, well, we're going on to some nightspot. Bella says I need my black shirt.'

'You moved out weeks ago.'

'It was stuck at the bottom of the laundry hamper.'

'You know where the closet is.'

'Sure. Don't let me interrupt.'

While Dan stood at attention, panting too audibly for Jane's comfort, Joe thrashed and slammed his way around their bedroom.

'This might not be the best time for introductions,' Dan observed.

Joe emerged, carrying a fistful of dirty shirts. 'Goodnight,' he barked. 'Nice not meeting you.' He slammed their front door and stomped down to the ground floor.

Dan looked more embarrassed for Joe and Jane than for himself. He bid her a quiet goodnight but not before advising that she chain the front door after he left.

'Did maybe he know I was here tonight?'

'My daughter might have mentioned it in passing.'

'Yeah. I don't think that was about a shirt, Jane. Men can get irrational when they feel their nest has been invaded—even the nice, decent types.' Dan gripped her by the shoulders. 'Trust me on this one. I've been in Joe's shoes, and let's just say I wasn't at my best.'

She chained the door behind Dan. Lorraine's DVD player could be heard still going upstairs and Jane applauded her mother for not walking in for a snooping nightcap.

Well, she had certainly done her homework this week! She'd followed Baldwin's Stratagem Twenty. She'd taken Sammie's two bits advising her to stop being the passive do-nothing. Joe was seething, suspicious, and wrong-footed but all the lobs in the world wouldn't confuse a solid net-player like Dan.

Sure enough, the waters were muddier, but with the rough and wonderful sensation of Dan's kiss still on her lips, did she feel like recapturing the old fish, even if she could?

Chapter Twenty-one, Shed Your Skin like a Golden Cicada

Six libraries in Brent were shut down that week over protesters' demonstrations. Even Alan Bennett's summary of the council decision as 'child abuse' couldn't stop the Tory tumbrils from rolling across the cobblestones.

Innocent of their luck to still have a library, the Rhyme-Timers followed Chris into the corner for yet another rendition of *Who Moved My Cheese?* (Jane couldn't get Chris to give up wildly mismatching readers and books but the kids seemed happy enough with a self-help book on managing change) while Jane reviewed renovation proposals with the Library Authority's visiting architect.

Mr Gumble, a short, balding man, unrolled his blueprints across the issue desk with the self-importance of an imperial emissary. Soon it was clear that Mr Gumble had his own tale to tell Jane, along the lines of Who Stole My Library.

'This big surface will go to make space for extending the computer bank—you'll get the very latest computers, of course—and we can probably squeeze in another printer station over here.' The architect tugged at the mandarin collar of his black wool tunic. He peered at Jane through very round spectacles with thick black rims. He was a *Wind and the Willows* character, Mole in specs.

'Then where will the borrowers—?'

'No, no, Ms Gilchrist. *Customers.* The Secretary of State for Culture insists we call them customers. Think Waterstones, film centres, or coffee bars. It's all part of the new library philosophy based on retailing principles.'

'If you remove this central desk, where do our readers check out their books?'

'We're replacing the desk with a prefab pod. Your customers will access their materials at the pod stationed over here, to free up the entrance. Makes it more welcoming. Removes the social barriers. A big desk puts people off.'

'But you're using that social barrier right now to spread out your blueprints. A lot of our borrowers—'

'Customers, Ms Gilchrist, customers.'

'They're elderly. This whole block is full of them. This is where they leave their shopping and let me watch their handbags while they explore the shelves. We put their books to one side, over here. They want to see me when they come in. They want to know who's on duty. Sometimes, Mr Gumble, all they want is to rest in that chair and enjoy a bit of a chat. I might be the only person they talk to that day.'

'Well, I'm afraid there's no changing the pod. It's part of a job lot.'

Mr Gumble bent towards Jane, as if to suggest they tunnel down for safety together. 'If you're quick, you might hang about when the moving team comes and ask them to bung the desk in the back room until after the reopening ceremony. Then sneak it out again. But I've got to allocate you the pod.'

'Excuse me, Mr Gumble, only one pod? Surely, we get two?' Jane tilted her head towards Chris.

He peered at his inventory sheet. 'Oh, I see. I do see. He's staff, too? Dear me. Well,' Mr Gumble knocked over Chris's placard lettered, *Kidnapping! School shootings! Organ transplants! Read Jodi Picoult now—before it happens to you*! He propped it back up. 'We'll be giving you wall display cabinets, too.'

'I don't want display cabinets. This isn't a shopping mall! Who should I talk to?'

'I wouldn't peek over the trenches right now. The government is forcing the councils into huge budget cuts and they're closing more than a hundred libraries—your older branches are a soft target if you don't keep up.' He whispered, 'Some libraries are entirely volunteer-run now or going self-service. I've seen one in Yorkshire where all that was left was a shelf of paperbacks in the village local, next to the toilets.'

'Trained librarians replaced by machines and bartenders.' Jane shook her head.

'I know what you mean, Ms Gilchrist. The Big Society makes me feel littler than ever, but perhaps that's just me.'

Mr Gumble acted friendly, as friendly as the guy announcing the invasion of the monstrous Triffids in John Wyndham's story. Desks replaced by pods, skilled professionals by machines? Could a machine guide a child to Noel Streatfield?

Worse, who was marked out for redundancy? Chris was better with teens and younger adults, but his short story workshop for seniors had never been repeated. Jane was adept with the elderly, but if they were 'customers,' they had a very short shelf life compared to Rhyme-Timers.

She watched the happy litter of five-year-olds listening to Chris. Her mobile rang. She left Mr Gumble with his measuring tape and sought privacy in the foyer. She braced herself for Joe's voice—angry, disapproving, or conciliatory.

It wasn't Joe, but Bella trilling, 'Jane, is that you?' Her vowels sank their rounded fangs into Jane's neck through the cordless air.

Bella sounded breathy, even for someone who'd built a career ventilating over ripe aubergines: 'Jane, please, please, *please* don't ring off. I must be the absolutely last person you want to speak to but we really must chat, you know, to clear the air.'

Jane held the speaker away from her scorched ear.

'Jane? Are you still there? Jane?'

'You want to *chat*? Bella. Do you equate stealing someone's mate with borrowing a recipe?'

'How droll. I'm so glad you haven't lost your sense of humour. But Jane, I'm not calling for myself. I wouldn't dare. I'm calling for someone we both care so much about.'

'Sammie. I'm dealing with that. Dr Landis isn't worried, if we keep her on track.'

'Well, no. Of course, I care about Sammie, care terribly, I always have, and this horrible eating business, well, I know you must be absolutely frantic. I'll loop back to you on that later. No, I was referring to Joe, actually.'

Jane managed a hoot of derision. 'What makes you think I care about Joe?'

'He's absolutely beside himself. Was up all night. Drinking straight from the bottle. I found him passed out in the Jacuzzi. Does he normally go on binges, or is it just Sammie and Lorraine who over-imbibe? Darling, is this a family hobby?'

So poor old Joe had come untethered by the sight of Dan embracing Jane. Or as Baldwin might put it—he'd been *muddied*. It was laughable—wasn't Jane the one who was supposed to be beside herself? In Sammie's defence, if not yet her own, she felt stronger every week that passed without her chugging down some insecticide, or trying the head-in-oven routine. For all the beauty of *The Bell Jar*, Jane had outdistanced Sylvia Plath for resilience off the page.

'Jane, you still there? Joe says he doesn't feel well enough to come to work today, and we're schedded to do the New Russian Cuisine tomorrow and we can't get the jellied borsch with Oestra—'

'Well, that's too bad but he's got an assistant director. Or he can collect his sleeping tablets while I'm at work. Or just tell your guest to serve up some polonium pancakes.'

'Jane, how can you crack jokes? He can't go fall apart on me, he can't!'

'Actually,' Bella adopted a superior tone, 'Actually, this *is* about Sammie after all. Sammie needs stability. We've got to sort things out for Sammie's sake. How long do you expect her to live with us? Weekends work better for me when I have time to spend with her. I'd like to go back to weekends.'

That was a deft dodge, dragging Sammie back into it.

'Yes, Bella. We must work it out, sooner or later—'

'Tom Aiken's new place—? This week?'

'Top floor, Harvey Nichols.' Jane was damned if she'd let Bella surround herself with gourmet toadies. 'I'll book us for my birthday, as usual, in my name, of course, to avoid any fuss. Maybe by then, Joe will be himself again.'

'*Your birthday*? That's in *January*! Forget that old birthday tradition. We've got to sort this all out sooner than that. I'm on my knees *now*.'

'I'm too busy, Bella.' (Feeding Bulgakov, restacking Hellers and Chevaliers, studying for Baldwin's exam, helping Lorraine hang up her smalls to dry.)

'Oh, pul-ease. You can't possibly be that busy. Well, I just hope there won't be more nights like last night. Sammie can't afford her father having a complete breakdown.'

Jane held her ground, like an insect evading the predator's detection by standing stock still.

Bella backed off from outright defeat. 'So! Fine. Fine! We'll do lunch in January. It's marvellous of you to be so adult about it, Jane. I assumed I'd have to appeal to your better self.'

'Don't worry, Bella. Some of us only have one self.'

Jane had surpassed herself, and before she lost her courage or wit, she ended the call and collapsed in the wobbly chair next to the big desk just like one of her palsied 'customers'. She felt as shaken as the Second Mrs de Winter receiving a cheery tinkle from the late *Rebecca*.

January gave her weeks to arm herself for the Harvey Nichols battlefield. Agreeing to meet Bella looked like she was accepting Joe's defection—when she was not. As Sammie said, why be a passive victim seeking succour from a pile of books on the bedside table? Whatever happened to the Lotus of Revenge? If Baldwin was right, fighting without fighting was the only strategy no one prepared for: If everyone was geared up for hysterics and self-pity, Jane would armour herself in indifferent dignity until she was ready to strike.

For once, Jane was doing her homework ahead of time. Friday night, they'd be discussing Stratagem Twenty-two. When you're in danger of being defeated and your only chance is to escape and regroup, create an illusion. While the enemy's attention is focused on this artifice, remove your men, leaving behind only the facade of your presence.

The point of the cicada gambit was to give the appearance of no change whatsoever, total inaction, the original pose, the Loser Jane trapped in her librarian's knit trousers with the elasticized waistband, left as bait. The new Jane was going to escape Bella's counterattacks undetected.

Bella mustn't ferret out Jane's determination to lure Joe back or so much as buy a new blow dryer on discount. She must lie like a cicada skin while the refortified Jane scuttled off with Dan to exploit Joe's jealousy.

It struck Jane like a Chinese gong that Bella could not have rung her out of concern for Joe. Bella had practically grovelled, and grovelling signalled need. Need was always Bella's Achilles Heel. Bella had never done anything that wasn't self-serving. Years ago, this trait had amused Joe and Jane observing Bella donate her slim paycheque to a charity only because it was sponsored by a talk show host she hoped to snare. Bella's flaky narcissism had now matured into something canny in its ability to disarm and paralyze. Bella hadn't lost a wink over Joe.

No, Bella sought only things important to Bella—but what? It had to do with Dan, of course. Bella wanted to judge for herself how Dan's love might clear Jane from the field, might signal that the appearance of Dan on the scene permitted—what?

What did Bella want that she didn't already have?

It was a worrying question and the sooner answered, the better. But the fact that Bella needed something still unnamed repositioned Jane's psychic forces. She actually looked forward to that January lunch, to donning her dowdiest cicada skin to fade into the background of the bleached tranquillity of the all-white dining room at Harvey Nichols. She would evoke nothing but pity from Bella Triumphant.

She intoned to the library's bathroom mirror. 'The ideal general is patient. The ideal general is inscrutable. She waits for the enemy to give her the opportunity to win. Thank you, Sun Tzu.'

Her mobile rang again. 'Mum. Can I come home? Bella makes me run all these errands after school. Do her home filing. Fetch her coffee, dry-cleaning, even her shampoo. She says I'm her little godsend.'

'Exactly the opposite of what she just told me. And besides godsending is Rachel's job.'

'Rachel's twisted her ankle on a pair of heels like stilts. Do I have to do all this shit for her? I've got homework every night. One minute she won't leave me alone, then as soon as she's got her bloody shampoo, she acts like she doesn't want me around the flat.'

'Oh, darling, she's still devoted to you in her sick, twisted way. What do you mean, she doesn't want you alone in the flat?'

'I didn't say alone.' Sammie paused, 'Dad's here, sleeping it off.'

Jane sniggered, 'She's afraid to leave you alone with your own father?'

There was a revelatory intake of breath. 'Mum, that must be it! Oh, how weird. That's why she keeps calling me. She's afraid to leave me alone with my own father. Like she's jealous?'

It seemed Bella not only wanted something from Jane, she feared something in Sammie.

'Sammie, you promised Grandma and me you would hold the fort. Stay there, take care of Dad when he wakes up, give him a cup of tea, aspirin or Alka Selzer. He needs you.'

'Yes, Mum. But I'd rather move back home. I've got an exam in probability on Tuesday.'

'Sammie, you can do both.'

Jane came back from the library to find her mother fussing in front of her dressing table mirror on to which she'd taped three photos of Princess Alexandra of Kent.

'Darling! Guess what! We've got a part!'

So many years had passed since Jane had last heard that ringing announcement, she felt thrown back against the wall of time.

Lorraine's story tumbled out between powder-puffing, hair-pinning, and chin-taping. St John's nephew's school friend—who did something or other at Buckingham Palace—had bungled one of his first royal bookings—well, it all came down to some impossible conflict of scheduling, so 'The upshot, my darling, is that to save his little hide, he needs an experienced double for Princess Alexandra at the Factory for the Blind in Bermondsey. If I can pull it off, the Palace won't find out, and the little twerp won't lose his job.'

'That's not a part, Lorraine,' Jane said. 'Is it even legal?'

'Well, it's a performance.'

'For blind pensioners—?'

'Well, that's the genius of it. This way Her Royal Highness can do the other engagement and no one's the wiser. All I have to do is give an award, shake a few paws, say *thenk* you awfully, and head home. Now this is her, in this photo.'

Already Lorraine's jaw was hardening to a convincing royal clench and her soul was devoted to outdoing Helen Mirren. 'You know, I really spent too much time going after mature leads. I missed my calling as a character actress.'

Always her most reliable coach, Jane checked her mother's reflection in the mirror. 'You're still moving your mouth. And don't look down your nose so much that you turn cross-eyed. Thank God you don't have to do Princess Michael. How tall is Alexandra?'

Lorraine sighed, 'Jane, you never really understood acting. One can act royal, one can act superior, and one can act tall.'

Oh, dear, that was familiar too, that sensation of exclusion back into the wings. How often had she detected her mother's disappointment emanating like toxic radiation from behind the chummy actress-y facade? If Jane had changed over these last weeks of Baldwin's coaching, her mother still saw only the old cicada helper.

Jane scoffed, 'Why doesn't the Princess just send them a singing telegram? Would the Royal One set the table in costume, please, while I reheat the tamale pie?'

'Of course, darling. Oh, I'm so excited!' Lorraine set out the trusty Hirschfeld theatre cartoon place mats. 'St John has promised there'll be someone's arm to hang on to right up to the presentation and then over to my seat for the home band.' Lorraine tested her royal wave, side to side. It was amusing to see Mrs Ogilvie's face shining out from under Lorraine's own shaggy blonde waves.

'Can't the organizers see?'

'I hope they've been warned.'

'And there'll be a bathroom nearby, just in case—'

'Her Very Own, in case I have a little emergency.'

Lorraine had worked up quite an appetite and after pie and salad, finished off a bag of microwaved popcorn. She was brimming with plans for getting the voice into character, blocking out the stage moves, and testing the hair and costume.

Sunday broke grey and quiet. Jane went upstairs with Lorraine's morning tea. Exhausted by a late night of studying old Edward Fox videos, Lorraine lay snoring in her satin pyjamas with the piped lapels, some putty attempt at a regal nose still stuck on. Even in sleep, the old woman clutched the duvet's edge for fear of rolling off her mattress and breaking a hip.

Jane gazed down at the beloved face. It was actually good to see Lorraine in character—truly her mother again—getting ready for one last hurrah. Long ago, the backstage child had learned to recognize her mother beneath any combination of false eyelashes, greasepaint tans, rubber wattles, ill-fitting wigs, artificial wrinkles, and padded bosoms. Onstage or off, in costume or dressing gown, she remained Lorraine to her daughter. Jane's years of silent vows she would grow up to be Anybody-But-Lorraine were wearing on. With the passing of time, both pity and patience had polished down the daughter's resentments.

The doorbell rang. Sammie yelled from the landing below, 'Hey, Mum, it's *us*. I need my wellies!'

Clever child to alert her. Sure enough, Joe waited below, a careful distance from Jane's front door—waiting to be invited in.

'I thought I'd bring her back myself, instead of a taxi. We talked a little. It wasn't the best weekend in the world.'

'Well, it was an exception because I had a date.' Jane didn't ask him in.

'Um, would it be totally lame for me to apologize?'

'For ruining our lives? No problem,' she tossed off with surprising élan.

'I mean for making a fool of myself Friday night.'

'You're making fools of us both all the time.' She made to close the door. He reached out to stop her.

'Not of you Jane. Nobody ever took you for a fool. Except maybe once.'

Jane couldn't help, 'When was that?'

'The night Sammie was born and I proposed. And Lorraine pranced in on us with a couple of her cronies. I think you wanted to say yes, but then you saw Lorraine, and all you could think was her string of divorces.'

'I ignored your proposal for fear of becoming Lorraine?'

'Half of everything you do is a reaction to Lorraine—not that I'm not fond of the old bird.'

Jane resented Joe's doorstep psychotherapy. 'Good-bye, Joe. I'm going back upstairs to give Lorraine her medicine.'

'How is she?'

'In fine fettle, thanks to an engagement as a royal ribbon-cutter at some factory for the blind. The only critics to worry about will be Seeing Eye dogs.'

She sounded better than she felt.

<hr />

Monday Sammie reported to Dr Landis in the late afternoon—she hadn't gained any weight, but at least there weren't any more slashes on her arms—and after a late tea, she headed back to Bella's flat with a determined tread.

Jane met Dan for an after-dinner drink that night in the Sir Richard Steele. It was so relaxing to chat idly about unimportant things after Joe's jealous crisis and Bella's even deadlier, if stealthy aggression.

They were leaving the pub when she asked Dan how the bookstore stakeout was going.

'Oddly enough, it's like Stratagem Twenty-one,' he shrugged. 'Gilbert's afraid he's been tagged as a ringer. For his sake, we can't risk any more contact. For all intents and purposes, he's dead to us. He does nothing, sees nobody, and doesn't make a move. The cicada skin, just lying there. There's no way we can find out what's going on in there.'

'But Twenty-one says that while you're leaving your shell untouched, you're actually regrouping your forces.'

'Yes, but against what? Against what?'

They walked back as far as the centre of the square where the two red benches stood empty. The warmth of the coffee and Grand Marnier weren't quite enough to offset the frigid air brushing the plane trees. She rubbed her hands together in the chilly evening and Dan put his arm around her shoulders. It was cold enough for her to accept his warmth without protest, but the square was centre stage of a public space that had entertained the neighbours' curiosity for all the decades she'd lived there. To Dan it was just a small park in a foreign city. The English half of her hoped he wasn't going to make an exhibition and the American Jane longed for a passionate kiss.

'Just remember when you're on surveillance, you're under surveillance,' he teased. Together they sat in silence. Jane realized that Dan's sights were just as much focussed on the darkened storefront as on her features polished by moonlight.

'As you said, regrouping, but for what, Dan?'

'There are no explosives, no contact with our neighbourhood bomb maker, no incendiary cells meeting to get their blood up with horror tapes. I have a feeling that some plan is brewing, but not what we expect. Maybe, while our Gilbert is lying low, leaving his cicada shell unmoved, *so are they.* We're watching them. They're watching us.'

'It's pretty cold, Dan,' she shrugged a little to loosen his embrace, 'And I still have to finish a book for tomorrow night's Bookworm meeting. Another 9/11 masterpiece.'

'Not before you help me out a little more with this stakeout.'

'Meaning?' By the lamplight she caught a spark of mischief in his dark eyes.

'Make it look like we're doing nothing more than a little romance out here. We could make it a lot more convincing.' Dan enclosed her in the thick folds of his coat and started kissing her goodnight with a lot more skill than that first kiss She felt her body leaping up right out of its weathered old cicada shell—but whether it was with unfamiliar lust or merely girlish alarm that Sir Bernard's wife might be amused by this unusual view of 'ol Jane from her bedroom window overlooking the square—that was hard to say.

Chapter Twenty-two, (Shut the Door to Catch the Thief

While Jane waited for the Bookworms to arrive, she worried about paying bills, sorting out Christmas only two weeks away, and scheduling urology tests for Lorraine. Rupert arrived first. Jane watched him extract silverware from his old Fortnum's hamper. His mottled hands worked quickly and he transformed the same table destined for the rougher treatment of Mr Gumble's moving men.

The aroma of lemon cake wafted across the pages of Khaled Hosseini's latest novel up for the evening's discussion.

Jane hadn't finished Hosseini, but no matter, Carla would hold forth all evening, quoting from *The Times Literary Review* and *The Telegraph*. Any Bookworm who ventured an opinion still risked Carla's wrecking ball: Ruth had been steamrolled, Alma blitzed, and Catherine pulverized. Thanks to his secret preparations, Rupert was still standing, just.

'You know,' Rupert said, 'I finally located that website Carla loves, *The Dustjacket*. It took forever. It looks like nobody connects over to it, or from it, or quotes it, except, of course, dear Carla herself.' He thumbed through the curling pages of his morocco leather notebook to show Jane the web address. 'It has long been my impression that *The Dustjacket*'s bloggist—'

'Blogger—'

'Is not just contrarian, but downright dismissive of any views but his own.'

'Some book blogs are pretty widely read, *The Shelf Life* or *Reading Matters*—'

Rupert's eyes twinkled. 'There's a tally box on *The Dustjacket*'s front page—'

'Home page—'

'Yes. Now, I wouldn't want to dent Carla's enthusiasm in front of the others, but *The Dustjacket* hasn't attracted many strikers.'

'Hits, Rupert, not strikers—'

'Only twenty-seven.' Rupert glanced over his wireless rims. 'That's not very many, is it?'

'Lonelier than a sundeck on Pluto.'

'Still, I can see why Carla puts great faith in him. They always agree. Jane, a mean suspicion has snuck up on me. I fought it off, but here it is; I think Dustjacket is Carla herself. That's why Dustjacket backs her up on every book. She's not getting insights from him, she's claiming her views are more credible because she plants them in this blog!'

'Posts them. Anyway, that would make her the most insecure person in the group!'

'So often true of bullies.' Rupert was five foot, three inches in his Lobb handmade shoes.

He finished excavating his hamper, while Jane studied the second of her two stratagems for this week: Shut the Door to Catch the Thief, and its variation, Shut the Door and Beat the Dog. Force the small enemy into a quagmire if you calculate you can handle him alone. She imagined herself a sturdy Chinese woman tilling her rice, without a worry beyond putting dinner on the table—no book clubs, bulimia, or Bellas to wrinkle her sunburnt brow. Better to swing a handheld scythe through the paddies than to be caged up all day in a prefab pod. On Rupert's return from the men's room, the image faded. She was only a student of Chinese wisdom. There was no escape.

'Still in that Chinese evening class?'

Jane slid her notes across the table to Rupert.

'Skilful questions can drive an opponent into a corner,' he read. 'In negotiation, nail down your opposite number to a position. Hmmm. That's how I got my little Matisse sketch. I offered cash on the condition we settle the sale hours before the auction because I had a medical appointment. I refused to deposit a bid and leave it to chance: I gave them my offer, and took out my wallet, and kept fussing with the folds of my umbrella and checking the skies. It threatened to be a stormy day and I asked them how bad weather and the looming transport strike might affect the sale.'

'You scared them about low attendance.'

'We shook on the price. By two, the sun was shining, the strike was averted and the gallery was full. But the Matisse was mine.'

'Yes, Rupert, but every stratagem has a risk. Read on.'

'The cat forced into a corner may turn into a tiger, or the hunted dog may jump over the wall.'

'And these days, I am the hunted dog. I've got bad news. You remember the big cuts affecting everybody?'

'I read The British Library is considering charging reading fees! Shocking!'

'I've tried to keep this group together, even if it meant fighting to keep Carla inside the fence but now, my job might go and with it, the Bookworms.'

'Oh, dear.' Rupert adjusted his glasses, as if to correct the bad news.

'The library supervisor warned me that if it comes to more cuts, she'd keep the Rhyme-Timers as they meet during Chris's hours. That was a boulder-sized hint that my own hours won't matter much longer.'

'Well, I'm afraid I must report a distressing development myself.' He glanced over his shoulder, in case someone lurked between the shadowy book stacks. 'Carla is trying to organise a new reading group, with a visiting book reviewer each week to guide us—there being in Carla's universe only informed opinion.'

'I don't believe it. Yes, I believe it.'

Rupert whispered, 'The idea is, we'd put questions to the reviewer—'

'Questions vetted by Carla for depth and sobriety.'

Rupert nodded. 'She asked me about renting little chairs and, Jane, imagine,' his face paled, 'A lectern.'

'That's not a reading group!'

'So far, she has only suggested defection to me, probably just for my cakes. I refused out of loyalty to the Bookworms, but Jane, she'll seize any opening. Can't we ask this supervisor for an extension?'

'On the basis of what?'

'You're right. Better to make a clean cut.' Rupert slashed into his cake. 'I'd rather take Ruth Wilting out to tea once a week and hear what she's enjoying, than attend Carla's salon, listening to the latest thing her reviewer hated.' His hands shook. He'd leaked Carla's plans with good intentions, but it was more in his nature to calm things down than stir them up.

The group tackled Hosseini in predictable fashion. Alma and Catherine enthused about 'being right there in Kabul, bombs going off,' while Ruth Wilting analysed the author's style with erudition, but so little confidence, (waiting to be interrupted by Carla at every breath,) that Catherine turned up her hearing aid up until it whined.

Carla seemed unusually relaxed, 'being Mother,' and suspiciously solicitous of Ruth, making sure the elderly lady was first to have napkin, fork, and teacup. She even gave Ruth extra sugar, so there was no need to shout at Catherine to pass the bowl. As the librarian in charge, Jane would step in only when Carla's bullying charged too far into outright blitzkrieg, but oddly, Carla even let Ruth mispronounce Mr Hosse-eenie's name.

Catherine tried to parry Carla's game this week. She'd not only finished Hosseini, she'd also read another of his novels, and imitating Rupert's example, brought a *Times* interview.

'Well, done!' Rupert shouted into Catherine's better ear. This put Alma out of sorts until Rupert mentioned he'd spotted his first robin on the heath. He suggested that Alma walk with him over Primrose Hill to see if they could spot more. Alma blushed magenta at the idea of strolling in the open air at Rupert's stooped but dapper side.

The Bookworms moved through Hosseini's narrative of two Afghani women to negotiations of the Rawalpindi Agreement in 1919 in which Alma's great-uncle had played a pivotal role to the weave of Afghani versus Persian rugs—

Still no call-to-order from Carla? No demolition gambits? No thrusting of her capacious bosom towards Alma, just then deploring the unreliability of sell-by dates on shrink-wrapped pork chops?

Carla's complacent posture alerted Jane there was no time to lose. The others dithered like fat gazelles lapping at a pond while a hyena smirked behind a bush. My God, Carla was regrouping behind a capacious shell just like Baldwin's proverbial cicada. She would declare herself already gone any day now—with or without Rupert's cakes. Alma, Catherine, and poor Ruth would have no welcoming shelter for their literary pursuits.

Leave the door open to lure the thief . . .

'It's getting late,' Jane yawned. 'Before we leave, I'd like to ask Carla, who's done such a marvellous job of vetting that demanding list of books I gave her, whether she'd like to take on another little assignment for me?'

'No, no, Jane, not another list of tomes like that! It was a labour of love, I tell you! And I hope you all like the final choices I've brought back from that mission!' Carla chuckled at Alma, still ploughing through Trollope's *Can You Forgive Her?*

'No, actually, I'd like to delegate you, Carla,' Jane glanced at Rupert before continuing, 'to . . . reorganize our reading group.'

Rupert's slender hands covered the 'O' of his mouth. Carla shot him the expression Brutus might have worn hearing that Cassius had dropped by Caesar's on March 14 to say, 'Keep an eye peeled for sharp objects.'

Jane pressed on, 'You see, the district has moved again on reducing our branch services. If there are to be further cuts, it's just as I feared, at the expense of the Bookworms rather than the Rhyme-Timers.'

Foolish deaf Catherine nodded, pretending she'd heard. Even Ruth—who'd heard the bad news perfectly well—capitulated: 'Well, it's very important that the next generation learns to love the written word. I know only too well that at times of grief or loneliness, how nice it was to have a book.'

Carla blustered, 'A new group, Jane? Or reforming the Bookworms under some new sponsorship?'

'At least a bigger group, recruiting new members as quickly as possible, to persuade the district that the demand from senior borrowers is growing, not shrinking. Feel free to use the library's bulletin board. And knowing they're likely to say we can't open the library expressively for evening meetings in future, I also deputize you to find us a new, convenient location. I can think of no one else so energetic and capable as you.'

Carla glared.

'The new location must be within walking distance, especially for Ruth. What with walking frames and fixed budgets, using hire-cars or taxis every week is out. If they do shut down the Bookworms as an official reading group here at Chalkwood, we'll meet at my flat, but that's already four extra blocks for Ruth, and in the really poor weather—'

'Oh, we can't disturb your family, Jane! Your mother! Your daughter's exams!' Rupert glanced wildly at the gossipy women, but to no avail.

'And not with all your personal problems!' Alma jumped in. A pained look shadowed Rupert's brow. A Bookworm had breached the code of omertà on Jane's sorrows.

'I've told everyone to boycott that woman's show,' Alma said.

'I threw away her garlic press,' Catherine added. 'And I had some choice ideas of what to do with her mortar and pestle.'

'That's quite all right, Catherine. Joe didn't leave me for a pestle.'

'Just a pest,' Alma chirped and everybody laughed.

Jane continued, 'All right. Rupert's house is too far, and Alma's studio too tiny. Catherine, I know your daughter-in-law would never agree to us—'

Step by step, Jane backed Carla into a corner. If the Bookworms were shut out of the branch, the next-best location was none other than the spacious and elegant den in which Carla dreamed of seating literary lionesses feeding hungrily on Rupert's cakes and a guest appearance by James Naughtie from Radio Four.

Without any prompting, Ruth squeaked, 'Don't you live in the mews around the corner, Carla? I could manage that.'

Rupert was polishing one of his knives with a clean handkerchief to evade Carla's accusatory look. Had the librarian caught the thief and slammed the door? Carla sat undecided whether to bolt or play the game out. Jane hadn't cornered Carla completely, and it would be some days before she detected whether the conspirator could escape. Pulling up her head matron's torso with a deep breath, Carla shouldered her heavy satchel and promised, 'I'll see what I can do,' before marching out the door and into the night.

The dangers of Stratagem Twenty-two lay nestling in Jane's lap: If you have the chance to completely capture the enemy then you should do so, thereby bringing the battle or war to a quick and lasting conclusion. To allow your enemy to escape plants the seeds for future conflict.

On her walk home, Jane checked Joop's Painted Angel. Lights were on in the dormer window, but the Angel's windows on the first floor were dark. Joop had outlined his wings with gold paint, so that they seemed to shine alone, hovering like a bodiless carapace, promising flight, or escape, once the future was better illuminated.

She crossed the square, her footsteps weighed down with unanswered questions: Would Sammie pass her A-levels? Would the Mr Gumbles of government turn Chalkwood Library into a disco?

Her dark living room beckoned like a welcoming womb. She dropped her bag full of library correspondence on the sofa. Only the beams of the street lamp and a half-moon bathed the room in soft light. She closed her eyes.

The pounding of someone's fist—insistent and ferocious—started up right behind her.

'Anybody there?' A voice came from the bathroom.

'Joe?'

'Jane! Open this door, will you?'

Jane turned the bathroom knob but the door didn't budge. 'Pull the bolt!'

'The knob broke off. I can't get it to budge.'

'Joe, nobody's used that bolt in years.'

In the old days, they'd made happy, if awkward love in the bathroom, the only room where they could barricade themselves from a child curled up in their bed Sunday mornings. Then Sammie had learned to knock, the passion for love behind the shower curtain had waned, and the bolt had warped and rusted.

'I did not *intend* to lock myself in, Jane.'

'Well, find some tool to push it back.'

'Thank you, Miss Goodall, but I passed the chimpanzee-and-tool test years ago. I've broken two toothbrushes and a nail file.'

Jane went into the kitchen and sat down at the table. She felt powerful. She felt perverse. She boiled water for tea.

'Jane! JANE?'

That impotent bellowing reminded her of somebody locked up to feed someone revenge? Or course. Edgar Allan Poe's *Cask of Amontillado*. *'The thousand injuries of Fortunato I had borne as I best could, but when he ventured upon insult, I vowed revenge . . . Montresor, luring his enemy to view a precious liquor in the dank wine vaults . . . walling in Fortunato, brick by cold-blooded brick. What was the family motto again? Nemo me impune lacessit. No one assails me with impunity.*

Funny how Jane could recall Poe while fetching milk for her tea. She poured some into Bulgakov's bowl and scratched him under the chin. The cat cowered, his ears pinned back against Joe's howling.

'Jane? Goddammit, where did you go? JANE! WHAT ARE YOU DOING?'

Jane was sipping her tea. She hadn't lured Joe to any danger. Baldwin was always urging his class to trust the wisdom of the written word. Was it tempting to imitate anything just because it was printed? Here she sat, enjoying her soothing drink, while Joe shouted for help. Were the stratagems disconnecting her from her better self? There might be downsides to identifying with Poe's protagonist. Being Montresor was delightful, but after a few minutes, rather creepy. After all, Montresor was a madman and worse, at least from a librarian's point of view, an unreliable narrator.

She would liberate Joe . . . eventually. He'd inflicted a thousand injuries on her, or at least a thousand minutes of imagining him rolling around Bella's designer sheets.

'It's all right, Joe, I'm coming,' she called. She slid a roasting skewer through the narrow crack under the door.

'Too soft. Get something harder.'

Jane slipped him a knitting needle and a frosting knife.

Joe had a brief eureka moment when he tried a fingernail clipper to unscrew the whole latch head off the door but the aged screw threads just turned in circles.

'Can you please call a carpenter?'

While any London locksmith would leap with glee at an overtime job, Jane discovered London carpenters were a sleep-loving tribe.

Am I going to spend the night in here?' Joe screeched. Jane slipped him some Swedish crackers.

'Where are all the towels?'

'In the dryer.'

'How am I supposed to sleep without any pillows or towels? I suppose you think this is proof there is an avenging God.'

'Why are you in my bathroom, Joe?'

'You would ask.' She heard him lean against the door in resignation.

'Does it have to do with Sammie?'

'If you must know, I came to snoop for clues of how far you've gone with that American. I heard Lorraine singing on the stairs. I didn't want her to find me rooting around your things, so I ran in here, locked the door, and broke the bolt. I shouted for her to get me out but she'd gone upstairs. I think the old dear is ready for a hearing aid.'

Jane started to laugh and couldn't stop. She slumped down on the carpet against the bathroom door. They sat back-to-back divided by oak, like an estranged and disenchanted Pyramus and

Thisbe. Did Joe's paranoia about Dan feed on love or guilt over Bella? Whatever Jane had hoped to gain using Stratagem Twenty to muddy the waters, she'd never imagined turning Joe into a stalker.

'You can't have it both ways, Joe. You left me more than a month ago. Longer than that, by some accounts.' She rubbed at the discoloured carpet pile but the fluff stayed flat and stiff from a thousand damp treadings. 'Let me go.'

'It's not easy. You're a part of me, Jane. I worry about you. A lot. I know it sounds crazy, but I still feel like your mate, your protector, your—I know I should stay away. So people tell me.'

'Starting with Bella. You know, she wants to have lunch with me? I put it off until my birthday. A cleansing ritual to put the New Year on a different footing.'

'You don't have to see her.'

'Isn't that what sophisticated London ladies do?' Bitterness crept into her voice. 'Parade my insouciance to the whole world?'

'Nobody's that nice, not even librarians.' Joe's sardonic laugh came from under the door. 'I'll tell her to leave you alone.'

'Having lunch is the least of my problems. Besides, we both know her. Of course, you so much better now than I.'

'Bella can't imagine a world where she can't get everyone 'round to her way of thinking. She's like a terrier that way.'

'Which is why you left me for her.' Jane drove the thief into the corner with no escape. Now was the moment to get at the truth, no matter the pain, to hear Joe say it; I love you but I'm in love with Bella. Jane had to stop living from hour to hour on hints from a daughter full of wishful thinking that her father would come to his senses.

But Joe didn't say anything. He was ransacking the standing cupboard crammed with expired medicines and abandoned beauty treatments for a towel to soften his makeshift bed. Jane wished him goodnight.

Around midnight, Joe's BlackBerry chirped the Beach Boys' song, 'I Get Around,' which was hardly an improvement on the *Goldfinger* theme. The phone was still tucked into Joe's carryall, dumped behind the front door. It rang at intervals of ten minutes for the next hour or so.

Jane let it ring and ring. She could have answered it and put Bella out of her misery, but Joe was right—even librarians weren't that nice.

After a while, the Wilson brothers gave up and Jane heard Joe's snores echoing off the bathtub tiles. She couldn't help thinking it was a lovely sound before wetting her pillow with tears.

As an ennobled architect of global renown, Sir Bernard could pull strings as tautly in the sleazy underbelly of London's construction circles as Bill Sykes. After a few phone calls from the home office of Number 17 next door, Windsor Design and Restoration sent a Polish carpenter to Jane just before nine. Even so, negotiations with Jurek took some time, as the hardened professional insisted on cash in advance.

Listening to their haggling outside the bathroom door, Joe exploded when he heard Jurek's estimate: 'Tell him only Nureyev got paid gold in advance!'

This pleased Jurek. 'Yes. This is it. I am the Nureyev of carpenters. This door is valuable. I will not harm her.'

Twenty minutes later, the obstinate hinges were loosened and the door lifted away without a scratch. Desperate for a chance at the bathroom herself, Jane left Joe to his tea and toast with Jurek, who hinted that he wouldn't mind a boiled egg alongside.

'One thing I do not understand,' Jurek said, wiping the corners of his mouth with slow majesty. 'You could have just gone out the window and crawled along the balcony to come in here through this window. Thank you. I appreciate it.'

The Pole lathered more fresh butter on to his whole-wheat. The stupidities of an estranged couple preferring a night of chilly separation to a careful crawl of two metres along a Georgian balustrade were of less interest than another pot of coffee.

Joe and Jane avoided each other's questioning look. Why had that not occurred to them? Joe quickly recovered his satchel and embraced Jane very formally, both of them aware that the most casual gestures carried new significance.

'I know we have to sort out the money and stuff, but please don't do anything crazy, Jane,' Joe murmured. Jurek yelled from the kitchen, 'Toast is burning!'

Joe dragged Jane to the doorway, out of Jurek's hearing. 'You haven't contacted a solicitor or anything?' he asked.

'Not until her exams are over. For Sammie's sake, you can trust me to keep things civilized.'

'Well, please don't do anything precipitous. I worry about you all the time.'

'Hardly enough.'

'You mean I never loved you enough. I've been thinking about you, worrying a lot.'

Was this just remorse fuelled by heights of passion with Bella that he'd never experienced with Jane?

Was she confusing jealous possessiveness with renewed affection?

Why were they whispering as if they had something to hide?

Jane flushed with the urgency of his good-bye—her morsel of triumph mixed with indignation at the patronizing edge to his apology. Joe's ability to hurt her seemed diminished. He was jealous, worried, and wounded while her battle wounds were starting to heal.

She hurried him out the door. Stratagem Sixteen said, to catch something, first let it go. It was the sunny twin of Stratagem Twenty-two's sinister lesson: If they succeed in escaping, be very wary of giving chase. She was learning Baldwin's lessons well.

Too well. She had to talk to Baldwin—alone.

Chapter Twenty-three, Befriend a Distant Enemy to Attack One Nearby

Baldwin's sighs filled their tiny classroom. 'Keith, my dear boy, how do you always manage to get the wrong end of the stick? If the Qin Emperor had attacked the weaker states, their powerful neighbours would have been alerted and rushed to their aid.'

The professor scratched his brow for a clearer explanation. 'It's a question of taking it in stages. It's far better to forge scattered alliances with distant states and thus allay the fears of your larger rivals. So when the Qin did attack their nearer neighbours, the small states didn't interfere.'

Keith waved his list of Warring States in frustration. All of Baldwin's visual aids, time charts, and case studies were so much, well, Sinology to him: 'I get so confused with the Qin, the Qi, the Chu and the Wei kingdoms. I only remember the juicy bits, like that jealous concubine Lady Zheng, the one who told her emperor that his latest girlfriend didn't like his smell, so the emperor cut off the new girl's nose?'

'There's a Top Shop buyer who acts just like Lady Zheng,' Kevin said. 'She'd cut off my nose if she could.'

By way of explanation, Baldwin chalked a constellation of small and larger states around a central circle.

'Looking at this diagram of Stratagem Twenty-three, please give Keith an example, Winston.'

Chu the Younger turned as rigid as an undefended deer facing imperial headlights. Jane had just about given up on him when he burst forth with, 'I know! I've got one! Microsoft!'

They all waited for more. Was this cryptic reference all Winston could muster?

'When Microsoft was developing its X-boxes, it started working with small, independent software manufacturers. Why did they do that?' Winston asked. 'Microsoft could have squashed those independent developers like so many little bugs. But putting out a wide choice of games meant Microsoft could compete with the giant enemies like Sony and Nintendo for market share! They even sent out development kits to small companies for free. So, Microsoft made alliances with small states to attack the nearby strong states.'

'Wow!' Kevin applauded, 'Winston, you're hot tonight. I don't see why your father won't let you run things.'

'Not bad,' Dan agreed. 'All I could think of was Mao using Nixon to offset the Soviet threat. But then, you wouldn't describe the US as a small state.'

'Well, actually Nelson told me all about it—'

'Doesn't matter.' Baldwin broke him off. 'You, not Nelson, spotted the application and that's what counts.'

Bella and Joe were certainly Jane's nearby enemies. Where were her small, distant allies?

During the Tuscan food shoot, Rachel had proved more a bumbling enemy enabler than any ally. Joe's brother in Canada, Sterling, loved Sammie and had always approved of Jane, but the heir to the small Gilchrist lumber company lived so far away. He'd never left Canada for so much as a week in Florida. Jane knew childless Sterling would love to hear from them. She felt guilty that Joe hadn't kept in closer touch.

Even if there were a distant state slightly closer than Canada, the very idea of roping in marginal allies seemed like, well, exploiting innocent people. There was someone . . . but she hesitated. Jane had never been a 'user.'

It was one of the things she put to Baldwin during the break.

'Here you give us all these stratagems guaranteeing we win whatever we want, but they tempt us to do anything. What do you do when you've thought up a stratagem, but it goes one step too far? As if you're about to stretch some moral restraint past breaking point? Supposing one day, you wake up, look in the mirror, and realize you've become good at this, you've become a real winner, but a totally amoral shit?'

Baldwin smiled. 'You've thought of a small ally in your struggle against Joe? But you don't want to take advantage of someone? To draw them into a battle that isn't their own? Is that it?'

Keith and Kevin were ribbing the cash register ladies. Their loud laughter bounced across the expanse of empty tables. Baldwin led Jane to a quiet corner in the canteen so dark that a sad, brave glow of a single string of Christmas fairy lights over the buffet queue reached only the upper strands of his steel grey hair. His long, narrow features stayed in deep shadow. Jane couldn't read what he thought of her question. She hoped questioning the morality of the ancient tactics didn't offend him. She wasn't suggesting he was immoral.

'The ally you made me think of is hardly a small state, certainly not by her lights. She's at the BBC and always turning down Joe's programme ideas. Light-years ago, when I worked at the Beeb, she used to like me—or at least respect me. She's distant in the sense that she's removed from the Bella landscape and, what with all these cuts in library services, I need to start hunting for a new job. I was thinking of asking her for a job in television.'

Baldwin seemed perplexed as to the immorality of what sounded like a perfectly inoffensive plan.

'Immoral, because it crossed my mind that if I were back at the BBC I would be in a position to screw up Joe and Bella's project for a new series. Oh, I have the right! It was my idea in the first place. I thought it up to help Joe. Now, I might use Camille's help to ruin things for Bella.'

'It might rebound on you, if it were too obvious,' Baldwin warned.

'Oh, you've taught me a lot. I could use a borrowed dagger, or sacrifice a plum for a pear or openly repair the path and march all the way to Chencang and back before anybody suspected simple little Jane. But if it worked, how would I live with myself? It's hardly the Christmas spirit.'

'Christmas spirit never troubled the Lady Zheng.'

'That's my point. Do you think the stratagems can turn you cold or evil until you confuse winning with revenge for its own sake? These lessons can seem so calculated, so unethical, or underhanded.'

Baldwin buttered a muffin with precision. 'Jane, the Confucian philosopher Mencius puts it very well: All cleverness and wisdom are in vain if you do not know how to use your situation, just as the plough and the axe achieve nothing if they aren't used at the right time.'

'But you might get carried away and cut off somebody's nose, like Lady Zheng.'

'Well, that's true. An axe can be a very lethal weapon and you have been betrayed by the people you trusted most.' He ate with care and wiped his chin. Jane's question was something he wanted to take time with. 'You know, I live alone and I'm something of a chef myself.'

'Sorry, I don't follow.'

'Even I watch cooking shows. And when I watch Bella Crawford, I see a desperate woman, offering herself to everyone, in her kitchen and in her audience.'

'Oh, yes, she's famously sexy.'

'Sexy? There's a difference between meeting an attractive woman at a dinner party and being collared by a stranger swinging from a lamppost, murmuring "Hello, sailor." That kind of aggression invites a defence. No? I haven't convinced you that moral people have to strategize? More coffee? Wait here.'

She watched Baldwin cross the room. What made him such a lonely figure? He had regular features, nice hair, tall stature, but it all seemed to be in the process of crumbling on the frame, like the veneer of an old sculpture flaking off.

He brought back fresh cups for both of them. 'I know, I know, it's a vile brew, but I forgot my thermos. Perhaps next semester, we'll install an espresso machine.' He shot his cuffs, 'If I still have a class, that is. Returning to our moral dilemma, I've noticed you're very good with quotes, Jane, a skill honed among so many books, no doubt. Who said this: "Be as shrewd as snakes and as innocent as doves"?'

'Machiavelli? No, that can't be. He wasn't innocent. Severus Snape?'

'Here's a clue,' Baldwin winked. 'It's a very seasonal citation and it will answer your question once and for all.'

'Seasonal? Hum. The Queen's Christmas speech? Oh, I give up.'

'Jesus Christ, Matthew 10:16. Even Jesus warned us that cunning was a morally neutral instrument, like a car that can kill or speed you to the hospital. You know how we divided the thirty-six stratagems into groups of six?'

Jane recited: 'The Winning Strategies using concealment, the Enemy-dealing Strategies using disclosure, the Chaos Strategies using confusion, the Proximate Strategies to gain ground using simulation, and the Defeat Strategies—which we haven't got to yet, and I don't want to know about anyway.'

Baldwin laughed with her, 'Very good. But they can be grouped another way, into four types. One, damage stratagems, like those used by white-collar criminals where the destructive, egotistical element prevails, or two, destructive stratagems which only lead to short-term results. A third set could be called merely service stratagems, where honest opportunities are exploited, or four, light-hearted joke stratagems like the harmless humour in clever advertising that captures the intelligence.'

'But—'

Baldwin laid a parchment hand on her plump one. 'Wait. The Chinese sage Hong Zicheng said, "You must not have a heart that harms people. But a heart that is wary of people is indispensable." Now as far as I can see, your heart is quite intact. You claim intellectual ownership of your programme idea and it's your right to determine its outcome. So far, you haven't told me anything that will harm Joe in the long run, although in the short term, it might disappoint him for his own good. So, as far as my class is concerned, you should ask yourself, is it a damage stratagem, a destructive ploy, a service tactic, or a joke?'

'You're saying it's a service stratagem, although it seems like a damage one? It's all right to try?'

'Consider it homework,' he smiled.

Love and the Art of War

It was astonishing how eager Camille was to set some time aside to see her old friend Jane, think of it, after all these years—anyway, things were slow over the days before Christmas.

Jane braced herself for a return to her past. She dreaded bumping into one of Joe's or Bella's colleagues. She wondered how former office mates might greet the discarded Jane—with indifference or over-effusive pity? It would be hard enough to mingle later, if she got a job. Without one, she was an untouchable.

She prepared herself for a shock but not a complete Rip Van Winkle trauma. Taxiing up to her old office building, the BBC's Kensington House, she discovered a sleek businessman's hotel in its place. Well, that said it all. Joe had so forgotten Jane's old career there, he'd never mentioned that even Ken House was no more.

She lost valuable minutes phoning Camille's office and getting another cab to the White City headquarters. She announced herself to reception and then proceeded down the corridors with a Ninja's stealth, dodging the doorways of gossipy PA's and at one point, retreating into the Ladies' like a cat burglar when she spotted the head of Science Programmes, five stone heavier than she remembered him, rounding the corner, beer belly first.

Even with all the dips and detours, she reached Camille's office too soon. She sat on a small chair in the outer office while Camille's personal assistant and secretary silently appraised her dull skirt and sweater.

Camille finally blew in, a decade older, yet with her hair—no, actually her face—pinned back against her temples as if she were re-entering the stratosphere. She wore a concoction of garments far trendier than Bella's staple cashmeres. Years ago, Camille might have relied on power suits and expensive jewellery to compete with department heads, but she didn't need shoulder pads now. A quirky antique brooch fastened her bodice with artful casualness underneath a hand-knitted bolero. Camille must have become a very powerful fifty-year to shun office garb for the dress of an heiress doing graduate studies in Early Norse.

She'd reverted to her original artsy style. On first meeting Camille at a dinner party given by a *World About Us* producer—a dinner in honour of an Igbo Nigerian activist—Camille had worn a velvet drop-waist sheath and dramatic make-up of a wealthy adventuress from the 1920's. 'Gudrun,' Jane privately tagged her as she watched Camille demolish the arguments of her dinner partner with the appetite of a hungry lioness. *Women in Love.* Camille is a D.H. Lawrence heroine so eager for experience she self-destructs.'

After all these years, Camille's hair was still the same, a preternaturally shiny Louise Brooks bob with silicone conditioner but smelling, this afternoon, of Bolognese sauce and red wine.

'Jane! Jane! Jane! I was so touched you rang me.'

In Chanel slippers festooned with black velvet piping, Camille paced her office and chattered away at least five of Jane's precious allotted twenty minutes. She regaled Jane with details of a shoot in Tunisia that went so badly, they had to helicopter in their own *medecin sans frontières*. So much aggro, you can't imagine.'

Camille finally fell back into her leather throne and examined Jane across her broad desk. 'You're very brave. I know it's not easy to ask for work.'

This was a little rich. How could Camille know anything about it? Camille had worked non-stop at the BBC since coming down from Oxford as a production trainee. She'd climbed up the Beeb's greasy editorial pole and just stayed put, while dozens like her left to form independent production companies. She was like those bright things who get a fellowship and while everyone else goes down to work in London, looks up one day and finds herself middle-aged, still coaching Oriel undergraduates in Thomas Hardy.

Camille ran her finger down Jane's updated but still slight CV and mumbled, 'I don't really need to look at this. I know how good you were. These library cuts. Dreadful really, Melvyn was up on his hind legs droning in the House of Lords about it.'

Camille was stalling. 'You know darling, this place has really gone to the dogs. Good people come and try to put

Documentaries back on top, but they leave after a year or two. Anything we want to do in depth, you know, really commercial film quality, is given to Current Affairs . . .' She was lining up ways of giving Jane a gentle no. 'It's all about the bottom line now. I mean, these days what is television for when the kids are watching YouTube? That's what we should be asking ourselves. But do they know that over at Broadcasting House?'

Camille twiddled nervously with a wrist bangle. 'I mean they keep handing down new slogans as if Stalinistic thought campaigns could change anything.' She wiggled quotations marks in the air, 'Making It Happen? What does that mean when I'm fighting for intelligent programmes? Does that give me better audience share? My God, even Television Centre is up for sale!'

Jane knew she should exit with dignity. Camille's performance would soon embarrass them both. But she felt trapped in her chair. Camille chattered, 'They're losing 490 slots in the news divisions alone. Delivering Creative Futures, they call it. In other words, Think up a new future for yourself, mate, coz you haven't got one here.'

Jane thought of the poor library in Bow now tagged The Ideas Store. Did bureaucracies always cover up their demolition of civilization with jazzy branding?

'Creative Futures . . . Is that the latest slogan?' Jane whispered. She really must go now.

'Darling, I can't even recall the latest, they change with every new regime.' Camille's subject became the larger Decline of Western Culture. How could she offer work, when the BBC corridors ran red with the slaughter of hundreds of ambitious egos, sacrificed to the Great God of the Digital Future? There was Dantean wailing and gnashing of teeth from every studio.

Joe's name hadn't come up. Out of Camille's sense of discretion? Embarrassment? Some wacky worry about management guidelines on employing couples? Camille should have remembered she wasn't dealing with a married couple. Jane was about to remind her, when Camille rose from her chair like a hardened general dismissing the doomed.

Jane's twenty-minutes were up.

Jane sat tight. She forced a breezy smile. 'Camille. Joe has left me, the Library is cutting back, the Council taxes are in question, my mother's bladder is acting up, my child is applying to university. I'll take anything.'

The force field of Jane's determined inertia broke through Camille's defences.

'You don't mean anything?' Wouldn't you feel humiliated with a three-month free-lance contract?'

'Sounds brilliant. I only get three days at the library as it is.'

'You'd work from home? I only ask, as the alternative is sharing an office with a 21-year-old git who thinks he knows everything, thanks to a 2.2 in Media Studies from Loughborough.'

'I don't need a desk.'

Camille sank back into her chair. 'Really? There was an idea, but it was a bit feeble when we tossed it around.'

'Try me.'

'About posting whole books on the Internet. We've already done the Downside of Downloading music but it occurs to me this is a baby you might rescue. You could look into the Author's Guild who sued Google, copyright lawyers, that talking-Kindle thing and audio rights, rhubarb, rhubarb. That brouhaha about The Hathi Trust robbing everyone's copyright—'

'I can start tomorrow.'

Camille's carefully re-contoured eyes opened wide. 'You've changed, Jane. You were always clever, but a bit of a doormat. You seem to know what you want now. What did Germaine Greer promise us in our failing years? Oh, right, Crone Power.'

With malicious warmth, Camille went on, 'I could almost imagine you giving Bella the cold shoulder in the canteen. Oh, don't worry. She lives in her own Battersea bubble these days and she might even be moved up to Manchester. With cooking shows, it's not only the food that has a short shelf life. Mince from a tin? Delia should stick to her beloved footballers.'

To think Jane had suggested to Bella over lunch months ago that there might be a changing of the guard. Was Camille Harper actually hinting that Bella might really get the boot?

Camille continued, 'Course the threat of cancellation isn't the only thing that has Bella's knickers in a twist. I heard she's seeing some fertility man on Harley Street. She's a ticking womb.'

With machine-gun relentlessness, Camille was testing Jane's resilience. The subtext of all these references to Bella was clear: Are you tough enough to come back to work? Girls like us have to compromise with reality, even passing a pregnant Bella in the Ladies'.

Jane didn't flinch.

'You know, Jane, I'm truly sorry about what happened. Just to get that out of the way, as you're here.'

Jane would ride out this Bella humiliation, starting now. 'It happens.'

Camille explained, 'It didn't mean anything. Not to Joe. It came close, but in the end, he got cold feet. Because of the baby, he said. But I knew better. He was going to get back at you for not marrying him. Then he turned all honourable on me. Well, what did I expect? We'd just finished that Wayward Priests thing.'

Shock spread across Jane's brow but Camille ploughed on.

'You know what happens on these shoots, Jane. Anyway, as I said, we didn't actually *do* the dirty. When we got to the Big Weekend, he declared his love for you and retreated to the sofa. Such a gentleman! Don't laugh, Jane. Oh, you're not laughing . . . well, anyway, I was furious! And I certainly didn't expect our flirtation would damage his career.'

'How exactly do you mean?'

'Well, don't you remember? He wasn't on the job that election night. He was in Birmingham with me—well, on my sofa. That's why he got bounced to obits. I'm not surprised he packed it in and went independent.'

Camille's unexpected confession slammed into Jane like a lorry out of a blind alley. Joe had been bounced from *Panorama* for missing election coverage because he was almost having it off *with Camille? In Birmingham?*'

'But now, you come to me,' Camille cooed. 'I'm touched. You turn to me. You trust me. This means more than you know, Jane, offering me this closure. Joe still has loads of good ideas, but I had to turn them down, you see? I've recovered from sitting in my La Perla watching him snore on the sofa, but . . . I didn't want to worry you.'

Words froze in Jane's throat. Now she recalled phone calls in the night from mystified reporters looking for Joe and production assistants hanging up when they heard he wasn't home.

'God, I feel better! It's all right now, isn't it? Let's look at his famine pitch. Mind you, I don't care for the book tie-in.'

'Sorry?' Jane squeaked.

Camille fished around the bottom of her in-tray. 'You know. Bella's recipes mixing milk powder, aid supplements and dried roots. Here it is: *Cooking from the Refugee Larder.* I ask you. Does that woman have a scintilla of shame?'

Jane's thoughts raced elsewhere. How would Joe feel if he knew that all of his pitches were queered by Camille and her colleagues out of worry for Jane's feelings?

Then she thought of that comment about Bella's ticking womb.

Bella wanted Joe's baby? The devil's spawn, indeed, with Bella casting poor old Joe as Rosemary's Sperm Bank. Primeval anger surged through Jane. Riding on Joe's filming talent and filching Jane's famine outline—these were mere *hors d'oeuvres* compared to the theft Bella really desired. Jane's last hesitation about Christmas spirit disappeared.

She leaned across Camille's desk and smiled at her new ally. 'Actually, Camille, before we go over your Internet idea, and I am taking that assignment, I'd like to talk to you about that famine pitch . . .'

Stratagem Twenty-three was really easy once you got started. Without further compunction, she telephoned Joe's brother as soon as she got home.

'Joe wouldn't dare bring this woman along, Sterling, and it would be just bearable for me to know that if we three, well four with Lorraine, if we can't be together for Christmas, at least Sammie would have a real break with her father and genuine relatives.'

It was marvellous the way Sterling said yes—he'd love to see little Sammie again. He'd talk to Susan tonight and put it to his little bro' tomorrow. Joe would do the right thing, at least on this one. The small distant ally came through.

Putting down the phone, Jane slumped her head on the kitchen table in relief. She had hated the idea of Bella waking up with Joe on Christmas morning, showering Sammie with expensive gifts, and then, of course, feeding them something extra-terrestrial for 'their first family Christmas together:' roasted swans in cherry-meringue sauce or buffalo filet mignons garnished with Perigord cheese curdled by the virgin breath of cloistered nuns.

A flood of goddamn holiday season tears welled up, unleashed by tapping into an unexplored well of old-fashioned Canadian solidarity. Jane felt the larger spirit of Christmas, the balm of forgiveness, and the strength of clan solidarity. Sterling and Susan, with their modest dreams of new snowblowers in December followed by January blow-out bargains on winter tyres for the delivery fleet, had accepted long ago that they lived on the very margins of Joe's glamorous television life in London. That Sterling didn't hesitate at such short notice to host his brother and niece for a spell was kindness beyond the London Gilchrists' deserving.

Sammie looked over her shoulder as she collected warm clothes from the back of her wardrobe and jabbered on and on, about skating and real maple syrup. The days moved by swiftly, as Jane spent the break from Baldwin's class and library duties running up and down Oxford Street getting presents to shove into Sammie's bag. Joe could hardly say no, and with an almost miraculous ease, an airplane carried father and daughter off for one whole blessed week without Bella.

Christmas morning finally dawned on the square.

Jane heard her mother's marabou slip-ons tattooing back and forth across the ceiling as she readied lunch for her daughter. There would be chilled prawns in tomato-chilli sauce, Five-Minute Beef Wellington clipped from a McCall's magazine abandoned backstage in 1972, and Rocky Road ice cream smothered in warm Hershey's chocolate sauce.

Lying alone in bed, Jane started the merriment with a very delicious weep. It felt like Christmases of long ago, Christmases spent taking the coats of understudies who had nowhere else to go and pouring Manhattans and Bull Shots for tipsy 'aunties' while dodging the caresses of fawning 'uncles'.

Come to think of it, had there ever been a Christmas with only Lorraine—no uncles, no understudies, no Joe? Well, it was about time, Jane thought, as she carried her mother's requisite Youth Dew gift set upstairs. There stood Lorraine in a lamé caftan mixing up cranberry martinis. The rosy prawns waited on their cushions of crushed ice next to hot nibbles made by slathering Campbell's condensed mushroom soup on slices of white bread which were rolled up and grilled into bacon-wrapped bundles studded with toothpicks.

It looked absolutely delicious, a virtual take-away from the Rainbow Room circa 1963. Jane looked out her mother's dormer window and saw, like a benediction rare for NW1—a sprinkling of falling snow.

Anyway, there was one further consolation. If Jane's day was a territorial flight into the past, Bella's Noël celebration sans Sammie and Joe to admire her imported Blue Spruce designer tree was surely a signal defeat.

Chapter Twenty-four, Attack Guo by a Borrowed Path

Jane felt no victory flush when reading Camille's e-mail promise to rustle up a short-term contract for breadcrumb pay. One knew exactly what such temporary stints were worth during a recession. It would be up to Jane to prove through hard work and even harder lobbying that she could keep that series afloat or contribute something better after March.

Camille's 'closure' over Joe surely had a sell-by date.

Jane still felt nettled by the humiliation of Camille's back-handed confession, but less burning fury than the kind of indignation a librarian feels handed back a book that's a decade overdue—the news was too stale to provoke rage.

What she did see now was that Joe had more emotion invested in that proposal by her hospital bed than she had ever appreciated. He'd made it sound like an offhand suggestion, phrased as a joke that deserved nothing more than her scoffing mistrust. But if Camille's memory was even vaguely intact, Jane had scorched Joe's straightforward pride right into a flirtation costing him his professional reputation. She had not understood at the time that Joe was so proud.

Why, even Mr Darcy took Elizabeth Bennett's first rejection on the chin and proposed a second time.

The next day, Jane was running Thursday errands up in Hampstead when her brisk step slowed outside Daunt's. She stared unseeing at the new books display. Her spirits diminished to a morsel of shame. She had to admit, Camille's revelation about Joe wasn't a shock, more a revealed truth she'd elected to ignore so many years ago. Hit with catty rumours about Joe and Camille drifting down Ken House's draughty corridors, Jane had ducked and hid from everyone—including herself.

The gossip about Joe and Camille had surrounded Jane, even in her retreat. It never pounced, just lurked in an ugly way, circling the gentle ponds of work and leisure she frequented. Until, one horrible morning over a breakfast of bangers and beans in the basement canteen, Jane received an overt danger signal—an invitation to lunch with the BBC 'nuns.' From vestal virgins, these ex-mistresses had hardened into survivors of long-term office trysts. Married producers and faithless boyfriends had discarded them for perkier replacements, younger research assistants or secretaries. Swallowing their pride, they tended the BBC's various temple altars until the first pension cheque.

Jane ate one lunch with them, but their lined lips and out-dated hairdos made her shiver. She imagined her future without Joe as these harridans chummed it up like chthonic hyenas gnawing at her incipient plummet from status as the beloved of a coming man to cast-off of a confirmed high flyer.

Jane had declined membership in that grim club but fatally she'd also rejected an offer to take that Director's Course—a sure path to more career independence from Joe. She'd just finished her extended maternity leave, and then added sick leave. When she returned to work from her bout with the flu and Sammie's colic, she begged off any research trips or overtime. She'd folded her petals for a long winter's nesting with her tiny Samantha.

During those sunless months of night feeds and diaper changes, Jane caught little sight of Joe. It seemed from one night to the next, from the three-week recces to the month-long shoots, that Joe might take the opportunity of Sammie's birth to slip away from Jane altogether. She never demanded that Joe raise his flag in honest combat. She never questioned those rumours about Camille or that ignominious transfer to Obituaries—even to herself.

She survived that dark winter, shrinking down from a lively, curious young woman who expected laughter or love into a stubborn emotional adjunct asking only minimal loyalty. She brandished Sammie's caterwauling needs as more important than anything else.

In the spring, she finally abandoned her own broadcasting dreams to seek a 'proper' job as a librarian. She recruited Lorraine as an investor in Number 19, and offered to glamourize the attic flat's baby-frayed appearance so that Joe and she could acquire the first floor with its crumbling balcony. She presented Joe with half-finished plans already in the contractor's hands and paid for the redecorating with her final severance packet, all before Joe could sputter.

Had Jane planned to 'fight Joe and Camille without fighting,' Baldwin might well have applauded her. Instead, Jane had reduced her claims out of cowardice and worse, moved Lorraine in right over their heads, retreating to the very effacing, emotional routine that had bound her as a daughter. A newborn, a mother-out-of-law at home, and Jane off to the library stacks for good—Joe had taken all these changes on board without protest, losing Jane in the process.

The Northern line rumbled up to the Tottenham Court platform. Jane squeezed herself a sliver of space that left her face pressed against the door, her hand fighting for a hold on the pole, and her soul in the bottom of her shoes. She worked her way through the crush of Christmas sale shoppers and holidaying students to a seat at the end of the car reeking of beer and vomit. She settled in the half-seat cleared by an obese neighbour. She thought of foot soldiers press-ganged by warlords to the right and left, pitted against each other by ambitious noblemen in a merciless, endless quest for domination. She took out her class notes . . .

Like Jane, Baldwin so obviously never tired of plumbing the treasure to be found in books. At their last class before the holiday break, enthusiasm had radiated off the shoulders of his droopy tweed jacket as he chalked up ideograms and dates and turned with transfixed expression to convey the darkening mood of the late Spring and Autumn era;

'So evocative, don't you think, from the feudal time we associate with Confucius. As the era unfolded, larger states ate up the smaller ones. By the 6th century BC, most small states had disappeared. A few powerful princes dominated China. Take the leader of the Jin, aiming to swallow up Yu and Hu—'

'Yoo-hoo, watch out!' Keith mugged.

Baldwin wilted a bit, but he forged on: 'Aiming at the two small states, Hu and Yu, the prince of Jin borrowed a path through Yu territory to attack Hu. After taking Hu, of course, the Jin prince turned right around and destroyed Yu on his return journey.'

The small state of Joe yearned for success and respect, the powerful state of Bella wanted celebrity and an accessory baby, while Lorraine's lame fiefdom dreamed only of one last curtain call—even if the audience for this swan song consisted of blind welfare workers.

All Jane wanted was to be loved—to be at peace with Joe and Sammie again.

Jane's ruminations on Stratagem Twenty-four lasted until she crossed Primrose Hill Road and stopped on the kerb under Joop's Painted Angel.

After restoring the windowpane, Joop had repainted 'Thou Shalt Not Kill,' over a face more defiant than ever. The angel's wingspan touched the freshly painted wooden frame. One protective fist stretched straight ahead of his gaze. Joop encircled the whole portrait with painted barbed wire entwined with olive branches. How long would Joop remain in the square to embellish his avatar? The angel rose again from broken glass shards.

Jane's strength surged as she took in his renaissance and she finally admitted the hardest truth so far: Bella wasn't her true enemy. Nor was Joe.

Her true enemy was herself. In the same situation, Lorraine might pretend indifference, play dumb, gain time with a canny shrug, but Jane suspected Lorraine had never lied to herself, not about the quality of the character parts that paid their bills, nor the character of her men offstage.

Why hadn't Jane done what she wanted? Why hadn't Jane known what she wanted? Why did she just retreat from stronger souls who overwhelmed her and drove her into the escape of books? Even a painted angel showed more determination than she had.

In the dusk, Chalkwood Square glowed with the blue flickering of televisions, orange reading lamps, and grey computer screens.

Lorraine's lights were on, too. Jane delayed her homecoming, resting her purchases on one of the red benches in the cold square. Her life was a piece of this civilized arena; she could recall the winning battle to keep the library branch operating back in '98, the loss of the dear old 74 bus service, the compromise over paving off the top of the square to through traffic, the summer festivals, the Bonfire Nights and now, the departure of middle-class literati for hedge-fund glitterati.

The Greek restaurant had closed, the French restaurants changed hands and the butcher who opened early to sell you the bacon you'd forgotten for breakfast had died years ago—the very day after he retired. Businesses had started up and failed, a post office was lost and the park's opening hours extended.

But what about when it came to her defending the interests of the small State of Jane? Why hadn't she had that wedding? She'd never disdained weddings as bourgeois. That had been a convenient excuse borrowed from the times. She actually loved weddings. She always had. Joe thought it was her fear of failing at marriage like Lorraine, but now she thought it was something worse—she had been afraid of succeeding at something Lorraine had never managed?

Why hadn't she taken that Director's Course? Was she afraid of competing with Joe and succeeding without him?

She'd ended up a librarian—a very good one, some said—but yet, perhaps not good enough? The district boss had sidled up to her at the launch for the revamped reading room and asked, 'How long do you plan to work at this career, Jane?'

As she put on the kettle for Lorraine's tea, she felt a different person from the Jane who'd left the house that midday for nothing more than a few chops and vegetables. She saw things more clearly and from a greater distance—her mother's presence, kind but always overshadowing, and Joe—seeming so unfettered and confident but really as sensitive as a tropical plant.

And Dan? When her answering machine emitted Winston's bleating plea they meet for a snack and homework at the

Moonbeam that same night, she realized she'd hoped to hear Dan's voice instead.

After tea, she made her way back up to Belsize Park. Frying fish, stewing pork, and soy smells floated to Jane's grateful nostrils on a steam clouding the Moonbeam's dining room, but Winston's hunted expression would dampen any appetite.

'Of course, I get this Number 24, using an ally to attack a common enemy but I can't think of anybody who doesn't like Nelson.'

'Well, there's you, for starters.'

'Ha ha. The real problem is the sticky follow-up, the one where you turn around and betray your ally. What's the word Baldwin is so keen on—vanquish? I wouldn't want to vanquish anyone helping me corner Nelson. I'm a nice fellow, Jane. These tactics go against the grain, even for a useless piece of plywood like me.'

Jane reminded Winston through his distress to order some food. He chose the Menu of the Day, sliced beef in oyster sauce on a bed of noodles that had seen crispier moments.

Jane understood his distress. Prince Nelson acted more the coming hegemon of the Printing Kingdom of Chu every day, with more computer sales and software tutorials—and to Chu Senior's delight—ever bigger profits. 'Dad asked me the other night whether I was going to pass this class with honours. You know the joke about the Chinese Father, "You belong to 99%? Why you not 100%?" I've got one day left to use Stratagem Twenty-four.'

'How about Nelson's new girlfriend, Sabrina?'

'Selina.'

'Could you borrow her to attack Nelson?'

'Let me think. He's taking her out a lot, but there's something holding him back and that's his crush on *Hei Bai* Girl. Selina's bitching about it all the time.'

'Hey Bye Girl?'

Winston moaned into his tofu. 'Black and White Cat Girl. She's an Internet phenomenon.'

'Like Obama Girl?'

'Kind of. She wears a cat mask and a fur bikini with a long tail attached. She is the dream girl of millions of randy Chinese geeks, including Nelson. The words *Hei Bai* refers to Deng Xiaoping's old saying, it doesn't matter whether the cat is black, *hei*, or white, *bai*, as long as it catches mice, only Deng was talking about Communists and capitalists. When she uses it, she means, sort of, *whatev.*' Winston squirmed a little in his chair.

'What does she sing?'

'About lovers separated by forces beyond their control.'

'Separated by family feuds? Like Romeo and Juliet?'

'No, more like the Three Gorges Dam flooding their villages. Nelson stays up nights listening to her tinny voice through his earphones. When she called for earthquake relief donations, he emptied his entire savings account.'

He pushed his desolate stir-fry around on his cold plate. 'However, by day, the Nelson-Selina romance is hotter than ever. Which is more than I can say for these noodles.'

Brusque shouts and the banging of gallon-sized woks echoed through the emptying dining room and heralded the end of the Moonbeam's evening shift.

Winston shouted louder over the clamour, "Course Selina's mother, Dragon Lady Leong, is really pissed off about Nelson. Mother Leong had Selina practically engaged to a med student in Kuala Lumpur.'

'My son-in-law, the doctor, hmm?'

Winston scoffed. 'He'll have to become head of neurosurgery at the Royal Free to satisfy that ogress. Anyway,' Winston offered Jane the last two shrimp *har gow* congealing on a wilted lettuce leaf at the bottom of a steamer basket. 'Nelson made his move on Selina before Madame Leong could run interception.'

Through the noise of the kitchen clean-up, Jane heard the Moonbeam's front door chimes tinkle. Winston looked up and whispered, 'Oh my God, Jane. You're in luck. It's *her.*'

Three Chinese women entered the red glow of the dining room. The first, her face pale with thick white powder under a ruched turban, cackled into her mobile phone, while from her other elbow hung a Gucci handbag as big as an orange leather tugboat leading her into harbour. Her two cohorts followed, lesser court attendants with complexions closer to human tint.

'That's her,' Winston hissed. 'That's Madame Leong. God, I forgot, it's Thursday, their mah-jong night.'

'But aren't the Ng's closing up?'

'Wah, Cecilia's mother can't say no to Madame Leong.'

'Wow. A cigarette holder. Do you think it's real ivory?'

'Elephants slaughtered by special order.' Winston averted his eyes as the trio passed in a cloud of jasmine and nicotine. There was something un-Chinese about Madame Leong, something thick-featured and garish in style compared to the Ngs and their exhausted daughter. She'd stepped out of the pages of *The Letter*, the Somerset Maugham tale of Malaysian planters, mixed-blood mistresses, and hysterically jealous wives. Cecilia was clearing Jane's plate and bowl with her resigned discretion and left Winston undisturbed, still hunkered over his rice bowl. Jane asked why Madame Leong looked so different.

'The Leongs are Nonya—families descended from European, Malay, and Chinese traders on the peninsula.' Jane observed Mrs Ng fawn and cluck over the late arrivals with hot tea and little dishes of salted peanuts and pickled cucumber slices.

Disconsolate, Winston shook his head in wonder. 'I wonder if Selina really likes Nelson. Maybe she just wants to show that mother of hers she's not taking orders about Dr Kuala Lumpur.' He sighed, 'They act like the greatest love story since—' and at that, Winston lost grip of his chopsticks and a fat blob of oyster beef fell on his trousers, 'Shit, since—'

'Since Tristan and Isolde?'

'I don't know about them. I was thinking Becks and Posh.'

'Maybe Madame Leong's got the same worry you warned your father might happen to Chu Printers, only in reverse.' She sipped her cold tea, 'I've got it, Winston. I've got it!'

'What?' Winston dabbed cold water on his trousers, leaving a greasy splotch.

'Nelson teamed up with Selina on that pepper keychain promotion, right?'

'A hit. We had to reorder.'

'Now, if things go even better, Nelson might take over Sultana Software, not the other way around. He might subsume it into a whole Blossoming Garden of Vegetable Computer Products. So, Winston, it's obvious.'

'Not to me. I don't follow.'

Cecilia had refused to complete the quartet for mah-jong, pleading her studies. Mrs Ng took off her apron and filled the last seat. The rising din of the gossiping matrons amidst the sliding, shaking, and clacking of game tiles nearly drowned out Jane's words.

'Number Twenty-four. Make *Madame Leong* your temporary ally. It solves all your nice-guy hesitations. She didn't even notice your existence just now when she crossed the room. But,' Jane put down her teacup. 'You rope her in. Stoke her fears of Nelson for her own reasons, right?'

Winston whistled, 'I see. I warn Madame Leong that Nelson dreams of running her show.'

'That's it. That's it.'

'Hopes to manage her investments.'

'Yes!'

'Talks of her taking early retirement.'

'She'll hate him.'

'I tell her that Nelson's hero is Qin Shihuangdi, uniting China all over again. All he's missing is the clay warriors.'

'And the password to her online bank account.'

Winston rehearsed his stratagem. 'First, I leak the news that Nelson's really excited about getting engaged to Selina.'

'He talks all day about overhauling Sultana's operations,' Jane prompted him.

Winston's glance hit a Great Wall—the solid sight of Madame Leong's bright scarlet lips dragging on her cigarette holder as she lined up her tiles. 'She doesn't look like the kind of woman who panics easily.'

'You're right,' Jane admitted. 'She looks like she'd take matters into her own hands. Look at the points on those fingernails.'

'And go straight to my father to dictate terms—'

'With a pint load of honey on her knife.'

'He'd freak out if he saw her beady eyes on his company. He knows she'd eat him for dim sum. But he couldn't trust Nelson after that.' Winston's eyes suddenly brightened. 'It might work!'

'Attack Guo by a Borrowed Path, only Mrs Leong, not Selina, is your borrowed path to attack Nelson's credibility. Your father might think her offer is for real and panic, or suspect she's running scared and making a pre-emptive move. Either way, Madame Leong has got to be his personal nightmare.'

Winston's glee wilted like *bok choy* in the Sahara. 'It won't work, Jane.'

'Why not?'

'Well, for starters, none of this is *true*. And second, I'd have to talk to her.'

'First of all, it's all *possible*. And second, of course you have to talk to her. Tonight. Here. Now.'

Winston didn't budge. 'Let me get this straight. First, I spook her about Nelson's ambitions, she moves in on Dad with her devious defences, thereby getting Nelson into trouble, then I turn around and betray her to Dad? Number Twenty-four makes my head hurt.'

'Winston, get a grip. Baldwin will give you top marks on your homework, you'll pass the class, and your father will want nothing more to do with the Leongs. Nelson will be fried rice.'

'You'll hang around in case she shoos me away?'

'Of course not. This is a family affair.'

Winston still didn't budge. Jane stood up and whispered into Winston's ear, 'Vanquish your fears, Winston. She's not going to eat you. She's very well-fed already.' Madame Leong had just shoved aside her winning tiles to make room for a platter of curried fish heads.

'Well, for at least a few hours.' Jane shook her young friend's trembling hand good-bye.

Winston wobbled to his feet, brushed back his bangs, and marched into the fray.

PART III

For dozens of years after their ignominious defeat, the Han were compelled to court peaceful relations with the Xiongnu at the price of gold, silk, and occasionally, even an imperial princess.

Record of the Historian, Shi Ji, Volume 110, by Sima Qian (ca. 145—86 BC)

Chapter Twenty-five, Replace the Beams with Rotten Timbers

Was Jane no braver than Winston? Wasn't it high time she grappled with her own terrors and thrust herself into battle? All the while she Hoovered the living room, she chided herself; Winston and she might be two wimps on a battlefield where the ruthless prevailed, but neither was a total coward.

The time for Baldwin's 'chaos strategies' had ended. Tactics for gaining ground were next.

With the arrival of the new year, her sense of humour had started to revive and she even felt the blossoming return of physical desire. She dusted the window sashes and checked the soil of the daffodil bulbs she'd tried forcing in the refrigerator. Sure enough, she might even have paper whites in February. For the first time, she could imagine leaving Chalkwood Square, her life at the library, and everything that reminded her of the wimpy Jane.

Sammie returned rosy-cheeked from Canada to stay weekends at the square. Before every week at Bella's, the girl raided Jane's cupboards of all the snack foods banned from her godmother's pantry. Rejecting her godmother's cuisine had revived her appetite for Number 19's simpler fare. Her cheeks were filling out, plus she was bursting with fresh intelligence: Bella was to broadcast live from a street fair on Saturday afternoon—her audition as spokeswoman for the Free Tibet Campaign.

'She's hired a new marketing expert. Mr Robin calls the makeover her paradigm shift. Mr Robin says it doesn't get trendier than Tibet, what with all these poor monks setting themselves on fire, and Bella's counting on her monk to make her look more pertinent than some other chef from Ladakh.'

Sammie lathered Nutella on toast and mumbled, 'She gave me a list of things to prep by Friday night. Pulling little strings of shit off shrimps. Euuuw.'

Jane's blood simmered, less at Bella's phoney sympathy for Tibet than her exploitation of child labour.

'Why you and not Rachel?'

Sammie, her spine crumpled into an adolescent pretzel on the battered wooden chair, licked hazelnut chocolate off her fingers. 'Rachel is on some kind of strike. She told personnel she wasn't paid to be a dogsbody at fundraisers. So, this marketing person Mr Robin—and Mum, I use the word person advisably—says the demo will test Bella's ability to "connect kerbside." And he'll go forward with some kind of research poll after the show and, depending on the crowd response, devise a "holistic cradle-to-grave approach" with the right amount of "granularity in order to leverage Bella up his strategic staircase".'

'He can't be serious—!'

'Well, Mum, Mr Robin, unlike the rest of the universe, is behind Bella "500 per cent plus." Bella's been on her mobile all week lobbying everybody to watch her segment.'

Sammie would be Bella's *sous-chef* on camera too, so Bella had made her cut school to attend a meeting with Mr Robin. What colour cashmere would look best on video next to Mr Phuntsog robes of maroon and saffron? Which end of the fair's layout would guarantee the best pedestrian flow? Should Sammie wear an apron or pose as a bystander plucked from the anonymous hordes?

'Bella doesn't actually want me on the show, especially after Mr Robin raved about my youthful spontaneity.'

Jane was thinking dark thoughts: Stratagem Twenty-five, Steal the Beams and Change the Pillars had met its perfect moment, but needed a saboteur. She could no longer keep her Eastern inspirations from her only child.

'You remember at the Chinese restaurant, Sammie, Winston mentioned a tactic he was trying? Well, our teacher gives us a whole list of proverbs, which I've been trying to keep my spirits up, you might say. And now you've got to help.'

'God, that's cool. You're like some Jedi? You know I promised I'd be your man on the inside.'

Jane pulled out her dog-eared notebook of Baldwin's lectures and handed Sammie the master list of stratagems, indicating Twenty-five. 'Now, when Bella isn't looking . . .'

By the time an extremely sweet tea had been devoured and the table was littered with crumpled KitKat wrappers, Sammie's rucksack bulged with sugary bribes and her voluble spirits overflowed with mischief at the idea of being Bella's House Elf from Hell.

Jane commented. 'Brainstorming is good for your appetite.'

'Not brainstorming, Mum. Mr Robin calls it "sharing an idea shower".'

Underneath the mockery, Jane detected Sammie's anger—at her father's blind spot to Bella and thus, at his betrayal of common sense. Jane recognized the girl's desperation to be more than a powerless onlooker left in the wings of a self-destructing world. Nothing suited her better than this chance to misapply a few Blue Peter skills to the Tibetan fry-up.

Jane set off for Friday night class grinning at what Sammie was up to over at Bella's.

'You might call Twenty-five the architectural ploy,' Baldwin explained. 'An easy lesson for any of you with builders in. You'll recognize the pain inflicted when somebody shifts specifications behind your back—'

Keith then dragged the class through horrors inflicted by a Latvian plumber. 'And not just swapping hot water for cold, but brown sludge for drinking water. He hooked up the sewage pipes to the laundry room—'

'Keith? We must get on with—'

'Zelda tossed them out on their arses, but the whole basement needed to be re-piped, re-plastered, and repainted, and don't think for a minute we'll get our money back!'

'Keith, the details during coffee?' Baldwin wrangled them back to, 'The hollowing-out strategy and the last of our concealment group—what were the five others?'

Keith: 'Crossing the sea?'

Dan: 'Borrowed knife.'

Jane: 'Clamour in the west, I mean, east, no west.'

'Hiding the dagger with a smile, and borrowing a route through Yu to attack Nelson,' Winston shouted.

'Indeed, Mr Chu. So, in Twenty-five, your strategic house looks unchanged, but the content has been secretly swapped, downgraded, sabotaged or in the case of Mrs Phipps's laundry room, simply bungled, so as to bugger up your enemy.'

'Would deceptive packaging count?' Kevin asked, 'Not that we ever resort to such a thing.'

'What about the acquisition of a majority stockholding without much fuss, so that the ownership relationships of a company are altered while outwardly the company remains the same?' Nigel asked.

'Suppose an old team of managers has to step down from a governing board, could you replace them with a new team that looks different but thinks like the old ones? Oh, wait, maybe that's the reverse . . .' Keith looked muddled.

'Suppose a shop looks the same, but when the customers go in, they see new services?' Winston tried.

'Exactly what Nelson's done to your Dad's shop,' Dan warned.

'Oh, yeah,' Winston scratched his head.

Baldwin rescued Winston. 'Think in reverse, Winston. What are the risks of Twenty-five? How would you prevent it being used against you?'

'Oh, I'm very good at thinking up what can go wrong,' Winston nodded. 'You have to watch your beams and pillars or whatever, while they think you're looking the other way.'

'Very good, Winston!'

Nigel chimed in, 'In a banking negotiation, you'd watch how people quote your statements back to you, check the contract before signing to make sure they haven't slipped new "beams" into your position.'

Dan hadn't said much more than a warm hello to Jane, and already the class was more than halfway to the break. Nevertheless, tonight she felt an electrical buzz between them. And now she knew something that she hadn't admitted to herself when blow-drying her frizz into a soft cloud, borrowing some of Sammie's abandoned lip gloss, and pilfering some of Lorraine's No5 when delivering her Friday night tray with a Nicholas Ray DVD. Without saying a thing, Dan squeezed her hand as they trailed Keith and Kevin to the canteen.

Then he startled her with: 'I've outdone all of you with Stratagem Twenty-five but it took a whole team, and of course I can't tell the others. How 'bout I come over to your place tonight?'

'Some kind of recce?'

He nodded, 'If it goes well, no one's in danger, but tonight's the night. Your flat is the perfect place to signal the activity we've expected for some weeks. It would be a lot less conspicuous that some stakeout in a car or two straight guys sitting in the dark on the benches.' He winked, 'A lot warmer, too.'

Dan had spoken already of chemicals, of incitement. Could he be lounging like this in class—and not even sitting up very straight—with a bomb ticking away? He glanced at his watch like a man checking the delay dealing out a late-night poker game. Shouldn't the police circle the bookstore and arrest suspects? Shouldn't there be alerts to stay off the underground or buses?

Dan added too politely, 'Course, you can say no—'

'No. I mean, yes, all right.'

'It is all right. I'll explain later.'

The second half of the class on Stratagem Twenty-six, Point at the Mulberry and Abuse the Acacia, dragged on and on. When Dan and Jane escaped into a thick fog, the headlights of their minicab danced in the mist like beacons picking out a foreign shore. The cabbie favoured sharp curves through the soup with an alarming growl of pleasure. With each turn of the wheels, Jane's shoulder swung into the puffy cocoon of Dan's padded camping weskit and flannel shirt. He smelled of coffee grounds, leafy paths, and mossy wool. Jane hadn't really understood Dan's plans, yet here they were speeding northwards together through rain-washed streets to the square like an ordinary couple heading home.

She listened to Dan's mobile conversations with unnamed colleagues. Their cab screeched into the square, Dan paid it quickly, and rubbed his hands with impatience as she let them in. He never once glanced over at the bookshop.

'Want a drink?' She held up the sherry bottle and a can of beer before she realized it was a silly question to put to a man on duty. Yet Dan downed the beer with a quick slug and like a well-behaved Scout, laid the empty tin on the draining board. Then he turned on her television, lowered the volume, and sat down in Joe's big chair at the window, mobile in hand.

Was Jane his hostess, spectator, or co-conspirator? She detected contained excitement in the energetic efficiency of his movements. His impassive expression, his nice-guy thanks to the cabbie, his short nod conveying everything's all right, as they climbed the stairs—they were more than professional. The electricity radiating off him in the classroom hadn't been imagined after all, just not meant for her.

'Television lights are so homey, don't you think.' His sure command of her living room had a strangely arousing effect on Jane.

'So. We just sit here?' She tried leaning back into the sofa pillows in a relaxed and inviting pose. Dan took no notice. His eyes now stayed trained on the bookstore.

'Sure. What do you want to talk about?'

She sat up straight again, feeling almost jilted. 'Well, you were going to explain this, for one thing.'

'That can wait. How're things going with Joe?'

'Fine. He locked himself in the bathroom the other day, trying to spy on me. Well, on us, actually.' Even this didn't bring Dan around. 'Not that there's anything to spy on, I mean. Joe just thought there might be.'

'Huh, uh.' Dan pulled a pair of compact binoculars from his canvas book bag. He circled the room, turning out all the kitchen and hall lights, leaving only the blue glow of the television. Jane was plunged into semidarkness.

'Uh, Dan, some people might find all this mystery annoying.'

'Hmm. Sorry. Won't last long. Then we can have a real drink. Unless I have to go out.'

'Okay. Mind if I pop up to check on my mother?'

'Good idea!' Dan hopped up. 'Probably better from up there.' And he bounded ahead of her up to Lorraine's front door like a puppy delivering a newspaper.

Jane tapped on Lorraine's door to be nonplussed by another surprise. An elegant stranger opened the door and shook Dan's hand with Ruritanian formality.

Jane should have been used to Lorraine's character transformations by now, but she usually got more warning. Her mother's normally golden hair had been bleached pearl-white and shaped into a bouffant helmet of imperial command. There was a chiselled bump on her newly elongated nose and a swathe of ivory silk wrapped around and around her mother's neck, all set off by a breastplate of pearls and a white suit jacket, redeemed below the waistband by her poodle-print flannel pyjamas and leopard-fur mules.

'How nice to see you again, Mr O'Neill. Come in, darlings. Sorry, it's the latest Alexandra nose, thin and sort of hooky, except where it widens just here,' Lorraine turned her head from side to side. 'Not too Mountbatten, I hope?' Pasted on the dressing table mirror, Jane glimpsed half a dozen Alexandra portraits printed off the Internet by the Googling granddaughter.

'I'm not sure about the hair,' said Lorraine. 'This is from a reception to celebrate some anniversary of The Worshipful Company of Barbers. Now that's the look I want, kids. All fluffy. I'm not getting enough lift at the back. Maybe the hot curlers aren't small enough?'

'What's the Worshipful Company of Barbers, Mrs King?'

'God knows. Road company of Sweeney Todd? Doesn't matter. That's not our gig. Do call me Lorraine, sweetie. Now, this is the effect I don't want.' Lorraine held up a second snap of the hardworking princess, sporting wings of hair sprayed into spiky horns.

'Kind of Doctor Spock in *Star Trek*,' Dan agreed.

'I don't think We were trying that day. One of Our minor appearances.' Lorraine tapped at the photo. 'Now this is the best look. Last year's matinee at my factory.' She rested on the stool and peered into the mirror. 'They say blind people hear very well so as long as I get the voice right, no feelings hurt.'

'You'll do fine, Mother. You're going to save the royal bacon. I hope Buckingham Palace doesn't make a habit of this. You can't impersonate more than one royal at a time. I'm sure you could do Camilla.'

'Or that Duchess of Wimbledon,' Dan joked. 'Now, Prince Andrew might be a stretch.' He escaped to the living room.

Lorraine lowered her voice, 'Sammie says Joe's having kittens over that guy. Now, what's he doing standing on my window seat? At least he took off his shoes.'

'He's very keen to look out your window.'

'Attractive build. Still, I wouldn't waste time on anybody who ignores you like this. Go distract him, darling. I'm tired.'

'May I help?' Jane asked him.

'Shhhh.'

She sat down at her mother's kitchen table and pretended to read a magazine.

'What's happening?'

Lorraine was running herself a bath. Dan was growling into two mobiles at the same time, 'Lights are still on. Nope . . . maybe, wait. Okay . . . C'mon, c'mon. Lights off.'

'Dan, I think I'll—'

Dan wasn't listening. 'OK. Sedan's pulled up. Heeeeeere they go . . . one, two, three, OK, three. Yup, three. Yup, I think it was him. Heavy jackets, I'd say about twenty pounds, not more. They might've left some of it behind. Got'em? Okay, Lloyd has picked 'em up.'

Dan's head reappeared from the eaves and he hopped down to the rug.

'Thanks. We can go back downstairs if you want.' He grinned good-bye to Lorraine, 'That's great. Thanks.' Humming, he sallied out the door to wait for Jane in the flat below.

She cleared Lorraine's tray of half-eaten minute steak and mashed potatoes with a side order of Virginia Slims from the dressing table. Lorraine thrust a camera into her hands and posed for a snap of Alexandra Five to add to prints of Alexandras One to Four—with and without the Hapsburg nose, wearing a broad-brimmed ivory hat, in and out of various blazers and tailored dresses. Her mother was still a professional through and through.

'The hat works,' Jane said, echoing the backstage kid who wanted so much to be helpful, or at least not to be so very marginal.

'I don't suppose we're going to find out more?'

'About Princess Alexandra?' Jane counted out three kinds of pills and dropped them into a paper cup.

'No,' said Lorraine, stripping off the putty chin. 'About that Dan stalking around my apartment.' They kissed goodnight.

Back downstairs, Dan was turning the lamps back on. She poured a sherry for herself. Was he off duty yet?

'I wouldn't say no to another brewski.'

They toasted Baldwin's health, can to crystal, and sitting side by side on the sofa sipped in silence until Dan put the beer down and leaned towards her.

'Let me thank you properly,' he said, taking Jane into his arms. He gave her a tentative kiss that grew more wonderful once Jane made no move to stop him. She'd been waiting for the sensation of those arms around her since entering the classroom, and seeing him lift one flirtatious black eyebrow as she entered the room.

The kiss progressed in all directions. She feared knocking over the sherry, getting her jeans drenched in beer, but somehow the drinks scuttled away of their own accord. Dan certainly displayed a powerful appreciation for ten minutes spent watching the square.

Jane realized with happy resignation that nothing happening on her sofa was going to qualify for Rupert's Bad Sex Prize—quite the contrary. After many minutes of rising warmth and rushing murmurs, Jane relaxed. She forgot she was a leftover librarian. She was a lovely, soft companion of the campaigns of life, a woman ready to accept Dan's highest form of physical gratitude—unfamiliar in so many ways compared to Joe—but then quite satisfying after so many months alone. It went on and on, these waves of wonderful Dan.

Exhausted, they lay at last quite still on the sofa. Dan brushed Jane's hair from out of her mouth and eyes. Thank goodness he wasn't the sort of guy who did something contrived, like kissing your eyelids or asking stupid questions. He tucked her curls behind one ear and then the other, which was what she was dying to do anyway.

Jane rose as gracefully as a short, middle-aged and—regrettably at this moment—not very fit, woman could leave her couch of love. Was Dan gentleman enough to not eyeball her self-conscious glide out of the room? She fetched Joe's laundered bathrobe from the bedroom closet and tossed it to Dan. Knowing Joe had bought a new one to swank around Bella's flat didn't bother her tonight.

The plumbing groaned behind the wall as the water coursed over her. Dan was a sexy man. Dripping wet, she felt like ringing up Joe to tell him of a nice new body in her bed—well, on her sofa. She rubbed her dimpled thighs until they were pink and dried off her soft shoulders. How Rubenesque.

She found Dan watching TV. Although he kissed her again as she folded, tousled, perfumed and kimono'ed, into his waiting arms, did Dan really think the eleven o'clock news was ideal after-play? It was early days for the damp towel of suburban domesticity, but Dan watched so intently, so Jane stared, too. A crisp-suited blonde read to them, 'Failed Terrorist Attack on the Circle Line, Two Arrests, One More Under Suspicion.'

Jane gasped at the shots of floodlit police cordons, sirens and curious crowds pressed against police tape opposite the Tottenham Court Road Station.

Dan fell back against the sofa cushions, gratification spreading across his serviceable features. Jane hadn't witnessed so much satisfaction since Lorraine saw Sylvia Fingerlake fall flat on her drunken bottom in the middle of a Tony Awards ceremony, although Dan expressed his elation differently.

'Bingo.'

She whispered, 'Our bookstore people?'

'Yup. There they are, stupid turkeys.' Three mug shots flashed on the screen in a photographic bewilderment that would make Pollyanna resemble a heroin smuggler. One was none other than the young man who had addressed her on the kerb.

'I saw him coming out of the bookstore last October. He talked to me! I would never have guessed, unless . . .'

She stared at Dan. 'You *knew* they were going to bomb the station and you stayed here and—I don't understand.'

'Yes, you do, if you think about it.' His gentle hand ran her wet mop up off the back of her neck. 'You know, I love your hair. I can't tell you how often I've been listening to old Baldwin drone on and on, and just imagined doing this to these curls.' He bent over and kissed her neck, 'That's the perfume you wore when we had lunch in Camden.'

Joe had given it to Jane for her birthday, back when Joe bought presents she actually wanted—not just books on a three-for-two deal. Jane had wondered if her present was the third book.

The television news scene shifted to a stand-up report in front of Scotland Yard. Jane murmured, 'That boy seemed so nice, I thought he was your informer, Gilbert. To think he was one of the bad guys.'

And to think that Joe or Sammie or Lorraine or—oh dear, you couldn't think that way—you had to worry that any human being might have been hurt or killed. Then you realized that somewhere on the planet, someone else's child or parent was injured or killed. If not a rider on the Central Line, then some poor sod in a hellhole you'd never know about . . .

'That is Gilbert Sullivan.' Dan went into the kitchen. He settled for a banana, peeling it slowly and watching Jane with an amused expression. With a formidable chest covered in dark hair, he was like a forest animal, more badger than buck. Joe's torso had gone slack, weighed down over the years with long shoots, bad mattresses, late editing nights, and irregular meals. Then Jane felt a tender rush in absentia for Joe's familiar body.

'I'm so confused.' She wrapped her arms around her knees and took in the news report—the names, the talking heads, and the wrap-up without any better comprehension of why Dan's 'man' would blow up London.

'Jane, didn't I tell you, I did my homework with a team this week?'

He was pulling on his slacks with no more grace than Jane had mustered on her naked exit for the shower. There were moments when experience couldn't compensate for the clumsy readjustments of Hominem Post-Coitus. When his zipper snagged on his shirttail, Jane felt a swanlike superiority.

'I got it! You changed the beams. You changed something— wait, wait—you knew the explosion wouldn't go off. You knew nobody would get hurt. Of course! Because you changed their chemicals, didn't you? And you've only arrested Gilbert as a cover.'

She got out eggs to scramble, whisking them with cream and some sherry. 'And the whole time these boys were setting off to blow up London, you were making love like that?' She laughed and asked, 'How are you going to share your homework next week with Keith and Kevin and the other two?'

'Making love? I suspect they've mastered that without instruction from Baldwin or me. Except Winston. I worry about him.'

'I meant your Stratagem Twenty-five.'

'Oh, I'll make up something else. I always do.' Dan sighed. 'And anyway, the game's not over. That was the fun part. They're jerks, not even Grade B terrorists. Just wannabes. But the man that set them up is bound to be furious, losing three guys to interrogators, even losers like his New Jersey recruit. The boss, whoever he is, will want to recover his face, to protect any other cells.'

'Other cells? Other plots?'

Dan nodded. 'Even the good imam can't know everything. Other cells might not be such clowns.'

'What stratagem can you use against that?' Jane said, her whisk slowing down as she took in the implications. 'Await the Exhausted Enemy?'

'The NYPD doesn't pay *per diem* in British pounds for me to sit and wait.'

Joe hated paprika. Dan loved it. She added a tablespoon of Hungarian Hot. 'Beat the grass to scare them into betraying themselves?'

Dan turned sombre. 'London's a pretty big lawn for any snake to hide in. And we hear rumours of a pretty big target. It might be only a matter of days or hours. Umm, that sure looks delicious.'

Jane smiled, 'So do you. You know, I think you put your trousers back on too soon.'

Chapter Twenty-six, Point at the Mulberry and Abuse the Acacia

Late into the night, Jane and Dan snuggled and snogged, a pleasure for new couples that knows no age limit—though when the couple is older, the chatter may be more prolonged and the physical interruptions less frequent.

It was bliss for Jane to be in bed for the first time in the last six months without tormented thoughts of Joe and Bella. She could finally stop thinking of herself as the shortest side of a triangle.

They named their favourite cartoonists, the most disgusting ice cream flavours ever invented, how they voted, and the years they hadn't bothered.

Deeper feelings surfaced amid the rumpled sheets. Jane confided her worries about Sammie's self-destructive gestures and Dr Landis's encouraging treatment. Dan talked about daily life on the police force amidst the tribulations and aftermath of divorce—and with a conspiratorial trust—what Dan's London colleagues would do next about terrorist plots.

He rested comfortably against the headboard, holding her in his arms. 'The thing to remember is that anybody looking forward to blowing himself up must be off-kilter. You've got to spot that.'

'But some of them are smart—doctors and pilots—training to be inconspicuous?'

'Nothing to do with education. Education's not the same thing as wisdom or sanity. There's something in their soul—like a piece of gravel in their shoe—that throws them off. Makes them walk funny, so to speak, and you've got to spot it. They're needy or megalomaniac or just young. There're a lot of dumb clucks out there looking for a father figure. Not that everybody wearing a robe is an asshole. Thank God our friendly imam tipped us off. We just did the leg work.'

'You can't be that modest.'

'I don't want to spook you, but tonight was chicken feed. Amateur hour. For about ten minutes, you pat yourself on the back, go whoopee, something didn't go off, hundreds of people weren't maimed. But that wears off pretty quick. All in a day's work.' He hugged her. 'You're the real buzz of my news cycle.'

Jane pressed her head into the crook of his shoulder and echoed into the darkness, 'All in a day's work? That doesn't make me feel better.'

Did Dan hope to stay the night? That would be nice, but odd. What if she started snoring? She fought off her drowsiness. 'If you can't use the snake tactic to find out what they're going to do next, didn't Baldwin say that Twenty-six was the only disclosure stratagem left? You could lay charges to flush out the real culprits behind this gang?'

He sighed: 'Don't tell Baldwin, but I think ancient Chinese wisdom might take a back seat here to good old-fashioned surveillance, twenty-four-seven.' He nuzzled her ear. 'I feel nineteen years old with you.'

She loved chatting to Dan about Baldwin's class. Although everyone had done their homework this week, all but one had preferred Stratagem Twenty-five, the one about shifting beams and pillars, or proposals and inventories in order to wrong-foot their enemies. Nobody had used Twenty-six, no matter how hard Baldwin tried stoking interest:

'As one of the "indirect action stratagems," Pointing at the Mulberry can be quite subtle, Why the mulberry? Its leaves are used to feed silkworms. In China, the mulberry is very often compared to the acacia, a far nobler specimen. Your objective might be to criticize the acacia but in a way that only those around it understand your attack. Or the opposite, to convey criticism in such an oblique way that only the acacia itself takes your point to heart.'

'What if everybody, including your noble acacia, misses the point?' Keith asked.

'Isn't this just another version of killing the chicken to scare the monkeys?' Nigel pointed out.

'Your target might not be your competitor, Nigel, or your enemy, Keith, but your friendly consumer base.'

'I get it. I'll have a go,' Kevin perked up. 'Used to be, if you targeted the teen market with sporty clothes, they'd go for it. But recently the younger girls started buying the career line, you know, office gear. So we've restyled the older stuff with a hint of vintage—Paris Resistance photos, fifties neck scarfs, old photos of the Royals on 1920's hunting jollies, that sort of thing.'

'Exactly! Twenty-six is about innuendo, analogies,' Baldwin said. 'You see, Kevin didn't photograph teen-agers wearing business suits to school. He insinuated the romance of dressing more formally into a hidden message just within his targets' reach.'

'Too hidden from me. This one's too subtle,' Winston moaned.

'The implied message of Twenty-six might be indirect criticism, or strength and resolve, or as in Kevin's case, the lure of nostalgic sophistication.'

At which point, Winston dropped his head on to his desk with a strangled gurgle. Dan patted his spikey locks. 'Hang in there, li'l buddy.'

'Pretend to pursue one objective while going for another—or even its opposite.'

Baldwin tried one last angle. 'Think of it as the shadowboxing tactic. Or chaos theory? You know, the butterfly flapping its wings in China causing a rain storm in Los Angeles?'

Thus, Stratagem Twenty-six had concluded on a shared note of bewilderment for six colleagues that morphed into a wonderful evening for two new lovers. Dan's eyes were closed and his breath slowing as he fell into a doze. Jane stroked his chest and leaning on one elbow, whispered, 'Did you really need Lorraine's window to watch the bookstore tonight?'

'Nope. Stratagem One.' He mumbled happily into his pillow. 'Lucky for me you haven't reviewed much for your final.'

Jane's eyes popped open Saturday morning to the racket of Lorraine and Joe squabbling just outside the very bedroom where Dan now lay, a contented love bear snorting beside her. A carpet of plush stubble darkened his jowls. There was some touching moistness on his lips, and only an unkind soul would say he was actually drooling.

On the other side of the door, Lorraine jangled her set of keys like the watchdog Cerberus shaking his chains in warning. 'The child can't remember everything, Joe, not all the time, not with all this switching back and forth between houses, not to mention slaving as an unpaid assistant to the Queen of the Night! It was bound to happen, so don't raise your voice to me.'

'You're not helping, Lorraine. Sammie, how many times have I told you to keep lists? I don't have time for this.'

'I know it was here, Dad. I'd almost finished it when I left it on my desk. Or maybe . . .'

Lorraine: 'Can you call one of your friends, darling?'

Joe: 'Yes! Ring up a girlfriend before dragging me all the way across the city.'

Sammie: 'Do I have any time for friends? Now I spend my entire life on the tube!' Lorraine's reference to the Queen of the Night then triggered Sammie to give her rendition of Mozart's famous aria. Her high C's at ear-splitting pitch blotted out her father and grandmother's row.

Joe only shouted louder and Lorraine tried to hoot them both down. Tra-la-la'ing, Sammie kept hunting for her Latin textbook in her old room.

'Thanks very much, Lorraine. Sammie, we got the point. Now, shut up. Did you take her to see that?'

'*The Magic Flute* is part of her education. Kenneth Branagh's work is important.'

'More important than mine, you mean. Yes, I know, Lorraine, I've never been an *artiste* like you or an intellectual like your daughter. By the way, how's your no-name royal impersonation coming along?'

Jane lifted her head from her pillow and calculated exactly how wide the yards and how thick the lumber barricading mother, child, and Joe on the nether side of the door from Dan's furry rump exposed by the duvet slipping gently off their steaming percale love nest.

The quarrel hit a pause for air while Sammie's singing tooted solo from the depths of her cluttered closet. Jane heard shoeboxes hitting the other side of the wall.

Joe's voice broke the quiet with an ominous, 'By the way, where is Jane?'

'Jane?'

'Yes. Jane. Your daughter.'

'Am I my daughter's keeper?'

'No. She's yours. Where is she?'

'She's due at work by ten. Maybe she went early. Sammie, hurry up! Come upstairs, Joe, and I'll fix you something. A Bloody Mary?'

Nearly ten! Jane slipped out of bed and fumbled through her discarded jacket for her mobile. She would 'ring' from the library. Then she realized the phone was in her bag hanging right now from the coat stand in the hall.

'Lorraine. Jane's bag is hanging right there.'

'She has more than one purse, Joe.'

'Yeah. Sure. And each one contains, let's see, here's her wallet, Oyster Card, mobile, reading glasses.'

Joe bellowed through the bedroom door, 'JANE, COME OUT OF THERE AND GET YOUR DAUGHTER SORTED OUT! WE'RE DUE ON SET NOW!'

Dan leapt up, bug-eyed, all his manly assets shrivelling in seconds from languid torpor into panicked nothingness. Jane was sure she could see the wooden bedroom door bending in its frame under the force of Joe's pounding. Suddenly, Joe stopped thumping. After a few seconds of murderous suspense, the doorknob turned, and the door swung freely open.

Joe stared at Dan and then at Jane.

Standing behind Joe in her nightie, Lorraine shuddered at the sight of two naked bodies. She scuttled away like a crab in powder-blue lace.

'Great,' Joe heaved. 'My old bedroom. My old bed.'

'Your old Jane.' It wasn't fair to expect a rejoinder out of Dan, more exposed than anyone else. If ever there was call for a gold-embossed ceremonial robe garnished with two-foot plumes or a flame-coloured satin train, this was the moment, but Chinese wiles didn't supply wardrobe changes.

Joe's breath exploded in short warning snorts. He strutted back and forth like a peacock and spouted like Vesuvius. If he had been a deer with antlers, they would now be knocking against Dan's head. It was a mating standoff worthy of David Attenborough's cameras.

Dan rose to the occasion. He straightened himself, one foot forward, in a Florentine pose somewhat David-like in its naked pride. He held this duelling posture until Jane tossed him a threadbare bed throw. He wrapped it around his waist and braced himself again, a proud barbarian girding his loins in cherry mohair fuzz. Even under challenge without the benefits of a strong coffee, he mustered a respectable, 'Morning, Joe. Nice mattress,' barely audible over Sammie's squeaky soprano, 'Rejected . . . Neglected . . . Unprotected . . .' Her shrill voice trailed off again as her search led her through the cookbook crannies of the kitchen.

Dan gestured towards the bathroom with a polite, 'Do you mind?' It wasn't elegant, but at least he had the style to navigate through Joe's fumisphere without the indignity of placing hands over private parts. No, his vulnerable bits swinging away under great loops of pink yarn, Dan waited for Joe to step aside.

Joe hissed at his back. 'Is this what you want your daughter to see? Some hairy ape coming naked out of our bedroom?'

'Our bedroom? Reality check! Earth to Joe? Earth to Joe?'

Dan flushed the toilet. Jane hoped the threat of outright violence had passed with the gestures of banal human need. What would Baldwin advise? Not that Baldwin would ever find himself in Jane's predicament. This was a pretty tacky dilemma for

Baldwin's erudition. His romantic triangles would feature smoking jackets and Noel Coward quips. Instead of being a seedy Sinologist with fantasies of solving other people's problems with a few proverbs, better he were Gandalf the White descending on his stallion Shadowmail to vanquish all awkwardness . . .

Or was it Shadowpost? No, Shadowfax?

'JANE! Would you please pay attention to me?' Joe reached for her, and stumbled over Dan's jacket and trousers. With deliberate care, Jane smoothed the garments and laid them across her vanity stool. She caught her own panicked expression reflected in Joe's disbelieving gaze. It felt too much like Lorraine's bitter rows with Jack, but Jane could no longer play the child escaping into a dreamlike trance. She didn't want a full-blown row in front of Sammie, still so unstable, and God knows, Lorraine's personal plumbing might not hold up through a violent scene. Joe had never struck her, ever. He'd never even spanked Sammie—not even that night she crayoned all over his shooting script, *Drinking for Britain, Pregnant Mothers at Risk*. For God's sake, surely she was safe? Joe was Canadian.

Yet . . . Joe had never looked so mad—not peeved, not irritated—mad, I tell you, mad. Jane was about to shout, 'Don't Joe! Get out! How dare you?'

Baldwin's voice came to her, 'Stratagem Twenty-six can be used to discipline, control, or warn others whose status or position excludes them from direct confrontation.'

You wouldn't want to confront someone who had grabbed the vanity stool and was about to throw it through the window. Joe was acting like Heathcliff on amphetamines, Frankenstein plugged into double voltage, Hannibal Lecter with indigestion. Jane knew that if she yelled at him, Joe would only drown her out with louder yelling, and then Sammie would stop singing and start bawling or screaming or grab a razor again, and Dan would rush in to defend Jane, at which point Joe just might shove that stool into Dan's most sensitive parts.

No, Baldwin wouldn't holler. The famous general Han Xin wouldn't shout. The Duke of Huan never, ever raised his voice.

Jane sank back down into the messy bedding in a position of complete submission. She folded her robe neatly across her knees and stared at the stool legs hovering inches from her nose.

'You're right, Joe. I made a terrible mistake.'

Time for Stratagem Twenty-four to Clear a Path to Guo, or at least to the safety of the bathroom . . . Attack the smaller state . . . 'How could I know Sammie and you were coming over? Lorraine makes me furious—she just walks in and out of here without knocking. It's time she realized I have my own life to live. I could brain her with that stool myself.'

Joe peered around the stool. 'You're blaming Lorraine?'

'Of course.'

Now for some Twenty-six-style analogy. Jane plunged on. 'Just marching into my flat day and night, night and day. It's like being invaded. This must be how Georgia feels or those poor Tibetans. God! It's like Poland waking up from a sound sleep to German soldiers ordering breakfast downstairs.'

'You're comparing me to a Nazi stormtrooper. Isn't that overreacting?'

'If the boot fits.' Now, for some innuendo from both barrels. 'I don't think I'll resort to the old pot-and-kettle defence, but no doubt it would have occurred to Camille Harper, if she'd ever found herself in the same situation . . . in reverse . . . if you see what I mean . . .'

The stool lowered some inches. Jane had removed some of the wood under his fiery pot, thanks to Baldwin's Number Nineteen.

'Camille Harper?' Joe's breath whooshed out of him like a punctured balloon. Stratagem Twenty-six flashed in front of Joe's expression like a rapier. 'What does Camille Harper have to do with this?'

'You do see what I mean. Sofas of yore and all that.'

Now Joe lowered the stool. 'You know, Jane, you've always been a bit scatty, a bit vague. But now, you're really losing it.' His tone was now more protective than angry, almost tender. Guilt and love criss-crossed his face.

'You're right.' She shook her head, all dismay and confusion. 'I hardly know this man.'

'From what Sammie says, he's not the sort of person to stick around. I mean, doesn't he live in New England?' Was that love she saw on Joe's face, or pity?

'New York.'

'He's just using you, Jane.'

'I know, I know.' Jane hugged her knees with provoking satisfaction.

'And now you're babbling about Camille Harper.'

'Am I?'

'I found it!' Sammie waved her Latin book from the living room with a kind of perverse triumph. 'I had it all the time. Come on, Dad. I want to get to the street demo! Bella's counting on me!' She pranced down the stairs.

Joe yelled after her, 'We'll talk about this in the car.'

'Talk about what? Bye, Mum,' she called from the lower landing. 'Don't forget to watch me cook on TV! Free Tibet! Free Tibet!'

Her parents looked at each other in disbelief. Sammie hadn't heard or seen Dan. Jane smiled her most gracious good-bye. 'You can go now. Don't forget to take your indignation with you.'

His eyes narrowed. 'This isn't the same as with Bella.'

'Oh, how true. I'm happy with the family I have. I have a child already. But I'll be careful not to make any mistakes.'

'Jane, are you taking mood-altering medication?'

'Tranquilizers? Or birth control pills? I know. Fifty per cent of births in England these days are out of wedlock. Good to keep that in mind, Joe.' If Baldwin's advice was to attack the mulberry to abuse the acacia, Jane wasn't sure she'd employed the stratagem very well, since she'd pretty much cast herself as the mulberry.

Joe shook his head, pointing and fumbling his way backwards, 'Jane, you should see somebody.'

'Sammie's waiting.'

'Promise me. You'll talk to someone.'

'Well, I expect I'll spend the morning talking to Dan.'

Joe slammed the front door, shaking Number 19 to its very foundations.

><><

Bella waved and cooed to a handful of onlookers clutching their jackets and scarves against a brisk wind. 'I'm here today in Notting Hill Gate at the 'Save Tibet!' Demonstration and what a crowd of enthusiastic supporters behind me. Hellooooo there!'

'Hey, darling, can you do it in ten minutes like that *Telegraph* babe?' a yob taunted from the kerb. 'Yeah, we're hungry, sweetheart!' his pals joined in.

'I'm absolutely honoured to introduce our chef, just flown in from Dharamsala, am I pronouncing that right?' Bella steadied her makeshift kitchen table wobbling in the wind.

She read off a Post-It stuck to the bottom of her rice vinegar cruet, 'So, welcome, Mr Phuntsog! Mr Phuntsog is going to demonstrate a traditional vegetarian dish from Kirti monastery in Southwestern Sichuan.' Bella extended her microphone to a wizened brown monk in maroon cotton standing next to her. He bowed his shaven head towards the crowd behind them.

'The camera's over there, Mr Phuntsog. Now what can you tell us about our delicious demo dish?'

The monk embarked on his own script, 'The Chinese government says they allow religious freedom and improve living standards in Tibet. But our monks are immolating themselves because they have reduced our monastery to a prison, torture us and make living impossible for us—'

'Yes, Mr Phuntsog, can you tell us about the dish you're going to cook for us today?'

' . . . They say that I'm a terrorist and that explosives were found in my room. Those are nothing but lies, LIES!' The monk pounded his fist on the cooking table and a bag of rice fell on the pavement. 'I was forced to flee.'

Tying a *Travelling Kitchen* apron around the monk's waist, Bella strangled his flow with a tight knot and stepped on his cue, 'And of course, on the road, nothing is more delicious than an easy stir-fry, right?'

Suddenly from behind Bella, Sammie's freckled face popped into view. Watching from the safety of Number 19's kitchen, Jane saw her daughter was already wearing her *Travelling Kitchen* apron, but the child had scrawled across Bella's imprinted image, 'Free Sammie!'

Sammie set out small bowls of condiments and mixed spices as Bella continued, 'Now, Mr Phuntsog, we have our oil, our garlic, our ginger, all cut up—'

'*Your* ginger? *Your* garlic? Personal possession of material things is ephemeral. Owning even the smallest grain of salt is an illusion.'

'Yes, sorry, the oil, the garlic and the ginger were whizzed up in the food processor,' Bella fell back on her girlish simper, 'I so hope that doesn't ruin my karma.' The monk gazed at Bella with like a *bodhisattva* examining a reincarnation that had misfired. Bella lit the portable gas ring. It sputtered in the wind and went out. She tried another match and finally a pocket lighter. She shook condiments into the oil.

'Well, uh, Mr Phuntsog, could you tell us a bit more about this dish?'

The monk was silent. Jane could feel Bella's panic rising as the camera roved across the ingredients and back to her anxious, pleading expression.

The wok started to smoke. An ominous plume of grey fumes rose into the frame and circled Bella's shoulders.

'Mr Phuntsog, Can you tell us anything about this dish? *Please?*'

'That is mustard oil. It is burning too fast. You should use peanut.'

Bella glared at Sammie and grabbed the smoking wok to swab out the scorching oil.

The monk faced the camera squarely: 'My father is a carpenter and my mother is a market trader. We are poor, but we had enough to eat—'

'Yes, and you ate——?' Bella pulled him back on topic but the monk had chosen his own course.

'Ever since I was a child, I wanted to become a monk. I entered the Kirti Monastery in Aba when I was twelve and was admitted as a monk at twenty years of age. When my abbot there could not teach me anything more, he sent me to Lhasa——'

'So, there's our peanut oil, heating up nicely.' Bella scanned Sammie's row of little bowls. 'And now we add our, sorry, *the* spices . . . turmeric, clove, salt, cinnamon, ground red pepper, five-spice, a touch of Sichuan black pepper and——' Bella's nose reared back, 'My! That smells original,' she grimaced. 'But of course, thrillingly Tibetan!'

The Venerable One sniffed the billows of dark spicy smoke circling his shaved head.

'Smells like burning detergent to me,' he observed. 'The Kirti Monastery has been under tight surveillance since the protests of 2008. Our movements are restricted. Our home has become a prison. The people agree with the monks, something must change in Tibet. We are waiting for the right moment——'

'And this is the right moment for *bok choy!*' a desperate Bella screeched at the audience. 'Sammie!? *Bok choy*, please?' Sammie's little fist shot out from behind Bella's capacious torso and tossed a bunch of greens into the sizzling wok.

'That is not *bok choy*,' Phuntsog said. Bella's eyes widened as a clump of iceberg wilted into brown slime. She grinned like a crazed clown. The dwindling crowd behind her mumbled and shook their heads. 'Well, substitutions make for creative cooking. I always say, don't be afraid to make it your own.' She caught the monk's withering gaze and hurried to add, 'But not in any possessive material sense, of course.'

The spirit of Mr Robin was working to save Bella's neck. 'So what's the next step, Venerable, uh Guest?'

Mouth open, Jane watched the screen. Sammie was following their agreed strategy to change the beams, but they hadn't bargained on this delicious double surprise—a jet-lagged Tibetan dissident monk stealing Stratagem Twenty-six to broadcast his own freedom message as a substitute for cooking on Bella's airtime.

'Our country is in a great crisis, Bella Crawford. The people are starving.'

'And what could be better than a side of curried vegetables, RIGHT?'

'Horrible human rights violations are taking place under the military dictatorship. Tibetan religion and culture are under such unthinkable repression that we have reached a point of desperation! People would choose to die rather than go on living. This is why we demonstrate until we win. We will not give up.'

'And we aren't giving up on this stir-fry! After the greens, we add a drop of stock, Sammie? SAMMIE? THE CORNFLOUR TO THICKEN THE SAUCE, PLEASE?'

Arms flailing between her bowls like a fairground spiv playing a desperate shell game, Bella seized the bowl of white starch from Sammie's fingers and tossed the contents into the wok.

The blackening sauce began to pop and rise in a bubbling mass.

Phuntsong stared intently at the camera, 'Each monk folds his robe precisely according to the rules of the clergy, like this. Which enables us to immediately recognize government spies pretending to be monks—'

'Yes, Mr P.' Bella snapped. 'And now, some rice vinegar—' Sammie threw a cup of vinegar into the wok, and with that, the whole bubbling mess erupted like a volcano, spewing foam all over the table and sending a river of bilious lava streaming on to the pavement. The audience shrieked with delight.

In her kitchen, Jane hooted as she, along with mothers everywhere, recognized the playroom delight of mixing bicarbonate of soda with vinegar.

The crowd surrounding the demo table applauded wildly. Covered with foam, Bella sputtered in fury.

The monk lifted his maroon hem with delicacy to clear his sandaled feet from the waves of hot goo. He rounded the table and stepped carefully towards the camera. He leaned closer and closer to the lens until his smooth wide cheeks filled the screen.

He shook his shaven pate and said, 'I would like to make it clear to you watching today that this is not what we eat in Tibet. When we eat at all.'

With enormous dignity, given the howling hostess and the heckling crowd, Phuntsog brought his hands together in prayer for his people's liberation and calmly exited the shot, stage right.

From behind Bella's frozen stare, a gleeful Sammie waved both hands in the air, her fingers making a 'V' for Jane's unalloyed pleasure. Her daughter hadn't smiled that joyously in months.

Chapter Twenty-seven, Feign Madness But Keep Your Balance

'I have never enjoyed an episode of *The Travelling Kitchen* so much,' Lorraine sighed. '*If we eat at all*. What a punch line! What an exit! Don't call them, Bella honey, they'll call you. If they call at all!'

'I think we can safely say Bella's calling to free Tibet is off.'

Lorraine chortled, 'Mission Unaccomplished!'

'Another good thing came out of the weekend,' Jane added. She set her mother's tea tray by the pillow. Lorraine spent more and more time in bed these days. Jane knew it was age, but agreed Lorraine should rest up for her solo as Princess Alexandra.

'You know, Lorraine, that constant pain in my chest is subsiding, that feeling that I get through each day with one arm in a sling, but nobody can see it? Spending the night with Dan wiped all that out.'

'Well, you look a hell of a lot better. Are you in love with this Dan or do you still love Joe? You forgot the pepper shaker.' Lorraine loved Jane's scrambled eggs, the dish that settled pre-curtain jitters.

'Here it is, in my pocket. Well, it's crazy. Dan's nice, but when I saw Joe's wild expression, I loved him more than ever. And I saw that he still cares.'

Lorraine shook her head. 'Don't get your hopes up. It was a territorial reflex, sweetie. Not-in-my-cave Syndrome.'

'You're probably right.' Jane didn't confide that with Sammie's help, Joe had snuck a Christmas present under her pillow, a scarf from Scotland wrapped around a pair of emerald earrings.

'Joe suggested that I'm losing my mind.'

'Well, if he isn't to blame, who is?' Lorraine spread cream cheese on her water biscuit. 'Tell him not to worry. You'll find your mind sooner or later,' Lorraine brushed crumbs off her nightie with a showy flair. 'Just stay centred, Jane. No matter what happens offstage, the show goes on. After a while, darling, you realize that life onstage matters more than offstage. Leave the complications in the wings.'

'Like me, for one.' Jane's sudden accusation landed, scattershot, like the cracker crumbs. Even she was appalled at her outburst but it was true and it had to be said sooner or later.

Lorraine tried playing deaf. 'Well, here we are, together and cosy. Isn't it a beautiful afternoon? So cold and clear.'

Jane wasn't willing to let Lorraine glide out of her sights. She waited. And waited.

'Oh, darling, that was so long ago,' was the best Lorraine could manage.

'I just don't want Sammie to feel like that. Shoved to one side.'

The third week of January arrived as clear as the frozen sky. Jane's horizon had lengthened. No doubt Mr Robin would have called this her 'paradigm shift.' To Jane, it felt like a *Star Wars* card game Sammie played with a pimply admirer. You turned a card and lo! You'd landed on a friendly hunk of asteroid safe from menace for one more round. Jane headed off to the library under a limitless azure sky all of six degrees Centigrade, but the wind on her cheeks felt like a reviving slap, a reminder that sooner or later, we're all dead. Just get on with it, bend with the winter gales so you won't break and stop fretting.

Monday evening's Bookworms meeting made little progress in the battle for survival, no one having sorted out the question of new space or expanding membership. If anything, the group seemed plumb tuckered out, as Lorraine would say. When their book discussion sputtered to a standstill, Mrs Wilting suggested they adjourn an hour early.

Tuesday Jane discovered from a florist's call that an armload of pink roses sent by Dan had landed by accident in the safekeeping of Number 15.

The old Jane would have suffered this error in polite resignation. The new Jane went to her neighbour's and found her flowers were already culled, clipped, and arranged in a priceless antique vase. Dan's card had 'got lost.' She hoisted the Ming into her arms and marched the gargantuan spray back home. Her neighbour was disarmed by her proprietary effrontery, but this week, what with the Feigning Madness strategy, Jane was learning the hidden strength in not giving a damn how crazy she acted.

She left the blooms with Lorraine. Extending the life span of bouquets was an actress's trade secret extracted from backstage dressers who had to manage whole jungles of Stage Door Johnny floral tributes.

Wednesday Jane committed another folly. She spent twice her budget for a sharp new Joseph outfit to wear to lunch on Thursday with Camille Harper. They would sign Jane's contract and plan *The Global Library* series.

'Actually, I was thinking of another working title,' Jane said. 'And *The Word was Digital?*'

'That's rather good,' Camille admitted.

'Or, perhaps *Turning the Digital Page?*'

'Why, that's even better. Reminds me of that Kindle Fire launch.'

'You know, Camille, I had an idea for the opening credits that might—'

'Jane! Order your lunch! You've got the job!' Camille waved the menu in jest. 'If taking off for a few years made all our researchers this eager, I'd insert an obligatory sabbatical into every contract.'

Jane ate her chef's salad and listened to how Camille's shooting schedule dovetailed with other projects. How tactful of Camille to relegate Jane's long retirement to 'a few years off.' Age and success had mellowed Camille. She wanted to hear about Lorraine's health problems, Sammie's food crises, and the pressures on libraries. She nodded with empathy over the tumbles and setbacks the accumulating years handed to all middle-aged women, whatever their paths.

If Camille muffled her ambition under a light-hearted, even flaky demeanour, Jane perceived by the time coffee and tiramisu arrived that the sharp edges of C. Harper, veteran producer, hadn't dulled. An entire generation of television styles and battles had passed Jane by as she hid herself in the library while Camille had toughed it out through all weathers. She didn't go so far as to feign 'madness,' but like Stratagem Twenty-seven, Camille hid acute competence and competitiveness behind a superficial chumminess.

Jane's stylish Joseph jacket survived three courses of Camille, a midday meeting with the Camden Library Authority, and all the way to Baldwin's class.

'Avoid triggering a concentrated force which can generate an opposing force. Wild gestures can alert the enemy that something's wrong. Be still, hide the size or formation of your troops and don't explain manoeuvres to your men. Pretend to be a pig in order to eat the tiger. Play dumb. Hide behind the mask of a fool, a drunk, or a madman. Create confusion about your intentions and motivations. Lure your opponent into underestimating your ability until he drops his guard. Then you may attack.'

'Never let them know what you're thinking,' Dan intoned.

'Sun Tzu?' Winston asked.

'Nope,' Dan shook his head, 'Michael Corleone.'

Nigel perked up: 'Do any of you remember Richard Branson launching Virgin's transatlantic flight? Branson dressed up in a pirate costume and filled the airplane with movie stars and champagne. British Airways took him for an idiot and didn't see his threat until it was far too late. Wouldn't that be Twenty-seven?'

'An excellent example, Nigel. Let your enemies take you for an idiot. Exactly!'

'My father *knows* I'm an idiot,' muttered Winston.

'Put it to good use, my dear fellow!' Baldwin fired back. 'Tell us, Winston, what was the outcome of your rumoured conference with the Dowager of Mah-jong?'

'Madame Leong.' Winston avoided Jane's querying expression, 'My plan went wrong. Again. AGAIN! Now they're dating.'

'Nelson and Selina? But we already knew that,' Jane said.

Winston shook his head. The rest of the class stared. The alternative was too horrible to utter. Winston's father had taken up with Widow Leong? In Winston's world, all forces re-aligned in love and harmony despite his very best efforts—Nelson with Selina, the widower Chu with the Malaysian entrepreneur—leaving poor Winston's future hung out to dry in the Gobi winds.

Baldwin seemed set back himself for a moment. 'I see. Well, turn it to your purposes. If both young and old are busy romancing, you may not gain ground, but you'll be needed, not sacked. You have all the more room to manoeuvre behind their backs, while they ignore you like a feeble-minded also-ran. Think of poor old General Cao Shuang who was co-regent in the state of Wei with the great Sima Yi.'

'Hey, yeah,' Winston perked up. Dynasty Warriors 6!'

'Beg your pardon?'

'Sorry, professor, but for once, I actually know what you're talking about. Sima Yi is in one of those hack 'n' slash video games Nelson bootlegs from under the counter. There's no European edition yet.' Winston warmed up to his topic, 'It's a game manufactured by Koei, based on all this stuff the professor talks about, like *The Romance of the Three Kingdoms*. The Japanese bundle it with PlayStation 3.'

Baldwin leaned back and amused, merely sipped his tea.

'In the game, the character Sima Yi is cunning, ruthless, and extremely arrogant, boasting over every little victory. If you play him, you can't accept defeat. If he loses, he claims it's just another little trick he planned, part of some grand tactic. The graphics are so cool.'

'Yeah?' Kevin played video games with his eight-year-old.

'He wears all these amazing robes and shoulder guard-thingies and he wields this black fan,' Winston rose from his chair and pointed his pencil at Nigel's Adam's apple, 'The "Dark Feather," which bestows superpowers—'

Baldwin laid down his mug, 'And which has nothing to do with history. Thank you, Winston, back to our lesson . . .'

Winston took his seat, all superpowers snuffed out. Everybody but Nigel laid down their pens, because they had learned weeks ago that once Baldwin was going to tell them a story, it would be all they could do to simply remember the outcome:

'We go back to the Third Century.'

'The Three Kingdoms period,' Dan prompted.

'Yes, with two regents, General Cao Shuang and Sima Yi, ruling over the adopted heir to Emperor Cao Rui, the young Cao Fang, Prince of Qi . . .'

Keith groaned.

'. . . Now General Cao Shuang craved great power and prestige, and sought total control over the Wei kingdom. His first move was to persuade the young prince to promote his rival regent Sima Yi to personal imperial instructor, an honorary position giving Sima Yi no political authority, although he maintained his military command.'

'Obviously,' Keith interjected, somewhat facetiously.

Baldwin smiled with his habitual tolerance. 'In 241, Zhu Ran of the Wu kingdom laid siege to Fancheng, here.' He pointed to his map of China. 'Sima Yi broke the siege and drove off the attackers. Then he defeated Zhuge Ke of Wu, which in the year 243 was more or less around here.'

'More or less,' Keith echoed.

'That's enough of that, Keith. In contrast to these successes, General Cao Shuang's attack on the Kingdom of Shu ended in failure. The difference between Sima Yi's talent and General Cao's lack of it was more obvious with each battle.'

'I'm beginning to feel sorry for this Cao Shuang chap,' Kevin nodded.

'Sensing danger from too much success, Sima Yi took sick leave in 247. He was getting on in age, but was he really so ill? General Cao Shuang sent a spy to watch Sima Yi who pretended to be senile until Cao Shuang finally felt secure.'

'Sima Yi bided his time and while the general took his ward Cao Fang outside the capital on an official visit to the deceased emperor's tomb in 249, Sima Yi sprang into action in order to save the kingdom from Cao Shuang's irresponsible rule. He moved on the imperial palace with his own men and convinced the emperor's mother to give an order to arrest General Cao Shuang. With an imperial order declaring him a rebel, Cao Shuang and his allies surrendered because they expected their lives would be spared.' Baldwin added, almost as an afterthought, 'Of course, Sima Yi executed every one, and without a magic fan of black feathers, Winston.'

Kevin turned a little green. 'Oh, no, not again. Could I just say, Professor Baldwin, without implying anything personal, your stories turn my stomach and I'm in *insurance*. I've heard some stories. But does it always have to end in cutting noses or arms or mass beheadings, group massacres, walking corpses?'

'I had no idea a management course could be so stomach curdling,' Keith nodded.

'But I can't convince my father of Nelson's mismanagement,' Winston protested.

'Can you convince him you're ill?' Baldwin asked.

'Why not senile?' Winston retorted, to which everybody laughed.

'No, Winston, but you've given me an idea for your final exam. In the meantime, try acting as superlatively debile as possible. Nelson, your father, and the insidious State of Leong must never suspect what you're planning.'

'That's easy. I'm not planning anything.' Winston shrugged.

Jane worried that Winston would fail Baldwin's class. With every week, Winston's ploys only drew the Chinese and Malaysian families closer into a web that shut him out. As far as the coming exam was concerned, Winston was encouraged by Baldwin to bone up on his defensive positions and risk-reduction tactics. Perhaps Winston's best hope was in keeping his father in a holding pattern until Nelson outgrew his ambitions for the Chu shop.

He might dream of wielding a black fan, but in real life, Winston was what Lorraine might call one of life's gold-standard bit-players. Jane began to suspect Chu Pater was playing games of his own, sending his son to study tactics the old man had employed for decades in his petty-minded way. As long as Winston ignored the call of escape out from under his father's disapproval, as long as his endearing if slightly pathetic real-estate agent ambition remained in the kingdom of dreams, there was little victory in sight.

As for herself, Jane had tired of Baldwin's concealment and confusion strategies. She'd resolved that in only a few days, she was going to make a move that no one expected of the mousey librarian crazed by jealousy and abandonment and now rendered unreliable by middle-aged lust.

She was going to use Stratagem Twenty-eight—on herself.

Chapter Twenty-eight, Lure Your Enemy on the Roof, Remove the Ladder

Jane sat in the offices of Higgins, Higgins & Wraigth the next Tuesday at ten o'clock. KP Higgins was running late, so Jane shuffled through a pile of golfing mags. The librarian in Jane noticed how well-thumbed the magazines were. Apparently, Solicitor Higgins kept a lot of clients waiting—perhaps much-divorced men skimping on alimony for golf memberships?

Jane had long postponed this day; just sitting in this antechamber of oak walls and green plush, so sequestered and confessional, amounted to an admission that things between Joe and herself would never be reversed.

Then, last Friday night, Baldwin had taught them something that had sounded an alarm bell deep inside Jane.

Their teacups and smelly snacks aloft, the class had squeezed back into the little room and settled down like willing children at bedtime. During the break, Baldwin had outlined a business deal on the board. Evidently Nigel's weekly howl for more commercial applications had registered with the professor.

'Lure Your Enemy on the Roof and Remove the Ladder—the fourth of our six Gaining Ground strategies. Of course, it sounds like something you do to the enemy, but perhaps not always, hmm?'

The professor scrutinized Jane's face, shook his head, and turned away. Not for the first time, Jane found his doleful expression smacked as much of self-pity as academic frustration.

'Let's take an ancient example. The famous Han general, Han Xin, rode off against two rebel kingdoms, the Qi and the Chu. Chu sent out General Long Chu with two hundred thousand men to intercept the Han. The two armies met on opposite sides of the Wei River. General Han ordered his men to fill over ten thousand sandbags and carry them upstream to dam the water's flow. The next morning General Han led his army across the lowered river and attacked Chu, but after a short engagement, he pretended defeat and fled back across the river. General Long announced, "I always knew Han Xin was a coward!" He led his army across the river in pursuit.'

'General Long isn't long for this world,' Keith quipped.

'Exactly,' Baldwin poured a cup of jasmine tea from his thermos.

'Chu Long's army was just midstream, when at a prearranged signal, General Han's men removed the sandbags and freed the pent-up waters which drowned half of Chu's troops. General Han then wheeled around his retreating forces and attacked the advance guard of Chu, killing General Long. The remaining Chu troops were captured by the pursuing Han soldiers.'

'You were going to give us a business example, Professor.'

'Don't worry, Nigel. I'm ready for you. Get the enemy into a position where he can't back out. The so-called "ladder" could be any enticement. I've written here on the board the chronology of a Sino-German business negotiation. The names of the companies and the negotiable items in this column over here are for Nigel, as he's probably the only one of you who cares at this point.'

'Hang on,' Keith protested. 'Swiss Re isn't some corner newsagent.'

'Forgive me, Mr Phipps. This is the point, here, where the Germans wrong-footed the Chinese.'

'The *Germans* used Twenty-eight on the Chinese?' Keith marvelled.

Baldwin lifted an eyebrow: 'Indeed. One wonders if the Germans even knew they were using Twenty-eight at the time. They didn't leave enough time between their arrival in Beijing and their abrupt departure for anyone to complete the Chinese translation of the contract—although a preliminary draft in English had been agreed. Normally Chinese joint ventures insist that the Chinese-language version is the only basis for arbitration in case something goes wrong. And as you've learned in this course, things always go wrong. But it was too late for the Chinese side. Their choice was to let the contract fall apart at the last minute or allow the Germans to depart with the English version serving as the definitive text.'

'So Twenty-eight is a sort of locking-in tactic, securing the ground you've won?' Keith asked.

Baldwin nodded. 'Exactly. Quite useful in insurance, I should think, or sales of any kind. You entice your insuree up on to the roof with attractive premiums and generous coverage until he has no way down. You hope he never needs to find out that your coverage had a loophole or that he needed to add more coverage at a later stage when he was less insurable. You make special offers with hidden snags.'

Watching Keith scribble this down with such enthusiasm was bad enough. Jane winced to see Nigel jump into the flow: 'Or slap fines on premature withdrawal of funds but keeping that in the small print?'

Kevin loved Twenty-eight too: 'Offer customer discount cards and loyalty programmes that don't have any entrance fee, but require a minimum purchase for annual membership renewal?'

'Also in fine print?' Winston suggested.

''Course, Chu. That's the idea, innit?'

'My, my, this strategy certainly appeals to our high flyers! Can the rest of you spot a catch? Any particular danger?'

Dan's hand shot up and knocked over his empty paper cup, but these days, Baldwin gave him a wink and a pass. Everybody knew that Dan knew—well, whatever it was he knew. Baldwin preferred to pick on the others: 'Winston? Jane? Oh, go ahead, Kevin.'

'When a tiger is cornered, it turns ferocious. Its energy is totally focussed on getting out of that corner.'

Keith mugged, 'Speaks the Great White Hunter.'

'Hah! You just try going into the ladies' dressing rooms to stop a seventeen-year-old in the middle of her shoplifting spree.'

'Good point, Mr Filgrove!' Baldwin said. 'Trapped, the shoplifting kitten turns tigress. Remember the corollary from Sun Tzu, Principle Seven? If you burned your own bridges and threw your own troops into a position from which there is no escape, you could count on them to fight like hell. Now, can any of you think of another strategy that would come into play as Kevin's shoplifter unsheathes her claws?'

Dan raised his hand again. Winston pulled it back down.

Jane tried, 'Shutting the Door to Capture the Thief? No, that's too similar. And I expect a dressing room is escapable.' Joe's night on the floor of the bathroom had burned Number Twenty-two into her memory.

'Pretty obvious,' Keith chortled. They all hemmed and hawed. They were getting better at this game and wanted to offer Baldwin something subtler.

'Number Sixteen,' Keith tried. 'If you want to catch'em, let'em go? That way, Kev, your teen-ager tells all her friends what a nice manager you are. How you let her off with a warning. You avoid a hassle with her parents and get some good PR as the store that understands.'

Baldwin checked his watch. 'So, we have just enough time for the most subtle interpretation of Twenty-eight.'

They waited, curious. He teased them, 'Think of General de Gaulle. As president of France, he made every referendum a vote for or against himself. Thus—?'

Thus, four days later, Jane found herself staring at a threadbare carpet, in a solicitor's office tucked next to the Wallace Collection on Marylebone High Street. The venerable partnership of Higgins, Higgins & Wraigth came highly recommended by Lorraine's friend St John: 'Excellent, my dear, for the sorting-out of tedious complications off-stage.'

An elderly man in a three-piece pinstriped suit dotted with dandruff coughed and shuffled past Jane and disappeared into the loo at the end of the corridor. He might be Higgins senior—he was slow enough. Jane took up her bag, but the old man passed her a minute later, blind to her presence. She cleared her throat, and he jumped a little, then peered down at her through rheumy eyes. 'Waiting for KP? Won't be a moment.' He shuffled away.

She swallowed back despair. Why, after all these months of forbearance and watchfulness, after agreeing with Joe that neither one of them would rock the boat, was she here? Because she'd taken to heart Baldwin's description of Twenty-eight as 'the device that works best when used in the solitude of private battles, against oneself. You manoeuvre your own back against the wall to spur yourself on to the highest achievement.'

Last Friday Baldwin had barked out commands in their faces and filled the tiny room with the spirit of a Warring States desperado. 'Break your cauldrons! Smash up your boats! Roast your oxen using your own wagons as firewood for a final feast! Know when it's time to leave your own men absolutely no escape, nothing but a ferocious fight to the death.'

He peppered the blackboard with a flurry of advancing arrows shooting back and forth, 'Burn the bridges behind your advance! Now! There's no escape!'

He leaned down at them, his eyes fiery and his light hair silvery in the overhead light. Jane heard the battle cry of hundreds of clashing swords advancing to the final showdown and Baldwin's crescendo, 'There is NO WAY BACK!'

'Ms Gilchrist?' A dozen tinny bracelets jangling in Jane's ears brought her back to the law office.

KP Higgins was leaning out of her private chamber. Jane followed the plump Indian woman, draped in fuchsia silks and a Maharajah's worth of bangles, into the inner office. A desk neatly stacked with manila folders dominated the centre of the room.

'How do you do? My father-in-law is a bit tired, these days. I'll be consulting you. We receive a lot of referrals from Mr Stevens.'

Higgins extended a manicured hand with shimmering shell-pink nails. Jane started her story and KP Higgins was quick to catch the gist. She swiftly recited back a thumbnail summary of the Gilchrist evolution; they'd gone from a hip media couple with one child out-of-wedlock in defiance of bourgeois values to tired-out middle-aged-nobodies with no time or energy to change their situation.

'Until now.' Higgins shook her head.

'Well, now I need to know where I stand,' Jane explained. 'It's time I asked someone.'

'No adoption discussion, at any time?'

'Adoption?'

'Was there ever a surgical interventions that could be used to establish paternity? Any insurance coverage linking father to daughter? There's always DNA testing if it serves. I wish I could say it was more extraordinary, but if both names are on the leasehold . . . We'll have to protect you and your mother there. Is it possible you never discussed regularizing this situation, at any point, in all these years?'

Where had the years gone? They rewound in Jane's mind, days of chores and hours at the library, Joe and Sammie coming and going. Those years must count for something, she thought.

'Mrs Higgins, what are the rules about common-law-marriage? My mother and Joe joked about it from time to time.'

Higgins sighed. 'A rather poor joke on you, if you were counting on that. Joe is Canadian. Your mother is American.'

'Meaning?'

'Quite simple, really. Common-law-marriage exists in Canada. The Ontario Family Law Act specifically recognizes common-law spouses in Section Twenty-nine dealing with spousal support issues. The requirements are living together for three years or having a child in common and having cohabited in a relationship of some permanence. In America, many states recognize common-law marriage.' Higgins chirped, 'In some states, it's harder to get out of than to get into.'

'Are you saying they were both wrong about England?'

'Oh, yes, completely, I'm afraid. Quite amusing.' Higgins's expression stayed serious. 'I'm afraid the extent of women's rights are widely misunderstood, particularly in this society. Western women lack many social and cultural protections that less-developed countries would find abhorrent. You enjoy no protection of the law. Now, it is my job to see if we can turn that to your advantage, somehow.'

Clearly Higgins found the romantic posture of media artists or misguided feminists just a tiresome ignorance that again and again required the illuminating beam of her law books. In front of this professional amazon armed with eyeliner, hairspray, and kilos of peachy embroidered pongee, Jane felt a fool. KP Higgins clearly had no problem with bourgeois style, disposable income, or womanly rights.

'In England, Common-law Marriage ceased definitively with the Marriage Act of 1753. You cannot demand child-support payments from Mr Gilchrist. A father who was not married to the child's mother when that child was born will not automatically have parental responsibility for that child—no matter what the DNA says. He can acquire that responsibility by agreement with the mother, which you say you never obtained, or by applying to the court. He could have acquired it by marrying you after Samantha's birth. So your situation is now quite ambiguous on the child-support, especially as he's moved out, which implies far less commitment to your family unit than before, and it was already quite minimal by legal standards.'

'Although he's assuming partial custody of her now?'

'Oh, Ms King, no one talks of "custody" these days. The law regards "shared parenting" as beneficial to the child and would wish it to continue. You're not here to stop that, are you? Because your history might enable you to cut off his contact, but as long as both parents are fit—'

'No, I suppose not.'

Jane wasn't sure what she wanted, but she was startled to learn how the law stood. Higgins was already moving into financial matters. Jane found it hard to keep up. The speed of the consultation made it clear that Higgins Minutes were very costly units.

'. . . Having said that, removing a name from a joint account isn't always as easy as it sounds. Some banks will only take the instruction from the "main account holder", who is simply the person whose name was put first on the form that opened the account. Yourself? Higgins clapped her dainty brown hands together, 'Oh, we can thank the gods for small favours and lucky accidents. That does make things easier. To save you any inconvenience, I'll write a quick note to your bank manager straight away whilst you are sorting out your split, explaining what you want them to do, and we'll get you both to sign it . . .'

Jane was following Higgins with one mind and wondering at the same time how Joe would take all this.

'How do you think Mr Gilchrist will react?' The Asian woman's telepathy was unnerving. Or was it just that she did this every day, every week, for all districts of London, in all colours of the rainbow?

'Oh, he won't agree.'

'Very good. Very good.' Higgins ticked off a small box on her interview form. 'Irreconcilable differences. But how will he behave? Comport himself?'

'Oh, I see what you mean. That depends on his state of mind. He was nearly violent the other day. Practically smashed my face in with a stool.'

Higgins thrust her jaw forward and eyes blinked faster, as if she and Jane were now sisters joined at the dhoti. 'Do we need a court injunction?'

'Gosh. I don't know. He never stuck a stool in anybody's face before. You see, he discovered me in a compromising situation with another man.'

'Oh, no, no, no,' the shaking bangles chastised. 'That attitude will not do! Anything more compromising than his living with the godmother of your only child? We find that ironic, no more. We must make it clear to him that he enjoys no rights under your roof. No rights at all. No, no, no. Also, I wouldn't encourage him to chauffeur Samantha any longer, if you want to press this point—'

Jane could only think of the night Sammie had deliberately binged on alcoholic pop drinks for attention, or the discovery Sammie was toying with bulimia and cutting her arms—all those times when Joe and she had forgotten their rift long enough to share the grief and worry of parents. She thought of the relief they exhaled together when Bella brought Sammie home. Joe would always be there for his daughter, no matter how deep his discomfort with Jane.

Jane also remembered the fleeting calm that swathed Number 19 as she listened to Joe spend the night in the locked bathroom, the obvious window of escape somehow ignored. Perhaps Joe wanted to be there for her, too, in some subconscious way.

'Mrs Higgins, I don't want to waste your time. Perhaps I'm here too soon. I'm not sure what I want. I was hoping that once I got into your office, I would harden up, feel pushed to cut the ties, barricade him out. Feel strong enough to—'

'Wipe the slate clean?'

'Yes. Muster my forces better. Well, at least keep him from coming to the house at all hours—'

'We can do that.' Higgins nodded her balloon of shining, lacquered hair.

'At least make it clear to him that if there's another baby, I mean, a child by Miss Crawford, that my own child's interests won't be hurt—'

'Yes, yes, an important point. We must spell it out. I'm afraid Samantha's situation is linked to the status of any other theoretical child, especially if your ex-partner marries Miss Crawford or adopts infants with or by her—'

'That's possible. She's been displaying weird Angelina Jolie fantasies lately. Well, what should I do?'

'Well, I can write Mr Gilchrist a letter: We propose adoption of Samantha, mindful of her interests as defined by the Children Act 1989, with its expressed support for shared residence and keeping in mind there might be future issue. In which case, her financial claims on Mr Gilchrist's estate should be formally established.'

Higgins widened her limpid brown eyes and cocked her head, a Bollywood Bambi with a steel trap mind.

'I thought you said she has no claims on his support.'

'That's between you and me. I won't spell out in writing that Joe has absolutely no legal obligation to offer financial support. Let his solicitor do his job. We stress our moral claims, of course. Joe might suddenly stumble on a huge pot of gold. His childless Canadian brother might divorce and make Joe heir to the family timber business.' The bangles rattled, but the diction was pure cut glass.

There were various fine points of the law to wrap up. The gleaming Higgins briefed Jane Gilchrist with a dispatch only softened by a patronizing gentleness—like a veteran aid worker in the Third World dispensing her legal remedies to an ignorant client lacking all feminine wile.

At last, Higgins reached the end of her checklist. She placed Jane's fresh dossier on the top of her pile and folded her hands as if to signal, another day, another European sister saved from the ashes of feminist folly. Sweeping layered metres of rustling pink, gold and peach silk around the corner of her desk, she escorted Jane back to the outer office.

'I'll send the letter right away. Neutral wording, nothing acrimonious,' Higgins assured her. 'If you might accept one comment. The man who can't stay away from a house where he's not wanted, and the woman who doesn't change the locks the very day after he leaves her, these two people just might love each other after all.'

'Take her advice, woman,' barked the elderly Higgins, carrying a battered teapot through the waiting room. 'My son didn't listen to her. Now she owns the whole partnership.' He held the heavy office door open for Jane and waved her off with the indifference of the truly aged.

Joe had asked Jane not to do anything rash, and she had asked him not to upset Sammie with public displays until after exams. Now she'd used Stratagem Twenty-eight on herself and rode alone into that mysterious land known as 'legal proceedings.'

Charred bamboo bridges that once linked her to Joe smouldered in her wake.

Chapter Twenty-nine, Tie Silk Blossoms to a Dead Tree

The first thing Jane did after the Higgins meeting was to change Number 19's front door lock, an antique that required the attention of a specialist in nineteenth century hardware.

'Easier just to swap the whole door for a new one,' the grizzled Mr Wardle sniffed. He jiggled the warped wood. 'I mean, whot's to keep me from doing this?' He kicked the 1860-circa antique planks hard with his boots. 'Or this,' he drove his screwdriver into the hairline fissure between the peeling frame and a bit of plaster patching up the old wall. He shrugged, 'I'm willin' to take it off your hands for nuthin.'

A greedy glint in Mr Wardle's eyes dodged Jane's glance. Was the old door worth more than firewood scrap? In the old days, a sturdy handyman might have given Joe sage advice at the kitchen table in exchange for a cup of tea. But Jane lived alone now and Mr Wardle seemed convinced that a woman alone in the square was either a celebrity or divorcee with money to burn. Jane knocked down his original estimate by twenty per cent and saw off the disgruntled Wardle with honeyed thanks and private relief she still had any doors to lock behind him.

That Thursday afternoon, as a matter of course, she carried up a new spare key along with the tomato soup and Wisconsin cheese on Lorraine's tray. Her mother's A *Little Night Music* DVD blared through her front door. Balancing the tray in her arms there on the landing, Jane was about to give a loud knock when a devilish thought popped into her head. For a second, she almost held the wicked proposal back from herself. Then she let the possibility swim around for a second—do a lazy breaststroke, not exactly a determined crawl.

Still, *why not?* There would be consequences, but how bad? When and how Lorraine discovered she couldn't swan in and out of Jane's flat without first ringing down, she might take it hard, throw a wobbly, do a bit of Amanda Wingfield from *The Glass*

Menagerie or even channel some maternal harridan from Eugene O'Neill.

Yet, why should everyone have access to Jane's home? Why had it always been a given that she knocked on her mother's door, but the daughter got no privacy?

In the end, Lorraine didn't answer the door and Jane found her snoring in her sagging chintz chair near the dormer window seat, her face unguarded. Almost motherly. On the television screen, Diana Rigg was spitting out the cynical Sondheim's 'Everyday a Little Death,' 'Love's disgusting, love's insane . . .'

Jane switched off Diana. She deposited the tray on a footstool and laid Mr Wardle's shiny key next to the crackers. Then she pocketed the key again. If anyone needed it, it was Sammie.

Downstairs, she stretched out on the sofa, just as Joe used to do time and again, and watched the dull grey clouds skitter beyond the tops of the shivering plane trees under a late and indecisive January sky.

It was an ideal time to catch up with her research for Camille— plans by Google, Microsoft, and Amazon to scan millions of books on to the web. She reread her notes for coming interviews with the New York Public Library, Carnegie Mellon's Million Book Project, Tufts University's Perseus Press specializing in Greek and Latin text, the Alexander Street Press digitizing the letters and diaries of American immigrants, the University of Michigan's controversial Hathi Trust, the Library of Congress, the British Library. . .

Could the digitizing of human knowledge be the most profound cultural event since the invention of the printing press? Could it democratize the third century BC Alexandrian ambition of collecting all the world's knowledge in one place? If you believed London *Times*, this rampant revitalization of millions of forgotten volumes would 'encourage more people to go in search of the real thing.'

On the other hand, *The New York Times* sounded a gloomy death knell, 'The end of the book as we know it.'

Where should their new programme put its sympathies? With the Kindle or valuable leather volumes collecting dust? Jane didn't want the end of the book as she knew it but she liked this dream of books reaching everyone—not just people who could visit libraries or afford Waterstones. Was it a librarian's utopia or nightmare—if all texts, past and present, multilingual, on any subject, were viewable? At long last, there could be a universal archive, the cosmic library.

Jane shivered. Who would curl up by the fire with Holmes, Moriarty, and a glass of sherry? Who would forget to set the table because Wonderland was more wonderful? Was it up to the quaking librarians to lead the charge headlong into the infotopia battle to help readers simply survive?

She wrapped her imagination around the library of the future. How could they present these arguments on screen? The project absorbed her for hours. The muffled roar of traffic off Regent's Park Road mixed with the happy shrieks of children braving the chill outside. Ten years ago, the noisemakers had included Sammie, a red-cheeked urchin child rushing up the stairs for dinner in an animal gust. Jane's ears used to comb through that traffic noise for the churn of one special engine into the square signalling Joe's return.

Now all the hubbub had subsided into a neutral hum. The new lock was in place—barricading her from possessive Joe, her intrusive mother and even Dan's distracting interruptions. This unfamiliar solitude felt like safety, not loneliness.

The trees' pointed black claws scraped at the fading light. Would they ever sprout tiny nubs of brown, then little hooks of green, and at last, whole gloves of leaves, then puffed sleeves of foliage? Her face upturned to the graceful windows framing the falling dusk, Jane wondered: were things grinding to a halt for her, in some irrecoverable way? It wasn't a question of ageing—even Lorraine had booked herself for one last performance.

'. . . Attach lifelike silk blossoms to a dead tree. All but the most discerning will assume your tree is capable of bearing flowers,' Baldwin instructed them the following evening. He wagged a long finger, 'Don't even ask, Kevin! It's come down to us through the ages, and I'm sure that at some point, during some dynasty, somebody tied silk blossoms to a tree. Yes, Nigel? Your quibble *du soir*?'

'Boosting your strength by resorting to outside forces, yet again. Twenty-nine is so similar to killing with a borrowed knife.'

'Both stratagems, Nigel, demonstrate the East's preference for indirect action over direct confrontation. But they aren't the same, if you study the extended uses. Killing with a borrowed knife is considered one of the Concealment strategies, while Twenty-nine is a Simulation ploy. In other words, you use something at hand, yes, it might be an ally, Nigel, or it might be quite neutral—the weather. Twenty-nine aims at getting your enemy to believe something that isn't true. Maximize tiny resources into gigantic weapons.'

Winston started to raise his hand, but Baldwin cut him off, 'Bear with me, young Chu. The ancient sources mean we flaunt strength or potential we don't possess and thus delay the enemy's attack. I might splash water on the ground to freeze into ice under the feet of enemy troops. Or train monkeys to surprise the opponent's camp. Or a personal favourite, make ghosts appear or people vanish.'

'Make people vanish,' Winston dutifully noted. 'No problem.'

'Through the use of artifice or disguise, make something of no value appear valuable.' Baldwin smiled down at Jane. 'Make something of no use seem useful or someone of no threat appear dangerous.'

Nigel ventured, 'Like those fellows who invite potential clients to expensive restaurants they've already checked out. They've learned the waiters' names or met the chef ahead of time so they can impress gullible clients.'

'Yes, Nigel! That's the idea!'

Kevin joined in, 'Oh, this bloke I know claims to be all matey with Jamie Oliver . . .'

Jane doodled the bare branches of a wintry tree on her notebook. She added little flowers, one by one. She felt sheltered by Dan's energy. Overall, she felt better because of Dan. She even felt slimmer. Nonetheless, this fling might be a fake flower only useful to wave under Joe's nose. Once Gilbert the informer had helped Dan to save the unwitting New Jersey Javed and round up the bookstore's hapless band, Dan's time in London might be up.

He would be gentle about it, but sooner or later, Dan would go home.

What if he asked her to go with him?

Baldwin's brow shone with the tale of a besieged city during the Warring States Period: 'Tian Dan distributed the last food to his troops and prepared for the final showdown.'

'The final showdown? That bloke's premiums just shot up,' Keith quipped.

'Oh, Tian Dan wasn't waiting for any insurance adjustors, Keith. He rounded up all the bulls inside the city walls and ordered them draped in purple silk and fastened daggers to their horns. The troops painted the bulls' faces fantastic colours and bound oil-soaked reeds to their tails. Then they waited for night to fall. When the complacent men of Yan were fast asleep in their camp, Tian Dan gave the command to set fire to the reeds. Tails aflame, the bulls panicked as one wild beast, thundering and roaring through breaches cut through the city walls. The maddened herd ran towards the enemy—'

Kevin chortled: 'Who laughed to see a bunch of cows in Guy Fawkes gear running towards them?'

'No, Mr Filgrove,' Baldwin corrected him dryly, 'On one of the blackest nights in fourth century BC China, the troops of Yan woke up to a deafening roar breaking through the walls of Jimo, a city they had pulled to its knees, the last holdout of the state of Qi. Victory had been in sight. Soon, they'd be going home. And what did they see now, beyond the smouldering embers of their campfire? An army of flying dragons with livid faces in five colours, their hideous raiment from the underworld whipping around their red-hot blades. The people of Jimo had recruited an army of vengeful demons exploding out of their besieged city to trample the sleeping men of Yan. Which is exactly what happened.'

'Blimey!' Kevin shook his head.

Nigel scoffed, 'You don't actually believe these fairy tales, do you, Professor Baldwin? They're just folk myths, like Excalibur or the Round Table, aren't they?'

Baldwin scowled. 'I'm not teaching theology or mythology. These are the accounts found in the *Record of the Warring States*, a history compiled early in the Han Dynasty.' Baldwin's tone implied that the events that fiery night in Jimo were as precise and no less painful than his last dental appointment.

Nigel wasn't backing down: 'That makes them reliable?'

Baldwin's usual patience gave way. 'Yes, Nigel. We don't have time in this course to cover the whole range of Chinese strategic writing. In addition to Sun Tzu's *Art of War*, there is also Jiang Ziya's *Six Secret Teachings*, *The Methods of the Ssu-ma*, Wu Qi's *Wu-Tzu*, Wei Liaozi, *The Three Strategies of Huang Shigong*, and *The Questions and Replies* of Tang Taizong and Li Weikung, the last being written more or less eight centuries after the end of the Warring States. More than twenty-three hundred titles of military writing from ancient China have survived. Perhaps you'd like to dismiss them all as fairy tales, Mr Deloitte?'

'Sorry.'

Dan and Jane sneaked off at the break. They cut the rest of Baldwin's class to have dinner together, happy truants celebrating the eve of her birthday. She knew, even if he didn't, that an appearance at Odette's was more than a healthy step, it was a statement. This romantic spot, with its mirrored walls was not only a popular haunt for illicit lovers, but also Joe's favourite neighbourhood eatery. A very satisfying fuss was made at her appearance in the dining room. The waiter who served her Grand Marnier soufflé lit up with a lilac birthday candle treated Dan like a Primrose Hill regular.

One diner stared, mouth agape, across the room like a beet-faced puffer fish. An awkward wave of a pale hand revealed it to be Bella's PA Rachel Murty, enjoying a date, if she could enjoy anything at all in her current condition. She was suffering from a sunburn that left two white sunglass shapes around her washed-out grey eyes.

Jane resolved that Rachel would not cramp her evening. Dan and she were going public. If that public included a direct hot line to Joe and Bella, so be it. She hadn't spoken to Rachel since their Greek lunch last November.

Jane reached across the table, took Dan's large hand in her own, lifted her chin, and smiled adoration. It was easier than she thought and the meal proceeded like one of those dream dates Sammie talked of having any day now. Champagne, *chèvre chaud*, turbot in white wine sauce, and white chocolate *soufflé*.

Rachel stared and stared. Clearly, Puffer Fish Murty wasn't going to let it rest. While Dan settled the bill, Jane headed off to the Ladies'. She heard Rachel's clopping footsteps dogging her down the wooden stairs.

'Jane, is that you?' She pressed her nose against a toilet door hinge and peered right into Jane's cubicle. 'Who's the hunk?'

'Rachel, you must be drunk. May I please pee in peace?'

'Jane! Do me a favour? I'm having an awful evening. Can you two join us? You know how they say they're either married or gay? Well, I'm stuck with one who turns out to be married *and* gay. He wants me to take him dancing at the Trojka.'

'So, go. Ring me next week.'

'Please, Jane.'

Jane emerged from the cubicle, and stared at Rachel's feet.

'What are those?'

'Shoots. Half boots, half shoes. They don't fit.'

'What have you done to your face? Haven't you heard of sunscreen?'

'They took my fifty off me at Luton security. Tossed it in the bin. My only week off in six months and after one afternoon, I ended up in Emergency. Take it from me, Jane, there are certain resorts in this world where you should avoid Emergency. I saw things that still haunt me in the dead of night. Next time, I'll say, no thank you, I prefer to die right here from my third-degree sunburn with Room Service.'

'Well, get well.' Jane brushed Rachel's burning cheek and made for the door, but Rachel grabbed her arm.

'Is that the guy Sammie told Bella about? And Bella told Joe? The antiterrorist expert?'

Jane slowed. 'What were they saying?'

'You really want to hear?'

'I'm not sure.'

'Well, they had a flaming row in Editing. Bella told Joe to calm down, why should it worry him? She was getting shirty that he was so fussed about it. Aren't men unbelievable? Masters of the Double Standard. I didn't hear the rest of the fight 'cause they went off to lunch still going at each other, but judging by their conversation, Joe's knickers were in a twist. Bella came back all red-eyed from crying.'

'Good.'

'Well, no, not about, well, yes, that too, but Joe was mostly afraid you might run off to the States with this guy. Move away. Take Sammie with you. Have this American's baby.'

'Sammie?'

'No, you, of course. Joe was thinking you might want more family.'

Was he indeed?'

'Of course, Bella told him bollocks. You couldn't be serious. Not with Lorraine and Sammie to take care of.' Her boiled-egg eyeballs widened. 'Is it serious?'

Jane knew it wasn't. Of course she wouldn't. Jane hadn't even thought about having another baby, ever. She wasn't even sure she could. She was probably like those bare wintry trees in Chalkwood Square just scraping for a little happiness against a dusky sky.

Of course, it was the last thing she would admit to Rachel, teetering with one unsteady hand on the washbasin.

'My plans are nobody's business,' Jane said with dignity. Of course, the solicitor Higgins's letter was vague, but not opaque. Joe had no formal custody responsibilities, but enjoyed no rights, either. Jane could take Sammie away from England forever. With these racing thoughts, Jane fixed a gaudy silk blossom to a branch of her barren reality, then added another, and yet another. Maybe there was still time to have another child. A whole football team. Let that image gum up the works of Bella's ticking biological clock!

Within seconds, she'd fashioned a whole arbour of ridiculous possibilities to her future. She had no intention of letting Rachel know it was just a feint.

Rachel lurched against the mirror, hoping for yet more juicy news. Jane steadied the girl, and beamed a smile of fertile potentiality. Two glasses of birthday bubbly fizzed through her imagination and within seconds, Jane mustered a girlish blush.

'Who's to say? Sammie would love a little brother. According to Yogi Berra, it ain't over 'til it's over.' She shrugged. 'I am tired of London, it's true. As for Lorraine, she misses New York so much, Rachel.'

Rachel clung to the cubicle door, whether dizzy from sunburn, booze, or Jane's astonishing manner, who could tell?

'You know, just chatting to Dan brings back all those happy times when my mother was playing off-Broadway.' Why tell Rachel those were the unhappiest years of Jane's life?

'Guh-awd,' Rachel said. 'So Bella's wrong?' She stuttered, 'I mean, oh, Jane, you aren't preggers already, are you?'

Jane feigned embarrassment. 'Oh, no. At least I don't think so. Sorry, we can't join you, darling. Skip the Trojka and go home to bed. Try some aloe vera on that burn.'

'Oh my God,' Rachel gasped. 'Joe's gonna freak.' She sank down to the cool moist tiles and collapsed against the wall, stared up at Jane. 'If Joe freaks, Bella will panic. If Bella panics, my life is going to be one fresh hell, for weeks and weeks.'

'You don't have to tell Joe anything that isn't true,' Jane said, salving her own conscience and lifting Rachel to her feet.

'It's no good asking me to keep secrets,' Rachel moaned. 'Bella will just put my feet to the fire if she hears I bumped into you.'

'Don't worry, Rachel. Bella and I are having lunch soon. And I'll tell her all about it.'

She left Rachel wobbling her way back from the Ladies' room and watched to make sure she didn't tumble over and break her neck. Rachel was already fumbling in her handbag and pulling out her mobile.

Was it the magic of Strategy Twenty-nine or just humdrum human nature? Whatever it was, Baldwin was right yet again. You could dress up a barren tree with silk flowers, especially if your target was too sozzled to see straight. At long last, Jane suddenly felt she herself stood on higher ground, even though the view of the valley below had misted over.

Chapter Thirty, Reverse the Positions of Host and Guest

Despite everything, Bella's plea 'to chat' had meant that their traditional birthday lunch date stuck to Jane's calendar—rather like a blob of stew frozen for months to the innards of the fridge. Harvey Nichols' fifth-floor dining room remained the appointed field of engagement.

Reassuring Bella by e-mail that there was no reason whatsoever to cancel their biannual fête, Jane insisted she was looking forward to it.

Bella parried with a warning she was coming down with Brisbane flu but Jane persisted; she even had a favour to ask. She booked the table herself for a duel waged over lettuce leaves, sun-dried tomatoes, and fat-free desserts.

Dan fortified the start of her birthday with a coffee served bedside. She hadn't felt so physically spoiled in ages. There was a great deal for Jane to catch up on, sexually speaking. Perhaps if Dan stayed in her bed more, she'd miss Joe less. Not that Dan lacked for enthusiasm or interesting little ways, but still, even washed-out and washed-up, Joe remained her sexual habit. Was she hard-wired to Joe for life? For the moment, it came down to the difference between a new partner and beloved missing mate.

Sipping the frothy brew, she was tempted to stay home and give the sexual purging of Joe more of a concentrated effort. Really put her back into it, so to speak. She glanced at the time. She could still ring and leave Bella a get-well message, (after all, cordiality could be cruel, Jane thought, mindful of Caroline Darcy's icy pen) to the effect that she was tied up with library headaches. Theoretically, Jane could cancel Bella for lunch again and again—if not for life. Would dodging their encounter signal cringing defeat or victorious indifference?

Her telephone interrupted this strategic meditation. 'Happy Birthday, Jane. I hope I'm the first to remember.'

If Rachel had gabbed, Joe probably suspected Dan was on birthday duty ahead of him. News about Dan crossed London faster than the Eurostar ploughing into St Pancras. There really was no underestimating the toxic uses of 'well-intentioned' onlookers.

'Oh, no, I'm well into forty-three already.' Dan was half-listening, circling the bed, his electric shaver mowing up and down his jaw.

'Oh. Is that James Bond I hear in the background? Listen, I just wanted to offer my happy wishes for the day.'

'Thanks. You know I'm enjoying a midday meal with Bella?'

Joe protested, 'She promised me that was off! I told you already, there's no need to expose yourself.'

'Don't worry, we're not going to claw like cats.'

'I'm hardly worth fighting over.'

'And I'm not afraid of her.'

'No, it's just I wouldn't want to see her try to—I mean, she can be pretty—I mean, I just don't want to see you—'

'Joe. I *know* Bella and I'm no saint. For Sammie's sake, I'm determined to make the best of this situation.'

Joe's voice lowered. 'I'm sure you are, Jane, and I'm grateful, but Bella's a little high-strung since the street fair, you know, Sammie and her explosions. I'm caught in the middle—day and night. *The Travelling Kitchen* set is hell. The flat is hell.'

Jane gave a cold chuckle, indifferent to updates from Hades. 'Well, everything's fine at this end. How are things going with your own work?'

'The budget's cut, again, all the money is going to digital for Poland, France, Germany. Sorry, I shouldn't bore you, not on your birthday.'

'And high definition for Japan, South Korea, Mars and Venus . . .'

'How do you know all that?'

'Haven't you heard? I'm Camille Harper's researcher now. She bent my ear off about it last Wednesday.' Jane struggled to keep her tone breezy.

'Well, I have no right to expect you to make this easier by meeting Bella and I am really grateful. I hope you've got something nice on for this evening.'

'Just Lorraine and Sammie. At forty-three, why not?'

Joe turned a little indignant. 'Why not? Because Lorraine hasn't remembered your birthday in the last ten years. Sammie's idea of a present is some White Stripes CD. It was always me who reminded them. Why not? Because you've spent the last six months planning Lorraine's Big Eighty party? Have the final invitations gone out?'

'Oh, yes. Lots of acceptances.'

'Sir Brian?'

'Still working on him.' In fact, Sir Brian MacKelling's people had never come back to Jane's people. Ever since Lorraine had scribbled Sir Brian with that childish longing in her eyes, Jane had pestered production companies, agents, and personal assistants and finally schlepped to Sir Brian's fabled Limehouse hideaway. She left an invitation, one of Winston's gold-edged stiff cards, already wilting in the murky fog of the river when Sir Brian's neighbour leaned out of a window and told her, 'He's on a shoot. Won't be back for donkey's years.'

Dan had finished shaving and was giving her a shoulder massage. She wished Joe could view that in close-up. 'Of course, Bella's catering is no longer required.'

'I think she guessed that. Uh, I didn't get an invitation. I assume that means I'm also scratched off the list.'

'It's Lorraine's party. She'll have you if Sammie insists.'

'Um, Jane, I got a letter from a solicitor—does this mean I won't see Lorraine any longer?'

'Well, you could take her out. She always loved your walks up the hill.'

'I miss those walks.'

'I was never sure how much walking you two managed. Lorraine never gave me details on how much time you spent braving the elements, and how much in the pub.'

'I miss the Queen's.'

There was a very long silence.

Through that heavy space, Joe expressed more than he had in months. Physically brave and always talented when working with visuals, Joe's clumsiness with words had trained Jane to listen hard to his pauses.

Finally, she said, 'I have to go to work, now, Joe. Thanks for calling.'

She'd expected to feel more anger inside and hear more defensiveness from Joe. There were provocative things in that Higgins parchment, like the cold suggestion he needed to formally adopt Sammie. Even from Bella's, he'd stayed as caring a father as he'd been in the square.

She bundled Dan off with a kiss and sped to the library for an emergency morning meeting of the Bookworms. The gloom of the noose hung over their desultory treatment of Julian Barnes. At last, Rupert touched on the dreaded subject: 'The problem is that we don't count. We're invisible. We're old.'

Ruth Wilting said, 'The newspapers always discuss what the young are reading. We're like guests that overstayed—'

'The aunties nobody wants at the wedding reception,' nodded Alma.

Jane cut off their droning. 'In my Chinese philosophy class we've been studying a strategy, reverse the position of guest with host. Supposing . . .'

Rupert rose a little from his seat: 'We don't stay readers on the sidelines? We become arbiters of taste instead?'

'As if anyone listens to me,' Carla said.

Rupert persisted: 'Carla, you poopoo'ed us out of reading the Bad Sex list, but that contest got oodles of publicity.'

'Sorry, Rupert, I don't quite follow.' Jane glanced at her watch. Less than two hours before lunch with Bella.

'Is Rupert babbling about sex again?' Catherine looked up from a doze.

'Yes,' Alma crooned.

'Turn your hearing aid back on!' Carla belted into Catherine's ear.

'Jane, you said the Bookworms needed to show they were worth preserving.' Rupert looked around. 'Suppose we sponsor a contest for senior writers?'

'To write about sex?' Alma scattered biscuit crumbs all over *The Sense of an Ending*.

'He means old people writing short stories about arthritis and Alzheimer's,' Carla scoffed.

'"To write about life with wisdom.' Jane followed Rupert's drift. '*Rem acu tetigisti* as Jeeves would say. You hit the proverbial nail.'

'Jane will judge the entries?' Ruth asked.

'No, you'll judge,' Jane insisted. 'That way, you'll stop being library consumers competing with teen-agers for budget money. You become library promoters, hosts instead of guests. Rupert, could you be the contest's public face?'

Alma nodded. 'Such a nice face.'

Carla looked crestfallen.

Jane would alert the Camden authorities and Rupert would produce a press release.

Jane suddenly realized, 'It won't work, Rupert. The budget meeting is in two weeks. There's no time to get the word out, draw in submissions, just not nearly enough time to run a competition.'

Alma said, '"We'd need a pile of entries in front of us right this very minute so we could announce the prize by next week.'

They sat in doleful silence. A couple of motorbikes gunned their engines outside.

'But we have a pile of entries!' Jane bolted to the back of the stockroom. 'Yes, here they are! Short stories from last year's workshop, "Pensioners' Prose." Chris said everybody there was an absolute Methuselah! We can start with these. Next year, we'll have time for proper submissions.'

She riffled through the sheets, counting, 'We've got at least eight here.'

'Our instant shortlist!' Rupert took them from Jane. 'We'll pass them around as we finish. You're sure these people are still alive? My goodness, "by Leon Trotsky"?'

'Well, Chris insisted on pen names to make the critiquing less painful,' Jane explained. 'Everybody knew who Trotsky was.' The cantankerous Mr Slobotsky had stormed out the door when Chris deemed the work of L. Trotsky 'Derivative Isaac Singer.'

'We've forgotten the prize,' Ruth said, her hands trembling. 'Will there be a prize?'

'A date with Rupert?' Alma tittered.

Rupert was almost as quick: 'No! Dinner for the winner, with all of us, of course, and Mariella Frostrup, and . . . an author. An old author. Could we get P.D. James?'

'John Mortimer!' Alma sighed. 'Oh, sorry. Too late.'

'All right.' Rupert cleared his throat, 'I propose Jane locate a famous old author who's still with us, and Carla, you invite Ms Frostrup? I'll work up some publicity and pay for the meal.'

'Claridges?' Ruth rhapsodized.

'No, Mrs Wilting,' Rupert said. 'The Ivy. After all, we want to be seen.'

Alma twitched her head like a robin. 'What'll we call our prize?'

If you can bear to be a little un-British, why not the Robert Frost Prize?' Jane suggested. 'He kept going 'til ninety or thereabouts.'

'Brilliant!' Rupert crowed. 'My dear ladies, we are about to award the world's newest literary plum, The FROSTY!'

Jane rushed back home to change. After five long months, she braced herself to face that estrogen-peachy complexion, those silicone-coated curls and famously boosted bosom. The warrior librarian arrayed her weaponry on the still-rumpled bed—a cross-your-heart silken T-shirt, trendy trousers, and a handbag so studded and bolted and nailed, so bloated with evil power, it looked like something Lady Macbeth stuffed with her used daggers.

Jane rinsed out her grey roots in twenty gooey minutes and then fired up Sammie's mysterious hair appliance. After a few false starts, the contraption coaxed Jane's mop into a sleek and shining curtain. That left only minutes for make-up, a slash of blood-red lips that looked ready to sink her teeth into Bella's neck. She pulled

322

on new boots with heels as high as an unabridged Roget's Thesaurus.

In the full-length mirror, there stood a mini-Amazon. The preposterous platform soles raised her more than three inches and the trousers draped like a dream. She must have lost weight. With Sammie gone half the week, she was living mostly on Lorraine's menu of Ritz crackers and Cheesewhip.

The cab moved almost too fast southwards and she found herself, as gorgeous and composed as the forty-three-year-old Jane would ever be, seated on Harvey Nichols' white upholstery. She braced herself for Bella's grand entrance, the *mwa, mwa* on both cheeks, before a full house.

But oddly Bella was not tardy. Jane watched the familiar hourglass figure hover and weave around the entrance, quickly check the bar, her sunglasses moving from side to side as she scanned the social lawn for potholes. She couldn't locate Jane at first. From behind her Jackie O Bug-Frames, her glance skimmed right over Jane's head, like one of those Nazi camp searchlights that just misses the hero digging under the barbed wire. A perplexed frown struggled to register on the Botox-ed brow. The horrible possibility penetrated her Celebrity Lizard brain that she, Bella Crawford, might have to wait, in public, for someone else.

Jane saved her with a royal wave. Bella hurtled across the room: 'Why, Jane, I didn't quite recognize you. It must be the hair or—'

'Relax, Bella. It's my birthday and I'm the one who's ageing, not you!'

Actually, Bella looked like she'd swallowed a sponge. Was it the reported flu bug or the translucent blue-lit ceiling casting her complexion into such puffy paleness?

'Just saw my skin man. I'll be a bit swollen for a few days.' They got through the air kissing, the soft press of the PETA-approved-fur biker-jacket, 'I think he might have injected too much. I have a searing headache and I feel a bit faint. I skipped breakfast because of this awful flu.'

'Bella, please relax. Everyone's staring at us. I'd forgotten what it was like, eating with you. Here's a menu to hide behind.'

'Thanks.' Bella received these unexpectedly kind words with a wary half-smile.

'I've ordered some bubbly. We'll just flush away the whole last year. And I'm going to have the snails in garlic butter and then the spinach soufflé. I just can't seem to keep the weight on.'

Bella blanched.

'I know, the camera adds a stone. Try the diet specials, down there.'

'I can't read this. I'm so dizzy. Maybe I am a little feverish. There's a norovirus going around.' Bella decided on bouillon and the Slimmer Salad. 'Oh, Jane, you're a darling to meet me like this to really talk. I have so many feelings I've wanted to express, but you know how I am about putting things on paper—'

'Totally dyslexic.'

'Well, it's just so hard to put things into words, and I know it's feeble to say this—such a cliché, really—but I never wanted to hurt *you*.'

'I know. To me,' Jane raised her glass and took a sip. She sank contentedly into the deep chair.

'Oh, yes, to you. Happy Birthday.' Bella downed the entire flute and coughed. She peered from under her sunglasses for a moment and said, 'I must say, you are looking slim.'

'Let's talk about Sammie.' Jane refilled Bella's wine glass.

'Oh, yes, let's. It's been hard for her, but I do think her doctor's helping. No more—' The suggestion made Bella gulp.

'And she's been difficult.' Jane sighed, 'I'm really sorry about the street fair. If you will put her on camera, be prepared for her to steal the scene. Girls that age just crave attention and she does take after Lorraine. Centre stage, etc, etc. Ready to order?'

The hovering waiter stared down at Bella, which made it all right for Jane to stare too. One of Bella's eyelids hung slack under a welter of inflamed needle pricks.

'Now, Bella, this favour I want to ask of you—'

'Yes, of course, what can I do, darling? You can ask me anything, anything.'

'I was wondering, could Joe and you take Sammie for the summer?'

Bella's working eyelid fluttered. 'June or July?'

'No, no, I can't be that selfish. The entire summer. June to, let's say, mid-October?'

'That's the favour?'

'Um, um,' Jane dug out a glistening snail and slurped up the garlic butter. She cut off Bella's panicked protests with exaggerated relief, 'Thanks, I'm so very grateful. I must get away. It would be so much better for all of us, don't you think? Especially Joe, given his feelings.'

'What feelings?'

'And for my project for Camille Harper—you've heard about that from Joe I expect? Oh, maybe not. I have to interview the big libraries in the States, Silicon Valley, Bill Gates up in Seattle—'

'You'll be gone for so long? Does Sammie go to summer camp? Or anything?'

Jane nodded, 'No, she'll holiday with you two, of course. What can I do, but turn to you? Lorraine isn't well enough to cope full-time. Someone has to supervise Sammie's revision for the exams she has to retake and Joe is hopeless at homework. You know what he learned in high school—hockey, beaver-skinning, maple-tapping—but you went through the British system—so no problem!' Jane confided, 'And I need time off.' She placed her plump hand on Bella's manicured claws. 'Woman to woman, I know you understand.'

'The whole summer?' Bella grimaced.

'It'll give you time to make up to Sammie for all this upset. Sorry, would you like a snail?'

'God, no.' Bella turned puce underneath her Jo Malone face powder. Perhaps the flu wasn't a fib. 'Jane, I know it's none of my business, but is there any other reason you might be leaving London?'

'Who's leaving London? It's only a long recce.'

'I mean, I know it's been hard for you, what with Joe and me, but is there any other reason?' Bella's hands shook.

'Oh, you mean Dan?' Jane curled her shoulders up to her earrings with the frisson of just thinking about Dan. She closed her eyes and sighed. She sucked on another snail. Bella leaned forward, her moulded tablespoon of cottage cheese untouched in its monastic nest of wilting lamb's lettuce.

Jane experimented with a lusty wink, although it wasn't very practiced. 'Really, Bella, I ought to thank you.' At the sight of Jane's greasy gastropodes, Bella swayed a little and closed her eyes but Jane wouldn't let up. *Thank you, Professor Baldwin.* She felt her attack gaining ground, her simulation leading to confusion, her disclosures and feints to the East and West working away at the overconfident star. Bella had assumed she would play hostess to Jane's submission but she found herself the guest at Jane's celebration.

'Let's drink to Dan.' Jane refilled Bella's wineglass. 'Wow, Dan . . . Bella, you have no idea.'

'I suppose I haven't,' Bella managed through her puffed-up duck lips.

'Things are so different with Dan but,' Jane turned demure, 'It's hard to explain. Anyway, Bella, don't worry about me.'

The snails lasted long enough to put Bella in the frame, so to speak, the portrait of Dan being a paragon of manly mind, muscle, and meaningful massages. Jane found this easy going since Joe's roaring jealousy had laid the ground, smoothed the tarmac, and readied the runway. She hinted at Dan's physical courage, his selfless generosity, and without going into details, well, Bella could guess the rest. Oh, yes, he always put the toilet seat down, never failed to load the dishwasher with the glasses standing the right way, and never, ever took a mobile call during a meal only to leave Jane staring off into the distance, waiting for him to finish—three of Joe's frequent venial sins.

Bella bore the stoic smile of someone suddenly stuck with librarian Jane's romantic leftovers.

Jane's soufflé landed on the table next, a vivid Martian green reeking of spinach, Parmigiano, and truffle oil. Bella was turning a strange green herself.

'Now, bring me up to date. I don't hear a word. How's the show's chef line-up? Lots of new cuisines? Still planning to save the world?'

Bella stabbed at her low-fat curd, but missed. 'Tibet fell through for reasons obvious. And as far as diseases go, it appears that even spleens in Sussex can do without me.' She gulped her champagne. She looked hot and dehydrated.

'Well, what do we need spleens for, except to vent them? I'm sure some disease will turn up. Have you tried flesh-eating bacteria? MRSA? That obesity virus's very trendy. Wuff, I'm so hungry, it's like I'm eating for two. I think I'll have some of that treacle tart.' She waved for the dessert trolley. 'Want to share?'

Bella glanced at her salad and said, 'No, I'm a bit off my feed.'

'And to think I had such a huge breakfast,' Jane smiled, 'But then Dan is a very energetic man. He needs a big meal to start the day. I do want to see how he lives at home. I expect we'll spend some time together while I'm in the States.'

There was a long pause. Bella's eyes drifted from side to side. She rested both hands on her temples to steady herself.

'Are you sure you'll come back?'

Jane refilled Bella's glass and said, 'Oh, well, I don't want to get ahead of myself.'

'Would you leave Sammie with Joe? I mean, with us? I thought he was worried that you might not let him see Sammie at all? Or he had to adopt her, or something, or, or . . . I'm really confused, Jane—' Bella choked on a carrot slice. Jane gave Bella a helpful thump on the back as the sad little salad was escorted off in disgrace by two waiters, their heads bent in horrified consultation.

'Well, it's good to get things straight, first. The flats, for one thing. Years ago, we transferred the two floors to Lorraine's name when she guaranteed the mortgage. Not that there's anything wrong with Joe's finances,' Jane admitted, and then glanced with solicitous worry at Bella's reddening face. 'Unless you're expecting too much? I wouldn't expect too much from him in any way. Oh, by the way, tell Joe his doctor's assistant rang—he missed his last check-up. He really shouldn't miss those.'

Bella gagged.

'I mean, I don't know what you're expecting. Don't press Joe on the subject of children—I mean it's obvious he doesn't want to lose you. And you'll always have Sammie. Although,' Jane noisily scraped up the remaining bits of soufflé with zest, 'I might take Sammie to the States, if I decide to move for good. But then Joe wouldn't see her at all. That isn't fair to you two, is it, considering—?'

Bella's eyes flickered, 'I don't quite follow—'

'I know!' Jane exclaimed, 'You take Sammie through the whole school year too, so she doesn't miss out. I'll be so busy from now on, don't you think that's for the best?'

Bella looked desperate for an oxygen mask. 'For the best?'

Jane shook her head with tremendous sympathy, 'Your only chance at motherhood, Bella. How could I deny you?'

'What do you mean? Has Joe had an operation or something I don't know about—?'

'Well, Sammie was a bit of an accident but such a lucky one, in retrospect. Gosh, you look faint. Waiter, a glass of water, please? Here Bella, drink this,' and Jane forced Bella's purple face back against the booth and poured half a litre of ice water down her gullet.

Bella started choking. Jane walloped her again, with the affection of a prison matron.

Warrior Jane was fast running out of thrusts to aim at Bella's bosom but her luck held. Just then a waiter sallied forth from the kitchen, booming out 'Happy Birthday' in his best audition baritone. He plunked a thickly iced chocolate cake in front of Bella. Diners across the room rose to their feet and belted out, 'Happy Birthday, To You.'

Bella shrieked, 'No, NO,' but Jane laughed off the error and laid the sputtering pink candle, melting wax, chocolate icing and all, on Bella's lambskin clutch. She picked up the check.

'No, no,' Bella gasped, 'It's your birthday. Really—I—'

'No, no, I ate twice as much! You're my guest, darling!' Jane shouted over the song.

Bella swatted at the candle scorching her bag. Jane grabbed her arm in a confiding gesture. 'You know, it's possible that this year, all my wishes might come true.'

Bella's nodding had turned into an alarming roll of the head, now a dip, and a deep gulp for breath. She was losing her struggle waged through a Botox migraine, a soaring temperature, garlic butter fumes, and cocktail of ice water mixed with *spumante*.

The crowd ascended to, 'Hap-py Birth-day Dear BEL-LA!' Her eyes rolled upwards to globes of white. Jane moved her new boots delicately out of Bella's way, for with a desperate swoop away from the table, London's most famous mistress of the soup pot returned her cottage cheese to Harvey Nichols in one ignominious go.

Chapter Thirty-one, The Beautiful Woman Trap

'Perk up, Chu the Younger! We've reached the final six strategies.'

'Why should I perk up? Your handout calls them the Desperation Strategies. I feel desperate, right?'

Baldwin rubbed his hands together, 'Are you all feeling desperate tonight? Not quite? Well, they can be also be tagged as the "self-protection," even "escape" tactics.'

He looked at Jane. 'You're looking very lovely tonight, Ms Gilchrist.'

'Thank you, professor, but if it's not Jane, I'd prefer Ms King from now on. My maiden name. I suppose everybody knows by now that my partner and I separated some time ago.'

They did indeed know. 'He left you for that cookery slag who threw up in Knightsbridge last weekend, right?' Keith asked. 'Euw, did you see her photo in the Mail? Somebody caught it on his mobile before they cleaned her up.'

'Fine Jane, Ms King it is, and just as lovely by any other name. And how appropriate, because tonight we study *Mei Ren Ji*, Number Thirty-one, the use of a beautiful woman to ensnare a man.'

'Hang on,' Winston interjected. 'Why doesn't Thirty-one have a four-character saying like the others? You know, something like, Touch Lotus, Eat Death.'

Keith agreed, 'Pretty Girl Trick just sounds naff. How'bout Lose the Race to Lovely Face?'

'Or, Taste Sweet Flower, Downfall Sour?' Kevin guffawed.

Winston cheered up: 'Share Her Bed, Wake Up Dead! C'mon, Nigel, you try one. Forsake Stamp Duty, Merge with Beauty?'

'Clearly, you've all got the idea,' Baldwin brought them to order. 'Now, I'll ask Nigel before he asks me: which strategy could Thirty-one compare or link up with? A true strategist combines tactics to maximum effect. But I get ahead of myself—linking them up is, in fact, a strategy all on its own, Number Thirty-Five. Well, Nigel?'

Nigel pondered in silence.

Jane raised her hand only a few inches. Dan didn't bother. Winston raised his hand high. Nigel wobbled: 'The cicada dressed in gold? No, that wouldn't be . . . Sorry.'

Winston couldn't wait. 'It's similar to Eighteen—the attack strategy, where you capture the bandit chief and weaken the core?'

'Yes, I suppose Winston's right, actually.' Nigel conceded.

'Good, Winston! The difference is that Eighteen is a head-on, go-at-'em tactic when used on its own, while Thirty-one smacks of corruption. It doesn't mean just seducing your enemy with a bit of skirt. You might bribe an ally or tempt an underling into executing your will.'

Dan nodded, 'How many virgins in paradise to get a dumb kid to blow up a train station?'

Baldwin pointed his finger back at Dan, 'A horrifying but pertinent example of combining Thirty-one with Number Three, Borrowing the Knife. Good! Now, let's put sex to one side: Thirty-one can refer to any kind of bait even, Keith, a fat sales commission. Here are three levels of use.' Baldwin had written on the board:

1. Enamoured enemy neglects his duties and allows his vigilance to wane.

2. Competition for the beauty inflames minor differences in the enemy's camp, hindering co-operation and destroying morale.

3. Enemy females at court, motivated by jealousy and envy, plot intrigues to make situation worse.

'These are rather obvious. Bimbos tossed in your lap!' Nigel tapped his pen with impatience. 'What are the preventive tactics?'

Baldwin turned severe. 'Obvious, is it, Nigel? Haven't you seen for yourself a bank deal finalised in Tokyo or Seoul by a team of skilled ladies entertaining so-called sophisticated men?'

Nigel huffed, 'As I said, rather obvious.'

'I knew a young man once, a civil servant posted to Hong Kong when it was still a British colony. He was an Oxford man, high-flyer, lots of promise at the Foreign Office, ripe for promotion, and happily married to a very suitable woman. Then one day, a new secretary was seconded to his outer office.'

Baldwin threw back his head and laughed with a bitter note that caught Jane's attention: 'Willowy, slender, a classical beauty. She'd studied her way into the civil service out of the back alleys of North Point where her Shanghainese refugee family ran a *daipaidong*, a noodle stand.'

Baldwin stared out the window and said, 'She was a girl who had stepped out of a Tang Dynasty poem by Li Po.' He recited to the dark pane:

Her robe is a cloud, her face a flower,
Her balcony, glimmering with the bright spring dew,
Is either the tip of earth's Jade Mountain,
Or a moon-edged roof of paradise.

Keith squirmed. Nigel stared at his cufflinks. Dan's jaw tightened as he observed Baldwin's faraway look.

'I suppose that's pretty fruity stuff in Chinese,' Kevin said.

'Fruity enough. Before he knew it, the poor man found himself without his suitable wife, without his promotion, and without any future on the Governor's team.'

'Just for shagging a local?' Keith asked.

'The girl was a plant, Keith! A spy groomed and then tossed into his lap, as Nigel would say, by the Chinese Communist Party's intelligence agents. Obvious, except to a man who loved Chinese poetry.'

Winston blurted out, 'What happened then?' when Jane kicked his ankle.

During the break, she scolded him, 'You twit! Baldwin was talking about himself! "What happened then?" Instead of being ambassador to Beijing, Baldwin ended up teaching idiots like us in a broom closet, that's what happened then.'

'Poor guy,' Dan sighed. 'Blown out of the water by a honey trap. It must feel like missing a basket in the final shoot-off. You replay it in your dreams until—why, that's what he's doing with our class! Replaying the strategic game he lost, over and over. It's kinda sad.'

'He said he was childless,' Winston said. 'So, I guess he's really on his own, just his class and Tang poetry books. Nigel's right—'

'Winston, did I hear you say Nigel's right? Forty lashes with a wet noodle!' Jane punched the boy's shoulder.

Winston protested, 'I mean Nigel's right when he says that Thirty-one is so obvious. I can just see Baldwin in a saggy tropical-weight three-piece suit in a back office—I know Hong Kong, remember? He's got just a sliver of a view through the pollution over Admiralty Station, with pile drivers in the harbour going *bam bam bam* all day, and a lunchbox of curried noodles at his desk. Then, one day, some babe comes on to him? The poor, deluded old scarecrow, trying to be a Tang lover.'

Jane watched Baldwin across the canteen. While he fished out some spare change for his tea, the teacher of 'Sane Separation' nobbled him for her table. A beaver-like woman full of teeth under a helmet of dark hair, she introduced the stooped Sinologist to her wan-looking ladies garbed in long skirts and hand-knitted sweaters.

"Maybe he wasn't always a scarecrow,' she said to Winston and Dan. She stared at the Mending Marriage group. *That could have been me. Should have been me, nesting among those desperate women. No tempting beauties there. I should talk. I'm pretty well separated from Joe, with no marriage to mend. Not even the satisfaction of a proper divorce—decent or otherwise. At least Baldwin's class kept me going.*

Dan said, 'He's a tragic figure, brought low by love.'

Good-natured Dan, never tortured like Joe by frustrated ambitions but strangely accepting of too much. Perhaps he wasn't for Jane in the long run, but there was no denying that if she had found the right classroom last September, she would never have felt so buoyant, not to mention even beautiful, with Dan this evening.

On Winston's suggestion, they ate a late dinner at the Moonbeam, their conversation fighting the clamour of the kitchen staff at the back. Cecilia bantered with Dan in Mandarin.

Winston shrugged, 'I should've kept up my classical Chinese. But it was all I could do to get my A-levels without Saturday mornings wasted on flash cards and stroke order.'

Dan chugged down his cold beer with zest. 'So how's the Romance of the Two Kingdoms going, Winston?'

Winston looked at his friends from under a clouded brow. 'Not quite at the double-wedding stage, but I wouldn't rule it out. Although Selina and Nelson did have a row. She asked him to go to Prague to check out cheap components but Nelson's waiting for delivery of some film-editing software. They argued for hours—components or I-Movie Ten? Whatev. Anyway, threatening Dad with a Sultana take-over was a complete non-starter.'

'Don't give up.' Jane said. 'If Selina starts to call the shots, your Dad could get cold feet.'

'Cold feet! Hardly. The transformation of my father into Belsize Park's Don Juan is terrifying! Not only does he not blanch at the suggestion of submerging Chu Printers into Sultana Software, he's outfitting his private office with a new sofa.'

Dan worried. 'Not a sofa bed?'

'Oh, don't go there. My poor late mother. Could I please have another Sprite, Cecilia?'

It was a sad reflection on Baldwin's class that Winston had learned so little about Chinese defensive or offensive strategy. He might even flunk.

'Oh, man, look who's here,' Winston cowered. 'See for yourself, Dan.'

The doorbells jangled to the entry of Nelson and a well-rounded young woman wearing a fake fur, jeans, and black patent platform boots. They took the first empty table without waiting for Cecilia to seat them.

'Well, well, well. So that is the enemy prince?'

'Please, Dan. Just ignore them,' Winston hissed.

Dan ignored Winston instead. He rose from his chair to introduce himself, shake Nelson's hand, greet Selina, and return with the cooing couple to Winston's side. Selina was charming, if a tad cagey. Nelson's blinding smile made it obvious that, as far as he was concerned, the Chu and Leong Empires were not at each other's throats, unless it was to leave those purple love bites on each other's gullets visible even now under the restaurant's garish lights.

Cecilia poured more green tea and disappeared through the swinging kitchen door. Slaving for her parents had left her hollow-eyed. Dan asked Nelson what he should order for the main dishes.

Nelson shrugged. 'Ask Winston.'

'You don't come here often?'

'Hey, no, this is Winston's hang out. I've never been here before.'

Selina bit down on a salted peanut. 'It's my mother's favourite mah-jong place,' she told Jane.

Cecilia served rice to a party at a table nearby. 'Have I seen that babe before?' Nelson winked at Dan, as if they were already bosom friends from back in the days when Xy-write was hot.

'You tell me,' the affable Dan replied. 'Here, try some crispie thingies.'

'Cute figure. She's familiar somehow.' Nelson's high, smooth cheekbones caught the glint of the cheap lanterns.

'She's just the waitress, Nelson,' Selina said.

A controlling type, Jane thought. Winston's tactics might yet work. Behind Selina's flawless complexion, flicked-ended eyeliner, and sticky lip gloss lurked Madame Leong II. She only lacked the cigarette holder from Penang and a turban in Day-Glo orange jersey to nail down Nelson's future fate as consort to the Leong matriarchy.

'. . . then you upload the finished video from your camera to your Google account and link it to your channel. YouTube tracks the hits . . .' Poor Cecilia hovered over Nelson, balancing platters in both arms. Finally Nelson made room for her to arrange the overflowing dishes around the table. She topped up everyone's glasses and refilled the teapot. Only Winston shrugged a sort of lopsided apology to her for his companions. Jane also noticed her, so young and tired, listening to the fun but left out and unnoticed.

Nelson kept up with his sales pitch. 'Dan, I bet you have a whole closetful of shoeboxes stuffed with old family movies. This way, you transfer them to digital, upload them for private viewing . . .'

Cecilia held the steaming kettle of tea to one side and interrupted Nelson softly, 'Excuse me, but you can't upload more than ten minutes unless you upgrade your account.' Nelson didn't appreciate Cecilia's pathetic attempt to cross the line from waitress to conversationalist. Seeing him scowl, the girl added, 'I'll get more rice, on the house.'

She scraped a plastic ladle around the sides of the rice pot for the last, crispy morsels as Nelson ploughed on: 'What's really cool, Dan, is that Google profiles your viewer hits by region, by country and URL address.'

'Nelson, I'm divorced. If I have a box of videos, I don't want to look at them again, much less post them on the Internet. I'm still in the Ice Age, fellah! My old video camera is so big, it wouldn't fit into this bag!'

'Oh, that's too bad,' Nelson commiserated. 'The new babies on your I-phone fit into your palm.'

'So, I'd jump straight to mobile technology if all you want is a few minutes on the run,' said Cecilia, smiling at Dan. 'And go for high definition. Don't get something out-dated fobbed off on you by a slick salesman.'

Nelson watched Cecilia clear another table. 'Slick salesman. She's got a nerve. God, who wears braids like that? Give me a beautiful woman in a fur bikini, not a greasy cheongsam, right, Dan?' He grabbed the rice bowl to his mouth and shovelled away.

Winston leaned over to Jane. 'See. I told you. He's got the fur bikini on the brain. Selina caught Nelson watching that *Hei Bai* chick a few nights ago. She practically strangled him with his earphone cords.'

Jane considered Selina, sitting opposite. 'She doesn't seem ready to break up with Nelson over a YouTube fantasy. I see the deposit of your whole inheritance into the Leong bank account before my very eyes, Winston. Pity you can't download *Hei Bai*

Girl into three dimensions to use The Beautiful Woman Trap and lure Nelson off into cyberspace.'

'To use Thirty-one on Nelson, I'd have to knock him out, envelope him in bubble-wrap, and express him to Shanghai, which you can see is where his table manners got stuck.'

Selina was nuzzling Nelson's ear. Winston covered his eyes. 'Oh, they're disgusting. My future as deputy manager goes right down the drain.'

At that moment, Selina's mother, Madame Leong, sailed into the Moonbeam with Winston's father hanging like an adoring, if emaciated handbag off her formidable elbow. Winston lifted a resigned hand in greeting and with futile filial piety, fetched two more seats.

'Correction. If I play my cards very carefully, Jane,' he said in a bitter tone. 'I'll work my way up to *assistant* deputy sales manager and all this.'

Chapter Thirty-two, The Empty City Scheme

Three weeks of Baldwin's class remained, to be followed by a long break while they prepared for exams. No more Friday nights with Keith, Kev, or Nigel for Jane. Even Winston would recede into the misty Territory of Chu to cram for his final. How did Dan expect their romance to evolve? Was his secondment from the NYPD to London fixed or open-ended? Was he growing sick of staking out amateur wannabe's while his colleagues back home cracked the conspiracies of hardened terrorists?

Dan's attentions to Jane had plateaued comfortably at the level you'd expect for a man on temporary overseas duty. He hadn't said anything one way or the other. He skirted Jane's fishing questions, as if he'd absorbed Stratagem Thirty-two, The Empty City Scheme, that recommended anyone under siege drop all pretence of military preparedness and act casually.

'When facing an advancing opponent, the commander opened the gates of the city. Sitting on the city wall in plain view of the enemy, he played music on his zither,' Baldwin taught them. 'Suspecting an ambush, his enemy withdrew.'

Despite her misleading hints to Bella and Rachel, Jane didn't need Dan's commitment. She enjoyed the ambiguity of their romance and the secrecy of his work. She needed room to rebuild her life at her own pace. It certainly was a change from the kind of tension she was accustomed to—being sucked into Joe's ambitions, enthusiasms, and disappointments. A lot of energy had gone into sharing Joe's moods, fighting for distance, and in the end, buffering herself from Joe's roller coaster needs.

Jane tried to imagine daily life with Dan. His work style and personality meant there might be city gates that would never open.

She stared out at the square and watched the arrival of one neighbour and the departure of another. So many were strangers these days. They knew nothing of the old days when, in the cause of scraped knees and borrowed birthday-cake tins, Jane had bounced in and out of homes on all sides of the square. Now the

Gilchrists were an anomaly, possibly the only middle-class family left. The square seemed immune to property bubbles and busts. Apart from the incongruous bookstore and Joop's Painted Angel, it qualified as a celebrity biosphere all by itself.

Nevertheless, it was still their home, or at least, nominally Lorraine's home for as long as she wanted, and that meant Jane and Sammie's, too. Yet, there was the possibility that like all of Lorraine's tours, life at the square must eventually see the curtain fall.

There was a respectful knock at the door that bordered on the facetious. Lorraine's recognition that Jane had changed the keys to the front door now produced a theatrical rapping right out of farce. Opening her door, Jane faced Princess Alexandra, The Honourable Lady Ogilvy LG GCVO, the youngest granddaughter of King George V and Queen Mary, in full Battle Dress.

Or not.

'Omigod, I don't believe it!' Jane was quick to curtsey.

'Not bad, eh? Ready for Curtain, Overture, and Beginners, please!'

Lorraine glided into the room on borrowed high heels. She extended her right hand in front of her as if parting a Red Sea of peasants.

'This is just a dry run. I just went up to the butcher's and he greeted me in front of all his customers as Your Royal Highness! There were three or four people standing around his shop and boy, did their dentures drop! I swear, they bought my act, kid!'

Indeed, Lorraine looked every inch the Princess. The wash-and-dry bleached bob was now a platinum bouffant topping bejewelled, be-hosed, and be-heeled blue blood. The complexion was powdered to a porcelain sheen and the red lips covered with pearly gloss. The putty nose was regal but just short of beaky.

'Listen to this.' Lorraine's tightened her jaw and clenched her teeth. 'I'm so gled to be here, among you ell, on this very, very, *emportent* occasion.'

'Works for me, but I've never heard Princess Alexandra. Do you know what she really sounds like?'

'Yep, thanks to archives fished out by Lloyd's cousin over at Bush House. She was recorded during a ribbon-cutting in Yemen in 1961, to break wind over some new town.'

'She might have changed in fifty years.'

'Royals don't *chenge* their *eccent*. Their range might drop a bit. Now tomorrow the car for Bermondsey picks me up at eleven—'

'Oh, Lorraine, I'll miss that. I have to be at the library tomorrow—'

'I thought it was closed on Tuesdays. Oh, don't worry, you'll hear all about it when you pick me up. You wouldn't want me to make my exit in a carriage pulled off by mice, would you? Here are the directions. Be there by two. We'll have a late lunch, a real post-matinee blowout. You know, darling, I'm actually nervous. How can that be? Stage fright over an audience that can't see me! Now I'm just stepping out to the High Street to give these heels more breaking in. Give the locals another shock. I'll try the newsagent next. One last dress rehearsal.'

Lorraine bestowed an aristocratic nod to their neighbour as she exited on to the kerb.

'Friend of your mother's?' Sir Bernard asked Jane.

'Yes,' said Jane. 'Theatre nobility.'

⤙⤚

The Bookworms' Frosty contest was swiftly underway. Camden Authority offered no objection and Rupert's old Winchester mate Colin planted a nice little mention in *The Sunday Telegraph*. Now they'd gone public, the pressure was on. They whittled away at the short story contenders like pros—but all the Booker badinage and Orange orations couldn't hold the fort against Carla's obstinate defence of 'My First Husband' by one Mrs Evelyn Smith.

Rupert battled for 'Text Me Now and Forever' by retired civil servant Peter Ffaulks. Rupert felt that Smith's story of a marriage cut short by war was too old-fashioned and too sentimental to attract the publicity Chalkwood Library needed. 'The Frosties

Contest should be all about proving we're grey-headed but with it.'

'Indeed, Rupert?' Carla retorted. 'I know we want to make a splash but with all those e-mails in unreadable spelling and text messages, it's too trendy to be credible as our choice.'

'Anything we choose is credible, Carla, if Mr Ffaulks is our age,' Rupert protested.

Jane worried a bit. 'Chris ran this workshop alone. We're taking his word for it that these authors were genuinely old. Anyone reading 'Text Me' might suspect a ringer of thirty crashed our list, just for the publicity.'

'I agree with Carla,' Catherine shouted. 'My First Husband moved me to tears. I read it over three times before I passed it to Alma. I was determined to find fault with it. Here are my notes:' Catherine fished out her reading glasses. 'Simplicity of language. Sincerity. Authenticity. Believable dialogue.'

Catherine continued, 'Not to mention searing honesty about the loneliness of all those years after he died. She doesn't sentimentalize the facts, Rupert. The husband died an ugly, wasteful death. Because that's what you did in our day. Did your duty.'

'Thank you, Catherine.' Jane glanced at her watch. 'I'm afraid we're not moving ahead. We've tallied it twice now, but we can't end with a tie. Everyone's second choice is 'The Examined Life.' It's well crafted, but just a bit too self-conscious to be my choice. I don't like being so aware of language that I can't lose myself in the story.'

They went at it through two more brews of Rupert's herbal tea without heeding the passing hours.

Mrs Wilting tried, politely, to deflect Carla from championing the Smith story, but for once, Jane was unimpressed with Ruth's superior ear for language or pace. Carla shook the other Bookworms' opinions away from them like a dog yanking at a soggy towel. Even Jane lost her patience with Ruth. Why was she using her last ounce of strength to make sure that Carla's choice took no prize?

Finally, Carla blew a gasket. 'I'm afraid I just have to spit out my mind this once without any sugary coating. No, Jane, I will say it. Ruth, you don't know the first thing about good writing. You never have. Sorry, but it has to be said. A "good read" just isn't enough. You're only pretending to enjoy all that modernistic rubbish, just to side with Rupert against me. Or to prove you're not ready for the crypt.'

There was an awful silence. Ruth looked close to breaking down. Carla braced herself to take on the rest of them, but no one defended their most aged colleague. The looming deadline of last trains, the eyestrain caused by the overhead strip lighting, and the hour for bedtime medications approached.

There was only time for one last vote.

Reaching into Alma's rain hat, Jane unfolded their ballots with discretion.

'One for 'Text Me.' A second for ''Text Me.' One for 'My First Husband,' and a second for Mrs Smith. A third for Mrs Smith and. a fourth for Mrs Smith. That's it. Two to four. First Prize goes to Mrs Evelyn Smith. Whew!'

'Read us a bit again, Jane, just to formalize our decision,' Alma entreated, to give Ruth Wilting and Rupert time to recover from defeat.

Mother said she might cling to the leftover facts, to help her endure later on. As soon as they'd left the registry, he'd held her tight against his serge and gold buttons, and asked with flippant bravado, 'So how's the first wife?' He was her first lover and her first husband. Now Clarissa resolved to content herself, for the rest of her life, to reading of suffering or loss and to experience the rest of her life only through books. To live a quiet life, a shadow's life among books. That kind of contentment had fallen out of fashion these days, but it wouldn't be passive. Her energy would go to keeping the books alive and for his sake, to prevent yet more death of the spirit.

That first afternoon Clarissa turned the heel of a sock he would never wear. She tried not to notice how the hardly-worn band on her finger lolled around her slender finger as she counted stitches.

As the years passed, the ring held faster to her thickening finger. Finally, as its gold wore down, a fraction of a gram with each decade, time lightened the pain in her heart. She grew frailer and the ring fell loose again, but was ever that much lighter. Pain survived and promises were lost, but both fell into a bearable balance.

Jane looked up. 'I love that phrase, "a bearable balance." Too bad the pensioners' workshop fell apart but next year we'll have time, for a long list.'

'And a real publicity campaign.' Rupert had loved his few days as promoter.

'But at least we have a winner. Well done!'

They needed to get the word out fast, to locate and congratulate Mrs Evelyn Smith and confirm the celebrity author. Rupert would start calling his contacts tonight.

Alma scraped up the last bits of cake icing. 'Why Ruth, don't sit there so angry. Carla didn't mean that bit about the crypt.'

'I put it too strongly,' Carla huffed, the head girl generous in victory. 'Sorry, Wilting.'

Catherine grabbed Mrs Wilting's hand and yelled, 'Feeling all right, dear?'

Tears poured out of Ruth Wilting's rheumy eyes in salty torrents. She'd lost control of her hands. Her right hand kept turning and twisting the old gold band on her left.

'Oh, good Lord,' Carla barked. 'What's got into you? Don't be so wet! I apologized, didn't I?'

Should Jane call a doctor? She stared at Ruth's compulsive fingers twisting round and round and the terrified expression on her crumbling face. Or—with sudden dismay and delight, Jane recalled Ruth's admissions of 'snatches of writing,' her allusions to 'bits tucked away in a drawer.'

It couldn't be. Chris should have warned her.

'Carla, shut up. Ruth. Evelyn Smith is your *nom de plume*, isn't it? You were in Chris's workshop last year. You wrote this story?'

Mrs Wilting nodded.

'*You're* the winner?' Carla bellowed.

Alma rounded on Carla. 'And all these years you've treated her as if she had nothing left in her head, nothing at all.'

'Well, she certainly fooled me, sitting there, half-vacant every Monday night,' Carla sputtered.

Rupert hissed like a wizened tomcat, 'It's called modesty, Carla.'

Ruth's shakes robbed her of speech. Jane held the frail woman in her arms for a long minute until Mrs Wilting managed, 'Oh, thank you. Thank you. Of course, I must recuse myself from the competition. The Frosty must go to the one about the professor. It's enough, well, it's really wonderful, actually, to know that I won in your eyes. Thank you, Carla.'

Rupert insisted, 'You shall present the award, Mrs Wilting, as you are the first choice.' They pestered her with questions: How long had she worked on her story? What was her 'process?' How many rewrites did it take? Had she ever tried to get published? Were there more stories, even enough for a collection?'

Ruth took some pills to steady her heart. With notable humility, Carla held Ruth's walker as the older lady struggled into her coat. Rupert and Alma insisted on escorting her the short distance to her front door. Jane watched them go, worried that their decision would overwhelm its author. If Jane had felt over the last few months that she herself might waste away from the low simmer of an aching heart, she recognized that Ruth was near drowning in happiness. What a triumph for the tiny woman who had prevailed over Carla's blustery expertise by instinctive use of Baldwin's stratagem of feigned harmlessness.

Later that night the Bookworms learned, one by one, that Jane's worst fear was borne out. The dependable Mrs Goodchild, the 'home help' who first urged her elderly charge to get some fresh air away from her desk, had discovered Mrs Wilting in her bed, her frail heart stopped.

'My First Husband' would take First Prize after all. Rupert rushed the news to editors' desks.

By early Tuesday morning, *The Telegraph's* graveyard shift had signed off on the lead for the Arts Section announcing the late Mrs Edward Wilting had won the first-ever Senior Story Prize awarded by the Camden Library Authority's community outreach programme. Rupert had supplied the subs with a framed photo of the shy bride over-towered by her Edward in uniform discovered at Ruth's bedside.

Not every Bookworm was pleased. Carla pounded on the locked door of Chalkwood Library after breakfast, shouting through the window, 'Jane, did you see this morning's *Telegraph*?'

'Oh, Carla, isn't it marvellous? With passages from the story, a mention for our branch and that quote Rupert got beforehand from Lady Antonia Fraser about next year's contest! How did he do it?'

'Won by the *late* Mrs Wilting, indeed! Like we gave our prize to a corpse! Next year Rupert gives our exclusive to *The Guardian*!'

Jane laughed. 'Camden called this morning to say that Chris can reopen the senior short-story workshop with the motto, Stories From the Oldest and Boldest.'

'Humpf. Well, better that than The-Kiss-of-Death Prize!'

Jane printed out the *Telegraph*'s story. She centred it on the display board next to a sign-up sheet for the next workshop.

True to her love of the written word, Ruth would have been the first to twinkle at what so outraged Carla: *The Telegraph* had been kind to the Bookworms, true, but the editors had had their mischief with the headline: *UNEXPECTED FROST FOR WILTING AUTHOR.*

Chapter Thirty-three, Turn the Enemy's Agents against Him

Tuesday morning had mingled enough excitement with sadness for a week, but Jane still faced a full day of grim library duties. The freakishly warm weather threatened rain and lightning.

All over England, libraries faced closure. Forty libraries across the country had locked their doors for good in 2007 and the disappearances only worsened with the coalition government's current cuts. In the West Midlands, Dudley Council marched another five on to the tumbril. Southampton readers protested a cut in library hours, the Croydon Council slashed another £12,000 from its budget. In Dorset, community volunteers were all that stood in the way of the closure of thirteen branches. In Kent, seventy-seven librarians received letters saying their jobs were going.

If 2011 was bad, 2012 looked worse. Dozens more branches lay exposed. When even the minister responsible for libraries asked how the needs of literate residents would be met, there seemed little that humble part-time librarians could do.

A letter for Jane arrived in the branch's post.

'Well, we knew it was coming. It was just a question of which arrived first—my letter or Mr Gumble's one-man pod. So Chris, I guess it's over to you.'

'I didn't study library science to run a DVD outlet. Look at this, Jane,' Chris read *The Daily Mail*: 'The Secretary of State for Children, Schools and Families declares this The Year of the Book. He says parents should spend ten minutes a day reading to their children. Reading what? Page Three?'

'Chris, read the rest of my letter. Not satisfied with cutting me, they've ordered us to cull twenty per cent of our books. I mean, the ones we can't sell.'

'Which books?'

'The letter doesn't say.' Jane's eyes widened. 'So there goes GB Shaw, and Keats.'

'Voltaire, Turgenev, Lawrence.'

'Trollope, Ibsen, Eliot, Poe, and Stevenson and, oh, Chris, how do we decide?' The stacks echoed Jane's despair. Her last act as a staff librarian was the destruction of books?

Chris put a hand on her shoulder. 'It's *Sophie's Choice*. Condemn some of your children. How about a full-fledged *auto-da-fe* with Barbara Bradford? Or do we do a Ray Bradbury? Call a book-burning squad in flameproof suits for a controlled blaze? Death to the Underborrowed?'

'Chris, do you remember how *Fahrenheit 451* ended? People like you memorizing Norman Mailer and Ian McEwan, and me repeating *Emma* over and over to myself, Human Books hiding out in a forest, keeping literature alive?'

'Jane, what was that discord tactic you mentioned the other day? Turn the Enemy's Agents Against Him?'

'Bribe enemy agents, feign ignorance, feed false information, but I don't see—?'

'Lead the enemy into his own trap. Do you realize, the Authority has just given us an excuse to cleanse this branch of all the dross we truly, madly, deeply loathe.'

Behind locked doors, they set to their task, ripping the covers off celebrity bios, Dukan diet books, and anything embossed with shiny letters. Children's classics were sacrosanct.

'We keep *Lord of the Flies*,' Chris passed judgement, '*Catcher in the Rye, The Diary of Anne Frank*.'

'Replace the enemy's flags and banners with your own,' Jane chanted.

The rain subsided and the skies cleared a little. Just before eleven, Jane raced to the top of the square in time to wave good luck to 'Princess Alexandra' headed to her 'appearance' at the Blind People Factory.

'Here I go, darling!' Lorraine shouted across the square. Jane exulted to see a doppelgänger of the Princess waving her royal salute across the square as a dark sedan passed Jane still panting as she reached the bollards a few steps from Joop's painted angel.

'Break a leg,' Jane shouted. 'Pick you up at two!'

A young man in polished black shoes eased her mother into the car. Wasn't it like old times, watching unseen from the stage wings as Lorraine made an entrance on the arm of her leading man? The years bounded past Jane like fleet-footed deer. 'Overture and Beginners, darling,' she whispered to herself, her youthful miseries now softened by the years.

Back at the book purge, despair was turning to glee. Management books would be sold. Keeping careful tally, Chris tossed outdated *Lonely Planets* and three copies of *Do Ants Have Arseholes?* He was determined to make the quota without risking Ian Rankin.

They ordered noodles from the Moonbeam, which Cecilia delivered on a motorbike still splattered with raindrops. She dropped to her knees at the edge of the book mountain. '*The Kitchen God's Wife?* You can't!'

So Amy Tan survived for sale, along with Jung Chang's *Wild Swans*. Jane pulled the plug on classics too long on life-support, including prize-winners only Carla admired. With a sense of fair play, a regretful Chris eliminated 'new' writers best known to *Granta* editors.

Time flew to the sound of covers ripped, tomes tossed, and the sound of bin bags filling up. Should they sell off *Life of Pi?* Did they need three copies of *The Autograph Man?* Did they need one? Suddenly Chris asked, Jane, 'Aren't you picking up your mother?'

Grabbing her bag and coat, Jane hurled herself into the path of a cab descending Primrose Hill Road but the traffic took forever. Princess Alexandra mustn't be seen—or heard—standing in a bus queue! The royal bouffant would end up clumps of peasant fluff.

Jane's cab pulled up at the Factory just as Lorraine waved in the direction of applauding blind workers. She hurried towards her daughter. 'Thank heavens you're here, darling. That silly aide Frederick had to go pick up the real princess ten minutes ago. First, find me a ladies' room.'

A jolly lady from the Action staff who was folding chairs told them, 'You know the way, Your Highness, to the director's? Hasn't changed since last year.'

Jane muttered, 'You must've been damn good. Is she blind, too?'

'Of course, I was damned good,' Lorraine turned her back on the dispersing gaggle. 'These shoes are killing me. Let's find the Royal Flush. Maybe this way—?' They headed towards a side entrance.

They were just entering the building when Jane felt an attacking *whoosh* behind her mother's back.

Men dressed in black plastic rushed in their direction and slammed into them. Four rough arms lifted Jane right off her feet and dragged her towards Verney Road. She heard Lorraine's imperial tones, 'Put Me DOWN!' and a grunt as Lorraine kicked one of the men in the groin. Jane dropped to her knees to slow them down, but still was dragged and finally tossed through the yawning doors of a mud-spattered van.

Lorraine was slung, still shouting, smack on top of Jane. One of the men whipped out a roll of duct tape and wound tight strips around Lorraine's mouth. Jane's head was yanked back as tape was wound so tight around her eyes she saw sparkling colours. Their eyes were bound shut by tight cloths.

'Lorr—!' she cried before the tape went over her lips. Lorraine's voice, lucid and cool mumbled, 'RP, Jane, my assistant.'

Jane was no actress, and this seemed a poor moment to argue accents, as she felt the kick of boots slam into her behind. Who'd seen this? Handler Frederick? Gone. The Action lady? Nearly sightless.

Sherlock Holmes always asked kidnap victims if they had listened to tell-tale noises, counted the stops, smelled landmarks along the route—rotting markets, curry shops, sea air, fertilizers— in order to retrace their abduction. Jane couldn't keep track of any smell, sound, or time. The racketing swaying of the van, the screech of wheels, and the muttered curses of the men only conjured up a bad Stella Rimmington thriller. Less than three hours ago, Jane had thrown Rimmington into the rubbish heap. She might rethink that decision—if she ever saw a library again.

'In there.'

They dragged Lorraine out first. Jane was next and after many minutes of rough handling, the men carried them down some steps and bound them, back to back, wired and taped.

Gasping and terrified, they were suddenly abandoned in the pitch darkness.

Jane forced out, 'All right?'

Lorraine mumbled out, 'I still need a toilet.'

Jane kicked out her legs and struck something wooden. She kept kicking for ten minutes at least. No one answered. The space was stuffy, humid, and cool, probably a basement. It stank. Jane rubbed her face back and forth on the concrete floor to loosen the tape. Lorraine did the same, and finally Jane could slur to Lorraine: 'Just tell them they've got the wrong princess.'

'They're probably going to make demands in exchange for me.'

'Who would kidnap Princess Alexandra? It's ridiculous.'

'I won't take that personally. Why should I tell them they've got an old has-been?'

'You're not a has-been. But you're right. Maybe we're safer as royal and servant.'

Lorraine harrumped, 'It was going so well! I deserve a better encore than this. Oooooh, my shoulder's so cold. Can we sit up again?' Inching around in a circle, they measured their space—just a small cell.

'We must keep our heads, darling. Oh, dear, remember what they did to that poor construction worker?'

Horrified, Jane said, 'I think they only do that in the Middle East.'

'Not in England,' Lorraine nodded, forcing Jane's head to nod as well. 'Not in the land of Henry the VIII.'

'You would cite him.'

'I'm sorry, I couldn't help it. Beheading made me think of summer stock and *Anne of a Thousand Days*. But Henry the Eighth wasn't a terrorist.'

'Anne Boleyn might differ.' Jane surmised. 'Let's be positive. We might be here for a while. How long is your nose going to stay on?'

Her mother groaned. Jane felt warm pee spreading underneath her hips.

'Oh, I'm so very sorry, darling.'

'Could happen to anyone, your Highness.'

They dozed, heads tilted back on the other's shoulder for as long as they could, leaning against a pile of packing boxes away from the puddles Lorraine's bladder had contributed to their predicament.

Jane lost track of time. Suppose what felt like hours was only fifteen minutes?

She worked up her solidarity with all the jailed people around the world right now, unable to stretch out, or see, or yell for rescue. It didn't work very well, and as she was a librarian at heart, she ended up thinking of *The Count of Monte Cristo* instead.

At what point did people start reciting poems or playing chess in their heads? She certainly hadn't memorized enough literature to stay the course. Damn, she couldn't even remember a single e.e. cumming's line of poetry. She'd taken it for granted there would always be books at hand. Happily, Lorraine's memory was good for a couple of seasons. There'd be Pinter, Sondheim, Rogers and Hart, Feydeau, Ibsen, Shakespeare and if it ever came to it, Lorraine's episodes on that daytime soap opera. You could do worse than be locked up with one of the most versatile actresses of her day.

But for now, they sat quietly. Lorraine even dozed for what might have been an hour, maybe two. Jane thought of Sammie and tried to reckon when her daughter would realize mother and grandmother were gone.

A door flew open. The tapes were ripped off their mouths.

'I need a bathroom. And a gin and tonic,' Lorraine barked, turning her blindfolded face towards the sound. Perhaps she was channelling Alec Guiness in *The Bridge on the River Kwai*.

'Alcohol is bad for your health,' said an educated man's voice. His accent caught Jane's ear.

'So is freezing in my own urine, young man. How long have we been here?'

'Four hours. You have eight more. They meet our demand, we let you go at dawn.'

'Demand?' Jane asked.

'Withdrawal of all British troops.'

'Oh, goodie.' Lorraine sighed. 'Home by teatime.'

'That's a ludicrous demand. From where?' Jane asked.

'Here is your soup,' Their captor unwired Lorraine's wrists and guided her fingers to a bowl of cold lentils.

'*Thenk* you, my good man,' Lorraine muttered.

'You don't sound like a foreign crackpot,' Jane said, gulping down her soup. 'Are you one of those local students with a loose screw?'

'We're moving you later tonight.'

More hours crawled by. Jane's neck was cramped and her wet thighs chilled. Lorraine was worryingly quiet. The door banged open again. Many rough hands again dragged them blindfolded into a quiet night. Jane smelled diesel fumes, rotting leaves, and foul refuse mixed with Lorraine's stale pee and the smell of old-lady terror. There was no whine of a siren or chop-chop of a helicopter, but the sounds of terrifying normality, just footsteps crunching gravel on either side of her and her mother's grunts of pain.

Counting on Trollopian storylines to sustain their empty hours had been outlandish optimism. These men might not be misguided liberators—just lovers of violence and death. How Jane regretted reading that last Martin Amis about nihilists. While she read her books, this sort of thing was happening all the time—only to other people.

Their van got caught in a traffic jam. Blindfolded into heightened sensation, Jane felt every metre of asphalt grind past. The two women were riding towards their death surrounded by life—chirpy, indifferent, London life. Loud music came from a car radio crawling ahead of them.

Now Jane realized a new danger—that as a useless palace assistant to a second-eleven princess, she might be cast aside and permanently separated from her more valuable royal companion.

Lorraine must have been seized by her own stage fright because lying rough on the jouncing metal, Lorraine muttered, 'In case they do close our show, darling, I'm sorry. So many things I did. Not something to go into now, as a princess, you understand, but you deserved better.'

'Nothing to apologize for, Your Highness. Just a bad script. You gave it your best.'

'Shuddup,' said a different voice.

'Yeah, shuddup.' said a third. They sounded like locals. One kicked Jane in the pelvis for good measure. Who liked kicking her so much? Given her aching spine, this was a bit of overkill—was he imitating rough thugs on telly? Where did criminals get their role models, anyway, if not from bad writing? If only they'd all been forced to read, then at least the city's social underbelly might be a fanciful kaleidoscope of Ed McBain hoods, Ian Fleming villains and Conan Doyle nasties.

What did these guys read?

Did these guys read?

It was soon apparent that they read prayers. Quite often. Once Jane and Lorraine had been repackaged with fresh tape and settled on two seedy mattresses in blackness, they heard for the third time now, a handful of male voices in recitation. Chanting shouldn't sound menacing, but in the end, Jane could only agree with Lorraine's own personal prayer, a disgusted, 'Oh Lord, not again,' through taped jaws.

The two women dozed on and off, but deep sleep was impossible. The sound of fraying tempers in a room somewhere on the same floor roused Jane from a deep doze. Apparently despite the issuing of their 'demand,' not so much as a regimental beagle had been withdrawn from combat.

Two of the men argued over when to kill the women. Another asked whether they should be allowed a bathroom visit. Which one first? Somebody yelled over the racket that it wasn't his turn to cook and who had left his wet towel on the floor?

Tension, anxiety, fear and venality veered between the vicious and the petty.

354

Outdoors, traffic sounds faded down to an occasional passing car. Was it evening by now? How late? Someone untethered Lorraine's feet and led her away, still blindfolded, and more tightly gagged for good measure. Jane trembled and waited for screams of murder or triumph or both. Instead, Lorraine returned in better spirits, her hands reeking of cheap soap.

Jane was elated now by the tiniest thing, and not only at the idea of breathing fresh air. Had these boys chickened out, as one day was turning to the next? Would they extend the deadline, at least long enough for Jane and Lorraine to negotiate a trip to the loo together and crawl out a window? Perhaps not during the second full day or the third, but maybe after a week? Or after the first month?

Her turn for the bathroom came. Jane hoped the kidnappers were respectful enough not to watch a woman relieve herself. Taking a chance behind the closed door, she blindly ran her hands all over the tiles, up and down, back and forth, like a cleaning robot crawling in random diagonals across the gummy walls of a swimming pool. At last, her hands discovered the ledge of a window high above the loo. Unfortunately it framed an aperture so small only Bulgakov could have negotiated it, and then, only if he'd cut back on the Friskies for a week.

Defeated, Jane flushed the toilet, washed her face and hands, and half-stumbled out. She heard the placid, professional tones of a newscaster coming from a room nearby, ' . . . the Queen and her immediate family assure the British public that the government is doing everything possible to secure the release of an unidentified member of the extended royal household taken hostage. Meanwhile, in other news . . .'

'Tosser!' An empty plastic bottle bounced off the television screen. 'That's wot we get? Member of the extended household? Like we got her butler or sumfing? We got 'er bleeding cousin, that's all! I told you! We shoulda waited for a chance at the old bag herself. Or one of 'em wanker princes.'

'Naw. Too much security. Well maybe we could've got that Edward. Send Al Jazeera a photo of 'im wearing pink undies on his head, like at Gitmo.' Four or five of them laughed as Jane eavesdropped.

'Yeah, well, we got one at any rate. And her knickers are stinking awright.'

Someone slammed an angry hand on a table. 'They didn't even report our demands. Probably glad to see the back of this old piss pot.'

'They did, too,' said a younger voice. 'You heard it on Al Jazeera.'

'Not on the English service,' someone sneered.

Jane listened again. Not quite all locals. One was American—'undies' and 'Gitmo' betrayed him. They were now going at each other, tossing blame around as they soured on their crime. The bravado that had carried them this far seemed to be faltering. Jane had dozed longer than she thought. Their dawn deadline was approaching.

She was standing in what she guessed was a narrow corridor. She worried as they wrangled that, faced with frustrated dissension, someone might suggest more desperate action as a purgative.

Then, she smelled a sweetish perfume as someone shifted behind her. Like a mouse frozen by the tread of an unseen cat's paw, she paused. How long had he watched her from inches away, smiling in malevolence while she—? *Euuw*, that was too embarrassing to think about.

He wound the wire back around her wrists, cinching them behind her waist, and with an elegance she found more frightening than the rough accents of the others in the room beyond, asked her, 'More than you bargained for?'

His warm breath brushed the hairs on the nape of her back. 'Still pretending you work for a princess?'

Should she nod yes or no to a man primed to murder and now humiliated by royal indifference? It was a deadly mix on which to hang your future.

She said nothing.

He pushed her ahead of him, past the doorway giving on to those voices arguing away and then back down a few steps. She stumbled, wishing she could only see and with a shove from behind, found herself back with Lorraine.

'We've got another meal, darling,' Lorraine muttered. 'Lentils with a side of lentils, I think, or cat food. Have we got to breakfast yet?'

'Call it the Last Supper,' said the velvet voice.

'Call it inedible,' she said and tossed her spoon on the floor.

After the 'meal,' Jane and Lorraine were left blindfolded, but hands and mouths free. While Lorraine expressed her relief, Jane's apprehension grew. She heard suspiciously frequent trips to the bathroom, one set of footsteps, a shower, then another and another. Compared to the haphazard execution of their kidnapping so far, this regimental queue for the shower was creepy and ritualistic. They dozed for what Jane reckoned was about two hours, then the prayers started up again.

Suddenly Lorraine was dragged up and away, protesting. Jane grabbed her mother's ankles and screamed into the fetid air. Someone yanked Jane to her feet and she too was dragged, bumping and kicking, until she was slapped hard across the face.

They forced Jane down on a stool and a young man barked, 'Stop struggling unless you want to explode.' They lifted her hands high over her head and pulled two straps past her elbows and down on her shoulders. They tied her into something. A heavy weight now nestled in the small of her back. Then they cinched her stomach and wrapped more canvas straps around her waist. She reached but they pulled her fingers out of the way. They wired up her wrists again.

'A new fashion in belts,' said the American voice. 'You're going to make another public appearance, you two.'

Jane thought of Joe, Lorraine, Chris, Dan and most of all Sammie. Sammie. Sammie. Then she heard Baldwin's voice interrupt her thoughts, saying of all things: *Lead the Enemy into His Own Trap . . . Turn the Enemy's Agents Against Him. The strategy of sowing discord.*

How far away his cultured voice echoed in her mind. How out of reach.

'You are such *amateurs*.' Jane taunted the darkness beyond her blindfold. 'You haven't forced us to beg the Queen to meet your demand.'

'Shut up,' said one of the men.

Jane had nothing to lose. 'That's what the *professionals* do. Film us begging. The Queen gets more blame that way.'

She got a sharp slap across her face.

'I'm sure one of you thought of a video,' she laughed. 'You can't all be nutters.'

'Shut up, you stupid cow. 'Course we made a recording. Here, where's that camera?'

'No! She's right. *That one* should have been in the film, begging her fucking royal guts out,' said the elegant man.

'You're blaming *me*? Wasn't *he* the one who wanted to be the star, and say good-bye to mummy? He posted our only memory card before we could stop'im. Anyhow, who got us all put under surveillance? For all we know, you spilled the beans. We're prob'ly all being watched right now!'

'Bitch's right. We should have a statement from her, holding a newspaper in front of the camera, showing the date 'n'all!'

'It's not too late, you clowns,' Jane said. 'Once the shops open, you could do it again. Get it right this time.' She delivered her frostiest librarian tone.

'Yeah, we'd get more play if we put the old princess in a recording!'

'YouTube it. It'll go viral within minutes,' Jane added.

'Whose side are you on, you cunt?'

'I just can't bear stupidity,' Jane hissed. 'And some of you are stupider than others.'

Jane's reward was to hear the elegant-voiced kidnapper chuckling to himself and then shouting, 'So who's going out to the shop is what I want to know? Who buys another memory card?'

Stratagem Thirty-three bought them more minutes. Jane and Lorraine sat in their heavy harnesses while the gang argued long and hard about who would feature standing on either side of Lorraine and what killers wore in kidnap movies—hoods with eye holes cut out, or just scarves wrapped around their noses and mouths under a pair of sunglasses.

They couldn't find any scarves. Black plastic bin bags didn't seem quite the thing.

They drew lots to see who would draft the plea and then disputed over the result of the pull.

They rowed over who had misplaced the camera and then lost their tempers completely when the battery wasn't charged.

For the first time since their abduction, Jane started to think that these boys really were hopeless amateurs after all. Her hopes were dashed when she heard sirens coming into their earshot and the screech of tyres outside.

'Deadline's passed. Put on your belts,' the elegant voice cut off their bickering at last. 'I got an audience all arranged while you gits were arguing. They're on their way. Let'em film her live in the street. Let everybody in England see the old bag beg, live and in colour.'

There was a terrible finality to his announcement that caught the whole room in its web.

'Bloody hell. Look out the window.'

They were impatient, scared, and fed up with each other. Suddenly Jane could smell the intoxication of celebrity suicide suffocating them into action.

'. . . Yeah, watch the Queen's cousin grovel and then we *do it.*'

'We're gonna go anyway, after this.'

Someone opened the front door. A chill drizzle hit Jane's face and hands. A bird twittered and a set of tyres swished on the wet street past her. A few raindrops dripped their way down her collar. The belt hung like two sacks of flour at the stiffest part of her aching spine.

'FREEZE,' came a megaphoned bark from far off in front of her.

Jane wanted to run, but in which direction? She reached out in all directions, hoping to get hold of Lorraine. She put her face to her knees to stop shaking, like an animal hoping to sink into a safe cleft in the field. Even if she could reach Lorraine, a loving embrace might trigger their deaths.

Violent hands pushed her down and her knuckles were ground raw across rough asphalt. Was the person pinning her down also rigged for dismemberment? Or were he and his friends postponing the panting virgins for another day?

Out of an eerie hush, Lorraine screamed and a car braked somewhere to Jane's right, its rubber wheels screeching like a cornered animal. Had they thrown Lorraine in front of a speeding car? Were they wired to a detonator? Would it be petrol and a lighted match?

Loud shouts came at them from right and left, all from across the street. Blindfolded, Jane couldn't make out what to do. She didn't dare jerk herself away from her captor or even turn her head too fast.

Jane thought of praying but just then the kidnappers started up a loud chant in unison which made a mockery of her own appeals to the Divine.

Sammie. Sammie. Joe. Sammie. Joe. Sammie. That was close enough to a prayer and this time, no tactic of Baldwin's came to interrupt her grief. Now she burst into tears, clogging up the sticky tape pressing on her lids.

Jane trusted Joe. She knew him in and out. If she died in the next few minutes, he'd put Sammie above everything else for the rest of his life. That there was no doubt in her heart on that one point was welcome comfort. Knowing that and loving him for that, at least, gave her some peace.

The ominous chanting ended. Even the official shouts off in the distance fell away, leaving rain spattering Jane's forehead and a gurgling of innocent water running along gutters somewhere near her knees. She made out the anonymous thrum of early morning traffic, the sound of London's throbbing lung, set behind the rumbling of diesel engines running low and steady not too far off. But in the immediate empty space around Jane there was only a lethal hush.

A walkie-talkie squawked, then nothing. Lorraine and she must be in some kind of standoff. They were kneeling, dead centre in the deadly eye of a security hurricane. Perhaps no one dared extend a hand for fear of triggering explosives.

'C'mon!' a kidnapper jeered from some ten feet behind Jane. 'C'mon, Princess! Beg for mercy.'

'Do as they say,' Jane urged Lorraine. *Anything to buy more time.*

Lorraine's voice came from about four or five metres to Jane's right, filled with sobs, 'I can't! I'm a blank! I can't think!'

Jane turned her face in Lorraine's direction. 'Course you can, darling. It's just a speech.'

'Not this time. Don't you realize? They'll kill us as soon as I finish.'

'That's nothing, compared to that critic from *The Times*,' Jane soothed her. 'They just want you to plead for mercy.'

'I can't do it, Jane, I can't go on!'

'Come on, bitch. Beg the fuckin' Queen to save you!' a kidnapper taunted.

'I'll prompt you, darling.'

'My lines, sweetheart,' Lorraine's gasp came almost inaudibly through the quickening rain.

'Remember Manchester? The festival? Your Portia?'

'Portia? Portia. Yes. Yes.' Lorraine started, 'Yes, I've got it, now. *The quality of mercy is not strained* . . .' But the old woman faltered.

'*It droppeth* . . .' Jane prompted.

'*It droppeth as the gentle rain from heaven . . . upon the place beneath . . .*'

'Bloody bitch! You promised to beg! They can't hear you!'

'She's talking about the bleeding rain—?'

'We should've done her in the basement when we had the chance—'

'Well, she's begging for mercy!' countered the American voice, 'And shit, it is fuckin' raining!'

'It is twice blessed,' Lorraine's voice swelled. '*IT BLESSETH HIM THAT GIVES AND HIM THAT TAKES: 'TIS*

MIGHTIEST IN THE MIGHTIEST; IT BECOMES THE THRONED MONARCH BETTER THAN HIS CROWN . . .'

The great actress Lorraine King had found her motivation and hit her stride, declaiming Shakespeare to the rising winds, although Jane detected in Lorraine's delivery more of Jack King's failing Lear than anybody's Portia. If Lorraine's strength and memory didn't give out, at least her mother would go out in character. No doubt to the kidnappers it all sounded like the kind of wackiness a stressed-out Windsor might come up with: *'IT IS AN ATTRIBUTE TO GOD HIMSELF—'*

'List our demands, you cow! Oh, right! That's great! She's peeing herself again. That's it!' One of the kidnappers sounded seconds from blowing himself up when Jane heard a voice full of authority shout down his megaphone, 'Good Lord, the bastards sliced her nose!'

There was an ear-splitting shout, a response, shrieking ululation, heavy footsteps racing toward Jane from the humming engines, barks of 'Watch out! 'Take cover!' 'RUN!'—then a deafening *BOOM*!

A tidal wave of gravel and loose branches thudded into Jane's soggy back, flattening her across the asphalt.

Bullets thudded into a wall on Jane's right and a kerbside to her left. She slowly curled her legs up, a terrified snail about to die on a London side street. She voided into her trousers with terror. Rather than feeling shameful, it merely felt like her life's guts draining out of her.

Groans floated through the wet breeze. Low grunts and awful animal squeals of pain punctuated a horrible silence.

'Mum?' Jane yelled out into the blackness.

'*Take up the bodies*, darling girl. *Much amiss* . . .' Lorraine's voice died away.

Chapter Thirty-four, Inflict Injury on One's Self, Win the Enemy's Trust

'Did she do that on purpose?'

'What?' The explosions seemed to have robbed Jane of half her hearing.

'Pissing herself?' The Assistant Commissioner in charge of special operations added, 'Quite normal under the circumstances, but if it was a trick to distract them, it was brilliant.'

Their ambulance wheeled and screeched its way to an emergency ward. In the back of the van, Jane managed a wan smile at the officer's stream of compliments: '*The Merchant of Venice* certainly wasn't something those idiots bargained for!'

On a stretcher between their benches, Lorraine lay swaddled in blankets, barely conscious, with her phony nose still dangling by a rubbery string off her lolling head. She resembled an Egyptian mummy coming unwrapped. Her condition was stable but at her age, it was hard to predict her survival of shock. Her mother's senses had been knocked for six.

'They didn't seem to have any plan,' Jane yelled, clutching her police-issued rain cloak over her soiled trousers.

'None worth mentioning. Of course, that's the worst kind of criminal—unpredictable,' the officer nodded. 'Once we ID'ed your location and monitored their bickering, we knew they might do anything. Seems one of them had spotted your mother masquerading as Princess Alexandra at the butcher's shop? He thought nabbing the Princess was the best comeback from the humiliation of a botched bombing. Of course, it all went pear-shaped. They were just stupid kids.'

'But who was managing them?'

The officer checked her bandaged brow where a graze from the explosion still seeped faint red. 'No one. At least no one our informer could nail down. God knows, he waited 'til too late trying to nail down some evidence.'

'An informer? With us?'

'Of course. He's the only reason your mother's final appearance wasn't some grisly item on *Newsnight*.'

'I must thank him,' Jane shouted over the traffic. It must be the man with the velvet voice, the one who brought them food and who had raised her hackles with a whispered warning that she might be unmasked at any moment. He'd known the risks of that to Jane, to Lorraine—and to himself.

The officer's eyebrows shot up. 'He died a few minutes ago at hospital.'

At Jane's startled look, she explained, 'Oh, we didn't shoot our own man. He swapped the dummy belt he'd prepared for himself, and put it on you. He had to take the suicide belt along with the others and he managed to defuse Lorraine as best he could when no one was looking. His priority was saving you, the mother of a teen-ager. You kept saying "Sammie," over and over again. Well, they would certainly trust him now.'

Jane's hands trembled with guilt. She flashed back to that fierce-faced young man greeting her outside the bookstore. She'd scurried away, nervous, while all along, she'd been gazing at the *wrong angel*—Joop's blond windowpane warrior was only a painted reflection of her true protector, the dark-haired guardian chatting on the step.

She shouted back to the AC: 'I met him before. I was looking up at a painting of St Michael on a window. And he told me Muslims believe in St Michael, too—just like Christians—only they think his body is covered with tiny hairs begging Allah for mercy.'

'Oh, that was our Gilbert. Always the cultural go-between.' The officer yelled, 'All I know is, St Michael's the patron saint of policemen. Good enough for me.'

Their ambulance whined into the Emergency entrance.

'Would the government have withdrawn any troops? I mean, if Princess Alexandra really had been nabbed and the Queen had asked?'

'I rather doubt it somehow. Here we are. Mind your step.'

The hospital kept Lorraine for two nights to run tests. It was a blessing for Jane who was too fagged to unwrap bouquets, mix drinks, or otherwise run interference with the inevitable flock of old acting birds who fluttered to the ward to check Lorraine's pulse in person.

Jane faced a first session at Scotland Yard, so even as wrap-ups of the story ran on the evening news, another version of the events—every rustle, sound, smell, and phrase—was extracted from Jane. Dan was permitted only to look in for a hug. The debriefing was the purview of two Englishmen who took nothing Jane said at face value. Perversely, sitting in her own waste in front of two tight-lipped interrogators required almost as much patience as lying gagged and bound with wire on a dirty cement floor.

Finally, she was released, exhausted, and still stinking, despite a shower and change at the police station. Their car delivered her gently around the familiar red, pink and blue facades of Chalkwood Square and pulled up outside her door.

Now Jane wept again, but this time with joy at seeing in the chill light what was almost ripped away from her by violent, illiterate youths. Number 19 waited there—its whitewashed Doric columns, nineteenth-century porticoes and crumbling cornices, Lorraine's dormer window—all dark. Only the single desk lamp by Joe's chair blinked its glowing vigil. Sammie was no doubt waiting for her.

She expected Dan would be there too; there was still so much to say to each other once her fog of confusion cleared away like the frost that was just now melting off the glinting grass. Whereas Special Branch had insisted on questioning Jane alone—uncoached and uncomforted—Dan could explain how their hiding places had been traced, who'd given the orders to hold fire or shoot and how and when he'd realized that his bungling bookstore bombers had hatched such a foolish last bid for infamy.

Love and the Art of War

Somewhere between the Bermondsey Factory for the Blind and the brink of death, Jane had mislaid her latchkey. Her police escort knocked.

Jane looked up as Joe answered the front door. He took Jane into his arms without a word. The policewoman followed them into the living room, studded by traces of an Ops Headquarters. Tea mugs and ashtrays stood draining upside down like scrubbed down soldiers at attention next to the sink. Discarded paper plates and empty chips packets told their story of thwarted hours and a helpful child kept busy by strangers doing their terrifying and impersonal duty.

'Joe, I wasn't expecting you, to be here, right now. Where's Sammie?' Jane's elation collapsed. She wanted to crawl into a bath and under the duvet. The front door closed behind the departing officer.

Joe nodded in the direction of Sammie's back room. 'She kept vigil until you were safe and then, well, I forced her to bed.' He folded up a blanket into a polite square and laid it on the sofa. He went into the kitchen and started the kettle.

'Sammie's all right?'

'She is now. She was incredibly steady. You remember when she was three and lost her beloved anteater? Remember that brave face?'

'Wylie the Anteater.' She accepted the steaming mug of coffee spiked with Grand Marnier from Joe's hand. The warm liquid ran down her aching gullet. She'd forgotten Wylie. When dusk fell on the square, three-year-old Sammie would clamber up the stairs of Number 19 with Wylie in her arms, their hair and fur stiff with mud and dead leaves. More than once, Jane had thrust her nose into Wylie's matted coat to drink in the rich sweetness of Sammie mixed with detergent and rich nature.

'And remember the look on her face when I found him in the boot?' Joe asked. 'If you'd seen Sammie these last two days! The bravado—those King genes performing away! The show must go on! And also that practical Gilchrist streak. She must've made twenty pots of tea.'

Jane laughed.

'But I could read her,' Joe went on. 'She was in terror of losing everything. It wasn't Lorraine or Sterling's expression. I saw her mother's face, *your face*, Jane, with that expression you wore all this winter. We were so afraid we'd never see that face again . . .' His voice cracked and he turned away.

Jane stared up at him. Suddenly abashed, he looked out at the square and shifted to something easier. 'You were unbelievably brave.'

'Oh, it was Lorraine's show. As usual.'

'No. I hear you were the brave one. Everyone says so.' Joe insisted. 'You kept her going. *As usual.*'

'You don't have to be nice, Joe. It's enough that I'm alive.'

'You don't understand, Jane. You don't realize you're at the centre, you're at the core of this family. You're not supporting cast. You know what Lorraine once told me when we were strolling up Primrose Hill? That what kept her going during the darkest years was you—you waking her up as soon as you got home from school, you packing her sandwiches, you running her bath, ironing her blouses, and setting her hair . . . and you hiding the booze when the good parts dried up.'

'She knew I did that?'

'Jane, you have always been her measure and her judge. She said you were the only critic whose reviews she cared about. All those years, she played to an audience of one—her baby.'

'But—but—I've always felt so dismissed. So sidelined. I could never live up to her billing.'

'She tries to steal the limelight, but let's face it, the old girl's more than ready to go. When I took her to Boots one day for medicines, she looked at the diapers for seniors and joked that one of these days, I should just take her out behind the barn like a worn-out cow and shoot her—her exact words. But you aren't ready to go. You had everything to lose last night. You were the brave one. And we're not prepared to lose you. I've never had to endure what you've just gone through. You have all my admiration and—' Joe hesitated.

Jane put her hand over his mouth and finished her coffee with a gulp. She tried to get up from the sofa but couldn't find the strength.

'I mean it. I've filmed people in war zones, but I was always nice and safe out of the frame, buffered by the cameraman. I accused you of hiding in books, but actually, you know? I was just as bad, always one remove from danger. You were about to lose your life,' He laid his hand on hers, 'with your plans for the future, and all. Funny, I only started to notice you even *had* plans once we weren't together every day. I guess I used to try to monopolize your attention by keeping you as my production assistant. Otherwise, you seemed closed off. I didn't feel so important in your eyes . . .'

How many years had she watched his brow furrow over drafts of proposals, shooting scripts, and recce schedules? If he had clamoured for her attention by needing her as his sounding board, how many years had she taken him for granted, only to look up over these recent winter months to see nothing but her lonely reflection in the dark kitchen windows? She turned away from her ghastly reflection now. Small wonder Joe fell into the arms of a bosomy housewares goddess, swooning one minute over future broadcast triumphs, seducing him the next with love hot and fresh from the oven?

She pecked him lightly on one cheek. 'I'll send Sammie over in a few days and maybe I'll take a little trip by myself to rest. Visit libraries in Cornwall or Edinburgh for Camille.'

'Yeah. You don't need me. You want me to call . . . Dan?'

'No,' she waved him off. ' I want to be alone with Sammie, just the two of us.'

'For a minute there, it felt like the three of us.'

Jane held her ground in silence. As the door closed behind Joe, she felt affection both weary and wary, all mangled up with sentiment, stale anger, and untethered misgiving. To track back to the origins of this muddle, to launch some kind of emotional archaeological dig, to excavate the skull bones of a rift that led to dishonesty and ultimately disloyalty—it was all too sad and late for that. She was bleeding somewhere, she felt truly injured, but when she checked in the bath an hour later, she couldn't locate the wound.

><>~<><

'Well, we're getting there,' Winston said, checking his revision sheet. The two friends faced each other across a pot of coffee. The kitchen table was scattered with to-do lists for the Grand Production of Lorraine's eventful eightieth year. Lorraine wasn't missing her big day, even if the doctor had relegated her to enforced bed rest until the very morning of the celebration.

As far as Winston was concerned, the party was in the bag—a takeaway bag from the Moonbeam Café. Gone were the fancy canapés promised a year ago by Bella, along with the cocktail menu Chris had patched together from cookery books in the library. With Cecilia's input and the goodwill of the Ng family's overworked staff, Winston had completed the menu, hired spare tables, chairs, glasses, plates, and silverware.

'Where are the chopsticks?' Jane checked his list.

'Your guests are too arthritic to manage anything but spoons.'

'We'll double the rice portions and slice the spring rolls into bite size pieces. And nobody needs teeth to eat almond gelatine. They'll manage with chopsticks.'

'I hate chopsticks, Jane. So fiddly.'

'It's not *your* birthday, Winston. Put the chopsticks back.'

Jane still had to sort out the hire cars and small vans for so many luvvies equipped with wheel chairs and walkers. Many would come with caregivers, but thanks to Sir Bernard's offer to serve sandwiches in his basement kitchen next door to the help, Lorraine's oldsters could revel a whole evening away from offstage feedings, changings, and nursing. They would return, for one day, to their authentic selves: hero and heavy, dame or ingénue, second banana, gravedigger, porter, and it went without saying, every single one of them a star.

Winston poured himself another coffee. 'Stop worrying about the party, Jane. Let's go over our notes. One week to the practice test. Right. Name all the Simulation Stratagems.'

'Oh, that's too difficult,' Jane yawned.

'I did it.'

'You did?'

Winston nodded. 'Just run your mind down the list. Which ones involve simulation?'

'Something out of nothing, Number Seven. Your father almost fell for that one, didn't he?'

'Until Nelson spotted the cards pre-printed and hidden under the desk.'

'Feigning Madness, Decorating a Barren Tree, Opening the Gates Wide, and . . . um . . .'

'The one you missed, playing hooky being kidnapped. Think masochistic.'

'That reminds me of the party. I've got fifty-seven women and only eleven men—'

'It's Inflict Injury on One's Self to Win the Enemy's Trust, the strategy of the suffering flesh. Prince Hu Lu sent his adviser Yao Li to spy on the Wei Kingdom. In order to convince the Prince of Wei that he could trust Yao Li, Prince Hu Lu sliced off Yao Li's arm, beheaded his wife and children—'

'My God!'

'That's the tactic. Self-mutilation to win the enemy's trust. Weaken yourself. Play the victim just to get sympathy.'

Jane copied Winston's notes.

'And don't forget preventive strategies, Jane. Baldwin says I'm good at those. Keep your eyes peeled for self-styled victims, underdogs, or anyone angling for the sympathy vote. And the counter tactic: if you put yourself at a disadvantage, just make sure it's not irreversible.'

'We're supposed to be learning survival. Baldwin's idea of winning is we cut off our limbs?'

'Not to mention committing suicide when your leader wins and you're unmasked as his spy. That's what Yao Li did.' Winston frowned. 'Not much of a happy ending, is it?'

Jane sighed. 'Who expects happy endings these days?'

Considering his stratagems always backfired, Winston sounded surprisingly upbeat. 'You know, Jane, I'm going to pass this practice exam and I'm going to pass the final. I'm going to wave my results in my father's scrawny face and then leave Belsize Park for good.'

'Oh, no!'

'Give up on Chu Printers or Raisin Pixels or whatever Nelson's going to christen it. I'm leaving the Kingdom of Chu for good. To follow my stars into the property business, my one true dream. An exile in the finest tradition of the ancients.'

'You're leaving London?'

Winston had grown up. Just a few faded apricot tips remained of his 'fun' fringe. 'Moving to Hong Kong. I'll stay with Auntie Lo, daughter of Grandma Two.'

'The monkey owner?'

'The very one. I wish I had some capital, but when I think of Madame Leong as a stepmother, I realize I'm lucky to escape with the shirt on my back.'

'Does your father know?'

'He's too busy running around like an old rooster in heat. I told Nelson that for all I care, Selina and he can turn the whole shop into a software circus.'

'Was he happy?'

'Yes, but I'm not sure he heard me under his earphones. He was ogling *Hei Bai* Girl's latest video.'

'Are you sure it's the right decision? Just walking away is a pretty big sacrifice.'

'Stratagem Thirty-three.'

'My goodness, Winston.'

'Look who's talking. Didn't Joe hint that he'd stay the other night, if you had swallowed your pride and asked? That he liked being the three of you again?'

'I couldn't go back to the way it was, Winston. I see now that it was like there were bits of Joe and me attached, here and there, but always with other people filling in the gaps.'

'So, you let him walk out. Wasn't that rather a big sacrifice?'

Jane rinsed the crumbs off their cake plates. 'I couldn't take advantage of a crisis and exploit Joe's sympathy. It would only backfire once the romance of my rescue faded. I could only live again with Joe on one basis, the way it should have been from the very beginning when we were first in love—wholeheartedly, as husband and wife. And that's not going to happen, even if ironically, my mother's trail of divorced husbands doesn't haunt me anymore. That was her life, but not mine. So, yes, I shooed him away.'

'Still, it must hurt. Like Yao Li watching his family beheaded.'

'Actually, Winston, it still hurts like hell.'

Chapter Thirty-five, Chain The Enemy's Ships Together

A February hailstorm pelted Jane as she locked up the library branch, navigated the slippery pedestrian rail bridge and reached the tube station. She'd stayed up late the night before polishing her proposal for Camille and so muddled through a Friday's shelving, her tired mind now on Baldwin's practice exam.

The course was coming to its end and so was her job. So far the signals on an extension of her BBC contract were good: the outline of episode themes had fallen into place, the proposed summer research trips were almost scheduled, and a pared-down budget stood close to approval.

A hollow-eyed Dan kissed her with a sigh of relief before they went into the classroom. Over the last ten days he'd attended an emotionally draining memorial service for the heroic Gilbert Sullivan, supervised the bureaucratic mop-up of what was left of the botched conspiracy, and debriefed grieving families in the company of his English counterparts.

Still, the London team and he had come no closer to building a case of solid evidence against any ringleader. He worked long days with the Brits and spent exhausting nights on the phone to New York. They had to make sure all avenues were explored before concluding that this particular 'international terrorism' plot was nothing more than an amateur fiasco turned deadly.

The latent schoolgirl in Jane hoped to please Baldwin. Nigel wanted to gain more corner office space using the tactics, and Winston dreamed of showing up a father who taunted him for ineptitude in All Things Chinese. Even Keith and Kev planned on finessing their jobs with newfound inscrutability.

Dan was just along for the ride, and by meeting Jane, he'd solved the loneliness of his empty evenings, even if he hadn't prevented his New Jersey quarry from self-destructing.

Baldwin passed out the question sheets: 'More than any of the other tactics, I'd like to see Number Thirty-Five.' Thirty-Five was

Link the Enemy's Ships Together, using a mix of stratagems to achieve a goal.

Jane scribbled away; she grouped her strategies, worked her defences, listed protective feints, and historical examples. She was doing well until the essay section. She tried writing about the Bookworms, but it wasn't working, so she tried describing how the strategies had, for a time at least, offset complete domestic collapse at Number 19.

Finally, halfway through her second draft, her pen slowed as she realized a deeper truth: this hapless band fighting for elbow space in their cramped closet, Baldwin's own class, had lived the wisdom of the Chinese ancients.

They had created something out of nothing, Number Seven—weaving a web of affection among strangers to face down a discouraging winter. Baldwin's assignments had distracted Jane's attention, leaving her subconscious time to overcome the shock of Joe's defection, a Noise in the East, Number Six. Over time, Jane and Dan had become lovers, while in class they posed as mere buddies, the proverbial cicadas leaving their skins in place—Number Twenty-one.

She started over and sped through her essay to the scratch of Nigel's fountain pen and Winston's groans. Stumped by the essay, Keith stared into the distance—as if one of his insured lay dying under Baldwin's stool.

'Don't sit there on your Jack Jones, Phipps!' Kevin jabbed his friend. In fact, Kev was working faster than any of them but was cheating; Jane saw Baldwin spot the stratagems coded on the label of Kev's water bottle, but do nothing. Perhaps Kev would explain his ruse as a stratagem.

'Time!' Baldwin collected their papers with a paternal pat on Winston's shoulder. When Winston wouldn't stop, Baldwin pried the pen from his fist. 'It's only a practice, dear boy.'

'Well, that wasn't so bad!' Kevin leant back, nearly knocking over the tell-tale bottle. 'You all right, Deloitte? Did you link'em up all into one fiendish chain of hedging, investing, disinvesting, merging, and cut-throat robbery?'

'Oh, zip it up, Filgrove.'

'Relax, Nige, it's just a warm-up.'

'I've got other things on my mind right now.'

'Eeoooow, aren't we touchy?

'Sorry, but I haven't had a very good week.' Nigel's knuckles went from dry pink to blanched bone. 'If you must know, I've been made redundant.'

Everyone stared at the banker.

Kevin looked a bit shamefaced. 'Oh, God.'

Baldwin shook his head. 'I'm very sorry to hear this, Nigel. You've been one of my best pupils in the entire history of this course.'

'Well, some things are beyond any strategies. The bank's writing down £1.2 billion because of pricing errors on asset-backed securities. It's an excuse to clean out anyone in sight of his pension.'

'The bastards!' Winston slammed his fist. 'Claim unfair dismissal.'

'Oh, I'll get a handshake, Chu, though it won't be golden,' Nigel said. 'They promised to carry me for six months, so Joyce and the children should be all right until I find something else.' He cleared his throat. 'I guess you all know I was a bit cross at first that this class wasn't full of City people. Now I admit, I've learned from all of you to think outside the box a bit more. From now on, I'll apply any strategy I can think of. When one fails, I'll fall back on the next. Unlike the rest of you, I've made one fatal error over the entire winter.'

'Assuming that you knew where the battleground was,' Baldwin said with sympathy.

Nigel's snorted. 'Absolutely correct! I wasn't leading any attack. I was completely under siege and I didn't even know it.'

Something was up. Bella's message, an imperial summons, was unequivocal—that Jane collect Sammie from *The Travelling Kitchen* studio in Battersea without delay. Jane rang Sammie, then Rachel, then Bella's mobile, to no avail. A secretary said Joe was ensconced in 'one of those meetings,' which struck Jane as odd because it was a taping day; Joe should be on the set, not in the production office.

Why couldn't Sammie taxi her way to Bella's flat? Or hop on the Northern Line back to Chalkwood Square? If Sammie was injured, Bella or Rachel should alert everyone on the way to hospital without delay. Jane chugged southwards in a taxi towards the South Bank. Only a forced march to Bella's cookery temple in Battersea would resolve this mystery. That was motherhood. Whatever lay tattered because of three adults' ambitions and blind spots, her child mustn't suffer any more. Sammie had finally started eating square meals again.

Bella's refitted factory space was touted on London's feature pages for being her 'self-realization sanctuary.' Its industrial gates admitted only a few privileged souls. Book reviewers of *Bella's Bistros, Bringing Home the Flavours*, and *Travelling Without a Ticket* had all answered the Cooking Queen's bidding to nibble and gossip—for exactly twenty-nine minutes.

Joe dismissed it as a 'girlie palace,' and worked from Shepherd's Bush as much as he could.

Jane trudged up two flights of steel stairs, her tread reverberating up and down the open stairwell. At the top of the third-floor landing, she found a mammoth lift for hoisting machinery. After ascending the last two storeys, its cage rattled open. Jane stepped into a minimalist foyer furnished in cinder blocks of heavy blue glass setting off a sleek desktop and chrome laptop.

Mundane office junk—telephones, filing cabinets, paper cups, cables, ashtrays—all the usual detritus of television studios, was banished from Bella's universe. Jane thought of Joe's rough and tumble décor for making documentaries—unwanted celluloid bits ground into the floorboards with old chewing gum and editors' cigarette butts.

Bella Crawford products sat in white box displays, lit and framed like precious museum pieces: pastel pepper grinders, hand-painted Tuscan platters, teak-handled woks, Korean condiment trays, Balinese salad forks, even a Mongolian grill sprouting dozens of sharp teeth for hooking shredded sirloin. A battalion of lethal sushi knives stood arranged by length and shape on a special rack near large double doors giving on to the interior studio proper.

Jane was just recalling Joe's joke that you needed a licence from Tokyo to wield those sushi slicers, when Bella's 'on-air' voice came from the dark cavern beyond. The star was hidden from Jane's view by banks of cameras, make-up artists and lighting technicians.

'I can't manage these gloves. They're far too clumsy.'

'Bella, can I have another sound level, please?' a soundman asked.

'I WON'T WEAR THESE GLOVES! Loud enough?' The amplifier whined its painful feedback.

Tiptoeing through the doorway, Jane nearly stumbled over two sheet-white legs stretched across her path. They belonged to Rachel, sprawled in a folding chair tilted against the wall.

'Hello, Rachel. Where's Sammie? What's wrong?'

'Haf a drinkie, Jane.' Rachel pulled a bottle out from behind her chair and poured some alcohol into a celadon 'BC' mug. 'Have a shot on the house. Some sort of Sri Lankan whisky. Brilliant stuff. Ordered it in Soho, the place we get the specialty beers. The Kaku—' she coughed, 'Sorry, the *whatever* duck is marinating in a bucket of it.'

Jane held the bottle up against a powerful spotlight shining above them. Rachel had pickled herself better than the duck. She knelt down to Rachel for a better look. The researcher was a bleached hue most often found floating in formaldehyde.

'Rachel, what's wrong with you? What's going on?'

'Joe just called from some meeting. They've cancelled the show. Finally.' Rachel suddenly leered. 'I'm liberated! Released! I'm not One Bit Sorry.'

Rachel's BlackBerry leaped around her ankles on the concrete floor like a Mexican jumping bean, its ring tones silenced for taping. Rachel waved it off. 'That, no doubt, is Personnel.'

'Have you told Bella yet?' Jane whispered. From the centre of the kitchen set, Bella was shielding her eyes against the blinding spots with one hand as she argued into the darkness about the dangers of blue crabs.

A man's elegant voice came from centre stage. 'I will wear the gloves. A single crab pinch can cause blood poisoning. Be very careful. Mrs Crawford should step on them like this, you see, and then pinch them with her thumb and index finger, this way.'

Rachel shook her head. 'I'm not going to tell her! Not in front of Chef Ragapaksa. He flew all night from Colombo and he's been such a good sport.' Rachel hiccoughed. 'I have a *shuper* idea.' She emptied her mug. 'You tell her. She already hates you, because she thinks Joe still loves you.'

Joe. This meant Joe was also out of a job.

'What happened, Rachel?'

'Delia's become flavour of the month with her cheesy all-English meals from packets. *Frugal Food's* been reissued. And Jamie keeps hammering on and on, grow your own, don't buy Hawaiian! Joe said they're already auditioning for a real English cook up in Manchester. *Salt of the earth* is what they want now.'

'Rachel, where's Sammie? I came here for Sammie!'

'Then the sales figures came in and you know, the sales on Bella Bunsen Burners are more important than viewers these days. Orders have just dropped off like that.' Rachel let a limp hand drop to her lap.

'Why so sudden?'

'Well, Gawd, Jane, do *you* have to ask? The Burmese street demo was bad enough. And then that photo in *The Daily Mail*. That's what did her in,' Rachel checked the whisky dregs. 'What's more hip now—a garlic press with her initials or Barf with Bella

Doggie Cushions off the Internet?' Rachel started sliding off the chair on to the concrete floor.

'You're pissed, Rachel. Go home.'

'I can't,' Rachel moaned. 'I'm waiting to swab up the festive lamprie segment before they do Duck Padré.'

'JANE!' Bella's voice roared out from all four corners of the studio, like the Wizard of Oz's 'great and terrible' from behind his screen. Fully made-up for taping, a vivid Bella materialized, looming at them through the shadows.

'Bella! Where's Sammie? What's wrong?'

'Jane, I have something to show you. And I want to hear from your own lips, immediately, what you intend to do about it. I have loved Sammie like a daughter, but I don't welcome any child into my home, the centre of my life-to-work balance, just to nourish a little viper. Not with the pressures I face—'

Rachel giggled, 'She has nooooo idea.'

'I found this in Sammie's school bag.'

Bella thrust a dog-eared piece of paper into Jane's face. It was none other than Baldwin's stratagems issued on that fateful first night of class. Shown to 'Your man on the inside' before the Burmese conspiracy, Sammie had scribbled the reverse side into a tangle of maths solutions, manga-style lettering, caricatures of Bella as a terrifying crone, and most heart-breaking, a four-line stanza dedicated to 'Mum and Dad'.

Jane thought fast, *Feign madness, play dumb.* 'Sammie draws well, don't you think? Look at this shading. I had no idea she could—'

'It's not the cartoon that bothers me. I worked out all that evil stepmother stuff at Kabala class. Look! There! What's that? A shopping list for substitutions she made on my Burma show. Oh, foolish me, I forgave it as a last-minute, spur-of-the-moment teenage prank. But it was all premeditated. Look, look, right here? Number Twenty-five, something about beams and pillars?'

'Sammie?' Jane called. Her daughter must be somewhere in that halo of the blinding spots and 'babies' illuminating the cooking island.

'Leave her out of this. She's busy getting crabs ready. This is between you and me. Your handwriting is on the front of this list.'

Jane wouldn't accept blame without a fight. *Turn the guest into host.* 'Bella, aren't you to blame for Sammie's hostility? She was ready to swallow the seduction of her father, even without the help of Kabala, but using the child as your weekend *sous-chef*, mop-up girl, factotum and all-round mule! Okay, it was a fun excuse for a few weeks, but even she realizes it's hurting her exams and her future. Which is more important than yours, Bella. Don't you think all this scrubbing the hearth might have been the last straw? It's something out of *Cinderella*.'

Nobody had ever nailed Bella yet for her crimes and got away with it. 'That's a lie. I've been kind and generous and–and— *inclusive.* I trusted her to be a team player. This is your revenge. To sabotage my career—'

Jane sniggered, 'Sabotage?'

'You trained her to use these tricks on me, didn't you?'

Jane hid her dagger behind a rueful smile. 'Bella, if only I could get Sammie to do anything. You know what problems Joe and I have with her. She wouldn't listen to me. She's completely besotted with your fame, your glamour, your generosity, your *everything.* I don't have a chance. But you do overwork her. Maybe she's just tired.'

Droplets of sweat broke through the make-up coating Bella's upper lip. 'You've played a really good game with me, haven't you, Jane? So accepting. So resigned. Pretending you understood what Joe and I have found together, acting like all you cared about was Sammie's welfare and shagging that American copper. Why, perhaps a little, and I do mean a little, of Lorraine's talent rubbed off on you after all. You probably arranged that whole kidnapping thing, just to get Joe's attention.'

Rachel mumbled. 'Try a plane crash next time, Jane.'

'It's really sad, you know? Bella grabbed Baldwin's stratagems and waved the paper in Jane's face. 'I'm going to show this to Joe. He'll see how pathetic you are, you and your kung-fu tactics.

Whatever misgivings he had—oh, poor Jane, so kind, so selfless, she only lives for books—wait 'til he sees this.'

Muddy the waters. 'Bella, I know you're paranoid but Joe already knows everything . . .'

'Paranoid?' Bella rounded down on Rachel, cowering at her feet. 'Phineas, am I paranoid?' she shrieked at one of the grips. Shielding his chest behind a coil of cables, Phineas scuttled past.

Jane spotted Sammie in the circle of light illuminating the show kitchen's work island. She was kneeling on the floor next to a plastic bin full of swarming blue crabs. Her small hands were slopping around in rubber fisherman's gloves. The crabs clawed her while she fumbled at their string bindings with poultry scissors and a pair of foot-long tongs.

The Sri Lankan chef stood at her side, his limpid black eyes observing Sammie's struggle. Wearing an immaculate apron, the enigmatic Mr Rajapaksa was a stunner with black curls oiled into a long ponytail. He was gorgeous enough to hurry thirteen hours straight from his tropical redoubt to stardom in Battersea, but too mindful of his debut to risk splashing crab muck on his toque.

Sew discord. Jane asked, 'Rachel, didn't I tell you I was taking an evening class? Didn't I show you this list?'

Rachel nodded. 'At the Greek restaurant. You said they were coping mechanisms.'

Bella peered closer into Rachel's ghost face. 'What's wrong with you?' She seized the empty whisky bottle. 'Oh, for God's sake! This is for the Padré Duck!'

'I have done my job. The duck is just as pissed as I am.'

Bella shook the empty bottle. 'But that was only Duck One! Where's the rest for Duck Two?'

Rachel flapped her hands a little and wobbled to her feet. 'It doesn't matter. Duck Two can go free. I'm free. You're free. Nobody is going to see this show. You are cancelled.'

'What?' Bella grabbed for Rachel but missed. The PA teetered away on three-inch Jimmy Choos. Bella headed pell-mell after her.

Now was the moment: *watch tigers fight, commit robbery while the house burns, and lead the sheep away*, in short, get Sammie out of this madness. Rachel and Bella had circled around to the microwave and were yelling at each other while Sammie stared at them from the other side of the island. Various production staffers fell back in retreat, removing headsets, and putting down clipboards as they hurried past Jane. Mr Rajapaksa disappeared in the direction of the toilets. Rachel rounded the island and headed back towards Jane, seeking safety in the foyer Jane had passed through. Bella soared past, yelling, 'Does Joe know? Who signed off on this?'

Jane ran to Sammie. 'Honey, take off that apron and come home. For good.'

'Oh, Mum, I have to stay here. I'm your man on the inside, remember?'

'Not anymore.'

'But then I'll hardly see Dad anymore.' Sammie's anguished expression spelled out how hard it had been. Jane was just searching for an honest reassurance about the future, when she heard Rachel scream.

'What is going on down there?' a voice roared from the director's booth hanging above them.

'She's got a KNIFE!' Rachel returned from the reception area and shouted towards the booth. She skidded and stumbled around the studio, the broken strap of one Choo slapping the floor. Bella followed, one manicured hand wielding a Kobe beef knife.

'Did you give this list to Sammie? Are you plotting against me with them? You're why my show is cancelled, you alcoholic cow! You tell me what Joe said or I'll use this!'

'Bella, put that down, for Chrissake!' *The Travelling Kitchen's* chief gaffer roared. He was a weekend rugby player when he wasn't doing Bella's electrical set-ups. He moved to tackle the star. In petulant surrender, Bella flung the razor-sharp knife straight across the set. To Jane's horror, it sank with a squishy *thunk* into a watermelon-sized jak fruit only inches from Sammie's ear.

In instinctive defence, the teenager slung her crab tongs straight back at Bella who winced at the glancing blow and lunged for her. 'You pimply little fiend!' She managed to grab Sammie's huge apron, which dragged across the island's surface. Melon ballers, *rambutans*, mallets, and paper towels went rolling and clattering in all directions.

With her mother pulling her in the other direction, Sammie jerked herself right out of the apron, and grabbed a colander to protect her face from Bella's blows. She hopped once, twice, and then sank a formidable kick into Bella's stomach. Grandma's expensive ballet lessons had finally paid off. But the force of her violent kick combined with Jane's anxious pulling pulled Sammie off balance.

She tripped and overturned the crab bin.

Gallons of salty water gushed across the studio floor. Phineas and his team raised the alarm. Like whirling cyclones, they ripped up the duct tapes webbing the studio floor as the sloshing tide threatened to short-circuit a fortune in equipment. Two dozen panicked crabs scuttled this way and that.

Jane pulled Sammie back to her feet and they flew towards the foyer, but not before an entire *batterie de cuisine*, including a tenderizing mallet and an eggbeater, whizzed past their temples. Bella's launch of dangerous missiles suddenly stopped with an unholy scream: 'AIIII! GET THEM OFF! GET THEM OFF!'

Jane grabbed the doorframe of the foyer to catch her breath and they looked back at Bella clinging to the edge of the island. She was jerking her right leg back and forth like a Thai boxer doing a warm-up on meth.

Two vicious blue crabs dangled from her ankle.

'I'LL GET BLOOD POISONING! GET THEM OFF!'

But unfortunately for Bella, union men have higher priorities. They were busy sandbagging the bank of mains with flour bags.

Just then Chef Rajapaksa sauntered back from the men's room and noticed Bella.

A panting Rachel stumbled into the foyer. 'The crabs got her.' Jane and Sammie held Rachel steady and the three of them listened to the industrial lift rising slowly to their rescue.

'I will get water,' Rajapaksa shouted with reassuring authority to the studio at large. 'We will immerse her ankle to release their claws.' He filled a spaghetti pot with water and poured it all over

Bella. Even through her hysteria, Bella smiled and turned and batted her lashes at her handsome rescuer.

Ah, Thirty-one, The Beautiful Woman Ploy. Creaking down in the lift to the sanity of the street, Jane kicked herself for forgetting that one.

Chapter Thirty-six, If All Else Fails, Run!

'Thank you so much for inviting me. I'm truly thrilled. I'm a real admirer.' Clumsy as a Stage Door Johnny, Baldwin wrestled with his umbrella. 'She once did a Christmas special on the telly— oh, sorry, excuse me—' A coven of ancient chorus girls jostled Baldwin in their rush to greet the Birthday Dame—'Though it was so many years ago, perhaps it wouldn't be tactful to mention it?'

'It's her eightieth birthday. As long as it's all about her, mention anything.'

Little Monica Chu helped Jane extricate Baldwin from his shabby mac. Glancing at himself in the entrance mirror, he patted down strands of loose hair. 'I've got your practice exam in that briefcase.'

Jane blushed, 'Oh, dear.'

'It was delightful to evaluate. I did yours after wading through Nigel's disheartening take-over tactics and merger machinations. You'll pass beautifully.'

'It's more important what I learned—that if I had had the right tools all along, I wouldn't have spent half my life shying away from every challenge. I would have lived my life facing forward, defending what matters—without fighting. I only learned it too late.'

Sammie bounced in. 'You're Professor Baldwin, aren't you? Will Winston pass his exam?'

'By a pink hair, if he concentrates on prevention ploys,' Baldwin said. 'And Jane,' he turned her by the shoulders away from the shrieks and greetings behind them in the living room. 'I want to confess something. I've felt guilty about it for so many weeks. Now, as you've done so well in the course, I don't feel so, well, duplicitous.'

'What do you mean?'

'You recall how passionately I argued that first night that the Thirty-six Stratagems could save your marriage? Well, they didn't work and I'm very sorry about that.'

'Oh, that's not your fault.'

'Well, it is, in a way. You see, I suspected they wouldn't help.'

'But you were so persuasive!'

'For my own selfish purposes, Jane. The truth is, if I couldn't register six students to my class, the absolute minimum, I'd be out of work.'

'Like my Bookworms!'

'Quite. Don't think the irony of that didn't strike me more than once. Just before you came into the classroom that first evening, I was preparing to tell the others that I'd have to cancel. Then you walked in.'

'I was the sheep that crossed your path. The serendipity stratagem, Number Twelve?'

'Exactly. But how to hold the sheep? Stratagem One. To save my job, I had to convince you to board the boat while concealing my true battlefield. If you had known how much I needed you, you might not have believed my lessons could solve anything. You'd realise I couldn't even use them to help myself.'

'You *tricked* me! Well, I'm glad you did. Now, there's Lorraine, over there.'

Baldwin looked relieved, 'Of course. I would have known her anywhere. Who's the tall man chatting her up?'

'Oh, that's Joe,' Jane said, a trifle drier.

'A very handsome opponent,' Baldwin said a little grudgingly; he still carried the bones of a once dashing figure.

'Joe was never really my enemy.'

She caught Baldwin admiring her reflection in the mirror. She saw an attractive middle-aged woman in a low-cut black dress looking straight back at her, taller by three inches in high heels. The dress had a white satin deep-V collar matched by French cuffs on the long sleeves. If not for the plunging décolleté, it called to mind the elegance of a Chinese scholar's gown. She looked not only sophisticated, but a quality rarely linked to Jane, *chic*.

The Christmas earrings from Joe set off her burnished curls, but the jade bracelet from Dan complemented her manicure. Dan wasn't there tonight. He'd flown back to New York to close the file with the New Jersey authorities, and then got sent to the Interpol headquarters in Lyon for another week to discuss the surge in female suicide bombings. Jane and Dan had bid each other Godspeed in the way two knowing and healthy adults enjoy. There was just enough time for Dan to give his final version of the hijacking nightmare: the scrambling trail of police work and delayed signals from Gilbert that got the police team set up in Bermondsey with only minutes to spare, the sad follow-up with New Jersey Javed's confused and bereaved parents, and the apologetic regret of the helpful imam who had never been able to set wayward acolytes free of the intoxication of death.

Dan might return to England sooner than officially planned, with no official cover this time but a declared and deepening interest in Jane. He'd suggested that she might visit him in the States. Sammie might even come over and join them between school terms. But somehow that particular hint had glanced off Jane the wrong way. The memory of Joe standing vigil with their daughter at Number 19 during the long hours of the kidnapping barricaded her thoughts like a sentry preventing passage into the future with Dan.

When Jane had begged for a little time to think, a frown of doubt crossed Dan's brow. 'If you're waiting for old Joe's blessing, you and I will never get anywhere,' was the American's warning when kissing her good-bye.

'So, Joe is passing around canapés,' Baldwin observed. 'Do I detect détente?'

'Oh, no, he's just here for Lorraine. Although, the night we got out safely he pretended—for ten whole minutes—that he wanted to come back. I saw that for what it was.'

Baldwin lifted an eyebrow.

'Just the sort of dramatic sentimental gesture you'd expect after a brush with death.' Or giving birth, she thought, remembering

Joe's proposal in the maternity ward so many years ago. 'Nothing more than theatrics.'

'Oh, dear, dear, dear, my lessons have failed. You didn't seize his offer? Grab the sheep that passed your path?'

'How could I? It's as if all the false fronts and feints, cover stories, and stratagems got mixed up into a huge stew of confusion. If I won someone's heart back, it would have to be more than just sliding into a compromise. You know Hans Christian Anderson's fairy tale about the Snow Queen? I've felt all year like Gerda, wandering far and wide, searching for the boy I once loved, and all the time I could do nothing to melt the chip of ice blinding his eyes to the Snow Queen's enchantment.'

Baldwin slipped his long arm through Jane's. Together they braved the noisy throng.

Lorraine was holding court in the far corner of the living room where Joe's desk usually stood. Framed against the tall window curtains and surrounded by a flock of wrinklies, she relived her terrors stretching from a basement cell in Bermondsey to the reassurance of a hospital drip. Out of her stuffed wardrobe, the old dear had resurrected a cheetah-patterned caftan, and added false eyelashes and a necklace of heavy amber stones. If she'd pulled Portia out of nowhere on that rainy street a few days ago, today she was one hundred per cent *Hello, Dolly!*

The party was up and running. Some fifty thespians trained to project to the back of the house were gathered together just to celebrate being alive. Despite all the bad reviews, upstaging understudies, tyrannical directors, heartless producers, botched entries, drunken exits, these footlight warriors were still strutting—or shuffling and rolling—across the stage of life.

Jane ushered Baldwin past the wheelchairs and walkers into a safe corner of the kitchen, where she could keep an eye on the flow of drinks.

'Joe's still a wonderful father and I still love him. But as long as Bella's in the picture, I want to be as far from it all as I can. I've come to terms with it, but I'm thinking it might get easier with more distance and time.'

'Ah, ha! You've tumbled to the positive use of Number Thirty-six.'

'Oh, I think I knew that one before taking your class.' The librarian in Jane couldn't help preening. 'Don't laugh! Agatha Christie wrote it down in one of her notebooks: "Of all the ways of avoiding disaster, running away is best".'

'Did she, now? I'll put her into my lecture. But running away gives Thirty-six such short shrift! Oh, gin and tonic, thank you. Here's my version. Surrender is complete defeat, compromise is half-defeat, but escape is not defeat at all. Retreat and regroup. As long as you are not defeated, you still have a chance. Oh, how do you do? You must be Joe! Your delightful daughter looks just like you!'

Jane eased away. Chatting about Sammie's studies gave Baldwin and Joe enough grist to move over to the buffet. Mr Ng and Cecilia were spooning out jasmine rice. Selina forked out Singapore noodles, thick with prawns and green peppers, and Nelson was in charge of Sichuanese tofu flecked with ground pork, chillies, and black beans.

Beyond all the dowagers' humps and doddering grey heads lay the frosty square that would burst into green in a few weeks. Jane felt she was hosting a rather topsy-turvy closing-night party, not just for all these tired troupers, but for her own disintegrating family's stint in Chalkwood Square.

Leaving might not be such a tragedy. Lorraine couldn't negotiate the stairs much longer. Sammie would be heading off to university and as Higgins, Higgins & Wraigth had warned, a fortune in Number 19 might vanish if they waited too long, bursting along with a property bubble already wobbly under NW1's celebrity weight and the recessionary winds.

Jane escorted one guest after another to the bathroom. Winston's little sister Monica stood loyal guard, as professional as any attendant in the Dorchester's powder room.

Passing back into the living room, Jane overheard Winston cheering up Nigel; 'Everybody *likes* me, Nigel, but I don't know enough about finance to make a go of it, while you know all about money. Which is not much good on its own, because let's face it, *nobody* likes you. I need you! You need me! Look, I'll be out in Hong Kong by June and I could let you know the lay of the land by, say, the beginning of August? You round up some capital and let your house on a short lease. Join me by October . . .'

Through the kitchen's French doors giving on to the small balcony, the wintry sun was warming up Sammie's act competing with her grandmother's: 'How long can she keep it up, he asked me? I said, Right, Commander, I can see why you're worried. My grandmother is an old woman with arthritis and a leaky bladder. On the other hand, there're some things you wouldn't happen to know about Lorraine King. One, she played the lead in the road company of *Applause* with a sprained ankle, two shows a day, for ten days, through a record heat wave. Two, this woman went on as Lady Macbeth on fifteen minutes' notice in Central Park in the rain and not one person,' Sammie wagged her finger in the direction of St John Stevens, 'Not one single person who had come to see Maggie Smith walked out or asked the box office for their money back.'

'How do you know that, dear?' asked a painted old dear in a flowered hat and support hose.

'Because she told me so.'

'She told you many times, I'll bet,' St John chortled from his prime seating in the balcony's sunniest spot.

Without warning, Jane felt Joe's hand settle on her shoulder. Together, they listened to their daughter's ringing tribute.

'Three. My grandmother played a nude scene as Cleopatra at forty-eight that had Glenda Jackson telephoning her congratulations the very next morning. And I know that because I've seen the clippings myself.'

'Dame Glenda. To my beloved MP and her margin of forty-two votes! Hear, hear!' St John Stevens raised his glass.

Sammie crowed, 'Four, I told the police, you can rely on Grandma to never go out of character. Dad always tells me, Sammie, your grandmother played the same divorcée for twenty-six weeks straight on a soap opera scripted by chimpanzees just to pay for your braces.'

The party was truly aloft. Joe standing so close overwhelmed Jane. She felt like escaping the warmth of his chest leaning into her and crawling under all the moth-eaten minks and nicotine-drenched Burberries piled on her bed. Unfortunately, she had to chaperone countless more expeditions to the toilet but just then Rachel came lurching toward them, gurgling, 'Oh my Gawd, Jane. Look who's here!'

The leonine head of Sir Brian MacKelling poked through the doorway. The room parted ways as best they could, limping aside, to make way for the Oscar-winning legend. Monica was jumping at his back in her futile attempt to snatch the camel cashmere overcoat draped across his towering shoulders. He stretched out his endless arms to salute Lorraine and shouted to the entire cast, 'Happy birthday, darling!'

Never one to play unfair with his leading ladies, Sir Brian held his entrance pose very patiently, giving Lorraine time to work herself forward and give her line with genuine joy, 'Oh, Bloody Good Evening, My Sweet Prince!'

Sir Brian's *ex-machina* descent from celebrity heaven and Lorraine's crowning ad-lib would have won over even the toughest reviewer's heart, but for an unscripted eruption behind the buffet table. Nelson had fallen on one knee in some kind of public ecstasy.

'Wah! I don't believe it! That's fantastic!'

Elderly faces leaned forward from their rented chairs. Sir Brian turned, all admiring eyes for the princely figure kissing Cecilia Ng's mucky hand daubed with soy and chilli paste. What was Nelson doing? Even all five-foot-one of Madame Leong strained to take in what possessed this same boy who only the night before had argued that her Nonya princess Selina should toss aside the fabled Malaysian med student for a life of prosperity under the standard of Sultana Chu Pixels.

'*You* are *Hei Bai* Girl?' Nelson shrieked. 'That pink bed is in Belsize Park? You shot those videos?' His eyes widened with delight. 'You digitalized and uploaded them all by yourself? Don't you know half of China is watching you online?'

Nelson's frantic eyes searched the crowd, 'Winston, Winston! Did you hear that? *Cecilia is Hei Bai Girl!*' He gazed in loving confusion at the waitressing student's greasy braids and stained rubber slip-ons. 'But you look so, so, different, I mean, without your black fur tail and bikini.'

Appreciative murmurs circled the audience of performers. 'Black fur?'

Lobster-faced, Cecilia stood exposed to her parents and some fifty senior citizens as a closet Internet temptress. She'd frozen as the room fell silent. Nelson shook her by the shoulders, 'Say something to me, Cecilia! No, no, please sing something for me. *River Runs Black as Your Heart!* Or *Burn the Red Flagpole for—*'

At which Cecilia dashed past Jane's withered guests and bolted out the front door. To the indignation of Selina, not to mention a comedian just then holding out his plate for a third helping of *choy sum* with almonds, Nelson chased down the stairs after his video vixen.

Jane looked down through the windows and caught sight of the couple as they emerged on the sidewalk below and stumbled across the mud and grass. Nelson caught Cecilia under the plane trees for a very public kiss. At the northern corner of the junction, Jane saw Joop standing on a ladder with a squeegee and bucket. Oblivious to the young lovers, the Dutchman was washing off the Painted Angel for good.

Jane's heart leapt at the thought of young love, lost love, deep love, even difficult love, but not the affectionate friendship that Dan offered, not just practical companionship and yes, Stratagem Thirty-six's solution of compromise.

The guests fell back into chatting and eating.

'I want to propose—,' Joe shouted. No one listened, so he shouted louder, 'Please—?'

'Oh, toasts later!' Lorraine waved her arms. 'Let me catch up with my darling Brian!'

Joe stretched out his hand to smother the hubbub, but a former Caliban thrust a flute of bubbly into his open fingers, with 'Relax, drink up!'

Joe persisted, 'Lorraine, for once, will you please shut up! I'm bloody well going to propose—! Mr Ng banged on the bottom of a clean wok until it sounded so like a gong, it even silenced St John's cronies out on the balcony.

Joe stared at the glass in his hand. 'I'm raising my glass,' he said and took a swallow.

'We can see that, dear,' said a biddy who had once understudied a Redgrave.

And that put-down made Jane burst into tears, for Joe and for all the years he'd tolerated Lorraine and her bitchy buddies, for the mixed blessings of their family, and most of all, for his own lost ambitions.

Joe stared across the room at Jane's wet eyes. His expression softened, 'I want to propose—to Jane.'

'To the hostess!' The old codgers raised their glasses and went back to buzzing away.

But Joe would have his monologue: 'Please, please! Jane, I've got backing by an independent for our series, *your* series, on politics and undernourishment. It starts with a shoot in North Korea, in remote areas nobody's filmed properly 'til now.'

Joe nodded in Lorraine's direction, 'It was Jane's idea for me to segue out of the cooking show back into work that could help change people's lives.'

Jane panicked. This was the worst possible Stratagem Thirty-six. Joe was fleeing to Pyongyang? He wanted to get out before she went to the US with Dan. *He's leaving us for good.*

She could barely listen to the rest of Joe's toast—'and it's also a good moment to make a fresh start. I don't want to do this program without Jane. It was her idea in the first place. She must be my full partner as co-producer for the series. I want her to use one of the visas, to take her with me to Pyongyang and all the other locations. To have her at my side as my wife.'

All eyes turned from Joe to Jane.

She wasn't sure she'd heard him right. He had proposed, again, in front of her whole world. As Sun Tzu promised, the worst thing could become the best thing. Perhaps it wasn't just the Snow Queen's blinding ice chip of ambition thawing from Joe's eyes. Jane herself saw Joe afresh—not as a character in a story—but just the person she'd loved all along, once again excited more about a project than about himself.

Jane said very softly, 'I never loved any man as much as you, Joe.'

'Good God, I've been upstaged, not once, but twice!' Sir Brian protested.

'Darling, we're all just poor players.' Lorraine patted his shoulder. 'And I think our little hour is at an end.'

The End

We're grateful for your time and hope you enjoyed this book. Please leave a comment on the reading platform of your choice, with our appreciation and thanks.

Also by Dinah Lee Küng

A Visit From Voltaire
Under Their Skin
The Wardens of Punyu (Vol. I, The Handover Mysteries)
The End of May Road Vol. II, The Handover Mysteries)
The Shadows of Shigatse (Vol. III, The Handover Mysteries)

Acknowledgments

The original painted angel was reported by Jane Kramer in 'The Dutch Model,' *The New Yorker*, April 3, 2006. Although that angel appeared in the window of a Rotterdam painter in 2004 on the day the filmmaker Theo Van Gogh was murdered, I see no reason why there shouldn't be other angels reminding us, 'Thou Shalt Not Kill,' in fiction—and in cities other than Rotterdam.

The Art of War, Sun Tzu, Delacorte Press, New York, 1983

The Thirty-six Stratagems for Business, Harro Von Senger, Marshall Cavendish Business, Singapore, 2006

The Book of Stratagems, (Tactics for Triumph and Survival), Harro Von Senger, Viking Penguin, New York, 2003

Sun Tzu and the Art of Business, Mark McNeilly, Oxford University Press, Inc., New York, 1996

The Wiles of War, Sun Haichen, Foreign Languages Press, Beijing, 1996

The Art of the Advantage, Kaihan Krippendorff, Penguin Group, U.K. 2003

The Art of War for Executives, Donald G. Krause, Berkley Publishing, New York, 1995

About the Author

Dinah Lee Küng worked for twenty years as a reporter in Asia writing for among others, *The Economist*, *The International Herald Tribune*, *The Washington Post*, and *Business Week*. She won the Overseas Press Club's Award for Best Humanitarian Coverage in 1991 and her comic novel, *A Visit From Voltaire*, was nominated for The Orange Prize for Fiction in 2004. She is the author of six novels and a number of plays, including the radio play, *Dear Mr Rogge*, which won a commendation in the BBC World Service Playwriting Contest of 2008.

She and her husband, a retired International Committee of the Red Cross delegate, have three adult children and live in Switzerland.

www.ingramcontent.com/pod-product-compliance
Lightning Source LLC
Chambersburg PA
CBHW022001090426
42741CB00007B/850